Social History of the United States

Titles in ABC-CLIO's
Social History of the United States

Social History of the United States

The 1980s

Peter C. Holloran
Andrew Hunt

Series Editors
Daniel J. Walkowitz and Daniel E. Bender

A B C ● C L I O

Santa Barbara, California   Denver, Colorado   Oxford, England

Library of Congress Cataloging-in-Publication Data

Holloran, Peter C., 1947–
    Social history of the United States : The 1980s / Peter C. Holloran and Andrew
Hunt.
        p.   cm.
    Includes bibliographical references and index.
    ISBN 978-1-85109-917-7 (alk. paper) — ISBN 978-1-59884-127-5 (set)
    EISBN 978-1-85109-918-4 (ebook)
    1. United States—Social conditions—1980–   2. United States—Social life and
customs—20th century.   3. Social history—20th century.   I. Hunt, Andrew E., 1968–
II. Title.
    HN57.H557   2009
    306.0973'09048—dc22   2008019996

12 11 10 09   1 2 3 4 5

Senior Production Editor: Vicki Moran
Production Manager: Don Schmidt
Media Editor: Ellen Rasmussen
Media Resources Manager: Caroline Price
File Management Coordinator: Paula Gerard

This book is also available on the World Wide Web as an eBook.
Visit www.abc-clio.com for details.

ABC-CLIO, Inc.
130 Cremona Drive, P.O. Box 1911
Santa Barbara, California 93116–1911

This book is printed on acid-free paper ∞
Manufactured in the United States of America

Contents

Series Introduction

Ordinary people make history. They do so in ways that are different from the ways presidents, generals, business moguls, or celebrities make history; nevertheless, the history of ordinary people is just as profound, just as enduring. Immigration in the early decades of the 20th century was more than numbers and government policy; it was a collective experience of millions of men, women, and children whose political beliefs, vernacular cultural expression, discontent, and dreams transformed the United States. Likewise, during the Great Depression of the 1930s, President Franklin Delano Roosevelt advanced a broad spectrum of new social policies, but as historians have argued, ordinary Americans "made" the New Deal at the workplace, at the ballot box, on the picket lines, and on the city streets. They engaged in new types of consumer behavior, shifted political allegiances, and joined new, more aggressive trade unions. World War II and the Cold War were more than diplomatic maneuvering and military strategy; social upheavals changed the employment patterns, family relations, and daily life of ordinary people. More recently, the rise of the Christian Right in the last few decades is the expression of changing demographics and emerging social movements, not merely the efforts of a few distinct leaders.

These examples, which are drawn directly from the volumes in this series, highlight some of the essential themes of social history. Social history shifts the historical focus away from the famous and the political or economic elite to issues of everyday life. It explores the experiences ordinary Americans—native-born and immigrant, poor and rich, employed and unemployed, men and women, white and black—at home, at work, and at play. In the process, it focuses new attention on the significance of social movements, the behavior and meanings of consumerism, and the changing expression of popular culture.

In many ways, social history is not new. American historians early in the 20th century appreciated the importance of labor, immigration, religion, and urbanization in the study of society. However, early studies shared with political history the emphasis on leaders and major institutions and described a history that was mostly white and male—in other words, a history of those who held power. Several cultural shifts combined to transform how social history was understood and written in the last half of the 20th century: the democratization of higher education after World War II with the GI Bill and the expansion of public and land grant universities; the entry of women, children of immigrants, and racial minorities into the universities and the ranks of historians; and the social movements of the 1960s. Historians created new subjects for social history, casting it as "from the bottom." They realized that much was missing from familiar narratives that stressed the significance of "great men"—presidents, industrialists, and other usually white, usually male notables. Instead, women, working people, and ethnic and racial minorities have become integral parts of the American story along with work, leisure, and social movements.

The result has not simply been additive: ordinary people made history. The story of historical change is located in their lives and their struggles with and against others in power. Historians began to transform the central narrative of American history. They realized that—in the words of a popular 1930s folk cantata, "Ballad for Americans"—the "'etceteras' and the 'and so forths' that do the work" have a role in shaping their own lives, in transforming politics, and in recreating economics. Older themes of study, from industrialization to imperial expansion, from party politics to urbanization, were revisited through the inclusion of new actors, agents, and voices. These took their place alongside such new topics as social movements, popular culture, consumption, and community. But social history remains socially engaged scholarship; contemporary social issues continue to shape social historians' research and thinking. Historians in the 1970s and 1980s who focused on the experiences of working people, for instance, were challenged by the reality of deindustrialization. Likewise, historians in the 1990s who focused on popular culture and consumer behavior were influenced by the explosion of consumerism and new forms of cultural expression. Today's historians explore the antecedents to contemporary globalization as well as the roots of conservatism.

The transformation of the questions and agendas of each new era has made it apparent to historians that the boundaries of historical inquiry are not discrete. Social history, therefore, engages with other kinds of history. Social history reinterprets older narratives of politics and political economy and overlaps both areas. Social historians argue that politics is not restricted to ballot boxes or legislatures; politics is broad popular engagement with ideas about material wealth, social justice, moral values, and civil and human rights. Social historians, naturally, remain interested in changing political affiliations. They have, for example, ex-amined the changing political allegiances of African Americans during the 1930s and the civil rights movement of the 1960s. So too have they examined the relationship of socialist and communist parties to working-class and immigrant communities. At the same time, social historians measure change by looking at such issues as family structure, popular culture, and consumer behavior.

For the social historian, the economy extends far beyond statistical data about production, gross domestic product, or employment. Rather, the economy is a lived experience. Wealthy or poor, Americans have negotiated the changing re-ality of economic life. Social historians ask questions about how different groups of Americans experienced and resisted major economic transformations and how they have grappled with economic uncertainty. The Great Depression of the 1930s, for example, left both urban workers and rural farmers perilously close to starvation. During the 1970s and 1980s, factories in the Rust Belt of the Mid-west and Northeast shuttered or moved, and many Americans began laboring in new parts of the country and working new kinds of jobs, especially in the ser-vice sector. Americans have also grappled with the unequal distribution of wealth; some people advanced new ideas and engaged with emerging ideologies that challenged economic injustice, but others jealously guarded their privilege.

As social history has broadened its purview, it has transformed our sense of how historical change occurs. Social history changes our conception of chronol-ogy; change does not correspond to presidential election cycles. Social history also changes how we understand sources of power; power is constituted in and challenged by diverse peoples with different resources. Social historians, then, look at the long history of the 20th century in the United States and examine how the terrain has shifted under our feet, sometimes slowly and sometimes dramatically and abruptly. Social historians measure change in complex ways, including but also transcending demographic and geographic expansion and political transformation. How, for example, did the institution of the family change in the face of successive waves of immigration that often left spouses and chil-dren separated by national borders and oceans? Or during years of war with rising rates of women's wage and salary employment? Or following moralist reaction that celebrated imagined traditional values, and social movements that focused on issues of sexuality, birth control, homosexuality, and liberation? His-torical change can also be measured by engagement with popular culture as Americans shifted their attention from vaudeville and pulp novels to radio, silent films, talkies, television, and finally the Internet and video games. The volumes in this series, divided by decades, trace all these changes.

To make sense of this complex and broadened field of inquiry, social his-torians often talk about how the categories by which we understand the past have been "invented," "contested," and "constructed." The nation has generally been divided along lines of race, class, gender, sexuality, and ethnicity. However, historians have also realized that analysts—whether in public or professional discourse—define these "categories of analysis" in different ways at different moments. Waves of immigration have reconfigured understandings of race and ethnicity, and more recent social movements have challenged the meanings of gender. Similarly, to be working class at the dawn of the age of industry in the 1900s meant something very different from being working class in the post-industrial landscape of the 1990s. How women or African Americans—to cite only two groups—understand their own identity can mean something different than how white men categorize them. Social historians, therefore, trace how Americans have always been divided about the direction of their lives and their nation, how they have consistently challenged and rethought social and cultural values and sought to renegotiate relationships of power, whether in the family, the workplace, the university, or the military. Actors do this armed with differing forms of power to authorize their view.

To examine these contestations, social historians have explored the way Americans articulated and defended numerous identities—as immigrants, citizens, workers, Christians, or feminists, for example. A post–World War II male chemical worker may have thought of himself as a worker and trade unionist at the factory, a veteran and a Democrat in his civic community, a husband and father at home, and as a white, middle-class homeowner. A female civil rights worker in the South in the 1960s may have seen herself as an African American when in the midst of a protest march or when refused service in a restaurant, as working class during a day job as a domestic worker or nurse, and as a woman when struggling to claim a leadership role in an activist organization.

Social historians have revisited older sources and mined rich new veins of information on the daily lives of ordinary people. Social historians engage with a host of materials—from government documents to census reports, from literature to oral histories, and from autobiographies to immigrant and foreign-language newspapers—to illuminate the lives, ideas, and activities of those who have been hidden from history. Social historians have also brought a broad "toolbox" of new methodologies to shed light on these sources. These methodologies are well represented in this series and illustrate the innovations of history from the bottom up. These volumes offer many tables and charts, which demonstrate the ways historians have made creative use of statistical analysis. Furthermore, the volumes are rich in illustrations as examples of the new ways that social historians "read" such images as cartoons or photographs.

The volumes in this series reflect the new subject matter, debates, and methodologies that have composed the writing of the United States' 20th-century social history. The volumes have unique features that make them particularly valuable for students and teachers; they are hybrids that combine the narrative advantages of the monograph with the specific focus of the encyclopedia. Each volume has been authored or co-authored by established social historians. Where the work has been collaborative, the authors have shared the writing and worked to sustain a narrative voice and conceptual flow in the volume. Authors have written the social history for the decade of their expertise and most have also taught its history. Each volume begins with a volume introduction by the author or authors that lays out the major themes of the decade and the big picture—how the social changes of the era transformed the lives of Americans. The author then synthesizes the best and most path-breaking new works in social history. In the case of the last three volumes, which cover the post-1970 era, scholarship remains in its relative infancy. In particular, these three volumes are major original efforts to both define the field and draw upon the considerable body of original research that has already been completed.

The ten volumes in the series divide the century by its decades. This is an avowedly neutral principle of organization that does not privilege economic, political, or cultural transformations; this allows readers to develop their own sense of a moment and their own sense of change. While it remains to be seen how the most recent decades will be taught and studied, in cases such as the 1920s, the 1930s, and the 1960s, this decadal organization replicates how historians frequently study and teach history. The Progressive Era (ca. 1890–1920) and postwar America (ca. 1945–1960) have less often been divided by decades. This highlights the neutrality of this division. In truth, all divisions are imposed: we speak of long decades or short centuries, and so forth. When historians teach the 1960s, they often reach back into the 1950s and ahead into the 1970s. The authors and editors of these volumes recognize that social processes, movements, ideas, and leaders do not rise and fall with the turn of the calendar; therefore, they have worked to knit the volumes together as a unit.

Readers can examine these texts individually or collectively. The texts can be used to provide information on significant events or individuals. They can provide an overview of a pivotal decade. At the same time, these texts are designed to allow readers to follow changing themes over time and to develop their own sense of chronology. The authors regularly spoke with one another and with the series editors to establish the major themes and subthemes in the social history of the century and to sustain story lines across the volumes. Each volume divides the material into six or seven chapters that discuss major themes such as labor or work; urban, suburban, and rural life; private life; politics; economy; culture; and social movements. Each chapter begins with an overview essay and then explores four to six major topics. The discrete essays at the heart of each volume give readers focus on a social movement, a social idea, a case study, a social institution, and so forth. Unlike traditional encyclopedias, however, the narrative coherence of the single-authored text permits authors to break the decade bubble with discussions on the background or effects of a social event.

There are several other features that distinguish this series.

- Many chapters include capsules on major debates in the social history of the era. Even as social historians strive to build on the best scholarship available, social history remains incomplete and contested; readers can benefit from studying this tension.

- The arguments in these volumes are supported by many tables and graphics. Social history has mobilized demographic evidence and—like its sister field, cultural history—has increasingly turned to visual evidence, both for the social history of media and culture and as evidence of social conditions. These materials are not presented simply as illustrations but as social evidence to be studied.

- Timelines at the head of every chapter highlight for readers all the major events and moments in the social history that follows.

- A series of biographical sketches at the end of every chapter highlights the lives of major figures more often overlooked in histories of the era. Readers can find ample biographical material on more prominent figures in other sources; here the authors have targeted lesser known but no less interesting and important subjects.

- Bibliographies include references to electronic sources and guide readers to material for further study.

- Three indices—one for each volume, one for the entire series, and one for all the people and events in the series—are provided in each volume. Readers can easily follow any of the major themes across the volumes.

Finally, we end with thanks for the supportive assistance of Ron Boehm and Kristin Gibson at ABC-CLIO, and especially to Dr. Alex Mikaberidze and Dr. Kim Kennedy White, who helped edit the manuscripts for the press. But of course, these volumes are the product of the extraordinary group of historians to whom we are particularly indebted:

The 1900s: Brian Greenberg and Linda S. Watts
The 1910s: Gordon Reavley
The 1920s: Linda S. Watts, Alice L. George, and Scott Beekman
The 1930s: Cecelia Bucki
The 1940s: Mark Ciabattari
The 1950s: John C. Stoner and Alice L. George
The 1960s: Troy D. Paino
The 1970s: Laurie Mercier
The 1980s: Peter C. Holloran and Andrew Hunt
The 1990s: Nancy Cohen

Daniel J. Walkowitz, Series Editor
Daniel E. Bender, Series Associate Editor

Volume Introduction

Even before the 1980s ended, observers invented a tagline to describe the era. They called it the "Decade of Greed." This catchphrase has withstood the test of time and continues to be used by scholars, politicians, media personalities, pundits, and ordinary people to evoke the excesses of the era. Ever since Oliver Stone's 1987 cautionary film *Wall Street* depicted Michael Douglas's character, Gordon Gekko, delivering a fiery speech on the virtues of greed, the decade has become associated in the popular imagination with the drive to acquire money. Gekko's electrifying speech reflected words and deeds of the day. A similar message echoed in the words of financier Ivan Boesky when he celebrated greed before an enthusiastic audience at the University of California at Berkeley's business school in 1986.

Since the 1980s, the theme of greed has dominated perceptions of the era. For their part, many conservatives bristled at the term "Decade of Greed," calling it unfair and insisting it does not accurately represent the realities of the period. They steadfastly defended Ronald Reagan, his supply-side economic policies, his tough Cold War stance, and his historical legacy. Even well into the New Millennium, talk-radio host Rush Limbaugh, for example, continues to attack the notion of the 1980s as a Decade of Greed on his popular nationally syndicated program.

Despite efforts of conservatives like Limbaugh to rehabilitate the era, the myth of the 1980s as a period of pervasive avarice and unregulated greed remains potent. Moreover, perhaps more than any other decade in American history, the 1980s became closely identified with the commander in chief of the time, Ronald

Reagan. In the 1980 presidential campaign, Reagan, a former Hollywood movie star and two-term governor of California, emerged a widely popular, larger-than-life figure with an uncanny ability to communicate his ideas to the American public. Even though Reagan championed some unpopular policies and his administration endured a series of well-publicized scandals, the setbacks never seemed to undermine his popularity. He was sometimes referred to as the "Teflon president," a term first attributed to Colorado representative Pat Schroeder and quickly adopted by other observers who insisted that scandals and controversies did not "stick" to Reagan. Beginning in the 1980s, and in the years since then, most accounts of the era have focused primarily on Reagan and his far-reaching influence. Chroniclers of the 1980s have routinely identified the decade's most significant milestones with key developments in the Reagan administration and U.S. Congress. Even now, most histories of the 1980s remain heavily political and top-down in orientation.

Regrettably, this focus on Reagan has perpetuated the idea of the 1980s as a Decade of Greed. Indeed, the very nature of the Reagan agenda—deep cuts to social welfare programs, tax loopholes for the wealthy, scaled-back regulation of corporations, a militantly anticommunist foreign policy, and the huge buildup in the arms race—tends to validate the persistent myth. A deeper exploration of the 1980s, however, shows it was a much more complicated decade than previously assumed, one that forever altered the very fabric of American society. By moving beyond the well-documented decisions of the Reagan administration and Congress and turning attention to previously marginalized players, we open up new vistas that provide striking views of a complex era.

Ordinary people faced new dilemmas unique to the 1980s and confronted unresolved tensions that still lingered from earlier periods in history. The 1980s assumed a wide array of meanings, depending on the subject one studies. Merely by rotating the historical prism, it is possible to glimpse the multitude of fragments that make up the diverse American mosaic. All histories have something to offer, whether one studies middle-class suburban teenagers and the challenges they faced, or Mexican immigrants crouched under canvas tarps in the back of pickup trucks searching for seasonal employment in Arizona, or Iowa farmers coping with crippling debts, or activists committing civil disobedience to protest limited government funding for AIDS research. In any history, the introduction of new viewpoints and voices further increases the possibility of understanding the nuances, contradictions, and transformations of the past.

It would be negligent of a broad narrative about American society in the 1980s—even one heavily weighted toward social history, as this one is—to overlook significant political developments. In a democratic society, the relationship between people and their government is paramount and cannot be ignored. This relationship ultimately blurs the lines between what is social and what is political. Thus, Ronald Reagan and other influential figures and the key events that have dominated the more traditional histories will appear in these pages.

But the primary focus of this book will be on the American people and how they lived life on a daily basis against the backdrop of the dynamic, changing world around them. Sometimes attention will turn to people overseas whose lives were transformed by policies and events in the United States. Whether at home or abroad, ordinary men and women in the 1980s felt the impact of policies formulated in the nation's capital.

It is difficult to pinpoint an exact time when the 1980s began. It is safe to say that the 1980s were born at an uneasy moment in American history, in the long shadow of the twin national traumas of defeat overseas in Vietnam and the Watergate political scandal at home. Still vexing the nation in 1980 were vivid images of Richard Nixon resigning in disgrace six years earlier, combined with the 1975 film footage of U.S. helicopters hastily evacuating embassy personnel, Marines, and frantic Vietnamese from the rooftop of the U.S. embassy as communists closed in on Saigon. Even as late as 1980, the Watergate scandal still tainted the public's faith in the political process. Cynicism stemming from its aftermath heightened voter apathy and fueled the alienation that a growing number of ordinary citizens felt toward government in general.

In the 1976 elections, 53.6 percent of eligible voters went to the polls. The people elected Jimmy Carter, a onetime peanut farmer, naval officer, and governor of Georgia, as their president. His chief virtue in the eyes of many voters was that he seemed to be a political "outsider." A so-called "New Democrat" who distanced himself from the liberal Democratic Party establishment, Carter doggedly supported a balanced budget and avoided any role in rebuilding the ailing New Deal coalition. Initially, he appeared to be a bold and innovative leader. He established a $1.6 billion Environmental Protection Agency "Superfund," pardoned Vietnam War era draft evaders, and created the Department of Education. He appointed minorities to key government positions, encouraged the creation of new Veterans Administration programs to assist Vietnam veterans, and placed 100 million acres of pristine Alaska land under federal protection.

But by the end of his first year in office, inflation began its meteoric climb. A new word entered the American household vocabulary: stagflation, the combination of spiraling prices, a stagnant economy, and rising unemployment. At the time of Jimmy Carter's 1977 inauguration, the United States still convulsed in the aftermath of the 1975–1976 economic recession. The cost of the Vietnam War and new social welfare programs in the late 1960s, combined with the energy crisis of the 1970s, contributed significantly to the huge leap in inflation during the Carter presidency, which jumped from 6.5 percent in 1977 to 13.4 percent in 1980. In an effort to stem the rising inflationary tide, the Federal Reserve board kept raising interest rates, which peaked in 1980 at a historic high of 20 percent.

President Carter's public approval ratings plummeted, approaching the level of Nixon's ratings during Watergate. Contributing to a precipitous decline in nationwide morale were crises overseas. The massive and alarming Soviet invasion of

Afghanistan in late 1979, coupled with the takeover of the U.S. embassy in Tehran by Iranian militants around the same time, heightened public concerns that America had lost its global eminence in the aftermath of the Vietnam War. Each night, people in the United States watched grainy images played and replayed on their televisions of Islamic radicals parading hostages through enormous crowds chanting "Death to America" and burning American flags. An attempt by the Carter administration to rescue the hostages on April 24, 1980, ended in disaster in Iran after a helicopter collided with a C-130 airplane full of fuel, killing eight soldiers. The malaise deepened and the nation grew increasingly disillusioned.

By 1980, the dominant mood in the nation had become increasingly conservative. Long gone were the upheavals and polarization of the late 1960s and early 1970s. The 1960s—with its unrest, experimental lifestyles, psychedelic rock, generation gaps, sexual revolutions, and florid fashions—seemed increasingly like ancient history to most Americans. Incredibly, only 10 years had passed since American GIs were immersed in the Vietnam "quagmire" and National Guard troops opened fire on students at Kent State in Ohio, killing four and wounding several others. Where, wondered some, were the upheavals, demonstrations, banners, and marches in 1980? Surely the 1960s had not exorcised all of the demons of racism, sexism, war, and materialism from the American landscape. Feminism, the main survivor of 1960s protest movements, continued to exercise a significant influence, particularly in its campaign for an Equal Rights Amendment (ERA). However, the American Left—what remained of it—was in a terrible funk, weakened by internal divisions, limited popular support, and the legacy of intense harassment and surveillance by federal and local law enforcement agencies.

The decline of protest politics in the 1970s coincided with the emergence of grassroots conservative social movements across the nation. The meteoric rise of the New Right came as a surprise to some observers. In 1964, when Lyndon Johnson enjoyed a landslide electoral victory over his opponent, Arizona senator Barry Goldwater, many political commentators prematurely predicted the demise of American conservatism. Such grim forecasts, though far from prescient, were understandable. Deeply fragmented, lacking a concrete agenda, and widely dismissed as extremist, the American Right seemed consigned to the fringes of society. After Goldwater's defeat, conservative activists across the nation quietly mobilized and coalesced. They learned valuable organizing techniques from the New Left, especially the importance of building single-issue organizations such as the National Rifle Association and Stop-ERA, and perfected new techniques, such as direct-mail fundraising. Behind the scenes, the New Right gained an astonishing momentum.

Meantime, the emergence of televangelists—a new generation of charismatic conservative ministers—filled television airwaves with sermons about family values and the evils of parental permissiveness, drugs, rock music, gay rights, abortion, and promiscuity. Jerry Falwell, the most visible of the televangelists, commanded an extensive network that included his television show *Old Time Gospel Hour* broadcast on the Liberty Broadcasting Network to 1.5 million subscribers, his Thomas Road Liberty Baptist Church, and Liberty University, all based out of Lynchburg, Virginia. Similar evangelical empires thrived under the leadership of Pat Robertson, host of *The 700 Club* on the Christian Broadcasting Network, and Oral Roberts, head of a $500 million religious enterprise that included Oral Roberts University in Tulsa, Oklahoma.

The New Right thrived by 1980. Activists networked, organizations linked together in common struggles, groups shared resources, and the leading intellectual, political, and religious figures of the movement regularly met to map out future strategies. The rise of the New Right mirrored the realignment of the Republican Party, away from the established Eastern conservative Old Right aristocracy and moderate Rockefeller wing, and more in the direction of Barry Goldwater's laissez-faire, anticommunist, anti–social welfare vision. The transformation undoubtedly benefited Reagan, who championed the New Right agenda in 1980 much more effectively than Goldwater had 16 years earlier. His presidential candidacy also enjoyed grassroots support from a wide variety of social movements that flourished in the 1970s. Sustaining the New Right was a backlash in the late 1960s and early 1970s against the Civil Rights, antiwar, feminist, and gay and lesbian rights movements. A statewide tax revolt in California in 1978 accelerated the ascendancy of conservatism. The California movement successfully campaigned for the passage of Proposition 13, cutting property taxes and ultimately jeopardizing the efforts of local governments to maintain education and various social services. Proposition 13 passed by a 2 to 1 ratio, triggering similar revolts in other states and fueling a multitude of New Right organizations across the nation.

Adding to Reagan's prospects in 1980 were demographic shifts in the 1960s and 1970s that relocated the center of the nation's political power from the Northeast and Midwest to the so-called Sunbelt states in the South and Southwest, a region extending from Florida to California. The Sunbelt states were once considered less important politically than the Midwest and Northeast. Political analyst Kevin Phillips predicted the coming primacy of the Sunbelt in his influential 1969 book, *The Emerging Republican Majority*. In the 1970s, the Sunbelt experienced 90 percent of America's population growth. Three Sunbelt states, Florida, Texas, and California, absorbed 40 percent of that growth and by decade's end boasted close to 25 percent of the electoral votes needed to win the presidency. By the 1980s, a family of four moved to Florida every six minutes, and one in five southerners had been born in other regions. The growing population of the Sunbelt tended to vote Republican, and a similar tendency flourished in the Western states by the late 1970s.

Candidate Reagan stood at the confluence of these trends, poised to take the White House in the fall of 1980. He was in top form in the presidential race, bolstered by an army of political advisors, advertising and public relations consultants, and influential Republican backers. He hit the vulnerable Carter hard, taking him to task for his foreign policy record and pronouncing him inconsistent and soft on communism. But Reagan reserved his sharpest attacks for the sour state of the economy under Carter's leadership, and fine-tuned his populist message.

On election day 1980, 52.6 percent of eligible voters cast their ballots. In the popular vote, 43.9 million votes (50.7 percent) went to Reagan compared to 35.5 million (41 percent) received by Carter. The electoral votes were much more lopsided: Reagan won 489 compared to Carter's 49. It was no accident that on Inauguration Day—January 20, 1981—Ronald Reagan was the first president to deliver his inaugural speech facing west, in the direction of the ascendant Sunbelt and Western states. He, perhaps more than any other president, understood the power of seemingly simple symbols and words. Many observers believed that with Reagan's electoral victory, the era known as the 1980s had begun in earnest.

By the end of Reagan's two terms in the White House, the nation had been altered in dramatic and irrevocable ways, emerging a very different place than it had been before his presidency. Virtually no part of American society remained untouched by the sweeping changes of the 1980s. Historians such as Eric Foner have characterized the 1980s as a "Second Gilded Age," a time of rising skylines, merging corporations, billionaires closing deals aboard Learjets, and legions of homeless people wandering the streets.

For ordinary people, the most striking transformation involved the introduction of new technologies into their daily lives. Fiber optics, automatic teller machines (ATMs), and microprocessors turned the United States into a wired nation and facilitated other advancements. Among the innovations that debuted in millions of American households during the 1980s were video cassette recorders (VCRs), cable television, compact disc players, camcorders, videogames, video disc players (the predecessors to DVD players), and, most importantly, personal computers, which were often accompanied by printers.

The early models of most of these devices were often primitive and too expensive for middle-class and blue-collar families to afford. In time, the technology improved and prices plunged, resulting in greater accessibility. Microwave ovens, for instance, began appearing in more affluent American kitchens throughout the mid-1970s, but their large price tag meant they remained far from commonplace. By the late 1980s, microwave oven ownership was almost universal and changed the way people from all walks of life prepared food. Likewise, VCRs revolutionized the way Americans viewed television in the 1980s, but VCR technology had already existed for many years. The early video tape recorders (VTRs) of the 1950s and 1960s were enormous and expensive, and used only in television studios and the wealthiest American homes. In August 1977, RCA announced that it would release its new top-loading VHS VCR to American consumers. The RCA VBT200 was intended to compete with the Sony Betamax, which first appeared in the United States two years earlier at a whopping price tag of $2,295. At a Manhattan press conference, RCA execs boasted that their model cost a mere $1,000, making it $300 cheaper than the current Betamax models. By 1983, VCRs flooded the market, and a solid, reliable unit could be purchased for less than $300.

Without doubt, though, the crowning achievement of the 1980s technological revolution was the introduction of the personal computer. In August 1981, IBM introduced its IBM PC model 5150, complete with 64 kilobytes of RAM, a single-sided 160K 5.25" floppy drive, and powered by a 4.77 MHz Intel 8088 processor. Retailing at $2,880 for a base model, the 5150 appeared in stores by the fall, in time for the Christmas season. Prior to the IBM PC 5150, consumers could purchase personal computers, but they tended to be bulky and expensive. In 1979, with six major companies distributing different types of PCs, computer ownership remained around 500,000 units nationwide. After the release of IBM's 1981 PC, the number of PCs across the United States increased to 10 million units within two years and kept rising. Adding to the proliferation was the new Macintosh 512K model, in stores by September 1984, the first computer to offer a mouse-driven graphical user interface that utilized icons (a forerunner of the Windows platform).

Paralleling the impact of new technologies on people's lives was the dramatic redistribution of wealth that occurred under the Reagan administration. Reaganomics, which George H. W. Bush referred to as "voodoo economics" in the 1980 presidential campaign, came under fire by some critics who feared that Reagan's economic policies favored the rich at the expense of poor, working-class, and middle-class Americans. Such concerns proved justified. The Reagan Revolution represented a radical departure from the priorities established by the 1944 G.I. Bill and other policies that deliberately sought to enlarge and buttress the American middle class. The result was a startling accumulation of wealth for the richest citizens, increased precariousness for the middle class, and a rise in the number of people living in poverty.

The coming of Reaganomics was swift and its impact was far-reaching. The Economic Recovery Tax Act of 1981 cut income and corporate taxes by $747 billion over five years while the Omnibus Reconciliation Act of 1981 mandated cuts of $136 billion in federal spending for the period 1983–1984, which had an impact on more than 200 social and cultural programs. Reagan appointed conservatives who shared his gospel of deregulation to key agencies. Deficit spending and a massive national debt both reached staggering levels in the 1980s. Gargantuan arms budgets were fueled by the growth of the national security state. The Pentagon's annual budget enlarged from $169 billion in 1981 to $239 billion in 1986. Over a period of five years, the Reagan administration's military spending budgets totaled $1.6 trillion. In 1984, Pentagon spending reached an astonishing $34 million per hour. In the meantime, Reagan cut the budgets of what the Office of Management and Budget classified as "human resources"—housing, education, urban, and social services—from 28 percent of federal spending in 1980 to 22 percent in 1987.

The effects of these dramatic shifts in federal priorities shaped different people's lives in varied ways. The outcome was not always as stark as Reagan's critics feared, although in certain cases, the scenario could be quite grim. Enormous defense contracts brought prosperity to communities across the country, especially in California, New York, Texas, and Virginia. Some communities thrived during the Reagan years while others became virtual ghost towns. In Santa Clara County, California, the center of the nation's vast computer industry—Silicon Valley—grew rapidly and saw its fortunes multiply. Elsewhere, in the steel towns of Pennsylvania, for example, or the industrial cities of the Midwest, conditions took a sharp turn for the worse.

Diversity remained one of the defining characteristics of American society in the 1980s. The nation experienced its largest influx of immigrants since the decade between 1900 and 1910. Roughly 8 million immigrants entered the United States in the 1980s, with a significant percentage coming from Asia and Latin America. Immigrant communities such as Koreatown in Los Angeles and the Cuban neighborhoods of Miami experienced dramatic growth. Some minorities witnessed their quality of life improve in the 1980s, and increasing numbers of Latinos, Asian-Americans, and African Americans moved into suburbs. Abject poverty and struggles over land rights and usage persisted on Native American reservations, although the establishment of the Indian Gaming Regulatory Act of 1988 permitted tribes to open casinos on reservations in states that allowed any sort of gambling, even charity gambling. It was not long before 75 tribes in 18 states had signed agreements to open reservation casinos.

The search for community, another long-running theme in American history, is woven through the 1980s tapestry. The ethos of the Reagan Revolution emphasized acquisitive individualism and encouraged people to make money and enjoy the material rewards that such enrichment could offer. The new technologies of the 1980s—personal computers, VCRs, and CD players—tended to reinforce the isolating and inward-focusing tendencies of the period. Yet the 1980s also furnished countless examples of men and women who sought to nurture and strengthen their communities. Sporting events and shopping malls brought people together in controlled environments, sometimes from great distances, for a shared purpose. Inhabitants of cities, suburbs, and rural areas alike coped, often collectively, with changes and maintained a sense of community cohesiveness.

The trend of moving to the suburbs that began after World War II continued, and by 1990, almost half of Americans lived in suburban neighborhoods. The suburbs expanded in ways that postwar social critics who warned about the decentralization of cities and suburban "sameness" failed to anticipate. By the 1980s, a flurry of neologisms developed to describe the evolving shape of suburbs, including "satellite sprawl," "new cities," "commuter towns," "bedroom communities," "urban fringe," and "multinucleated metropolitan regions." As businesses migrated out of aging central cities and into suburban downtowns, or "mini-cities," the urban–suburban dichotomy constructed by 1950s intellectuals became increasingly problematic. Suburban downtowns now offered a wide array of goods and services once confined to the business districts of central cities. As the end of the 1980s approached, there were a variety of suburbs dotting the American landscape, including working-class suburbs, "old" (pre-1960) suburbs, "exurbs" (or newer rings of houses beyond old suburbs), and "minority" (or so-called spillover) suburbs near cities, which tended to attract African American families moving out of the central cities. Minorities formed about 18 percent of the suburban population in 1990, although most minority suburbanites, African Americans in particular, endured continued segregation.

There were no major wars on the scale of World Wars I and II, the Korean War, or the Vietnam War in the 1980s. Still, the intensification of the Cold War and the looming threat of intervention in Central America made the possibility of a hot war seem very real at times and forced people to consider America's role in the world. At the same time, a host of smaller wars—at home and abroad—defined the decade. Throughout the 1980s, the Reagan administration aided anticommunist insurgencies and autocratic rightwing regimes around the world. The Iranian hostage crisis introduced a new adversary: Islamic fundamentalism. In America, veterans, politicians, historians, and cultural figures debated the Vietnam War, shattering a long silence that prevailed in the years immediately following the conflict, yet they failed to arrive at a concensus about the war and its meanings.

The deepest domestic fissures were caused by the so-called Culture Wars. Liberals and conservatives debated the role of the federal government, civic participation, religion, and culture in late-1980s America. Academics argued back and forth about the canon and whether to include more minority, non-Western, and female figures within it. Dissent was more robust than doomsayers claimed it was and protests occurred throughout the decade, including antinuclear rallies, Central America solidarity marches, and antiapartheid campaigns. Religious quarrels pitted fundamentalists against humanists. Within the Catholic Church alone, conservatives decried homosexuality, abortion, and secularism while adherents of liberation theology supported revolutionary movements in Latin America and gave sanctuary to Salvadoran refugees in their churches. American Jews grappled with their relationship to Israel. Muslims looked for mainstream acceptance against the backdrop of growing Islamic terrorist threats.

Social frictions crept into nearly all walks of life. Women and minorities benefited from certain advances in the 1980s, yet they also confronted the limited gains of the civil rights and feminist movements and considered new means of resisting discrimination. Workers in Austin, Minnesota, and Pittston, Pennsylvania, went on strike to improve their wages, benefits, and working conditions. Youths struggled with peer pressure, rising expectations, and, in some cases, limited job and higher education opportunities. Countercultures in the 1980s assumed a variety of forms, including gay and lesbian neighborhoods, enclaves of youthful punk rockers, and urban street gangs, each offering its participants fulfillment they could not find in mainstream society. By the late 1980s, another new term entered the parlance of the times—"political correctness"—which, although in theory it emphasized tolerance of diversity and multiracialism, nonetheless triggered intense and heated debates throughout the United States.

In many respects, the 1980s represented a dramatic departure from the decade that preceded it. The new music styles of the 1980s rejected the more hedonistic and self-indulgent elements of 1970s rock. The opening broadcast of MTV in August 1981 redefined the boundaries of music, spawned other cable television imitators, and often determined what songs would be Billboard Top 40 hits. New wave snyth-pop, dance music, "big hair" hard rock, and rap music saturated the radio airwaves. Movies tended to be more escapist in the 1980s then they had been in the 1970s, with films such as *E.T., Star Wars: Return of the Jedi, Ghostbusters, Top Gun,* and *Batman* setting box office records. Yet the decade also boasted some gritty, iconoclastic filmmakers—including Oliver Stone, John Sayles, and Jim Jarmusch—who challenged the cinematic conventions of the day.

The youth market was enormous and incredibly lucrative in the 1980s, as the sons and daughters of Baby Boomers came of age. Youth-oriented fashions were often an unusual mixture of outrageous and conservative, and were always quite distinctive. Spiked or feathered hair, parachute pants, *Miami Vice*–inspired linen jackets, stonewashed denim, checkerboard clothing, Camp Beverly Hills sweatshirts, fluorescent vests, Jordache jeans, Lycra bicycle shorts, Madonna-wannabe jelly bracelets, and striped miniskirts with legwarmers were but a few of the fads preferred by young people. Parents in the 1980s generally became more cautious and protective, especially following news of a rash of alleged sexual abuse cases at the McMartin Preschool in southern California in 1983, which touched off a wave of sex abuse hysteria across the country and heightened the anxieties of millions of mothers and fathers. Contributing to mounting fears were controversies over rising teen drug use, sexual experimentation by high school students, and youth violence. Predictably, conservatives spoke of deteriorating values while liberals raised concerns about the erosion of a higher collective purpose.

When Ronald Reagan died in 2004, the country's attention again turned to the 1980s. By this time, radio stations throughout North America featured "Eighties Retro Lunch" and "Eighties Saturday Night" shows. Websites and books dished up heaping helpings of Reagan-era nostalgia. Cable TV networks played and replayed 1980s movies like *Back to the Future,* television programs such as *The Cosby Show,* and "retro" music videos. In the aftermath of the September 11, 2001, terror attacks, the 1980s began to seem like a simpler time, and most people who took the stroll down memory lane ignored the problems and complexities of the era.

But the nostalgic trip, like the Decade of Greed myth, informs us very little. The 1980s were full of surprises and birthed countless new trends, but it would be a mistake to overemphasize discontinuity with earlier periods. At all levels of society, men and women engaged in a long-running debate—as old as the republic itself—over what sort of nation the United States ought to be. Central in the discussions were such weighty matters as religion, race, class, immigration, gender, sexual orientation, international relations, opportunity, the purpose of government and even history itself. In this respect, the 1980s remained consistent with other decades throughout American history as a battleground of ideas where men and women confronted the paradoxes and unfinished tasks of the day. Few of the dilemmas were satisfactorily resolved, and the arguments and counterarguments, the successes and failures, and the tragedies and triumphs that absorbed the nation's attention in the 1980s continued to shape the United States well into the new millennium.

Issues of the 20th Century

Beginnings

OVERVIEW

The beginning of the 1980s coincided with the resurgence of conservative politics and the unraveling of Franklin Delano Roosevelt's New Deal coalition. Throughout American history, successful political movements have often produced charismatic leaders, and modern American conservatism was no exception. Just as Martin Luther King Jr. emerged in the 1950s and 1960s as the embodiment of the civil rights movement in the mass media, so Ronald Reagan became the potent symbol of the rebirth of American conservatism in 1980. But the rise of the New Right in the 1970s, like the civil rights movement during the previous decade, was due to the efforts of countless men and women in communities across America. Demographic changes also played a role. Beginning in the 1960s, population shifts relocated the center of the nation's political power from the Northeast and Midwest to the southern Sunbelt states and the West, regions that up until the 1970s had been more marginal in importance politically. By the 1980s, a family of four moved to Florida every six minutes, and one in five southerners had been born in other regions. The growing population in the Sunbelt, as well as the West, tended to be strongly pro-Reagan. This chapter explores the spread of conservative grassroots struggles in the 1970s and the impact of those movements on American politics.

TIMELINE

1980   Inflation reaches 20 percent.

January 4: Jimmy Carter initiates grain embargo against the Soviet Union

January 7: Federal government approves $1.5 billion in loan guarantees to bail out ailing Chrysler Corporation.

February 2–3: More than 30 inmates are killed and 100 are injured during one of the most violent prison riots in American history at the New Mexico State Penitentiary.

March 21: President Jimmy Carter announces the U.S. boycott of the 1980 Summer Olympics in Moscow, citing the 1979 Soviet invasion of Afghanistan as the reason.

April: The Transport Workers Union Local 100 in New York City goes on strike demanding increased wages for contracted workers. The event—also known as the "Subway Strike"—shuts down the city's mass transit system for 11 days.

April: The Mariel Boatlift begins in Mariel Harbor, Cuba, and continues until the fall.

April 24–25: The aborted U.S. military effort to rescue American hostages in Iran, codenamed Operation Eagle Claw, ends in disaster as eight soldiers are killed and another four suffer severe burns.

May: Miami experiences race riots after four white former police officers are acquitted on charges of beating a black man to death.

May 18: Mount St. Helens (Washington) volcano erupts.

May 21: *Star Wars Episode V: The Empire Strikes Back* opens in movie theaters and drive-ins across the country.

June: Sixties radical Abbie Hoffman, who lived as a fugitive for several years, resurfaces in New York City, causing a media sensation.

June 1: Ted Turner's Cable News Network (CNN) goes on the air.

July 16: Former actor and two-term California governor Ronald Reagan is nominated for president at the Republican National Convention in Detroit, Michigan.

August 14: Jimmy Carter is nominated for president at the Democratic National Convention in New York City, defeating his opponent, Senator Edward Kennedy of Massachusetts.

Summer: A deadly summer heat wave strikes the United States.

November 4: Ronald Reagan is elected president of the United States, defeating incumbent Democratic President Jimmy Carter.

November 21: The nighttime soap opera *Dallas* reveals "Who Shot J. R.," attracting millions of TV viewers nationwide.

December 8: Former Beatle member John Lennon is shot and killed outside his apartment in New York City by Mark David Chapman.

THE CONSERVATIVE ASCENDANCY

A Shift to the Right?

Did American society become more conservative in the 1980s? This question was already on the minds of observers following Ronald Reagan's landslide electoral victory over Jimmy Carter on November 4, 1980. Conservatives rejoiced when they heard the news that their hero—the former Hollywood B-movie actor, two-term governor of California, and product of small-town Illinois—would soon be the 40th president of the United States. Predictably, most pundits on the right side of the political spectrum felt vindicated by the election of Reagan and believed that American society was at last becoming more conservative in the aftermath of the upheavals of the 1960s. The outcome of the 1980 election, explained the conservative *National Review* magazine, was indicative of "the plain fact that voters are rejecting liberal extremism" (*National Review* 1984, 14). Shortly after the election, liberal *New York Times* columnist Anthony Lewis glumly observed, "What happened in the 1980 election reflected a profound and general turn to conservatism in this country" (Lewis 1980). Not all observers agreed that the nation had moved to the right, however. Surveying public opinion poll data in 1983, economist John L. Goodman at the Urban Institute in Washington, D.C., found that "Ronald Reagan's election did not reflect, nor has he brought about, a change in the broad economic and social orientation of the American public" (Schwab 1988, 817). By the mid-1980s, a growing number of scholars began to concur with Goodman's conclusion. In Gil Troy's *Morning in America: How Ronald Reagan Invented the 1980s,* one of the first scholarly accounts of the decade, the author weighed in on the matter: "The great conservative realignment was chimerical. Only 28 percent of those bothering to vote identified as 'conservative,' only 13 percent as strong Republicans. Reagan's conservative ideology motivated only one Reagan voter in ten. Americans had not turned conservative regarding welfare, abortion, or the equal rights amendment. Voters wanted lower taxes and fewer regulations, but they still considered government the national problem-solver" (Troy 2005, 49).

Whether American society shifted to the right in the 1980s is debatable. Just as the very definition of conservative in its American context remains elusive and subject to constant revision, likewise it is difficult to determine whether an entire nation and its inhabitants moved in a particular ideological direction. One thing is certain: Reagan's rise to GOP presidential frontrunner in 1980 was due to a conservative shift within the Republican Party that had been underway since the 1960s. Since Barry Goldwater's dramatic defeat in the 1964 presidential elections, the forces of American conservatism had been mobilizing. This generation of activists has often been called the New Right, to distinguish them from pre–World War II patrician conservatives who were based mainly in the Northeast and focused primarily on economic issues. The New Right, by contrast, adopted more activist tactics by organizing grassroots mass movements, direct mailings, ballot measures, and referenda. They campaigned for conservative political candidates, supported influential think tanks, and created their own media outlets. Most importantly, the different conservative factions were able to locate common ground and advance a shared agenda that ultimately transformed American politics and society. "In 1945 'conservatism' was not a popular word in America," reminded historian George H. Nash, "and its spokesmen were without much influence in their native land. A generation later these once isolated voices had become a chorus, a significant intellectual and political movement which had an opportunity to shape the nation's destiny" (Roberts 1980, 23). Whereas the political trends of the early post–World War II years seemed to favor liberalism, the opposite was true by 1980. Liberals were now on the defensive and leftists were weak and divided. Meanwhile, conservatives wielded enormous influence and were poised to enter the halls of power.

No other event in the 1970s foreshadowed the triumph of Reagan as much as the heavily publicized California Tax Revolt. On June 6, 1978, California voters passed Proposition 13 by a margin of 2 to 1. The initiative cut local property taxes by almost 60 percent, capped property tax rates at 1 percent of a home's value, and capped the increase of a home's assessed value at 2 percent per year for the duration of ownership. The impact of Proposition 13 was immediate and dramatic. To many Americans, its passage seemed to herald a heyday of antigovernment sentiments. California's tax rate plummeted, and the media frenzy surrounding Proposition 13 helped trigger tax revolts in other states. Scholars thoroughly studied the tax revolt, and nearly 100 articles about the event appeared in academic journals between 1978 and 1980. The tax revolt also furnished Ronald Reagan with his supreme campaign mantra in 1980: "Government isn't the solution, government is the problem" (Morris 1999, 469).

Like the antibusing protests of the mid-1970s, the California Tax Revolt was a populist movement that attracted substantial numbers of ordinary people who felt disempowered, resentful, and vulnerable. Most of the rebels were blue-collar, middle-class Californians who had concluded that the state government had

Concerned parents and teachers protest the passage of Proposition 13 in Los Angeles on June 19, 1978. (Bettmann/Corbis)

raised property taxes too high and too arbitrarily. Overnight in the spring of 1978, entire neighborhood grassroots efforts emerged to campaign for Proposition 13. The movement had a charismatic leader, crusty septuagenarian Howard Jarvis, a retired California businessman who became a media icon in 1978 and could be seen on the cover of *Time* magazine that summer defiantly shaking his fist.

For the tens of thousands of rank-and-file activists who struggled to support "Prop 13" in their communities, the campaign for its passage represented their introduction to the world of political action. Long after the initiative was passed, the Prop 13 volunteers looked back on their efforts with a mixture of pride and nostalgia. In the spring of 1978, Belle Palmer was a volunteer who staffed a pro–Proposition 13 storefront in Van Nuys, California. She remembered: "When I look back, I realize how much fun we all had. We thought we were changing the world" (Orlov 2003, 16).

Televangelists and Christian Conservatism

Coinciding with the Proposition 13 movement, the emergence of televangelism further buoyed the New Right during the 1970s and 1980s. Televangelism was

Women and the New Right

The New Right would not have enjoyed the astonishing success that it did without the input of countless women. Intellectuals such as Suzanne LaFollette, a founder of the *New Republic,* historian Gertrude Himmelfarb, economist Rose Friedman, and author and activist Midge Decter, contributed significantly to ever-changing patterns of conservative thought. Women also factored prominently into conservative activism, often drawn into the movement during the 1960s and 1970s by their opposition to feminism. Thousands of libertarian women joined Young Americans for Freedom and organized on university campuses across the nation. Elsewhere, women participated in a number of key struggles: the pro-family movement, the antifeminist Eagle Forum, the STOP ERA campaign, and anti-abortion protests. Singer Anita Bryant, the spokeswoman for the Florida orange juice industry in the 1970s, raised the profile of conservative female activism when she launched a crusade in 1977 called "Save Our Children."

Undoubtedly, the most famous female conservative was influential activist and author Phyllis Schlafly, a role model for many right-wing women and a demonized figure in feminist circles. No other conservative—man or woman—worked as rigorously for the cause as Schlafly. A leader in the Eagle Forum, STOP ERA, and numerous other movements, Schlafly toured the nation, condemning feminism, homosexuality, and moral relativism from the pulpit. Born in 1924 in St. Louis, Missouri, to a Catholic family, she graduated in 1944 from Washington University and obtained a master's degree from Harvard the following year. She was active in Republican Party politics in the 1940s and 1950s, running unsuccessfully for Congress in 1952 and again in 1970. She emerged a leader in the conservative movement after her book *A Choice Not an Echo* was published in 1964. Her most notable political crusade occurred in the 1970s when she led activists in a struggle to defeat the Equal Rights Amendment (ERA), which she feared would have a harmful effect on women and family life. Many conservative women attributed Schlafly with bringing them into the movement. One female activist recalled: "[Phyllis] really changed my life. Everything that I had learned before in politics was just added to by another layer of sophistication because Phyllis is a sophisticated politician. . . . When you get into Phyllis's operation it's all women and we're all . . . running the office, we're running the campaigns, we're doing fundraising, we're doing everything" (Klatch 1987, 266–267).

part of a broader resurgence of evangelical Christianity across the United States in this period. By the end the early 1980s, a new generation of charismatic conservative ministers filled the television airwaves with sermons about family values and the evils of parental permissiveness, drugs, rock music, gay rights, abortion, and promiscuity. Rev. Jerry Falwell, the most highly visible televange-

Evangelist Jerry Falwell, founder of the "Moral Majority," greets GOP presidential candidate Ronald Reagan as he arrives to address the National Religious Broadcasters in Lynchburg, Virginia, on October 3, 1980. (Bettmann/Corbis)

list, commanded an extensive network that included his television show *Old Time Gospel Hour,* broadcast on the Liberty Broadcasting Network to 1.5 million subscribers, his Thomas Road Liberty Baptist Church, and Liberty University, all based out of Lynchburg, Virginia. Similar evangelical empires thrived under the leadership of Pat Robertson, host of *The 700 Club,* broadcast on the Christian Broadcasting Network, and Oral Roberts, head of a $500 million religious enterprise that included Oral Roberts University in Tulsa, Oklahoma.

With the encouragement of activists Howard Phillips, Richard Viguerie, and Paul Weyrich, Reverend Falwell founded the Moral Majority in 1979, a powerful political organization dedicated to advancing the goals of the religious right. Falwell's new foundation played a critical role in mobilizing conservative Christians to vote for conservative political candidates, especially Ronald Reagan, in the

1980 election. Between November 1979 and July 1980, the Moral Majority and other Christian groups closely allied with it registered 2.5 million voters. Predictably, Falwell aimed his assault against abortion rights, gay and lesbian liberation struggles, secular humanism, and political radicalism. Emboldened by Republican gains in the 1978 midterm elections, the United States' leading fundamentalist figures united behind Christian Republican political candidates. "We have enough votes to run the country," proclaimed Pat Robertson (Lienesch 1982, 405).

The founding of the Moral Majority occurred at a crossroads for Christian conservatives. Months later, on April 29, 1980, Pat Robertson and several of his most influential allies organized "Washington for Jesus," a massive prayer rally that drew 200,000 fundamentalists to the nation's capital and demonstrated the political clout of the religious right to the rest of America. This dramatic action paralleled a new offensive against the forces of "secular humanism," which was a broad but heavily used term in right-wing Christian circles to describe a host of things: homosexuality, feminism, a perceived unraveling of American families, the Democratic Party, the ACLU, the NAACP, the Unitarian Church, and any other people or institutions considered threatening. "Simply defined," wrote Tim LaHaye, a founder of Moral Majority, "secular humanism is man's attempt to solve problems independently of God" (Diamond 1989, 85). On a local level, Christian right activists spearheaded campaigns to remove "secular humanist" textbooks from school shelves. In 1975, Mel and Norma Gabler of Longview, Texas, launched their own attempt to screen public school textbooks and weed out any deemed by their newly created group, Education Research Analysts, to be excessively humanistic and irreligious. Other opponents of "secular humanism" joined in the crusade. For a time in the 1980s, book banning became increasingly common in fundamentalist-dominated communities, and sometimes it was endorsed by the legal system. In 1987, for example, a federal judge in Mobile, Alabama, banned 44 textbooks based on excessive "secular humanist" content.

By the early 1980s, Christian evangelism had moved into the mainstream. In 1979, a Gallup poll indicated that 40 percent of the population consisted of "born again" Christians. The following year, millions of white evangelicals who supported Jimmy Carter in 1976 voted for Ronald Reagan instead. Reagan repeatedly wooed the Christian Right to support him, including his participation in a 1980 Religious Roundtable, which featured a number of prominent fundamentalists as guests. Many "born again" Christians identified with Reagan, who, ironically, never fully embraced fundamentalism or evangelicalism. Still, Reagan in 1980 articulated the deepest beliefs of religious conservatives. "I have found a great longing in America for a spiritual revival," Reagan proclaimed, "for a belief that law must be based on a higher law, for a return to traditions and values that we once had. . . . We are a nation under God" (McLoughlin 1983, 103).

Grassroots Conservatism in the Age of Reagan

Chroniclers of the rise of post–World War II grassroots conservative movements have typically focused on key organizing efforts in the 1960s and 1970s. Most accounts conclude in 1980, with the presidential victory of Ronald Reagan, which many historians treat as the culmination of years of mobilizing on the Right. After the Reagan triumph, histories of conservatism in the 1980s usually switch focus, exploring the evolution and transformation of political conservatism in Washington, D.C., while neglecting grassroots campaigns. Such an emphasis, unfortunately, obscures the continued and complicated role that local grassroots conservative social movements played in communities across the country during the Reagan era.

The idea that conservatism "triumphed" in American society in the 1980s is itself a highly dubious notion. The dynamics of political power in the nation's capital often necessitated compromises from even the most stalwart conservative policymakers. Champions of the Reagan Revolution in the 1980s failed to balance the budget, dismantle the welfare state, or decrease the size of the federal bureaucracy. To win elections, conservative politicians often borrowed from the language of liberalism and populism to attract women, minorities, and working-class voters. Modified positions and recurring concessions led some conservative purists, such as Barry Goldwater and Richard Viguerie, to question how far to the right the country had really moved under President Reagan. In 1982, with the country still mired in recession, a public backlash against conservatism was already under way, as reflected in the outcome of the November midterm elections, which furnished several setbacks for Republicans. By mid-decade, an increasing number of politicians on the Right chose the term "populist" to describe themselves, which they found more flattering than "conservative." "Populism," explained Republican congressman Jack Kemp in 1983, "is basically the idea that you can trust people to make the right decisions about their own lives and about the country" (Peterson 1983).

Political shifts in Washington, D.C., reflected changes at the grassroots level. Local conservative organizations continued to mobilize in the 1980s and still wielded considerable clout, but issues of great importance to earlier generations of conservatives, such as anticommunism and nativism, became increasingly irrelevant in the 1980s. Especially robust were groups that emphasized social conservatism, such as the National Pro-Life Political Action Committee, the National Christian Action Coalition, Phyllis Schlafly's Eagle Forum, and the Moral Majority. While these organizations were not officially affiliated with the Republican Party, their members often campaigned for conservative Republican political candidates. In 1984, the grassroots Christian Voice, for example, mobilized a thousand men and women who were new to politics to serve as delegates at the state Republican convention. By 1987, GOP presidential hopefuls Jack Kemp, George H. W. Bush, and others busily courted grassroots antiabortion activists in Iowa.

With President Reagan in the White House during the 1980s, some conservative organizations slackened in their activities, confident that their agendas enjoyed increased support in the nation's halls of power. In 1984, a liberal activist noted, "When you're in power, you have a harder time raising money. People feel you don't need funds, that there is nothing more to achieve. Our side has a lot of devils to beat: domestic cutbacks, threats to Social Security, a Senate with Jesse Helms, environmental concerns" (Bonafede 1985). Some groups, such as the rightwing John Birch Society, actually experienced declining membership rolls in the 1980s. The so-called Birchers almost ceased to function in 1986 following the death of their longtime leader, Robert Welch.

By contrast, other conservative organizations flourished, especially those that adapted successfully to the changing times. Of utmost importance to the viability of a conservative organization were its methods of outreach. An especially potent means of attracting new adherents was the "direct mail" system championed by veteran New Right activist Richard Viguerie. His highly successful direct-mail firm in northern Virginia employed 300 dedicated conservatives in the 1980s. Using the latest database technology of the day, the direct mailers accumulated information about the age, sex, residence, education, income, lifestyle, and buying habits of different segments of the population. Sometimes they zeroed in on particular zip codes where residents were especially responsive to such appeals. The demographic information they accumulated over time helped them determine where to send mass mailings that appealed for support for a variety of conservative organizations. A typical direct mailing would consist of four pages of highly polemical, adjective-heavy language—often alarmist and over-the-top in style—and contained special inserts, mailing envelopes, decals, and other materials. Direct mail was also employed by activists on the Left, most notably by Public Interest Communications, a progressive firm owned by Roger Craver.

In most cases, the conservative movements that thrived in the 1980s were led by people who positioned themselves as outsiders. They successfully appealed to the resentments of ordinary people who feared that America was drifting in the wrong direction. Fears of homosexuality, secular humanism, feminism, "Eastern" elites, moral relativism, and excessive power at the federal government level all combined to drive ordinary people from all walks of life to participate in the varied conservative social movements of the 1980s. Grassroots organizing on the Right did not abate during the Reagan years. If anything, it grew increasingly sophisticated and attuned to the anxieties of marginalized Americans.

Conservatives played an instrumental role in mobilizing support behind Ronald Reagan in 1980. The various factions put aside their differences with one another, coalesced around key economic and cultural issues, and brought rightwing ideas that had previously been marginalized to the forefront of the national debate. Conservatism, which many observers had dismissed as moribund a mere 16 years earlier, was revitalized and made relevant again. Following

Reagan's landslide victory, he repeatedly praised activists for their efforts and carefully considered their input when it came time to make key decisions. A few years into Reagan's presidency, some zealous ideologues expressed disappointment that, in their view, the commander in chief had not shown sufficient dedication to the cause. By 1983, budgets were soaring, some federal bureaucracies were expanding, and most social welfare programs endured, despite some drastic cuts. Some on the right, especially libertarians, registered their complaints in the op-ed pages of newspapers or at public gatherings. Still, most conservative Americans welcomed Ronald Reagan's presidency as a positive step. When Reagan ran for the presidency a second time in 1984, many familiar faces campaigned for him yet again, and the conservative movement that so effectively assisted him four years earlier remained a force to be reckoned with in American society.

THE PIVOTAL YEAR: 1980

A Time of Transition

As the gateway into the 1980s, the year 1980 anticipated a number of the decade's most important developments. In 1977, Jimmy Carter's presidency initially appeared to follow traditional liberal patterns: the president pardoned Vietnam War–era draft evaders, created new federal bodies such as the Environmental Protection Agency, and emphasized the importance of human rights in the formation of U.S. foreign policy. Within a year, however, as economic conditions worsened and global conflicts flared, Carter jettisoned liberal priorities in favor of the more pragmatic, ideologically flexible centrism of the so-called New Democrats, which would characterize the remainder of his presidency and set the stage for the rightward shift in American politics. Sweeping changes were not confined to Washington, D.C. Far beyond the Beltway, the nation was experiencing economic, radical, gender, cultural, and social transformations whose ripples could be felt in even the remotest communities. This tour of 1980 will include visits to the following themes:

- The 1980 Miami riots
- The Iranian hostage crisis and American society
- The heat wave in the summer of 1980
- A study of immigration in America in 1980

Beginnings: The 1980 Miami Riots

On the afternoon of Saturday, May 17, 1980, one of the worst riots in American history exploded in the streets of Miami. Igniting the bloody event was the acquittal by an all-white jury in Tampa of four Miami police officers accused of beating to death African American insurance executive Arthur McDuffle the previous December. Immediately after the verdict was announced, a whirlwind of violence and looting swept through the streets of Miami. Snipers fired guns from rooftops and high windows, motorists purposely ran over fleeing pedestrians, arsonists set fire to local businesses and assailants began beating innocent bystanders. Several prominent African Americans called for the resignation of States Attorney (and future U.S. Attorney General) Janet Reno, whose office prosecuted the McDuffle case. In the meantime, the mayor of Miami, Puerto Rico–born Maurice Ferre, strongly condemned police brutality and called for amnesty for rioters who stopped participating in the unrest.

After three days, 14 people were dead, 371 were injured, and police had arrested 450 Miamians. A *Washington Post* reporter surveying the damage noted that "the blackened remains of drugstores, Dairy Queens, liquor stores, gasoline stations and an elementary school gave off the sickening stink from fire. Overturned cars sat unattended in the middle of deserted boulevards" (Hornblower 1980). Within hours of the outbreak of rioting, National Guard units were mobilized and deployed to the streets of Miami. Although some journalist and network news correspondents blamed the violence on the verdict of the McDuffle case, the riot had much deeper roots in the despair, lack of economic opportunities, and police abuse that were so pervasive in African American communities across America. Unemployment among African Americans was double that of whites in 1980, and relief seemed elusive to most African Americans. Poor blacks were becoming increasingly resentful, not only against whites but also toward Haitian and Cuban newcomers, who were perceived to be taking jobs away from native-born residents.

The presence of National Guard troops, coupled with heavy rains that fell on Miami, helped quell the riots. The worst of the violence was over within a few days, but riots would erupt again in Miami in June and July. When President Jimmy Carter's motorcade passed through Liberty City, a predominantly African American section of Miami, crowds of angry African Americans booed and threw stones at his limousine. The rioters had compelling reasons to be angry at the president. Long before the riots erupted in the spring of 1980, living standards had declined for most African Americans across the nation. During President Carter's first year in office, an estimated 131,000 African American families fell below the federal poverty level. His cuts in key urban programs resulted in continual deterioration of African American inner city neighborhoods. In 1978, his administration allocated an insufficient $150 million for urban social services, which sparked a public outcry by several mayors who condemned Carter for his

National Guardsman directs traffic away from fires burning during the riot in Miami, Florida, on May 18, 1980. (Bettmann/Corbis)

lack of support. The Miami riots grimly highlighted the nation's unresolved racial tensions. President Carter was visibly shaken when he visited the riot-torn neighborhoods of Miami in June. Yet his political and economic priorities exacerbated the already stark conditions in the riot-torn city. His rejection of traditional Democratic Party liberalism expedited the demise of the New Deal Coalition—a tenuous alliance of labor unions, African Americans, women, southern Democrats, and liberals—that had been declining since the 1960s.

A second riot occurred in the streets of Miami in July, when African American groups seized control of several neighborhoods for 48 hours and began looting, burning, and sniping at the police. In Liberty City, heavily armed SWAT teams enforced a 9 p.m. to 6 a.m. curfew while police counterattacked crowds of rioters. City officials met with community leaders, area residents, police representatives, and business owners to discuss solutions to the crisis. Modest amounts of federal money trickled into Miami to help rebuild some of the ruined neighborhoods. But despair would remain palpable on the inner-city streets for the next several years. "We have been made nonentities, non-human beings," remarked an African American woman in Miami following the May riots. "When you're a non-human being, you become an animal" ("Miami 1980"). The race riots were but one of many crises—both foreign and domestic—that would vex Jimmy Carter for the remainder of his presidency.

The Iranian Hostage Crisis and American Society

The grainy television images haunted Americans for years. Nightly news broadcasts beamed to millions of television sets across the country each night showed film footage of enormous crowds of chanting Islamic revolutionaries in Tehran, Iran, parading masked American hostages through the city. On the morning of November 4, a sprawling crowd of chanting students penetrated the gates of the American embassy, a compound thought to be impregnable against mobs and therefore nicknamed "Fort Apache" by the Marine guards. The student militants took 71 hostages, soon releasing 19 but holding 52 in captivity for the next 444 days. A young Iranian militant, asked by a hostage why he had taken over the embassy, replied, "To teach the American government and the CIA a lesson, so it will keep its hands off other countries, particularly Iran!" (Ebtekar 2000, 69).

Millions of Americans watched with a mixture of curiosity and outrage as the heavily televised drama unfolded. Few viewers understood the extent of American intervention in Iran that predated the embassy takeover. In fact, the origins of the hostage crisis extended back more than a quarter of a century. In 1953, the CIA orchestrated a series of upheavals that resulted in a coup overthrowing Mohammed Mossadegh, Iran's democratically elected prime minister. His government coexisted in Iran with the monarchy of Mohammed Reza Pahlavi, Shah of Iran, which was backed by the British and, later, the U.S. governments. Mossadegh, prime minister since 1951, established a reputation as a fiercely patriotic nationalist determined to transfer Iran's vast foreign-dominated oil markets to Iranian control. The prime minister moved dramatically to nationalize British oil companies, but his base of support consisted of a volatile combination of distrusting mullah's, militant students, the radical Tudeh (or Masses) Party and a few loyal military officials. The CIA planned a series of street protests, gradually leading to a military coup orchestrated by Theodore Roosevelt's grandson, Kermit, that restored the Shah to power in Tehran. By August 23, 1953, the Shah was firmly in place, following days of disorder. He welcomed Kermit Roosevelt to the royal palace and thanked him profusely. "I owe my throne to God, my people, my army—and to you!" (Halberstam 1994, 365).

For the next quarter of a century, the Shah, firmly backed by Washington, controlled one of the most repressive regimes in the region. In the early 1960s, the Shah began a process of westernizing Iran known as "the White Revolution," which included promises of land redistribution and allowing women to vote, but the reforms were largely superficial. Meanwhile, the Shah enjoyed a steady flow of military, technical, and economic aid from the United States right up through the Carter administration. When the Arab oil-producing nations enacted an embargo on oil shipments to the United States because of its support for Israel, the Shah saw to it personally that the flow of Iranian oil to America went uninterrupted. To consolidate the monarch's power, SAVAK—the secret police—arrested and imprisoned dissidents, resorting to murder in numerous instances. The Islamic clergy were among the most active resisters against the Shah. In 1963, Ruhollah Khomeini, a 60-year-old Islamic cleric, issued a *fatwa* or religious edict calling the Shah's westernizing reforms "a threat to Islam," and warned of the "imminent dangers facing the Koran and this country of the Koran" (Wright 1989, 50).

Riots erupted across Iran in late 1978, causing the Shah to declare martial law, and as the situation worsened, he ordered government troops to employ violent tactics to disperse angry mobs of Iranians. But it was too late. The Shah's rule was crumbling. Mohammed Reza Pahlavi, Shah of Iran, left the country in January 1979 for his own well-being, and on February 1, Khomeini left Paris for Tehran, stepping into the chaotic power vacuum. The mood in Washington was grim. A coalition of revolutionary councils now controlled Iran, demanding extradition of the Shah to Iranian custody, along with the vast sums of wealth he siphoned from the treasury. As long as the former monarch remained overseas, the new Iranian leaders reasoned, there was always a danger that the CIA might attempt to engineer a repeat of the 1953 coup.

The hostage crisis touched off a fierce outcry in America. Overnight billboards appeared along American highways featuring Khomeini's deadpan expression and bold words, "Fight Back . . . Drive 55!" Media coverage of the event was extensive, and the news show *Nightline,* hosted by Ted Koppel, began as a nightly television program focused on the hostages. A flurry of opinion polls in early 1980 indicated strong public support for military intervention in Iran to solve the crisis. The president's approval ratings climbed from 32 percent in early November 1979 to 61 percent by early December, his highest rating during his term in the White House. Pollster George Gallup called the jump in numbers "stunning" and "the largest increase in the four decades the Gallup poll has made measurements" (Sick 1986, 18). Responding to public pressures to act, President Carter froze $12 billion worth of Iranian assets in the United States, severed diplomatic relations between the two nations, and introduced an arms embargo on Iran. Intense diplomatic efforts occurred through the United Nations and private intermediaries. Days turned into weeks, weeks into months, and even though Carter initially enjoyed a temporary boost in public approval ratings, his support quickly declined as Americans began perceiving him as a restrained, "do-nothing" president (Johnson 1991, 35).

In April, an attempt to rescue the hostages orchestrated by President Carter and key military brass ended in disaster after one of the rescue helicopters collided with a refueling plane in the deserts of Iran. Pictures of the charred fuselages strewn across the desert were prominently featured in newspapers across the country, a stark visual that confirmed in the minds of millions of Americans their fears that the nation's postwar prestige and power had waned significantly since the end of the Vietnam War.

The disaster touched off a wave of anti-Iranian sentiment across the nation in the summer of 1980, which fueled prejudices against Iranians living in the United

A Student holds an anti-Iranian sign at a protest during the Iranian Hostage Crisis in Washington, D.C., on November 9, 1979. (Library of Congress)

States and occasionally resulted in violence. In New Jersey, straight-A student Tina Bahadori was selected to deliver the valedictory address at Atlantic City High School's commencement in June, but because she was an Iranian national, school officials rejected her at the last minute and selected a different speaker. At a federal prison in Otisville, New York, authorities imprisoned 171 Iranian men for four days without charges. An additional 20 Iranian women were also imprisoned in New York for several days. In cities across America, anti-Iranian demonstrations were commonplace in 1980. Predictably, such sentiments also influenced young people. A 1981 study by the Jewish Community Relations Council in San Francisco found an increase in hostilities against Iranian-born students in high schools throughout the San Francisco Bay area. In other parts of the country, newspapers reported an increase in incidents of bullying and intimidation against Iranian high school students.

The Long, Hot Summer

A deadly heat wave—one of the worst in American history—settled over the nation in early June 1980. A high-pressure system surged over the United States from the south, moving sluggishly over the Gulf of Mexico, and halting abruptly over the southwest. With it came a layer of thick, boiling hot tropical air that extended from California to Wyoming, from the Dakotas to Georgia. Cities experienced repeated electrical brownouts as people ran air conditioners to maximum capacity. Droughts plagued much of the Midwest, South, and West, hitting the farms particularly hard. Poultry breeders in Oklahoma, Arkansas, and Texas lost $4 million worth of chickens and turkeys to heat while agricultural losses in North and South Dakota exceeded $280 million by mid-July ("Killer Heat Wave," 29). In Arkansas, Gov. Bill Clinton declared a state of emergency due to the unrelenting heat. Rampaging fires engulfed western states, with the worst raging in Colorado's White River National Forest. Each day, firefighters wearing thick protective gear battled the flames while tanker planes droned over the surreal brown skies of Colorado, Texas, Arizona, and California, dumping thousands of gallons of fire retardants with each sweep. Where flames did not destroy, the sun scorched. The wheat farms of Montana suffered a drier year in 1979–1980 than the Dust Bowl year of 1936–1937. Corn stalks in Kansas and Nebraska wilted under the relentless 100-degree heat of the midday sun. At the center of the heat wave was Texas, which became a stark over-heated oven in the summer of 1980. The hottest month of June ever recorded in Texas history brought 45 deaths, and even more would eventually perish the following month ("Heat Wave" 1980, A12).

The poor and elderly were particularly vulnerable to the heat wave, yet nobody could fully escape the misery. Each day, some 60 cast and crew members of the hit television series *Dallas* consumed 30 gallons of Gatorade and 30 gallons of water, as well as "unaccounted cases of soft drinks" (Curry 1980, 16). So intense was the heat that *Dallas* star and sex symbol Charlene Tilton passed out from the high temperatures while posing for photographs for her fans. Fifty miles west of San Antonio, in rural Texas, farmer V. H. Neumann surveyed his withering fields. "We are just burning up. Everything is gone" ("Killer Heat Wave," 29).

In other parts of the United States, people did their best to cope with the stifling heat. Predictably, social class shaped options. Municipal workers in Chicago, Detroit, New York, Atlanta, Boston, and Philadelphia turned on fire hydrants so kids—often immigrant and African American children—could find relief and fun in the gushing water. Senior citizens without air conditioning died in their homes of heat exposure. A scene that repeated itself over and over happened in early July, when Dallas police entered the home of David Michaelson. Inside, the temperature hit a sweltering 110 degrees due to an air conditioner breakdown; 77-year-old Michaelson and his sister Sadie lay dead on the floor of heat exhaustion ("Killer Heat Wave," 29). In the meantime, middle class and affluent Americans escaped the heat in air conditioned suburban homes, enjoying new technologies such as cable television and top-loading VCRs. Political junkies, in particular, watched the presidential campaigns on Ted Turner's newly-launched Cable News Network (CNN). The movie theater also offered a cool atmosphere, and people lined up for city blocks to view *The Empire Strikes*

The Death of Disco?

In the 1980 smash hit comedy *Airplane!,* a distressed aircraft making an emergency landing knocks over the tall, steel tower of a disco radio station, thus cutting off the broadcast. The film was so full of gags that it was easy to miss, but this symbolized—in a humorous way—the demise of disco music. Born in the mid-1970s with such hits as the Hues Corporation's "Rock the Boat," Love Unlimited Orchestra's "Love's Theme," Average White Band's "Pick up the Pieces" and Van McKoy's "The Hustle," disco seemed to get off to a promising start. The genre combined blues, funk, jazz, rock, and heavy percussion dance rhythms for a unique blast of sound that was a welcome change from the turgid 1970s hard rock scene.

At the time, disco was celebrated as the most multiracial form of music in existence, in the composition of both its performers and their listeners. It was also widely embraced in urban gay enclaves in San Francisco, Los Angeles, Chicago, Philadelphia, and New York. As Casablanca Records executive Kenn Friedman proclaimed, "There's a big cultural difference between rock and disco, and it's gayness. Some people don't like to talk about it, but it's true. Disco began in gay clubs" (Kopkind 1995, 313). By 1976, disco clubs began operations in New York and soon spread across the country, and the airwaves were saturated with disco music. Even a disco version of the *Star Wars* theme by the band Meco became a heavily played single. Within a few years, a backlash was under way, which came close to sending disco to the music graveyard. However, the opening of *Saturday Night Fever* in late 1977, following the release of its best-selling soundtrack earlier in the year, rejuvenated the ailing genre and offered it a second life. For a time, disco again dominated the airwaves, and dance clubs did a brisk business. But the revival of disco also intensified the simmering backlash, and its rebirth proved short-lived.

The disco craze had largely run its course by decade's end, although certain disco hits still scored big on the Billboard Top 40 in 1980, among them Diana Ross's "I'm Coming Out" and "Upside Down," Kool and the Gang's "Celebration," and Earth, Wind and Fire's "Let's Groove." But a recent antidisco backlash had diminished the potency of the genre, and the output of hits declined steadily. "No other pop music form," observed *Rolling Stone,* "has ever attracted such rabid partisans and fanatical foes, dividing audiences along racial and sexual lines, even as its function . . . was to turn the pop audience into one big happy family" (Schulman 2001, 71).

A huge antidisco frenzy at Chicago's Comiskey Field in July 1979, sponsored by the Chicago White Sox and featuring an emcee blowing up a pile of disco albums, touched off an enormous riot as the primarily white crowd rushed onto the baseball field to join the destruction. Similar antidisco actions occurred at other sports events, bars, dance establishments, and concerts. Hostility toward disco reached a fever pitch, fueled by misgivings about the interracial nature of the music and the movement, as well as the popularity of disco in gay communities. Nevertheless, disco styles persisted in the music of the 1980s, especially the dance hits of Madonna and Michael Jackson and the synth-pop sounds of such new wave bands as New Order and the Bronski Beat.

Back, the long-awaited sequel to George Lucas's 1977 generation-defining zeit-geist *Star Wars.* By contrast, few Americans paid attention to the Olympic Games occurring in Moscow during July and August. President Carter had chosen to boycott the games in protest against the Soviet invasion of Afghanistan, which would prove to be an omen of future tensions.

In Atlanta, mecca of the ascendant Sunbelt, the revival of the Cold War and the high temperatures were the least of parents' fears. A serial killer walked the streets of Atlanta in the summer of 1980, murdering African American children. The killings began the previous summer with the disappearance of two youths and continued until the fall, ceased for a time, then resumed in March. All of the victims were abducted (including a girl who was kidnapped from her family's bathroom) and later found brutally murdered by stabbings or gunshot wounds. A few of the children were never found. The horrific Atlanta child murders—every parent's worst nightmare—triggered a firestorm of controversy in the city. In April 1980, parents, relatives, and friends of victims founded the Committee to Stop Children's Murders to lobby the police to do more. The Atlanta police complained loudly about the lack of cooperation from city officials, and every-body wondered why the Federal Bureau of Investigation (FBI) stayed out of the investigation as long as it did. Citizens groups suggested racist foot-dragging by the police while gossip circulated throughout Atlanta's African American neighborhoods about crazed Ku Klux Klan or Nazi Party members carrying out the killings. At last, in September, the FBI began conducting an extensive investigation into the murders and disappearances. Novelist Toni Cade Bambara painted a vivid description in her book *Those Bones Are Not My Child* of the ter-rifying atmosphere in Atlanta that summer. "City under siege. Armed helicopters overhead. Bullhorns bellowing to stay indoors. Curfew pushed back into the p.m. hours. Gun stores extending sales into the a.m. hours. Hardware stores scram-bling to meet the demand for burglar bars, deadbolt locks, alarms, lead pipes, and under-the-counter cans of mace and boxes of pellets" (Bambara 2000, 2).

Coming to America in 1980: A Study in Contrasts

The summer heat wave did not deter the flow of immigrants arriving in the United States every day. During the 1980s, six million immigrants came to Amer-ica, most from Asia and Latin America. The cover of the July 7, 1980, issue of *Newsweek* celebrated these so-called New Immigrants. The Refugee Act, passed by Congress in 1980, granted political asylum to those fleeing countries where their lives might be in jeopardy as a result of their race, religion, nationality, or political ideology. Immigration officials applied the act selectively, making it far easier for immigrants from communist regimes, particularly Cuba and Vietnam, to enter the country than those from autocratic, pro-U.S. client states such as El Salvador or the Philippines. The most dramatic and heavily publicized immi-gration influx in American history occurred in the spring and summer of 1980.

*Cuban defectors during the Mariel
Boatlift in 1980. (U.S. Coast Guard)*

In April, the first of thousands of Cubans who were part of the so-called Mariel Boatlift began sailing into ports all over the southern Florida coast, motivated by a loosening of emigration restrictions by the Cuban government. They came on ships, cabin cruisers, fishing boats, dinghies, rubber rafts, catamarans, and even inner tubes, braving the sometimes blazing hot, sometimes stormy 90-mile stretch of ocean between Cuba and the United States. Network news cameras perched inside helicopters filmed their harrowing journey for the nightly news. The immigrants' motives for coming to America varied. While thousands left to escape political repression, two scholars who studied the enormous waves of Cuban refugees arriving in Florida found "that economic motives were beginning to play a larger role affecting the decision to leave Cuba, certainly more so than had been the case in the early 1960s" (Boswell and Curtis 1983, 51). The *Marielitos,* as they were called (because their boats left Mariel Harbor, 20 miles west of Havana) eventually numbered approximately 130,000. Complicating matters was Fidel Castro's decision to deposit thousands of prisoners and mentally ill Cubans on America's shores. About 26,000 *Marielitos* had prison records while 5,000 (or about 4 percent) were hardcore criminals (Boswell and Curtis 1983, 53).

Once in the United States, the *Marielitos* inhabited makeshift refugee camps. Overnight, a massive tent city—encircled by a tall chain link fence with barbed wire—sprang up near downtown Miami, under the shadow of the towering concrete Interstate 95 overpass. Miami's Orange Bowl stadium became a temporary shelter filled with thousands of cots where Cuban refugees awaited resettlement amid boxes of canned goods and bottled water delivered by volunteer relief agencies. Other refugees ended up at Eglin Air Force Base in Florida. Certain *Marielitos,* usually the "problem cases" (the mentally ill, violent offenders, drug dealers, and so forth) were shipped off to heavily guarded refugee camps in other states: Fort Chaffee, Arkansas; Fort McCoy, Wisconsin; and Fort Indiantown Gap, Pennsylvania. Those released for settlement typically gravitated toward large urban centers: New York City, Philadelphia, Chicago, and Atlanta. The majority of new arrivals moved to the vibrant and legendary Cuban-American community in Miami. Little Havana, Miami's Cuban section, was a lively mixture of family-run grocery stores, fresh-seafood sellers, cigar manufacturers, *botanicas* (stores that specialized in ritualistic religious items, such as herbs, oils, and figurines), clinics, furniture stores, and restaurants. In the early 1980s, more than 18,000 Cuban-owned businesses operated in Dade County (Miami), many along the main thoroughfare in Little Havana, Calle Ocho (Boswell and Curtis 1983, 87).

The preferential treatment given to Cuban immigrants by the federal government highlighted glaring inconsistencies in U.S. immigration policies. Such double standards became evident in a particularly gruesome incident far from Miami. On July 6, Border Patrol officials in southern Arizona discovered the corpses of 13 immigrants—4 men, the rest women, and a two-year-old child—rotting in the blistering hot summer sun, among a cluster of paloverde trees, two of them lying face down on Bibles. The dead refugees came from El Salvador, a small, densely populated Central American nation. In the long and violent history of El Salvador, the years between 1979 and 1984 were among the worst. A civil war there pitted the Salvadoran government, beset by coups and dominated by the nation's far-right military, against Marxist guerrillas of the Farabundo Marti National Liberation Front (FMLN), based in the rural areas and mountainous forests.

For a brief period, hopes were high in October 1979, when a democratic-minded civilian-army junta overthrew an autocratic ruling general and called on both the right and left to lay down weapons. It soon became clear to observers that the junta could not control the murderous Salvadoran military, especially the notorious paramilitary death squads, which had close ties to the military and consisted almost entirely of soldiers.

The number of disappearances and murders increased in late 1979 and early 1980. In January 1980, the more progressive/centrist members of the junta resigned in protest against abuses by the military. The assassination of renowned human rights activist Archbishop Oscar Romero on March 24, 1980, as he said mass in his cathedral further polarized the country. He had been El Salvador's equivalent to Gandhi and Rev. Dr. Martin Luther King Jr.—a voice for the voiceless, and a critic of injustice—and he met their same violent end for publicly criticizing the government.

The disappearances and extreme bloodletting continued throughout the year, and political violence claimed the lives of 9,000 Salvadorans. The wanton murdering culminated in December 1980 with the murder of four American Catholic missionaries—three nuns and a laywoman—performing humanitarian volunteer work in the countryside. The savage murders prompted President Carter to temporarily halt military aid and organize a special mission, headed by William D. Rogers, under secretary of state in the Ford administration, to investigate the crisis in El Salvador.

Against this backdrop of terror, Salvadorans routinely fled their homeland, bound for what they hoped would be new beginnings in the United States. Tragically, they soon discovered that the politics of U.S. immigration policy discriminated against them because the Salvadoran government, although undemocratic and repressive, was anticommunist and enjoyed substantial financing from the

United States. U.S. officials would never orchestrate a Salvadoran version of the Mariel boatlift, even though the steady stream of Salvadoran refugees who left El Salvador daily undoubtedly would have welcomed such hospitality. The regime in El Salvador was at least anticommunist, U.S. officials reasoned, and fostered lucrative opportunities for American business firms.

So Salvadorans had to exercise great stealth in entering the United States. Such was the case with 43 Salvadorans in late June 1980, who paid $2,500 per person to smugglers who promised to relocate them to the United States. They traveled by chartered bus to the U.S.–Mexican border, from which point they expected to fly to Los Angeles. When the smugglers—known as "coyotes"— changed plans, two dozen nervous Salvadorans, fearing the sudden switch, backed out and decided to hike across the southern Arizona desert with the help of some other smugglers who promised safe arrival in the United States.

The error in judgment proved fatal. For days the Salvadorans wandered in the deadly 115-degree heat, and after their 20 gallons of water ran out, they began desperately consuming cologne, after-shave lotion, deodorant, and eventually their own urine. These were mostly middle-class men and women fleeing political repression and hoping—like the *Marielitos*—to find new beginnings in the United States. Some of the women began the horrific death march through the desert wearing high heels and ended up with their feet wrapped in rags (Crewdson 1980, 1). The smugglers abandoned the Salvadorans to search for water. One by one, the Salvadorans perished over the Fourth of July weekend, in the middle of scorching hot Organ Pipe Cactus National Monument in southern Arizona.

Border patrol officials found 12 survivors who lived by drinking each other's urine, and 13 baked, dehydrated corpses lying on ground that reached temperatures of 150 degrees ("13 Aliens" 1980, 1). The 12 men and women were treated for dehydration, then incarcerated to await deportation back to El Salvador. The costly welcome given to the *Marielitos* was denied to the Salvadorans for entirely political reasons.

A Nation in Transition

A tumultuous year, the events of 1980 reflected a nation in transition. President Carter had the misfortune of presiding over a nation in transition, still convulsing from the traumatic disasters of Vietnam and Watergate. The climbing double-digit inflation, a complex legacy of excessive government spending on the Vietnam War and Great Society social welfare programs without sufficient tax increases, as well as the Middle East oil crisis that began in the fall of 1973, raised fears of impending economic doom. The Soviet invasion of Afghanistan and the Iranian hostage crisis further eroded confidence in President Carter's ability to confront threats to American security and business interests abroad. Opinion polls indicated widespread support for U.S. military intervention in Iran to resolve the hostage crisis, and yet, paradoxically, the majority of the American people doggedly continued to embrace isolationist sensibilities. Defeat in Vietnam five years earlier fostered a phenomenon in the United States known as "Vietnam syndrome," a fear of intervening in protracted wars and needlessly jeopardizing the lives of American youths.

The arrival of "new" immigrants from Asia and Latin America diversified the nation, enhancing its multicultural landscape while also fueling nativism among people uneasy with new immigrants arriving at a time of economic stagnation. Within America, culture wars erupted between conservatives and liberals in 1980 over the nature of the family, religion, law, and the purpose of government. Popular culture, especially films, openly addressed themes of marriage, divorce, and sexuality—issues regarded as taboo a generation earlier. Music, too, played a vital role in cultural shifts. Disco deteriorated after years of dominating the pop music scene. In August 1981, MTV went on the air, signifying a shift in musical trends that would have far-reaching implications for the 1980s.

The times had changed dramatically since the upheavals of the 1960s had succeeded in dismantling Jim Crow segregation in the South and helped bring an end to the Vietnam War. The nation's political establishment had shifted rightward during the intervening 10 years since the 1960s, despite enclaves of committed progressives who sought to preserve the glowing embers of 1960s protest. The nomination of Ronald Reagan as presidential candidate at the Republican National Convention in Detroit in July anticipated the triumph of American conservatism. Most observers in the long, hot summer of 1980 thought the presidency was Reagan's for the taking. Liberals predicted disaster in the event of a Reagan victory while conservatives regarded him as a larger-than-life demigod. "We are off on a special adventure," predicted Hugh Sidey in a November issue of *Time* magazine, "for which there is no travel guide and no reassuring precedent" (Boyer 1990, 30).

REAGANISM TRIUMPHANT

The death of Ronald Reagan in May 2004 prompted millions of Americans to revisit the 1980s and reassess the 40th president's contributions. Critics and supporters remained divided about the meaning and significance of Reagan's accomplishments. The president's defenders have claimed that his policies ushered in a new era of prosperity, led to a reduction in the size of the federal government, enhanced the nation's prestige in the world, and helped topple communist regimes in Eastern Europe and the Soviet Union. Critics balked, insisting that Reagan's priorities enriched the wealthiest Americans at the expense of the poor and middle class, created massive debts to be paid off by future generations, escalated tensions around the world, and did not necessarily contribute to the implosion of communism abroad at decade's end. Even when Reagan died—more than 15 years after he left the White House—public opinion varied about his achievements and legacies. Themes in this section include the following:

- An examination of Ronald Reagan's effect on American politics
- A portrait of a Rustbelt city, Detroit, Michigan
- A portrait of a Sunbelt city, Atlanta, Georgia
- The 1980 election and the American people
- The Reagan Agenda: A New Direction

Ronald Reagan and the American People

One of the most popular and beloved presidents of the 20th century, Ronald Reagan came from a working-class background. He was the second of two sons born to Jack and Nelle Reagan in Tampico, Illinois. The first son, John Neil, was born on September 16, 1908, and Ronald Wilson arrived three years later, on February 6, 1911. Reagan's father Jack, an Irish Catholic and dedicated Democrat, described his second son as a "fat little Dutchman," and "Dutch" became Reagan's boyhood nickname. Jack nicknamed his other son "Moon." The family moved to various places, including Chicago, but eventually settled in Dixon, Illinois, by 1920. Young Reagan had a particularly troubling relationship with Jack Reagan. Hampered by alcoholism, Jack traveled from job to job and repeatedly turned up on his own doorstep inebriated. On at least one occasion, Ronald helped his unconscious father to bed. In his memoirs, Reagan tended to romanticize his youth, particularly the time he spent playing outdoors, skating in the winter, and swimming in the summer.

Numerous volumes have been written about Reagan's life and presidency. Reagan chroniclers have spotlighted the benchmarks of his story. Opening the narrative with his birth to Irish-American parents in small-town Tampico, they followed him through his adolescence and his early career as a Depression-era radio sportscaster, his move to California in 1937, and subsequent rise to Hollywood motion picture stardom in the 1940s. He appeared in 54 movies, many of them low-budget studio dramas. A milestone of utmost significance in Reagan's life was his political shift rightward in the 1950s, in the aftermath of a waning film career, failed marriage, and health problems. He married Nancy Davis in 1952 and became a spokesman for General Electric in the 1950s, hosting General Electric Theater on television from 1954 to 1962. Over time, he abandoned his faith in New Deal liberalism, switched party affiliations, and immersed himself in Republican Party politics. At the 1964 Republican National Convention in San Francisco, Reagan delivered a memorable speech on behalf of presidential can-

Republican presidential candidate Ronald Reagan smiles at a campaign stop in Columbia, South Carolina, on October 10, 1980. (Ronald Reagan Library)

didate Barry Goldwater. Thrust into the spotlight, Reagan went on to enjoy a series of stunning electoral victories, first to the California State House in 1966 where he served two terms as governor, and finally the White House in 1980.

The conflicting accounts of Reagan's achievements before and during his presidency are invariably shaped by the ideologies of his chroniclers. With few exceptions, intense partisan commitments and strong emotions have colored accounts of the 40th president. Generally, historians and biographers have either lionized Reagan or focused almost exclusively on what they regarded as his failures and disastrous legacies. Rarely has there been a middle ground between hagiography and criticism in Reagan's case. "He was a distinctive personality," wrote admirer Dinesh D'Souza, "not without flaws, but nevertheless larger than life. There is much about leadership that we can learn from him today. Our world is the one he made, and our challenge is to fulfill his vision for America" (D'Souza 1997, 32). By contrast, Sidney Blumenthal, journalist and senior adviser to Bill Clinton from 1997 to 2001, described Reagan as charismatic in style but a reckless conservative in practice who cut taxes while simultaneously overseeing enormous increases in defense spending. "Once he learned that the supply-side theory his advisers had advocated was backfiring," Blumenthal wrote, "producing deficits instead of the promised Niagara of revenues, he was pleased with the deadening effect. He revived the grandeur of the presidency for his stage set but put the executive branch to sleep" (Blumenthal 2003, 18–19).

During the 1980s, pundits, scholars, political junkies, and other observers tried to make sense of Reagan's popularity with the American people. Collectively, they scratched their heads and wondered why a leader whose policies were so blatantly supportive of the wealthy and the military-industrial complex could be so popular among men and women adversely affected by such policies. The nickname "Teflon President" was applied to Reagan in the 1980s because even though his policies often received mixed responses from the public, he himself always remained popular. Attempts by leftists and liberals to demonize the president always failed. Only a small segment of the nation's population vehemently disliked Reagan, and they tended to be on the left end of the political spectrum. Opinion polls taken throughout the 1980s showed that most Americans found Reagan to be a calming presence in the White House. Millions of people saw in Reagan what they wanted to see: a kindly grandfather, a militant Cold Warrior, a firm commander in chief, a man asleep at the wheel most of the time, a befuddled lover of jelly beans, a practitioner of "Voodoo Economics" (a term invented by George H. W. Bush) or an Abraham Lincoln–like statesman.

Like Franklin Delano Roosevelt and John F. Kennedy before him, Reagan's popularity was bound up in his style. He was a brilliant speaker and charismatic figure. He was a master of one-line, sound-bite statements. He rarely exhibited anger or any other strong emotions in public, and he surrounded himself by managers who were dedicated to perfecting his image. His jokes, anecdotes, folksy manner, and smooth voice even managed to win over critics who emphasized that it was his policies, not Reagan himself, they disliked.

During the height of the Iran-Contra Scandal in 1986 and 1987, Reagan's popularity eroded somewhat. A greater segment of the public seemed willing to dismiss him as an irresponsible, even reckless, president. Yet when Reagan left office in 1989, he enjoyed a level of public support that matched that of Franklin D. Roosevelt at his height. Interestingly, toward the end of Reagan's second term as president, conservative activists around the country circulated petitions to repeal the 22nd Amendment to the Constitution, which set presidential term limits at two. They hoped their efforts would enable Reagan to serve a third term in the White House. While the movement never really went anywhere, it is safe to say that without constitutionally imposed term limits, Reagan might have served as president well into the 1990s.

Detroit, 1980: Portrait of a Rust-Belt City

In the sweltering heat of the third week of July 1980, the Republicans held their national convention in Detroit, Michigan. At that time, more than any other city in America, Detroit epitomized the declining Rustbelt. If the southern Sunbelt represented regeneration in the form of exploding populations, thriving businesses, cowboy millionaires, and burgeoning defense industries, the Rustbelt—

covering a vast region from the Great Lakes to the Northeast—was its downward spiraling counterpart. A mere quarter of a century earlier, the region wielded such enormous political and industrial power that presidential candidates coveted its predominantly working-class voters as essential to victory. During World War II, the industrial heartland served as one of the centers of war production. In the postwar era, newsreel cameras focused on its humming factories to highlight America's might and determination in the uncertain Cold War world. The region's cities attracted impoverished southern African Americans and immigrants from around the world who brought with them hopes of starting new lives. These workers wrote home to relatives with vivid descriptions of job opportunities available in the steel and automobile factories of the Midwest and Northeast.

The alarming downfall of America's steel industry foreshadowed events in automobile production. In the 1960s, a combination of factors—diminishing demand and sliding profits, increased foreign competition, employee salary hikes and concessions won by the powerful United Steelworkers, and the lure of inexpensive labor elsewhere in America and overseas—led to a new era of organization and retrenchment in the steel industry. A series of plant closures sent convulsions throughout steel towns in Pennsylvania, New York, Ohio, and Indiana. Mass layoffs began in 1971 and continued throughout the decade. On Monday, September 19, 1977, the Youngstown Sheet and Tube Company announced that it was closing its enormous Campbell Works plant in Youngstown, Ohio, resulting in 4,500 jobs lost. For the residents of Youngstown, this event came to be known as "Dark Monday." The layoffs reached a fever pitch in the late 1970s and early 1980s, at the same time that automobile manufacturers were beginning to lay off their workers. Between 1979 and 1982, the auto and metals industries reported job losses of 1.9 million. The losses occurred against the backdrop of a declining production sector. From July 1979 to November 1982, the number of jobs in the private, goods-producing sector plummeted from 26.62 million to 22.95 million, a loss of more than 3.5 million or almost one in seven jobs.

The rusting of America's smokestack industries created precarious conditions for the nation's blue-collar workforce by the 1980s. In Detroit in particular, the rich and poor lived in stark, almost Dickensian, contrast with one another. Along the gentle beaches of Lake St. Clair, a lengthy stretch of road known as Lake Shore Drive separated the water from the vast, meticulously kept estates of Grosse Pointe, a neighborhood that drew many automobile company executives. Approaching downtown Detroit, the road suddenly turned into East Jefferson Avenue and ran through impoverished neighborhoods and a decaying, graffiti-stained business district. Entire neighborhoods stood as grim testaments to the deleterious effects of deindustrialization. Weed-choked fields surrounded the mammoth brick skeletons of what had once been thriving industrial complexes, many of which were, by 1980, enclosed by rusted and broken chain link

Robots perform functions once done by humans on an automobile factory line in Michigan, 1995. (Corel)

fences. City blocks of overcrowded projects and decaying, sometimes abandoned houses extended for miles. It was in these same neighborhoods where, a mere 13 years earlier, widespread desperation and hunger temporarily transformed into a firestorm of hopeless fury, shattering the illusion of a prosperous Detroit. The epicenter of the 1967 riot was further east, on 12th Street, an area of pool halls, liquor stores, and pawnshops, where the residents were desperately poor and had a difficult time finding affordable housing.

Changes in the auto industry profoundly altered Detroit. Increased reliance on automated, robotic assembly lines in automobile manufacturing plants led to additional layoffs of white and black workers alike. The American automobile oligopoly known as the Big Three—Ford, Chrysler, and General Motors—hastened the transference of manufacturing to Sunbelt states in the south or abroad to Mexico and South Korea, to take advantage of nonunion labor. The Japanese automobile industry, in the meantime, began aggressively moving into American markets, advertising their cars as more fuel-efficient at a time when gasoline prices had soared to unprecedented heights. For a while in the 1980s, the Big Three countered the bold Japanese efforts by appealing to economic nationalism, encouraging people in the United States to "Buy American," and lobbying Congress to establish high tariffs on Japanese-made automobiles. But the high quality of Japanese cars and the opening of Japanese assembly plants in the United States (starting with Honda's motorcycle factory in Marysville, Ohio, in 1975) at a time when American firms were relocating production overseas secured a permanent and growing demand for Japanese automobiles in America.

For most car buyers, the promise of owning a reliable Japanese vehicle at a time when American cars were regarded as inferior superseded their sense of economic nationalism. Few consumers cared whether their monthly car payments enriched Japanese or American capitalists. Cargo ships reached America's ports in 1980 and unloaded steady streams of Datsuns, Toyotas, Mazdas, and Hondas. The Japanese cars used more plastic, aluminum, and computer parts whereas American cars—cumbersome, heavy, and not always carefully constructed— seemed to break down more frequently, making them the brunt of many late night talk show jokes. In the 1980s, the Japanese auto industry made significant inroads into the United States, forever altering the American industry in meaningful ways. By 1987, 31 percent of passenger cars sold in the United States were foreign made. Citing the need to remain competitive, the Big Three downsized, which triggered waves of layoffs across the country. In 1980, a quarter of a million laid-off automobile workers searched for employment.

The smallest of the Big Three companies, the Chrysler Corporation, lost $1 billion in 1980 alone, despite the efforts of the company's leaders to reorganize it from the highest levels to stop the hemorrhaging. The company teetered close to bankruptcy at the time its chairman Lee Iacocca accepted a massive federal government bailout loan to save Chrysler in 1980. During the Republican National Convention in July, the automobile industry was still very much in a state of transition, leaving bewildered autoworkers—already living in a constant state of anxiety about job security—struggling to make sense of the dramatic shifts. Unemployment inflicted a devastating toll on Detroit residents, rising to about 20 percent by the time of the Republican National Convention. Morale in poverty-stricken neighborhoods virtually bottomed out as violent crime rates in the city increased sharply.

Contributing to Detroit's ailing economy was the exodus of whites out of the city, a trend that began in the 1950s. During that decade, the white population of Detroit declined by 23 percent, while the African American population rose from 303,000 to 487,000, more than 62 percent. Coincidentally, automobile manufacturers began constructing new plants in predominantly white suburbs outside of Detroit, such as Wyandotte. By the 1960s, the inner-city assembly lines could not keep up with newer automated production out in the suburbs, and plant closures fed economic decline in the city core. Shopping stores closed, landlords neglected their property, and young African American workers had an increasingly difficult time finding the sort of jobs that were once plentiful for their fathers and older relatives. Despite these problems, thousands of Republicans gathered in Detroit in July, hoping to transmit a clear message that theirs was the party of the people, no longer dominated by Northeastern patrician bureaucrats who were out of touch with the American people. Working-class Detroit, to party officials, seemed like an ideal setting to make the case.

Atlanta, 1980: Portrait of a Sunbelt City

Atlanta, Georgia, in the early 1980s furnished a sharp contrast to Detroit's ailing post-industrial landscape. Maynard Jackson, the city's first African American mayor, elected in 1973, liked to refer to Atlanta as "the buckle of the Sunbelt." His successor, Andrew Young, who was elected in 1981 during a short-lived economic downturn, strengthened relations between the city and the business community, which effectively revitalized Atlanta's economy. Throughout Atlanta, signs of prosperity were everywhere. The city's expanding skyline, which had been quite modest in 1960, boasted several new skyscrapers by the mid-1980s. In 1980, Atlanta's lavish new $750 million Hartsfield International Airport opened, handling 80,000 passengers a day and serving as the hub for major airlines such as Eastern and Delta. The first part of the city's new MARTA subway system opened in 1979, and construction on it continued at a feverish pace during the early 1980s. The convention trade flourished in Atlanta, as the city emerged the third biggest convention city in America. In 1978, the Convention and Visitors Bureau estimated that the main convention hotels—including the Hilton, Sheraton, and Peachtree Plaza—directly employed 18,000 people.

In the meantime, new suburban developments spread north of Atlanta, into communities such as Kennesaw, Alpharetta, and Roswell. Vast seas of spacious houses with freshly laid sod and newly planted saplings grew up around interstates and highways. Many of the new suburban residents of the 1980s benefited from the full-service governments in Cobb, Fulton, and DeKalb counties, which provided parks, municipal functions, fire and police protection, and independence from Atlanta. Adding to Atlanta's positive image in the 1980s was state of race relations in the city, which, on the surface at least, appeared harmonious. During the civil rights movement, local politicians referred to Atlanta as "the city too busy to hate." Yet by the 1980s, they cast their gaze higher, calling it "the world's next great city."

Numerous economic variables contributed to the growth of Atlanta. In addition to its thriving convention business, a strong federal government presence buttressed the city's economy. The *Atlanta Journal-Constitution* noted, "Atlanta has the largest concentration of federal agencies outside of Washington, D.C., of any city in the country" (Bernard and Rice 1983, 42). Located in and around the city were the Centers for Disease Control and Prevention, several military bases, including Dobbins Air Force Base and the Atlanta Naval Station, and several federal government offices. Moreover, when Atlanta became the state capital in 1868, replacing Milledgeville, state government bureaucracies also brought jobs to the city. Government jobs coexisted effectively with the private sector. Coca-Cola had its headquarters in Atlanta. Ted Turner's massive cable television empire was also based in Atlanta, which in 1980 included the "Superstation" (WTBS) and his newly launched Cable News Network (CNN), which went on the air on June 1. Thanks to WTBS, Americans across the country were able to follow Atlanta Braves baseball games during the 1980s.

Despite its many success stories, Atlanta remained plagued by a variety of social ills during the early 1980s. The city's economy soured during the hard-hitting recession at the beginning of the decade. Even before the 1980s, the process of white flight dramatically altered the demographic composition of Atlanta. In the 1970s, the city's population dropped 14 percent, and many of the people who left were white. As was the case in Detroit, whites moved out of Atlanta and settled in the new neighborhoods of the suburbs while African-Americans gravitated into the city. The economic downturn of the early 1980s hit the African American community particularly hard. Among African American males living in the inner city in 1981, the jobless rate climbed above 18 percent and surpassed 45 percent for African American teenagers. By the city's estimates that same year, one in four Atlantans—most of them African Americans—lived in poverty. Visitors to Atlanta in the early 1980s found the downtown dark and deserted at night. During the terrifying spree of brutal slayings between 1979 and 1981 that became known as the Atlanta Child Murders, 28 youths either disappeared or were found murdered. Many African Americans, most notably Washington, D.C., mayor Marion Barry, insisted that the reluctance of federal investigators to intervene to solve the horrific crimes was an example of racist double standards. At the height of the killings, plainclothes police officers performed an experiment. They lured African American youths into their unmarked police cars with promises of 10 dollars. Every child tested accepted the bait, which Mayor Jackson insisted was a sign of their desperation. Meanwhile, observers of Atlanta politics noted a distinct racial divide between voters living in the city, who often backed liberal Democrats, and those living in the suburbs outside of the city, who often elected conservative Republicans.

Despite a host of problems, Atlanta emerged as a Sunbelt success story, and the economic boom that began in the 1980s lasted well into the 1990s. "In recent years," wrote Larry Keating, "the Atlanta economy has experienced especially robust growth. . . . Between 1980 and 1998, the Atlanta regional economy grew by 906,929 jobs, a rate of increase of 99 percent. Much of this growth occurred in the service sector" (Keating 2001, 11). The suburbs of Atlanta continued to expand in the 1980s. The city attracted a sizable immigrant population (25,000 Jamaicans, 13,000 Koreans, and 20,000 Southeast Asians by 1995), adding to its diversity. Its emergence as an international city seemed complete when Atlanta was selected by the International Olympic Committee in 1990 to host the 1996 Olympic Games.

Who Shot J. R.?

While presidential hopefuls crisscrossed the campaign trail in air-conditioned vehicles, the masses seemed more concerned with the question, "Who shot J. R.?" A March 21 episode of the popular nighttime soap *Dallas* titled "House Divided" in which an unknown assailant shot filthy rich oil magnate J. R. Ewing, scored a record number of television viewers in the Nielsen ratings, not to mention 250 million viewers overseas. It had only been two years earlier—in the fall of 1978— that *Dallas* debuted on CBS, depicting the melodramatic saga of an aristocratic family dominated by the malevolent petroleum baron J. R. (played by *I Dream of Jeanie* alumni Larry Hagman). Several members of the Ewing family empire had motives to want to murder J. R., including his brother Bobby, wife Sue Ellen, rival Cliff Barnes, ex-mistress Kristin Shepard, and family banker Vaughn Leland. Across America, people from all walks of life discussed possible culprits and motives. Viewers would have to wait until November to find out who pulled the trigger.

Meanwhile, the show spawned a prolific cottage industry across America. Sellers hawked J. R. beer, a British rock album with an A-side song called "I love J. R." and a B-side song titled "I Hate J. R.," J. R. cologne, buttons, dart boards, and T-shirts with statements such as "I Shot J. R." and "Will Rogers Never Met J. R." In the Oklahoma presidential primaries, an estimated 600 voters cast their ballots for J. R. Ewing while Larry Hagman received 3,000 letters per week from fans. Every week, tens of millions of Americans tuned in, and *Dallas* seemed to be tailored for the times. Earlier generations of television viewers had grown up on idyllic depictions of middle-class life such as *Father Knows Best, Leave it to Beaver,* and later *The Brady Bunch.* Even the comfortable Ricardos of *I Love Lucy* avoided lavish trappings, opting instead to reside next door to plain Fred and Ethel Mertz. A few sitcoms of the 1970s explored working-class lives, among them *All in the Family, Good Times,* and *Sanford and Son.* By contrast, *Dallas* aired in the late 1970s, with its *Peyton Place*–like portrayals of the Ewing empire. The show's influence on television proved far-reaching. It inspired several imitators in the 1980s—most notably, *Falcon Crest* and *Dynasty*—and although each contained a character viewers loved to hate, the overall positive portrayals of the rich and powerful in such shows reflected changing attitudes about wealth and privilege in America in general.

At a time of rampant inflation and skyrocketing gas prices, with the process of deindustrialization triggered by the huge layoffs of steelworkers at United States Steel (13,000 jobs eliminated) and Bethlehem Steel (10,000 jobs eliminated), *Dallas* and its clones offered a weekly glimpse into a sexy, bubbling champagne world of private jets and sordid family machinations. The spotlighting of dysfunctional wealthy people, in particular, updated Horatio Alger for the changing times. The show conveyed a clear message to the American public: If people whose lives were this tawdry and confused can emerge as modern-day Captains of Industry, anybody could. Explaining the show's appeal, executive producer Philip Caprice noted, "Viewers love to see rich people more screwed up than they are. It makes them feel superior" ("Who Shot," 68).

American Voters and the 1980 Election

The 1980 presidential election, which resulted in a landslide victory for Reagan, inspired countless scholarly articles and books. Political scientists carefully study exit surveys, demographic statistics, polling data, and behavioral theories. Historians treat the election as a watershed. Most scholars, regardless of their partisan leanings, agree that the outcome of the 1980 elections was the result of widespread voter dissatisfaction with the policies of President Carter. Ordinary Americans bore the brunt of the suffering under Carter as inflation soared, the economy soured, and the process of deindustrialization accelerated. Increasingly morose by 1980, Jimmy Carter campaigned half-heartedly for the presidency and became a lightning rod for a variety of antagonisms and resentments. The once-mighty New Deal coalition, which had been unraveling since the 1960s, continued its downward spiral. A political realignment in the South, under way since the 1960s, was complete by 1980. Most southern white voters now supported the Republican Party, casting their votes for Reagan. Moreover, political scientists began to identify substantial blocs of traditionally loyal Democrats—many of them middle-class suburban dwellers—who voted for Reagan in the 1980 presidential election. Even greater numbers of Democrats backed Reagan four years later. The term "Reagan Democrats" was widely used by mid-decade to describe these disgruntled centrist Democrats.

Chroniclers of the 1980 election detected a "gender gap" in voting patterns. Only 47 percent of women voted for Reagan, compared to 56 percent of men, creating a gap of 9 percent. Moreover, women were more likely to disapprove of Reagan's policies than men. By the end of Reagan's first term in office, when opinion polls from the previous four years were averaged, 9 percent fewer women than men approved of his performance in the White House. In some regions, Republicans narrowed the gender gap, but it persisted through much of the 1980s.

Other voters who tended to remain loyal to the Democratic Party included African Americans, Hispanics, and organized labor. Throughout the 1970s and 1980s, Republicans could not muster more than 10 percent of the African American vote. By 1988, only 6 percent of African American voters identified themselves as Republicans while 83 percent referred to themselves as Democrats. Hispanics, too, leaned toward the Democratic Party. In the 1980 elections, Carter received 18 percent more of the Hispanic vote than Reagan.

Organized labor backed the Democratic Party, but nationwide union membership had been declining since the 1960s. Unions, with the exception of the Teamsters and the Professional Air Traffic Controllers Organization (PATCO), endorsed Jimmy Carter. But outside the halls of the AFL-CIO headquarters, a growing number of rank-and-file workers had become frustrated with Carter's economic policies, which often proved inimical to working-class Americans.

In many parts of the country, blue-collar voters turned against Carter. But with no real prolabor alternatives, Reagan—a determined foe of organized labor—

ended up receiving many of their votes. Such was the case in the steel towns of Allegheny County, Pennsylvania, where increasing numbers of workers defected to the Reagan camp. Even though Carter unveiled a steel-industry aid plan in 1980 to resuscitate ailing firms, many Pennsylvanians remained skeptical, fearing that Carter's actions came too late to do any good. Terry McQuillan, a 30-year-old furnace operator in U.S. Steel Corporation's sprawling Homestead works, protested:

Ultimately, few voters were inspired by Carter or Reagan. While Carter's public opinion ratings plunged in 1980, Reagan was not a particularly revered candidate either and would not enjoy widespread popularity for a few more years. An October 1980 poll showed that Reagan's 23 percent "highly favorable" rating was a mere two points above George McGovern's historic low of 1972. A Gallup poll taken after the election indicated that 37 percent of voters decided to vote for during the last week leading up to the election, and 10 percent of them made the decision on election day. Nearly all studies of the 1980 election reached similar conclusions: the electorate had not necessarily moved right but had instead voted against Carter, and party loyalty was at best fickle among the average American voter.

A New Direction

Speaking to the nation on inauguration day—January 20, 1981—Reagan broke with the tradition established by previous presidents by facing west instead of east when he delivered his speech. It was appropriate that Reagan aimed his words in the direction of the Sunbelt, where he enjoyed solid support. More than any other president in American history, Reagan understood the power of both symbols and words, and nowhere was his mastery of each put to use more effectively than in his first inaugural address. In his speech, Reagan repeatedly emphasized themes that would dominate his rhetoric during the 1980s. He warned that the nation was in a state of deep economic crisis. He insisted the federal government was too bloated and needed to be reformed and scaled back. He expressed concerns that global unrest threatened America's position in the world. "In the present crisis," Reagan proclaimed, "government is not the solution to our problem; government is the problem" (Boyer 1990, 31). Borrowing heavily from Rooseveltian rhetoric, the 40th president told the people that renewal was forthcoming if Americans would maintain faith in their nation and its possibilities. "The crisis we are facing today," he proclaimed, ". . . does require . . . our best effort, and our willingness to believe in ourselves and to believe in our capacity to perform great deeds; to believe that together with God's help we can and will resolve the problems which now confront us" (Boyer 1990, 34).

The triumph of Ronald Reagan represented the culmination of the post–World War II conservative movement. "We have one agenda," Reagan remarked. "We seek to put our financial house in order and rebuild our nation's defenses" (Edel 1992, 13). The new presidency created a level of excitement and anticipation in Washington, D.C., that rivaled the buzz surrounding Roosevelt's first 100 days in office. In his early months in the White House, President Reagan emphasized his economic priorities, which included deregulation, tax reduction, and cutting certain social welfare programs. Addressing a joint session of Congress in February 1981, Reagan revealed his economic plan. He took his cues from a number of prominent advocates of supply-side economics, including Michigan congressman David Stockman, New York congressman Jack Kemp, and *Wall Street Journal* editorialist Jude Wanniski, but he was especially influenced by the writings of Arthur Laffer, a supply-side economist at the University of Southern California.

Ronald Reagan's inaugural speech, January 20, 1981. (U.S. Department of Defense)

The so-called Laffer Curve, a chart the economist supposedly sketched on a cocktail napkin at a bar in 1974, established his theory that tax cuts would actually stimulate tax revenues. Reagan and other key figures in his administration took Laffer's theories seriously and sought to apply them to federal policies. Observers coined the term "Reaganomics" early on to describe Reagan's economic policies. Tax cuts proved central to the gospel of Reaganomics. The president and his advisors theorized that tax cuts would promote investment that would result in economic growth and, eventually, increased tax revenues. The new administration took aim at the federal budget deficit and hoped that tax cuts, coupled with cuts in government spending—particularly on social welfare and entitlement programs—would shrink the deficit. David Stockman, who had been a member of the radical Students for a Democratic Society in the 1960s and eventually became a conservative Republican congressman, was appointed by Reagan to be his budget director. Stockman proposed a 30 percent tax cut over a period of three years. Congress urged a compromise, which resulted in a 25 percent cut spread out to 5 percent in 1981 and 10 percent each year in

1982 and 1983. The impact of the tax cuts was dampened somewhat by spreading them out over three years.

The tax cuts—known as the Economic Recovery Tax Act—were supposed to coincide with deep cuts in federal spending. In theory, as government spending plummeted sharply, inflation would decline and the economy would enjoy an infusion of more capital. Reagan and his fellow supply-siders hoped the new capital would expand government revenues without having to raise taxes. Budgets were slashed, especially for programs designed to aid the most vulnerable in American society, such as Aid to Families with Dependent Children, food stamps, and unemployment compensation. But major entitlement programs, such as Social Security and Medicare, made it out of the cutting gauntlet intact, due in large part to congressional resistance against Reagan's policies.

The Reagan administration also aggressively advanced policies of deregulation, which involved scaling back or eliminating government regulations involving consumer protection, workplace safety, health care, and the environment. Between 1981 and 1985, for example, the personnel at the Consumer Product Safety Commission dropped from 855 to 502. Regulatory agencies had lost 12 percent of their staff and funding by 1985. Reagan often appointed new directors to various agencies whose views were hostile to the bodies they led. As head of the Department of Interior under Reagan, James Watt pushed aggressively to open up wilderness areas to mining, drilling, and real estate development. When criticized in 1983 for his decision to sell more than 1 billion tons of coal from federal lands in Wyoming, Watt showed his insensitivity by noting that his coal-advisory board included "a black, . . . a woman, two Jews, and a cripple" (Pemberton 1997, 122). Even though Watt resigned after making the comment, countless other officials in the Reagan administration shared his unwavering devotion to big business.

The Reagan-era tax cuts and deregulation accompanied the largest peacetime military buildup in American history. The president believed that his predecessor, Jimmy Carter, had allowed the military to become too weak and vulnerable. Therefore, one of Reagan's highest priorities was expanding the military and defense establishment. But Reagan's perception of his predecessor was inaccurate. In reality, Carter had committed enormous sums of money to military escalation, and Reagan simply continued the massive arms buildup that was already under way by the late 1970s. "Defense is not a budget item," Reagan announced to his staff, "you spend what you need" (Schaller 1992, 47). From 1981 to 1986, Reagan oversaw a $1.46 trillion defense buildup, including development of the B-1 bomber (which President Carter had scrapped), the MX missile system, and the Strategic Defense Initiative (SDI), or "Star Wars," a space-based satellite system that in theory would detect and intercept incoming missiles.

Resisting opportunities for arms control during his first term in office, the president and his administration, backed by Congress, assumed bold and provocative stands against the Soviet Union. They deployed close to 400 Pershing II

Rendering of the Strategic Defense Initiative design, created by scientists at Los Alamos National Laboratory in New Mexico. It shows a space-based particle beam weapon attacking enemy intercontinental ballistic missiles. Opponents dubbed this proposal Star Wars when scientists criticized it as impractical. (Department of Energy)

missiles to West Germany in 1984 and 1985, placed more than 3,000 cruise missiles on B-52s and B-1s, and thoroughly updated the entire nuclear program. By 1986, America's defense budget outlays had surpassed $300 billion, about double the 1980 level.

The enormous arms buildup signified Reagan's firm commitment to an anticommunist—particularly anti-Soviet—foreign policy. Since the 1950s, Reagan repeatedly stated that the Soviet Union was an aggressive world power determined to exert its authority around the globe. In keeping with this viewpoint, Reagan not only oversaw the proliferation of what Eisenhower called "the military-industrial complex" but he also advocated a global anticommunist policy known as "the Reagan Doctrine." The doctrine involved the U.S. government financing anticommunist guerrilla movements in various parts of the world, particularly the key hot spots of Nicaragua, Angola, Mozambique, and Cambodia. Moreover, the Reagan administration moved rapidly to buttress numerous autocratic, pro-U.S. regimes in Latin America and Asia. During the 1980s, dictatorships in El Salvador, Chile, the Philippines, and South Korea and a host of other countries enjoyed extensive support from Washington, D.C.

The policies of the Reagan administration would evolve and change over the course of the decade. Reagan proved to be somewhat more moderate in his approach to domestic and foreign policy matters during his second term in office, as détente and the Iran-Contra Scandal slowed the momentum of his conservative thrust. While some of Reagan's policies represented a continuation of his predecessor's priorities, others marked a decided departure. Just as Franklin Delano Roosevelt's New Deal shaped the lives of millions of Americans, so the ripples of Reagan's policies were felt in communities across the nation. The recession of 1981–1983 shook public confidence in the president. More than 11.5 million Americans lost their jobs during the so-called Reagan Recession, and millions more saw their wages reduced significantly. By 1983, however, an economic turnaround was evident; more people went back to work and millions of new jobs were created. Regardless of whether Americans benefited or suffered because of Reagan's policies, the 40th president remained strikingly popular among most people, as demonstrated in his landslide reelection victory in November 1984.

BIOGRAPHIES

Bella Abzug, 1920–1998

Women's Rights Advocate and Politician

Easily identifiable by her colorful wide-brimmed hats, Bella Abzug was a celebrated feminist pioneer and politician of the early 1970s. By the early 1980s, Abzug remained one of the most highly visible feminists in the United States and continued leading a variety of nongovernmental organizations (NGOs) dedicated to improving the status of women in America and the world. A lawyer with deep roots in radical Jewish activism, Abzug was one of the founders of the antiwar organization Women's Strike for Peace in the 1960s. She was elected to three terms in the House of Representatives (from 1971 to 1977) on peace and feminist platforms. In the late 1970s and early 1980s, she was one of the most highly visible supporters of the Equal Rights Amendment (ERA). In 1978, Jimmy Carter named her chair of the National Advisory Commission on Women but later fired her for her criticisms of his administration. Abzug, who continued to chair several feminist and human rights commissions during the presidencies of Reagan, Bush Sr., and Clinton, was an outspoken critic of Reagan's conservative politics throughout the 1980s. In 1984, she wrote *Gender Gap: Abzug's Guide to Political Power for Women,* a systematic and highly regarded study of the effects of the political gender gap in American society.

John B. Anderson, 1922–

Congressman and Independent Presidential Candidate

A moderate Republican from Illinois, John Anderson grew up in Rockford, served in the U.S. Army during World War II, and attended law school at the University of Illinois and Harvard University. In the 1940s and 1950s, he worked in a private law firm while active in the Republican Party. Between 1961 and 1981, he served 10 terms in the U.S. House of Representatives. He gained fame as a third-party presidential candidate in 1980, running against Carter and Reagan. As an independent candidate, Anderson attacked Reagan from the center of the political spectrum, claiming that the Republican frontrunner's economic programs were too extreme and irresponsible.

Republican U.S. representative from Illinois John B. Anderson campaigned for president in 1980. Running as an independent, moderate candidate, Anderson garnered 7 percent of the popular vote. (Library of Congress)

Anderson enjoyed a strong showing of grassroots support in communities across America, and the initial groundswell triggered by his campaign encouraged him. He won over a broad spectrum of voters who were impressed with his integrity and straightforward manner. Soon, though, Anderson would begin to falter in the polls, and he ultimately ended up receiving 7 percent of the vote in a popular election that saw Ronald Reagan defeat Jimmy Carter by a landslide (50.7 percent to 41 percent). Shortly thereafter, Anderson retired from politics and returned to his hometown of Rockford but continued to advise moderate third-party candidates.

Deborah Harry, 1945–

Lead Singer of the Group Blondie

Born in Florida, adopted at age three months, and raised in Hawthorne, New Jersey, Deborah Harry supported herself with a variety of jobs while she was growing up. She found employment as a cocktail waitress, secretary, store clerk, Playboy Bunny, and lead singer in a folk band called Wind in the Willows. Along with boyfriend Chris Stein, Harry founded Blondie in 1974, and the band played mostly small venues such at clubs and warehouses. Blondie assumed an important place at the vanguard of the American new wave/punk music movement. With her stark, punk beauty, revealing outfits, and acerbic humor, Harry became one of rock's most easily identifiable figures. By the late 1970s and early 1980s, Blondie emerged as one of the hottest bands in America, scoring several chart-toppers, including "Heart of Glass," "Call Me," "The Tide is High," and "Rapture." Like so many bands of the day, Blondie was plagued by internal conflicts, and the band broke up in 1982. Harry went on to an unsuccessful solo career and appeared in several movies, including John Waters' 1988 cult favorite *Hairspray*. She remains a cult figure and a celebrated pioneer of the new music sound of the 1980s.

Sonia Johnson, 1936–

Feminist and Equal Rights Amendment Advocate

In 1979, following a heavily publicized trial, activist Sonia Johnson was excommunicated from the Church of Jesus Christ of Latter-day Saints for, in the words of the Church, "preaching false doctrine, undermining authority of church leaders and hurting the church's missionary effort." Johnson had become highly critical of the Church, claiming it was excessively "patriarchal" and hindering the passage of the Equal Rights Amendment (ERA). A Mormon homemaker, Johnson converted to feminism and campaigned for the ERA in the late 1970s and early 1980s, leading a series of women's rights struggles across the country. In 1981, she published her autobiography, *From Housewife to Heretic,* which was ridiculed by Mormons and celebrated by feminists. After her marriage to her husband Rick unraveled, Johnson ran as a third-party presidential candidate for the Citizens' Party in 1984 and shortly thereafter founded a lesbian communal dwelling, which eventually folded in the 1990s. The author of several books in the late 1980s and early 1990s, Johnson had largely disappeared from the public eye by the early 2000s.

Ayatollah Ruhollah Khomeini, 1900–1989

Iranian Leader

Khomeini was an important spiritual figure in modern Iran and a Shiite cleric who founded the Islamic Republic of Iran in 1979. With his long white beard, flowing black robes, and never-changing dour expression, Khomeini assumed the role of the chief villain in the popular imagination of most Americans during the Iranian hostage crisis. He was born September 24, 1902, in the village of Khomein, about 350 kilometers southwest of Tehran. He was, by all accounts, a spirited boy who, according to a biographer, "beat other boys in wrestling, but his favorite game was leapfrog and in this he was considered the local champion" (Moin 2000, 14). The murder of his father while Khomeini was still an infant (which young Ruhollah blamed government agents), coupled with the death of his mother when he was 15, led him to devote himself intensely to theological studies and to become a *mujtahid* (jurist) in the 1920s. Though not widely known, Khomeini enjoyed wide respect in Iranian religious circles, and by the early 1960s, he was busily organizing a cultural *jihad* against the Shah. He gained fame in 1963 for issuing a *fatwa,* or religious edict, calling the Shah's westernizing reforms a threat to Islam. He went into exile in the 1970s and returned in 1979 to lead the revolution. For the remainder of his life, he played a vital leadership role in the new revolutionary Iran, which, unfortunately, began to rival the Shah's regime in its brutality and authoritarian policies.

Lane Kirkland, 1922–1999

President, American Federation of Labor-Congress of Industrial Organizations (AFL-CIO)

Head of the AFL-CIO from 1979 to 1995, Kirkland emerged as one of the most prominent prolabor spokesmen in the United States during the Reagan era. He was born to an affluent family in Camden, South Carolina, served in the U.S. Merchant Marine in World War II, and later obtained a bachelor's degree from the School of Foreign Service at Georgetown University. He went to work in the AFL-CIO's research office in the 1960s, and became close to George Meany's executive assistant. Kirkland was a cold-war liberal who supported President Lyndon Johnson's Great Society programs and the Vietnam War. In 1980, he urged union members to vote for Jimmy Carter, and he repeatedly supported Democratic political candidates in the 1980s and 1990s.

He strongly backed the Solidarity labor movement in Poland, and—thanks to his efforts—millions of dollars were sent overseas to the Polish organization. His own brand of centrist, nonconfrontational unionism, coupled with a militant cold-war ideology that often led him to support Reagan's foreign policies (including CIA efforts to destabilize antigovernment unions in Latin America), undercut the oppositional

Lane Kirkland, head of the AFL-CIO from 1979 to 1995. (Courtesy AFL-CIO)

agenda of labor unions, which left them vulnerable to assault by the Reagan administration and private industries.

Kirkland received the Presidential Medal of Freedom, the nation's highest civilian honor, from President Bill Clinton in 1994. He retired from AFL-CIO in 1994 and died in 1999. By that time, organized labor in America had reached its post–World War II nadir.

George Lucas, 1944–

Filmmaker

Lucas was a revolutionary filmmaker, one of a small group of young directors in the 1970s (including Martin Scorsese, Steven Spielberg, Francis Ford Coppola, and Brian DePalma) who transformed modern cinema in the aftermath of the 1960s. The son of a conservative businessman from Modesto, California, Lucas loved cruising and racing as a youth, which were prominent themes in his 1973 surprise sleeper *American Graffiti*. Almost single-handedly, Lucas invented the concept of the summer blockbuster when he set out to make a modern-day "Flash Gordon"–type movie with contemporary special effects. Several years in the making, *Star Wars* (1977) stunned audiences with its mythological storyline and stunning spaceship battles. Three years later, *The Empire Strikes Back* was the summer hit of 1980. Along with filmmaker Philip Kaufman, Lucas created the storyline behind *Raiders of the Lost Ark* (Lawrence Kasdan wrote the screenplay, Spielberg directed), the number one box office hit of 1981.

Lucas created Industrial Light and Magic to help enhance film special effects, continued cashing in on profits from *Star Wars* movies and merchandise, and oversaw the creation of four other *Star Wars* films (directing three of them) between 1983 and 2005. Explaining the success of *Star Wars,* scholar Andrew Gordon, who has studied Lucas extensively, commented, "Lucas created a pop-culture pastiche that borrowed from all over the place. The appeal isn't so much that it's high-tech or futuristic. The movie is a throwback. It has a gleaming post-modern surface and an old-fashioned core" (Hinds 1999).

Jerry Rubin, 1938–1994

Yippie and Yuppie

Activist-turned-entrepreneur Jerry Rubin gained fame in the 1960s for his clownish antics, outrageous blend of countercultural styles and radical political sensibilities, and his role as a defendant in the famous Chicago Seven trial. In 1967, Rubin was one of the founders of the Youth International Party, or the Yippies, along with humorist Paul Krassner and famed political activist Abbie Hoffman. In August 1968, Rubin and the Yippies protested at the historic antiwar demonstrations outside the Democratic National Convention in Chicago. By the early

1970s, Rubin had adopted abrasive, outrageous rhetoric, praising Charles Manson and calling for an apocalyptic confrontation with authorities. After his close comrade Hoffman went underground in 1973, Rubin began exploring yoga, Erhard Seminars Training (EST), and bioenergetics. In the late 1970s and early 1980s, he emerged as a stockbroker who organized networking meetings and entrepreneurial seminars. He exploited his status as a 1960s radical to spotlight himself and in the process became the archetype for an emerging myth that 1960s activists had "sold out" and abandoned leftist politics to make money. In fact, the very term "Yuppie"—a household word in the 1980s to describe young urban professionals—likely had its origins with Rubin, according to Chicago newspaper columnist Bob Greene. When Hoffman returned aboveground, the two men—now distant from one another—participated in a traveling debate show that drew crowds of thousands in cities across the country in 1983 and 1984. Hoffman remained a political activist through much of the decade until he killed himself in April 1989. Rubin was struck and killed by an automobile while jaywalking in Los Angeles in 1994 at age 56, leaving behind two children.

REFERENCES AND FURTHER READINGS

Allen, Frederick. 1996. *Atlanta Rising: The Invention of an International City.* Atlanta: Longstreet Press.

The American Conservative. http://www.amconmag.com/.

American President. http://www.americanpresident.org/.

Anderson, Annelise, Martin Anderson, and Kiron Skinner. 2003. *Reagan: A Life in Letters.* New York: Free Press.

Andrew, John A., III. 1997. *The Other Side of the Sixties: The Young Americans for Freedom and the Rise of Conservative Politics.* New Brunswick, N.J.: Rutgers University Press.

Bailey, Beth, and David Farber. 2004. *America in the Seventies.* Lawrence: University Press of Kansas.

Bambara, Toni Cade. 2000. *Those Bones Are Not My Child.* New York: Vintage.

Bernard, Richard H., and Bradley R. Rice. 1983. *Sunbelt Cities: Politics and Growth since World War II.* Austin: University of Texas Press.

Biskind, Peter. 1998. *Easy Riders, Raging Bulls: How the Sex-Drugs-and-Rock 'N' Roll Generation Saved Hollywood.* New York: Touchstone/Simon and Schuster.

Biven, W. Carl. 2001. *Jimmy Carter's Economy: Policy in an Age of Limits.* Chapel Hill: University of North Carolina Press.

Bluestone, Barry, and Bennett Harrison. 1990. *The Great U-Turn: Corporate Restructuring and the Polarizing of America.* New York: Basic Books.

Blumenthal, Sidney. 2003. *The Clinton Wars*. New York: Farrar, Strauss and Giroux.

Bolce, Louis, Gerald De Maio, and Douglas Muzzio. 1992. "Blacks and the Republican Party: The 20 Percent Solution," *Political Science Quarterly* 107 (1): 63–78.

Bonafede, Dom. 1985. Wielding Databases for Political Clout. *Adweek,* June 13.

Brennan, Mary C. 1995. *Turning Right in the Sixties: The Conservative Capture of the GOP*. Chapel Hill: University of North Carolina Press.

Brinkley, Douglas. 1998. *The Unfinished Presidency: Jimmy Carter's Journey Beyond the White House*. New York: Viking.

Bonner, Raymond. 1984. *Weakness and Deceit: U.S. Policy and El Salvador*. New York: New York Times Books.

Boswell, Thomas D., and James R. Curtis. 1983. *The Cuban American Experience: Culture, Images and Perspectives*. Totowa, N.J.: Rowman and Allanheld.

Boyer, Paul, ed. 1990. *Reagan as President: Contemporary Views of the Man, His Politics, and His Policies*. Chicago: Ivan R. Dee.

Busch, Andrew E. 2005. *Reagan's Victory: The Presidential Election of 1980 and the Rise of the Right*. Lawrence: University Press of Kansas.

Camardella, Michele L. 2005. *America in the 1980s*. New York: Facts on File.

Carroll, Peter N. 1982. *It Seemed Like Nothing Happened: The Tragedy and Promise of America in the 1970s*. New York: Holt, Rinehart and Winston.

Carter, Dan T. 1995. *The Politics of Rage: George Wallace, the Origins of the New Conservatism, and the Transformation of American Politics*. New York: Simon & Schuster.

Cockburn, Alexander. 1987. *Corruptions of Empire: Life Studies and the Reagan Era*. New York: Verso.

Crewdson, John M. 1980. "Aliens Tell of Their Desert Ordeal As Search for Smugglers is Pressed." *New York Times,* July 8, 1.

Crime Library: Criminal Minds and Methods. http://www.crimelibrary.com/serial/atlanta/.

Critchlow, Donald T. 2005. *Phyllis Schlafly and Grassroots Conservatism: A Woman's Crusade*. New York: Princeton University Press.

Curran, Barbara A. 2004. *25 Years of Dallas: The Complete Story of the World's Favorite Prime Time Soap*. College Station, Tex.: Virtualbookworm.com Publishing.

Curry, Bill. 1980. "Hell or Texas? It's a Tough Choice," part I. *The Los Angeles Times,* July 4, 16.

Dallek, Matthew. 2004. *The Right Moment: Ronald Reagan's First Victory and the Decisive Turning Point in American Politics*. New York: Oxford University Press.

Davis, Mike. 1996. *Prisoners of the American Dream: Politics and Economy in the History of the U.S. Working Class*. New York: Verso.

"Death March in the Desert," *Newsweek,* July 21, 1980, 55.

Diamond, Sarah. 1989. *Spiritual Warfare: The Politics of the Christian Right*. Boston: South End Press.

Disco History Page. http://www.disco-disco.com/disco/history.html.

Drew, Elizabeth. 1981. *Portrait of an Election: The 1980 Presidential Campaign*. New York: Simon & Schuster.

D'Souza, Dinesh. 1997. *Ronald Reagan: How an Ordinary Man Became an Extraordinary Leader*. New York: Three Free Press.

Dugger, Ronnie. 1983. *On Reagan: The Man & His Presidency*. New York: McGraw-Hill.

Eagle Forum Website (for the writings of Phyllis Schlafly). http://www.eagleforum .org/.

Ebtekar, Massoumeh, as told to Fred A. Reed. 2000. *Takeover in Tehran: The Inside Story of the 1979 U.S. Embassy Capture*. Vancouver: Talonbooks.

Edel, Wilbur. 1992. *The Reagan Presidency: An Actor's Finest Performance*. New York: Hippocrene Books.

Edsall, Thomas. 1985. "Onward, GOP Christians, Marching to '88," *Washington Post,* June 30.

Edsall, Thomas Byrne, and Mary D. Edsall. 1992. *Chain Reaction: The Impact of Race, Rights, and Taxes on American Politics*. New York: W. W. Norton & Company.

Ehrman, John. 2005. *The Eighties: America in the Age of Reagan*. New Haven, Conn.: Yale University Press.

Farber, David. 2004. *Taken Hostage: The Iran Hostage Crisis and America's First Encounter with Radical Islam*. Princeton: Princeton University Press.

Farley, Reynolds, Sheldon Danziger, and Harry J. Holzer. 2002. *Detroit Divided*. Albany, N.Y.: Russell Sage Foundation Publications.

Fraser, Steve, and Gary Gerstle. 1989. *The Rise and Fall of the New Deal Order, 1930–1980*. Princeton, N.J.: Princeton University Press.

Frum, David. 2000. *How We Got Here: The 70's: The Decade That Brought You Modern Life—For Better or Worse*. New York: Basic Books.

Goldberg, Robert Alan. 1995. *Barry Goldwater*. New Haven, Conn.: Yale University Press.

Goldwater, Barry. 1997. *Conscience of a Conservative.* Washington, D.C.: Regnery Publishing.

Halberstam, David. 1994. *The Fifties.* New York: Fawcett Books/Random House.

Harris, David. 2004. *The Crisis: The President, the Prophet, and the Shah–1979 and the Coming of Militant Islam.* New York: Little, Brown.

"Heat Wave Toll Rises to 65; Grain Loss Laid to Drought," *The New York Times,* July 2, 1980, A12.

Hinds, Julie. 1999. "Star Wars, Myth and Menace: How a Space Opera Conquered the World," *San Jose Mercury News,* May 6, 1G.

Hornblower, Margot. 1980. "Miami Violence Abates, but Blacks Simmer," *Washington Post,* May 20.

Horowitz, Daniel. 2004. *Jimmy Carter and the Energy Crisis of the 1970s: The "Crisis of Confidence" Speech of July 15, 1979.* Boston: St. Martin's Press.

Inness, Sherrie A., ed. 2003. *Disco Divas: Women and Popular Culture in the 1970s.* Philadelphia: University of Pennsylvania Press.

Johnson, Haynes. 1991. *Sleepwalking Through History: America in the Reagan Years.* New York: W. W. Norton.

Jordan, Hamilton. 1983. *Crisis: The Last Year of the Carter Presidency.* New York: Berkley Publishing Group.

Keating, Larry. 2001. *Atlanta: Race, Class, and Urban Expansion.* Philadelphia: Temple University Press.

"Killer Heat Wave," *Newsweek,* July 14, 1980, 29.

Klatch, Rebecca E. 1987. *Women of the New Right.* Philadelphia: Temple University Press.

Kopkind, Andrew. 1995. *The Thirty Years' Wars: Dispatches and Diversions of a Radical Journalist, 1965–1994.* New York: Verso Books.

Ladd, Everett Carl. 1981. "The Brittle Mandate: Electoral Dealignment and the 1980 Presidential Election," *Political Science Quarterly* 96 (1): 1–25.

Lewis, Anthony. 1980. "The Tidal Wave," *New York Times,* November 6, A35.

Lienesch, Michael. 1982. "Right-Wing Religion: Christian Conservatism as a Political Movement." *Political Science Quarterly* 97:3.

Linkon, Sherry Lee, and John Russo. 2003. *Steeltown USA: Work and Memory in Youngstown.* Lawrence: University Press of Kansas.

Marable, Manning. 1984. *Race, Reform and Rebellion: The Second Reconstruction in Black America, 1945–1982.* Jackson: University Press of Mississippi.

Martin, William. 1996. *With God on Our Side: The Rise of the Religious Right in America.* New York: Broadway.

McGirr, Lisa. 2001. *Suburban Warriors: The Origins of the New American Right.* Princeton: Princeton University Press.

McLoughlin, William G. 1983. "Faith." *American Quarterly* 35 (1/2): 57–58.

"Miami 1980," *The Nation,* May 31, 1980, 644.

Moin, Bager. 2000. *Khomeini: The Life of the Ayatollah.* Boston: St. Martin's Press.

Morris, Edmund. 1999. *Dutch: A Memoir of Ronald Reagan.* New York: Random House.

Nash, George H. 1976. *The Conservative Intellectual Movement in America Since 1945.* New York: Basic Books.

National Review Online. http://www.nationalreview.com/.

Orlov, Rick. 2003. "Jarvis Troops Still Proud of '78 Feat," *Daily News of Los Angeles,* June 6.

O'Sullivan, Arthur, Terry A. Sexton, and Steven M. Sheffrin. 1995. *Property Taxes and Tax Revolts: The Legacy of Proposition 13.* New York: Cambridge University Press.

Pels, Rebeccca. 1995. "The Pressures of PATCO: Strikes and Stress in the 1980s." In *Essays in History,* vol. 37. Corcoran Department of History at the University of Virginia. http://etext.lib.virginia.edu/journals/EH/EH37/Pels.html.

Pemberton, William E. 1999. *Exit with Honor: The Life and Presidency of Ronald Reagan* Armonk, New York: M. E. Sharpe.

Perlstein, Rick. 2001. *Before the Storm: Barry Goldwater and the Unmaking of the American Consensus.* New York: Hill & Wang.

Peterson, Bill. 1983. "As New Right Gets Old, Strategists Recast It as 'New Populism,'" *Washington Post,* March 12.

Pollack, Kenneth. 2003. *The Persian Puzzle: The Conflict Between Iran and America.* New York: Random House.

Reagan, Ronald. 1990. *An American Life: The Autobiography.* New York: Simon & Schuster.

Reed, Adolph, Jr. 1999. *Stirrings in the Jug: Black Politics in the Post-Segregation Era.* Minneapolis: University of Minnesota Press.

Remembering the Assassination of Archbishop Oscar Romero, March 24, 1980. http://www.creighton.edu/CollaborativeMinistry/romero.html.

Rieff, David. 1993. *The Exile: Cuba in the Heart of Miami.* New York: Simon & Schuster.

Roberts, James C. 1980. *The Conservative Decade: Emerging Leaders of the 1980s.* Westport, Conn.: Arlington House Publishers.

Schaller, Michael. 1992. *Reckoning with Reagan: America and its President in the 1980s.* New York: Oxford University Press.

Schneider, Gregory L., ed. 2003. *Conservatism in America Since 1930: A Reader.* New York: New York University Press.

Schoenwald, Jonathan M. 2001. *A Time for Choosing: The Rise of Modern American Conservatism.* New York: Oxford University Press.

Schulman, Bruce J. 2001. *The Seventies: The Great Shift in American Culture, Society, and Politics.* New York: Simon & Schuster.

Schwab, Larry M. 1988. "The Myth of the Conservative Shift in American Politics: A Research Note," *The Western Political Quarterly* 41 (December): 4.

Shorris, Earl. 2001. *Latinos: A Biography of the People.* New York: W. W. Norton.

Sick, Gary. 1986. *All Fall Down: America's Tragic Encounter With Iran.* New York: Viking Press.

Smith, Robert Charles. 1996. *Racism in the Post Civil Rights Era: Now You See It, Now You Don't.* Albany: State University of New York Press.

Smith, Suzanne E. 2001. *Dancing in the Street: Motown and the Cultural Politics of Detroit.* Cambridge: Harvard University Press.

Sugrue, Thomas. 1996. *The Origins of the Urban Crisis: Race and Inequality in Postwar Detroit.* Princeton: Princeton University Press.

"13 Aliens Cast Off by Smugglers Die in a Baking Desert in Arizona," *New York Times,* July 7, 1980.

Thomas, June Manning. 1997. *Redevelopment and Race: Planning a Finer City in Postwar Detroit.* Baltimore: Johns Hopkins University Press.

Thompson, Heather Ann. 2004. *Whose Detroit? Politics, Labor, and Race in a Modern American City.* Ithaca, N.Y.: Cornell University Press.

Troy, Gil. 2005. *Morning in America: How Ronald Reagan Invented the 1980s.* Princeton: Princeton University Press.

Viguerie, Richard A. 2004. *America's Right Turn: How Conservatives Used New and Alternative Media to Take Power.* Chicago: Bonus Books.

White, F. Clifton, and William J. Gill. 1981. *Why Reagan Won.* Washington, D.C.: Regnery.

"Who Shot That Nice Mr. Ewing?" *Newsweek,* November 17, 1980, 68.

Wirls, Daniel. 1986. "Reinterpreting the Gender Gap," *The Public Opinion Quarterly* 50 (3): 316–330.

Wright, Robin. 1989. *In the Name of God: The Khomeini Decade.* New York: Simon and Schuster.

Cold Wars, Hot Wars, and the World Stage

OVERVIEW

A massive military build-up in the United States during the 1980s coincided with escalating Cold War tensions between America and the Soviet Union. The largest peacetime expansion of the military in U.S. history occurred during the Reagan presidency, and its effects were felt across the country. Reagan's defenders later argued that dramatic military expenditures at home forced Moscow to spend into oblivion and ultimately caused the collapse of communism in the late 1980s and early 1990s. Such assertions represented, at best, a dubious rationalization for years of unchecked military spending. Without question, the U.S. build-up influenced decisions in Moscow, but the unraveling of communism had more to do with internal contradictions and economic problems inside the Soviet Union and its East Bloc allies that predated the 1980s. At home, this escalation in hostilities created a Cold War culture that revived fears of communism from earlier eras. Yet the domestic anticommunism of the 1980s proved much less potent than it had been during the 1950s. The upheavals and cultural transformations of the 1960s undermined the alarmist power of anticommunism and fortified the right of all Americans to dissent more freely. In the 1980s, Cold Warriors only partially revived the anticommunist consensus that existed before the Vietnam War.

At home, a host of issues related to foreign policy captured the attention of millions of Americans. The Cold War of the 1980s had lost much of the potency of its 1950s' counterpart. Men and women continued to debate the meaning of the Vietnam War, which was still fresh in people's minds ten years after the last American troops were withdrawn from the Southeast Asian nation. While there were no wars on the scale of Vietnam during the 1980s, the so-called "War on Drugs" triggered cultural clashes over drug use. The role of local, state, and federal governments—as well as law enforcement agencies—in the curbing and controlling of drugs took center stage with other important national issues by the middle of the decade. Finally, as the Reagan administration intervened increasingly in the affairs of Central American nations, citizens debated the merits of that involvement abroad and what do about Latin American immigrants arriving on American soil.

TIMELINE

1980–1981   Paramilitary death squads in El Salvador murder 30,000.

Archbishop Oscar Romero, the Martin Luther King Jr. of El Salvador, is murdered by death squads, March 24.

Three American nuns—Maura Clarke, Ita Ford, and Dorothy Kazel—are murdered by the death squads in El Salvador, December 2.

1981   Ronald Reagan becomes the 40th president of the United States.

Fifty-two American hostages released in January after 14 months in captivity in Iran.

Deranged gunman John Hinckley, Jr. attempts to assassinate President Reagan at the end of March.

Paramilitary death squads in Guatemala murder 11,000.

U.S. jets shoot down two Libyan fighter jets over the Gulf of Sidra, triggering a long period of hostilities between the two countries.

President Reagan approves of funds and CIA training for Nicaraguan Contras.

Reagan increases aid to the Salvadoran government.

1982   The Polish government bans Solidarity.

Soviet leader Leonid Brezhnev dies.

Yuri Andropov becomes the general secretary of the Soviet Communist Party.

In a military coup, Gen. Efrain Rios Montt comes to power in Guatemala.

U.S.-backed Contras, based in southern Honduras, begin attacking targets in Nicaragua; the Nicaraguan government declares a state of emergency.

In June, 750,000 Americans attend a rally in New York City's Central Park to protest against nuclear weapons.

In August, U.S. Marines arrive in Lebanon as part of an international intervention to supervise the withdrawal of Palestine Liberation Organization (PLO) forces.

The far-right National Republican Alliance (Arena) wins rigged parliamentary elections in El Salvador.

Gen. Gustavo Alvarez, chief of the armed forces in Honduras, cracks down on trade union leaders and political organizers with leftist leanings; Honduran death squads assassinate numerous suspected "subversives."

1983
President Reagan makes "Evil Empire" speech in March.

President Reagan announces the Strategic Defense Initiative (or "Star Wars"), which involves new state-of-the-art technology that will shoot down incoming Soviet missiles.

Korean Air Lines flight 007 is shot down by Soviet aircraft on September 1 after it strays into Soviet airspace, killing all 269 aboard, including a U.S. Congressman.

Terrorists attack the U.S. Marine barracks in Beirut, killing 241 U.S. servicemen.

U.S. Marines invade Grenada in late October.

ABC airs *The Day After* on November 20.

1984
Elections are held in Nicaragua; several political parties participate; FSLN leader Daniel Ortega elected president.

The Central Intelligence Agency (CIA) begins mining Nicaraguan harbors.

Jose Napoleon Duarte elected president in El Salvador.

1985
Mikhail Gorbachev becomes general secretary of the Soviet Communist Party.

The first summit meeting between Reagan and Gorbachev takes place in Geneva.

1986   The International Court of Justice (or World Court) in The
                   Hague, Netherlands, condemns the United States government
                   for mining Nicaragua's harbors and supporting the Contras;
                   the World Court insists the United States furnish reparations
                   to Nicaragua; the Reagan administration ignores the verdict.

                   Filipino dictator Ferdinand Marcos' U.S.-backed regime
                   topples in February.

                   Chernobyl nuclear reactor in the Ukraine explodes in April,
                   killing 31 immediately and exposing countless more to
                   radiation afterward.

                   Second summit meeting between Reagan and Gorbachev is
                   held in Reykjavik, Iceland.

                   The Iran-Contra scandal is revealed to the public in
                   November.

1987   American volunteer Ben Linder, a 27-year-old engineer
                   working in Nicaragua, is killed by the Contras in Jinotega.

1987–1988   Costa Rican president Oscar Arias wins Nobel Peace Prize
                   for introducing a peace plan that eventually helps end the
                   Contra War.

1988   In January, the Soviet Union begins a program of economic
                   restructuring known as *perestroika.*

                   Soviets announce troop withdrawal from Afghanistan.

                   USS *Vincennes* shoots down Iranian passenger plane, killing
                   all 290 aboard.

1989   Solidarity is triumphant in Polish elections in June.

                   The massacre at Beijing's Tiananmen Square occurs in June.

                   East Germany opens the Berlin Wall on November 9 and
                   enthusiastic Germans begin tearing it down the same day.

                   Hurricane Hugo ravages Nicaragua, leaving thousands
                   homeless and worsening the woes of the war-torn nation.

                   The death toll from the civil war in Guatemala reaches
                   100,000, with an additional 40,000 missing.

                   Far-right Arena candidate Alfredo Cristiani is elected president
                   of El Salvador in what many observers considered a rigged
                   election.

AMERICA AND THE WORLD

Reviving Anticommunism in America

When Ronald Reagan vowed in the 1980 presidential race to restore America's global prestige by strengthening its military and adopting a more militantly anticommunist foreign policy, millions of voters were reassured by his promises and rewarded him with election to the highest office in the land. The 1979 Soviet invasion of Afghanistan, President Jimmy Carter's decision to boycott the Moscow summer Olympics in 1980, and the deteriorating state of U.S.-Soviet relations convinced a large segment of the population that the Cold War had returned after the long lull of détente. The dramatic escalation of the arms race during Reagan's two terms in the White House merely reinforced these perceptions.

Signs of a new Cold War culture were visible in the United States by mid-decade. Nowhere was its presence more pronounced than in popular entertainment. On multiplex screens across the country, Cold War fantasies were played out in a variety of ways. American soldiers returned to Vietnam to save POWs and refight the war in such films as *Uncommon Valor* (1983), *Missing in Action* (1984), and the 1985 box office smash hit *Rambo: First Blood Part II*. Hypothetical Soviet invasions of the United States were depicted in such movies as *Red Dawn* (1984) and the 12-hour miniseries *Amerika,* which aired on ABC in 1987 as a right-wing response to *The Day After*. In *Rocky IV* (1985), the cinematic boxing icon took on an evil Soviet boxer called Ivan Drago. In the 1982 Cold War thriller *Firefox,* an aging Clint Eastwood sneaks into the Soviet Union to steal a deadly, radar-evading prototype jet and fly it back to the West to be examined by the good guys. Soviet defectors were celebrated in such films as *Moscow on the Hudson* (1984) and *White Nights* (1985).

Elsewhere in America, fears of communism assumed different forms. In the nation's high schools, impressionable students typically developed negative stereotypes of the Soviet Union, which were frequently reinforced by their teachers. A November 1985 *New York Times* poll of 1,277 respondents found that "53 percent of those questioned said that political differences—or the military threat from the Soviet Union—were the first things that came to mind when they thought of the Soviet Union" (*New York Times Magazine,* November 10, 1985). In academe, debates flared about the origins of the Cold War, the guilt or innocence of alleged atomic spies Julius and Ethel Rosenberg (who were executed in 1953), and the lessons of the Vietnam War. Such ideological skirmishes were especially apparent among historians. Apologists for the Cold War in the historical profession clashed with so-called revisionists, who insisted that America shared the blame with the Soviet Union for inflaming global tensions. In the meantime, right-wing watchdog groups such as Reed Irvine's Accuracy in

Media (AIM) and Accuracy in Academia (AIA) monitored the media and higher education in an effort to counteract what they regarded as a predominance of excessively liberal viewpoints in those professions.

To some extent, the groundswell of anticommunism in the 1980s was offset by nationwide fears of nuclear war. By 1982 and 1983, public opinion polls indicated that anxieties over the likelihood of a nuclear confrontation between the superpowers were widespread in American society. On November 20, 1983, ABC aired the controversial film *The Day After,* which graphically depicted a hypothetical nuclear war and its aftermath. The made-for-TV movie, which focused on the plight of a doctor from Kansas who survives a fictional nuclear exchange, was also a cultural event on a par with such influential television dramas as *Roots* and *Holocaust.*

In an unprecedented move, the network interrupted the movie with limited commercial breaks, and no commercials aired after the film's mushroom cloud scenes. The controversial content scared away advertisers and only a few intrepid companies—including Minolta cameras, Dollar Rent a Car, and Commodore Business Machines—purchased spots. Still, *The Day After* was an enormous success, attracting almost 100 million viewers. The National Education Association warned parents not to allow their children to view the film alone and encouraged family members to have open dialogues about nuclear war. Some conservatives who were unhappy with the horrific depiction of nuclear war, including Rev. Jerry Falwell's Moral Majority, threatened to boycott ABC. Former secretary of defense Henry Kissinger dismissed *The Day After* as "a simple-minded notion of the nuclear problem" (*New York Times,* November 21, 1983). By contrast, the film inspired foes of the arms race to redouble their efforts. Antinuclear activists organized several events and campaigns surrounding the film. As an aide to a dovish congressman pointed out, "Politically, the left is fairly unabashed about using this film to further the freeze and arms control" (*New York Times,* November 17, 1983).

Rally in memory of those who died in the downing of Korean Airlines flight 007, shot down by the Soviets on September 1, 1983. The KAL Boeing 747 was shot down after overflying Soviet air space, and all aboard were lost. (Wally McNamee/Corbis)

Public fears of nuclear war were heightened by the Reagan administration's increasingly militant anticommunist foreign policy. On the home front, such developments prompted conservatives to warn about the dangers of communism while liberals feared a revival of McCarthyism and civil liberties violations. The Cold War reached a deep freeze in 1983. In March, President Reagan denounced the Soviet Union as "the Evil Empire," thus borrowing from the language of the enormously popular *Star Wars* movies. This was followed by the shooting down of Korean Air Lines flight 007 by a Soviet fighter jet on September 1 when the plane veered into Russian airspace. The Soviets insisted the airplane was conducting spy missions, but most Americans were convinced it was simply a stark act of Soviet brutality.

The revival of Cold War tensions intensified when U.S. troops invaded the island nation of Grenada in late October to overthrow its Marxist government. By the time *The Day After* aired on ABC in the fall, the prospect of a nuclear war was perilously real, which is why the film struck such a deep nerve in the American public. The Korean Air Lines incident, in particular, hardened negative perceptions of the Soviet Union among large segments of the American public. Among the 269 passengers on the flight were 52 Americans; in the days that followed the downing of flight 007, the White House received thousands of telephone calls and telegrams demanding a strong response from President Reagan. As one outraged woman from Arlington, Virginia, proclaimed, "I hope Mr. Reagan gets the message. We have to take stronger action against the Russians" (*Washington Post,* September 12, 1983).

In the domestic scene, the revival of anticommunism in the Reagan era lacked the intensity, scope, and duration of the predétente Cold War. Simply put, the threat of internal "subversion" was never an important issue in the 1980s. The long, agonizing war in Vietnam prompted many people, even conservatives, to reevaluate the merits of anticommunism. At no point in the 1980s did Congress investigate domestic "subversion" as it did during the 1940s and 1950s. Some civil libertarians feared that the 1982 cancellation of the popular CBS television drama *Lou Grant,* which starred controversial leftist actor Ed Asner, heralded a resurgence of blacklists. Yet there was no evidence of a well-organized blacklist similar to the influential "Red Channels" pamphlet of the 1950s, which listed the names of alleged communists and their so-called fellow travelers, thus ruining the careers of numerous innocent people. The closest thing to a blacklist in the 1980s was a list of "subversives" maintained by the Immigration and Naturalization Service (INS) in accordance with the 1952 McCarran–Walter Act. Names appearing on the list were denied visas by the INS. Typical of those who were refused visas were leftists in Nicaragua's Sandinista government and supporters of the Marxist rebels in El Salvador. Despite these attempts to control the flow of radical ideas into America, the nation did not experience systematic civil liberties violations on the scale that occurred in the 1950s. While anticommunism

Rambo

The fictional Vietnam veteran John Rambo, played by Sylvester Stallone in three films during the 1980s, emerged as an important pop-culture icon in the mid-1980s that symbolized both violent machismo and the revitalization of American military might. His first appearance came in the 1982 action film *First Blood,* in which he was portrayed as a misunderstood veteran who wanders into a small town in the northwest searching for some old friends. Rambo is soon arrested by a violent sheriff who harasses and brutalizes him. But the adroit veteran escapes into the woods and creates several booby traps to prevent the local police from capturing him.

In his debut film, Rambo was not the comic-book action hero that he becomes in subsequent films. Rather, he was representative of the misunderstood Vietnam veteran who was treated poorly by the public upon returning home from Indochina; thus, he was a potent symbol of betrayal and rage. *First Blood* contained several violent scenes, but, unlike its sequels, its bloodletting was realistic and served as potent social commentary. The antiauthoritarian sensibilities of the film were readily apparent, and it lacked the implausibility and right-wing politics of the next two Rambo movies.

For the 1985 sequel, *Rambo: First Blood Part II,* the filmmakers transformed John Rambo into a comic book–style action hero who was sent to Vietnam to rescue POWs held captive by evil Vietnamese communists and their Soviet masters. The Cold War fantasy was the second-highest grossing film of 1985 (just after the box-office smash *Back to the Future*), and the name Rambo instantly became a household word. Rambo quickly assumed mythic proportions. By defeating his Vietnamese and Soviet adversaries so effortlessly, Rambo single-handedly achieved what millions of American military personnel failed to accomplish in Southeast Asia years earlier. Not surprisingly, President Reagan jokingly referred to Rambo when discussing his foreign policy at a press conference. A mid-1980s spoof of the *Rambo* movie poster showed Rambo's body with Reagan's head superimposed over it and the title changed to *Ronbo.*

But the Rambo phenomenon proved to be short-lived. Another sequel was released in theaters in 1988, *Rambo III,* but it failed to break into the top 10 grossing films of the year. Like the previous installment, *Rambo III* featured the super veteran battling communist enemies, this time in Afghanistan. But it suffered from the same bad timing as the 1987 ABC miniseries *Amerika,* about a Soviet invasion of the United States. Both films appeared as the Cold War was waning, both were panned, and both had a difficult time attracting viewers. Most filmgoers who bothered to see the third film regarded it as little more than a rehash of *First Blood Part II.* The Rambo craze had run its course by the end of the decade, and a fourth sequel would not appear again until 2008 (sans communist villains). Still, for a while, Rambo stood as a potent symbol of national pride and Cold War fantasy at a time when the sting of defeat in Vietnam was still widely felt.

remained a guiding force in the formulation of foreign policy, American society had become more pluralistic and tolerant of dissent within its midst by the 1980s.

The Military-Industrial Complex in the 1980s

In his famous 1961 farewell speech to the nation, President Dwight D. Eisenhower warned of the dangers of what he called the "military-industrial complex." Eisenhower worried that the federal government, military, and major corporations were in the process of forming a powerful relationship with each other that threatened the future of America's democratic institutions. By the 1980s, relations between the three sectors had grown even more sophisticated, overlapping, and mutually beneficial. "Trillion" became a household word during the decade, used often to describe gargantuan arms spending sprees of the era. Reckless Pentagon expenditures shocked some Americans as stories surfaced about $900 ashtrays and $4,700 coffeepots. "That something is terribly wrong at the Pentagon is now clear to every American," wrote former ambassador Douglas MacArthur II, "as the unfolding stories of waste and extravagance in military procurement become part of the daily news. This did not happen overnight, however, nor in the last year or so. The problem has been building steadily for years, but it has been aggravated by the way the Pentagon has been handled during the Reagan years" (*Christian Science Monitor,* June 7, 1985).

Not only did defense budgets skyrocket in the 1980s but the nature of defense spending also changed. Unlike earlier phases of the Cold War, when a higher priority was placed on conventional military equipment such as tanks, trucks, and rifles, the arms race of the 1980s focused more on the production of aerospace and electronic equipment. Economic stability became increasingly dependent on the staggering military expenditures of the Reagan era. Millions of Americans owed at least part of their livelihood to some element of government military spending. The peacetime build-up furnished millions of jobs and strengthened hundreds of communities across the country. In Stratford, Connecticut, the massive Sikorsky helicopter facility that constructed U.S. Army Blackhawk helicopters employed 12,500 workers in 1985. The sprawling McDonnell Douglas military aerospace plant in Tulsa, Oklahoma, employed 3,000 men and women by 1982. At the Hughes plant in Tucson, Arizona, 8,000 workers produced missiles and fulfilled a variety of huge military contracts. Many of these facilities were like small cities, complete with restaurants, gymnasiums, chapels, and stores. In some states, such as Virginia, California, Texas, and Florida, the abundance of military production facilities led to striking economic booms by mid-decade.

While numerous states benefited from such jobs, the defense production sector was vulnerable in certain respects, and its presence in many communities was far from permanent. Congressional investigations into allegations of misspending and corruption undermined some firms. Certain companies reorganized

View of the shipyard of the Newport News Shipbuilding and Dry Dock Corporation in Newport News, Virginia. (U.S. Department of Defense)

in the mid-1980s and shut down facilities, which proved devastating to local economies. Civilians and military personnel alike were susceptible to such downturns. In late 1988, a federal commission recommended the closure of 86 military installations across the country, which translated to a loss of 12,000 civilian and military jobs. New arms treaties and the easing of Cold War tensions by 1986 prompted the U.S. government to begin dismantling missile silos in the heartland, a process that accelerated in the 1990s.

There were very few strikes or labor disputes in defense industries, due partly to the high wages and extensive benefits packages offered by most of the larger firms. The rare strikes at defense facilities generated headlines. A 1979 strike at Newport News Shipbuilding Co., the largest privately owned shipyard in the country and largest employer in Virginia, resulted in a temporary halt to the production of sensitive U.S. Navy defense materials. For several months in 1984, about 6,500 workers at the Fort Worth division of General Dynamics, one of the largest defense firms in the 1980s, went on strike over a series of contractual disputes. The following year, more than 4,500 General Dynamics employees went on strike at five plants in Michigan, Ohio, and Pennsylvania, which temporarily brought production of tanks to a halt. In 1986, the management at the LTV Aerospace and Defense Company factory at East Camden, Arkansas, began hiring replacement workers to take the place of 550 unionized employees who were

Songs about the Cold War

While love songs dominated the radio airwaves in the 1980s (as they had in past decades), a number of bands also performed songs containing themes that reflected the Cold War tensions of the day. One of the most popular one-hit wonders of the 1980s, Nena's "99 Luftballons" (or, the English version, "99 Red Balloons"), was a strange, synth-pop new wave song from 1984 about a young couple that releases 99 red balloons into the sky, only to trigger a massive Cold War nuclear confrontation.

Some songs spotlighted repression in communist countries. Elton John's moving 1985 hit "Nikita" told the story about a Westerner who falls in love with a Soviet woman, only to see their love doomed by Cold War tensions. The disheartened protagonist in "Nikita" looks forward to the day when the Cold War ends and the woman can live freely, without "guns and gates" holding her in place. The rock band Styx performed a song, "Double Life," about people "on the other side of the Berlin Wall" who lived in secrecy and fear.

Other songs emphasized the threat of nuclear war. British rocker Ozzy Osbourne's popular song "Crazy Train" contained lyrics about "heirs of the Cold War" and "millions of people living as foes." "Maybe it's not too late," he sang, "to learn how to love, and forget how to hate." Other Osbourne songs contained antinuclear and pacifist themes, such as "Killer of Giants" and "King of the Bomb." The Clash, a popular British punk band in the late 1970s and early 1980s, sang several songs with Cold War themes, most notably their 1979 ballad "London Calling" ("Now war is declared," they wailed, and warned ominously of a "nuclear error"). Depeche Mode, a dark, synth-pop band from the United Kingdom, performed "People are People" (1984) about men who hate one another without really knowing each other. The video for "People are People" shows film clips of Soviet soldiers marching while the lead singer laments misunderstandings between cultures.

A decidedly more light-hearted approach to the Cold War–themed music of the 1980s was "New Frontier" (1982), by ex-Steely Dan lead singer Donald Fagen. The song spawned a humorous, oft-played video on MTV in the early 1980s, about a young man and woman, dressed in 1950s styles, descending into a bomb shelter and looking forward to a post-apocalyptic "wingding." In a similar humorous vein, the offbeat "Two Tribes" by British new wavers Frankie Goes to Hollywood, was a tongue-in-cheek song about nuclear war between the superpowers.

A more serious entry into the genre was "Russians," by Sting, ex-lead singer of the Police, which sought to humanize people living on both sides of the Iron Curtain. "Believe me when I say to you," he sang, "I hope the Russians love their children too." During the second half of the 1980s, there were fewer Cold War–themed songs on the nation's airwaves, perhaps a reflection of the détente occurring between the Soviet Union and the United States. A few Cold War songs continued to climb the charts in the later 1980s, most notably "Land of Confusion" (1987) by Genesis. But, for the most part, the short-lived genre of Cold War pop music belonged to those uneasy years in the first half of the decade.

out on strike and thereby disrupting the production of rockets and launchers at the facility. Within a matter of weeks of when the replacement workers were hired, LTV was once again operating at full capacity, fulfilling its lucrative government contracts.

During the decade, staggering defense budgets and robust military Keynesianism became the order of the day. In many sectors of the economy, defense industries proved to be engines of economic growth and expansion. Few Americans questioned the arms race and the intensification of militarism, especially when such policies ushered in economic good times. Men and women from all walks of life assumed that these conditions were necessary to ensure continued prosperity. President Eisenhower was indeed prophetic when he predicted that the military-industrial complex might one day wield an enormous influence over American society, although perhaps he failed to anticipate that such a state of affairs would become the norm in the United States so soon.

Terrorism Abroad, Anxiety at Home

After the 1973 oil crisis, in which the Organization of Petroleum Exporting Countries (OPEC) began boycotting countries that supported Israel in the Yom Kippur War, many Americans began developing negative stereotypes about Arabs and fundamentalist Muslims. In the popular imagination, Arabs became associated with rich sheiks who were responsible for rising oil prices while fundamentalist Muslims came to be regarded as fanatical terrorists determined to destroy liberal Western democracies. Like most stereotypes, such notions contained nuggets of truth. The Iranian Revolution of the late 1970s and the 444-day hostage crisis that followed it hardened American perceptions of undemocratic Middle Eastern theocracies. Polls in the early 1980s indicated that most Americans regarded Israel as a lone democracy fighting a life-or-death struggle against Islamic fanatics, and that it should be supported by Washington, D.C.

In May 1981, the Reagan administration expelled Libyan diplomats from the nation's capital after intelligence information was intercepted indicating that Libyan leader Muammar el-Qaddafi was planning to assassinate American diplomats in Rome and Paris. During the early 1980s, Islamic fundamentalists targeted U.S. personnel and troops sent to Beirut, Lebanon, as part of a peacekeeping force whose purpose was to separate warring factions. First, a suicide bomber in a pickup truck attacked the U.S. Embassy in Beirut on April 18, 1983, killing 17 Americans. Then, on October 23, a suicide bombing of the U.S. Marine barracks in Beirut killed 220 Marines and 21 other U.S. servicemen, and sent shockwaves through the United States. Following the attack, the Marines were quietly withdrawn from war-torn Beirut.

With a mixture of shock and surprise, ordinary Americans watched film footage on their televisions of terrorist attacks overseas. Especially jolting was the hijack-

Americans who were held hostage aboard the Italian cruise ship Achille Lauro, *returning to the United States on October 12, 1985. (U.S. Department of Defense)*

ing of Trans World Airlines Flight 847 in June 1985 as it flew from Athens to Rome. At the demand of the hijackers, the plane, a Boeing 727, landed at Beirut International Airport, and U.S. television news cameras captured dramatic images of terrorists holding the pilots at gunpoint through open cockpit windows. The terrorists brutally murdered a U.S. Navy diver, Robert Dean Stethem, but most of the hostages were eventually freed, which coincided with the Israeli government freeing numerous Shiite prisoners. The hijacking of Italian cruise ship *Achille Lauro* in October and the horrifying execution of 69-year-old disabled American passenger Leon Klinghoffer (who, perhaps not coincidentally, was also Jewish) outraged much of the nation. Adding to frustrations were news reports from the Middle East of American journalists and clergy who were being held hostage in Lebanon and other countries in the region. Images of American hostages such as Terry Anderson, Tom Sutherland, John McCarthy, and Terry Waite hardened the attitudes of most ordinary Americans toward the Middle East.

Throughout the United States, anxieties about Arabs and Middle Eastern terrorists assumed different forms. Novelty stores in the mid-1980s sold dart boards with the face of Qaddafi in the center. In 1984, presidential candidate Gary Hart warned that the American economy must not "be mortgaged to oil sheiks," and he argued that the U.S. government should avoid negotiating with the Palestinian Liberation Organization (PLO) "until and unless the PLO rejoins civilization"

(*New York Times,* November 21, 1983). The following year, the American Arab Anti-Discrimination Committee (ADC) reported the bombing of a mosque in Houston, broken windows at mosques in San Francisco and Potomac, Maryland, and threats received by Arab-American groups in Dearborn, Michigan; Allentown, Pennsylvania; New York; Los Angeles; and Washington, D.C.

In 1986, the Connecticut-based toy company Coleco introduced a swarthy Arab action figure called Nomad, to serve as an adversary to its best-selling Rambo doll. A series of well-publicized protests by Arab-American groups prompted Coleco to halt production of Nomad. The same year, Arab-American antidefamation groups successfully persuaded the record label Elektra to remove a 1979 song titled "Killing an Arab" from a greatest-hits album by British rock band the Cure. In 1987, Los Angeles agents with the INS arrested seven Palestinian resident aliens and the Kenyan wife of one of them for allegedly affiliating with a subversive organization. During the Halloween season in 1989, Spencer Gifts, a popular novelty shop with 435 stores in malls across America, sold Arab-bashing masks called "the Sheik" and "the Arafat."

Even though human rights organizations and antidefamation groups remained vigilant, it was a difficult time to be an Arab-American or a Muslim in the United States. Reports of harassment, beatings, racist slurs, and intimidation were common among Arab-Americans. Sometimes racist attitudes turned deadly, as was the case in 1985 when the regional offices of the American-Arab ADC were bombed in Boston and Santa Ana, California, and set afire in Washington, D.C. The Santa Ana explosion killed Alex Odeh, West Coast regional director of the ADC, whose violent death shocked Arab-Americans and left his wife and three daughters inconsolable. In some cases, anti-Arab prejudices were inflamed by the extremist Jewish Defense League (JDL), whose leaders targeted Arab-American antidefamation groups as enemies of Israel. The FBI, in fact, suspected JDL involvement in the bombings of the ADC offices. In other cases, such as the shooting of a Palestinian grocer in Milwaukee in January 1986 or the beating of an Arab newspaper editor in Philadelphia later that same month, acts of violence appeared to be the work of deranged, violence-prone individuals. Throughout the decade, Arab bashing proved to be cyclical. Heavily publicized terrorist attacks overseas inevitably added fuel to the fire and triggered hostilities across the country. Following such incidents, Arab-American groups often issued statements condemning the attacks, and high-profile Arab-Americans, such as James G. Abourezk, a former U.S. senator from South Dakota, and Casey Kasem, a popular nationally syndicated radio disc jockey and host of *American Top 40,* called on the public to exercise tolerance.

Fears of Islamic fundamentalism in the United States had a basis in reality. Overseas, radical terrorists posed a greater threat to American individuals and institutions than at any previous time in history. That threat would deepen and expand over the years, and eventually culminate with the horrifying terror attacks of September 11, 2001. In sharp contrast to these developments, though, Arab-

Americans always prided themselves on being loyal, patriotic citizens. They repeatedly condemned terrorist acts and supported the right of the United States to defend itself against violent adversaries. Despite this, many Arab-Americans experienced discrimination throughout the 1980s. While such prejudices never approached the intensity of anti-German sentiments in World War I or the scope of Japanese internment in the 1940s, still they left a scar on the country and contributed to a decline in the health of America's democratic traditions in the 1980s.

THE CENTRALITY OF CENTRAL AMERICA

Background

Central America in the 1980s was a volatile region filled with revolution, violence, and upheaval. Many of the region's ills were related, both directly and indirectly, to its troubled historical relationship with the United States. Ever since the 19th century, relations between the United States and most Central American nations had been problematic at best, tumultuous at worst. Over the years, a familiar pattern developed: High-level officials in Washington, D.C., supported Central American leaders who placed a strong emphasis on the sanctity of U.S. business interests in the region. From the late-19th century until the 1970s, few of these leaders had any interest in nurturing genuine democracy in Central America. On the contrary, most were autocratic and several came to power in military coups. Whenever popular uprisings occurred in Central America—and they happened often because abject poverty, illiteracy, and lack of opportunities were so pervasive—Washington, D.C., opted to support tyrants whose highest priority was remaining in power, rather than assisting ordinary men and women who were trying to transform their countries. Thus, few of the region's inhabitants had faith in the motives and actions of the U.S. government.

This troubling dynamic was in place long before World War II. However, in the postwar era, American presidents and elected officials transformed Central America into a key theater of conflict in the intensifying Cold War contest between the communist and noncommunist world. The CIA-orchestrated overthrow in 1954 of Jacobo Arbenz Guzmán, the reform-minded president of Guatemala showed Latin Americans in stark terms what they could expect from the United States. The Cuban Revolution of 1959 heightened fears among presidents, members of Congress, and the State Department about the spread of communism in Latin America.

Alarmed and defensive, Washington officials resorted to supporting regimes that sought to quell internal unrest and showed little interest in improving the living standards of ordinary people. The Cold War altered relations between the United States and the nations of Central America. Policymakers who were largely unaware of the troubled history of the region blamed the uprisings and turmoil in Central America on the amorphous and monolithic "specter" of communism. During the Reagan presidency, Guatemala, Honduras, El Salvador, and Nicaragua were each in a state of crisis. The situation had become explosive. War, repression, and death-squad killings swept across the region. A 1979 revolution in Nicaragua brought a war, fought by National Guardsmen who had been a part of the hated regime that had been overthrown and financed by Washington, to the impoverished and traumatized country. In the meantime, the U.S. government buttressed "friendly" regimes in El Salvador, Guatemala, and Honduras, which fueled internal violence and conflicts, and forestalled any possibility of real democracy arriving in those countries. This section will explore the conflicts in Central America from the perspective of ordinary people from that region and the United States. The following themes are discussed in this section:

- The Nicaraguan Revolution and the people
- The tragedy of El Salvador
- The Sanctuary Movement

The Nicaraguan Revolution and the People

On July 17, 1979, the embattled dictator of Nicaragua, Anastasio Somoza Debayle, announced on Nicaraguan television that he was resigning and would soon be departing from his native land. By the time his regime collapsed, Somoza was the most hated figure in Nicaragua. He had managed to alienate a broad segment of the Nicaraguan public, including landowners, urban dwellers, middle-class professionals, rural *campesinos* and Catholic clergy. By the summer of 1979, years of repression, violence, torture, nepotism, and misrule were finally coming to a close. Even Somoza's most generous sponsors in Washington, D.C., had run out of patience.

During the 1970s, a powerful revolutionary movement had spread across the land, and by decade's end, the momentum of events favored the guerrillas of the Sandinista National Liberation Front (FSLN), usually called the Sandinistas. Many of the revolutionaries came from Nicaragua's poorest families. To most Nicaraguans, the Sandinistas seemed to be the modern-day heirs of Augusto Sandino, a legendary Nicaraguan independence leader who wore a tall hat and led the guerrilla forces that resisted the U.S. Marine occupation of the country in the late 1920s and early 1930s.

The Sandinistas launched offensives from the jungles of Costa Rica and Honduras in the spring and summer of 1979, and Somoza's war-weary National Guard was no match for the hardened rebels. Somoza boarded a plane in Managua on July 17 that took him to Miami, and he eventually settled in Paraguay, where he was murdered while living in exile in Asunción in 1980. On July 19, celebrations erupted throughout Nicaragua as the triumphant forces of the FSLN swept

Street celebrations in the Nicaraguan capital of Managua after dictator Somoza's departure in July 1979. (Organization of American States)

into cities and towns across the country. In cities like Managua, Masaya, León, and Estelí, triumphant Sandinistas and ordinary people shared in joyous victory gatherings.

The idealistic revolutionaries of the FSLN inherited a bankrupt and war-torn nation. Nicaraguans had endured years of warfare and persecution, and most of them simply wanted peace. The Sandinistas established a junta that consisted of a wide segment of the anti-Somoza opposition groups, including prominent entrepreneurs, newspaper editors, and landowners. The goals of the revolution were highly idealistic, and included land reform, literacy campaigns, universal medical care, and equal rights between the sexes. President Jimmy Carter's administration briefly supported the revolution during its early months before turning against it due to alleged human rights abuses occurring under the Sandinista regime. In 1981, Carter's successor, Ronald Reagan, would take an even more aggressive stance against the Sandinistas by supporting the so-called *contras,* a rebel army consisting primarily of former members of Somoza's detested

Nicaraguan Contra soldiers raise clenched fists at a training camp in Honduras in 1989. The Contras were the armed opponents of Nicaragua's Sandinista National Liberation Front (FSLN) in the 1980s. The rebel group received clandestine military and financial support by 1981 from operatives within the administration of U.S. president Ronald Reagan. (Cindy Karp/Time Life Pictures/Getty Images)

National Guard. The Contras would also be joined by disaffected peasants and some powerful Nicaraguans whose fortunes waned after the revolution, and they received $19 million in support from the Reagan administration in November 1981. Before long, the CIA was strengthening its ties to the Contras, providing training and support for the counterrevolutionary army.

The Nicaraguan revolution had very promising beginnings. Workers in many key sectors of the economy began to see their wages increase, rural peasants benefited from land reform, and the desperately poor received much-needed medical attention and dental care. Idealistic volunteers came from all parts of the world, including the United States, Canada, East and West Germany, Great Britain, France, India, Japan, New Zealand, and Australia, to help rebuild the blighted country and assist impoverished Nicaraguans. Although many of the Sandinistas adopted a Marxist analysis of Latin American history and politics, they proved to be much more pluralistic than the Cuban communists. In fact, they bore a more striking resemblance in their rhetoric and policies to Western European social democrats. According to Thomas W. Walker, professor of political science and director of the Latin America studies program at Ohio University, "far from being a coterie of wild-eyed ideologues, the Sandinistas behaved in a pragmatic and, indeed, moderate fashion throughout the nearly eleven years they were in power" (Walker 2003, 43).

Millions of Nicaraguans benefited from the transformations that occurred under the Sandinistas. More than half of Nicaragua's arable land fell under the Sandinista's land redistribution project, and the program ultimately benefited more than 60 percent of rural families (Prevost 1999, 10). But the Contra war had an undeniably devastating impact on the country. The Boland Amendment, enacted by Congress in 1982, temporarily halted U.S. aid to the Nicaraguan Contras. The Reagan administration subverted the amendment by diverting aid to the Contras

Traveling to Nicaragua

Thousands of Americans traveled to Nicaragua in the 1980s to investigate conditions under the Sandinista regime. For the most part, the revolutionary government extended tremendous hospitality toward this special "Yankee" invasion. The Sandinistas reasoned that it made perfect sense to welcome such delegations into the country because once Americans saw for themselves that the country was not the totalitarian gulag the Reagan administration claimed it was, they would presumably return home and oppose the Contra War in Nicaragua. In some instances, the struggling revolutionary government even subsidized travel for groups of Americans. The travelers came from all walks of life: students, retired people, government workers, university professors, small business owners, homemakers, and countless others made the journey to Nicaragua. Each year, thousands of Americans visited the nation, most often in the summer months. There were even delegations consisting entirely of visitors from a single profession, such as physicians, lawyers, politicians, or motion picture celebrities.

Typically, planes carrying Americans would land in Managua and the journeyers would go on two-week tours of the country, which included interviews with trade union members, government officials, opposition leaders, newspaper editors, military brass, religious figures, and ordinary peasants, as well as some sightseeing. The trips were often organized by activists who opposed U.S. policies in the region and were affiliated with such progressive organizations as Nicaragua-Honduras Education Project, Witness for Peace, and the New York City–based Marazul Tours. The typical trip cost between $1,200 and $2,000.

Americans would often begin their stay at the Intercontinental Hotel in Managua, and they were advised to drink bottled water and take malaria pills. Just as the Sandinistas had predicted, the American delegations often returned home to oppose U.S. intervention in Nicaragua. Indeed, welcoming Americans to Nicaragua had the desired effect. In the United States, public opposition to President Reagan's Nicaragua policies was widespread, and recent travelers to the country spoke at high schools, community forums, and rallies and spread doubts about the wisdom of the Contra war.

Not surprisingly, authorities did what they could to undermine the practice. The U.S. State Department, for example, repeatedly issued warnings to Americans not to travel to Nicaragua. Certain organizations that planned trips to Nicaragua were harassed by federal agents. The San Francisco-based Tecnica, which sent delegations of technical experts to Nicaragua to provide high-tech training and expertise for humanitarian projects, was repeatedly visited by FBI agents, as were several individuals who went on Tecnica trips. In 1988, the New York–based Center for Constitutional Rights obtained classified FBI files through the Freedom of Information Act (FOIA) showing that the FBI routinely monitored and even harassed groups that opposed U.S. intervention in Central America. High on the FBI's

Continued on next page

Traveling to Nicaragua, Continued

"watch list" were such organizations as the Committee in Solidarity with the People of El Salvador (CISPES) and the National Network in Solidarity with the People of Nicaragua.

FBI harassment and State Department warnings failed to deter the small but robust movement of ordinary people who traveled to Nicaragua and returned to share their experiences with other people. Thanks in part to their work, U.S. policies in Nicaragua failed to attract enthusiastic support among the American public.

through the fundamentalist Islamic government in Iran, a covert strategy that formed the basis of the Iran-Contra Scandal. In 1986, the International Court of Justice at the Hague, Netherlands, ordered the United States government to "cease and refrain" from arming and training the Contras and mining Nicaragua's harbors. The Reagan administration ignored the ruling, and the U.S. government once again began financing the Contras.

Despite Reagan's claim that the Contras were the "moral equivalent of our founding fathers," the counterrevolutionaries routinely resorted to raping and murdering civilians and terrorizing entire communities. By the late 1980s, many Nicaraguans were tired and demoralized, and in the 1990 elections, they voted for the moderate candidate, Violeta Chamorro, who pledged to reverse many of the gains made by the Sandinistas. The Contra war left a lasting impact on Nicaragua and ultimately derailed what many observers considered to be an idealistic and promising revolution.

The Tragedy of El Salvador

An impoverished Central American nation roughly the size of Massachusetts, El Salvador suffered from a long history of violence dating back to the early-20th century. By the 1980s, it assumed a central place in the Cold War–geopolitical contests of the era. The crisis in El Salvador began even before Reagan entered the White House, during the final years of the Carter administration. A series of autocratic, pro-U.S. regimes toppled in rapid succession in the late 1970s and early 1980s. Coups and countercoups became commonplace in the capital of San Salvador, and each day seemed to bring news of power struggles occurring inside of new juntas. The so-called death squads—paramilitary units which had close ties to the Salvadoran military—routinely rounded up students, trade union workers, human rights activists, and anybody suspected of opposing the regime

Violence erupts in San Salvador, El Salvador, following the funeral of Archbishop Oscar Romero on March 30, 1980. The popular cleric, a vocal critic of the authoritarian government, was assassinated by the military on March 23, 1980. (Patrick Chauvel/Sygma/Corbis)

in San Salvador. Meanwhile, guerrillas with the FMLN, a Marxist rebel army, mobilized in the countryside and attacked government forces.

The mixture of political violence, government repression, and civil war in El Salvador created a volatile situation that exploded into rampant bloodshed in 1979 and 1980. The assassination of Archbishop Oscar Romero, a pacifist clergyman and outspoken critic of the government, sent shockwaves of fear throughout the country. Most observers suspected that the death squads were behind the murder of Romero. Thousands of Salvadorans began flooding out of the country, heading for Mexico and the United States, while others were driven by the repression into the ranks of the FMLN.

In the urban areas, thousands of men and women continued to disappear in the early 1980s while in the rural areas battles between government forces and guerrillas intensified. Even though President Jimmy Carter spoke of the need to promote "human rights" and find a peaceful solution in El Salvador, he suspended aid to the war-torn nation much too late into the crisis, and he did little else to help stem the rising violence. On December 2, 1980, soldiers in the Salvadoran National Guard pulled over a van transporting four American female church workers. The four women, Maryknoll Sisters Ita Ford and Maura Clark, Ursuline Sister Dorothy Kazel, and lay missioner Jean Donovan, were brutally murdered by the guard and their bodies were unceremoniously dumped in the countryside. News of the killings shocked Americans and prompted calls in the United States to reevaluate Washington's El Salvador policies.

The violence in El Salvador reached a grisly climax with a horrific massacre in the remote village of El Mozote, carried out by the government's armed forces. On December 11, units of the Atlacatl Battalion systematically murdered more than 200 innocent Salvadoran men, women, and children in an orgy of gruesome bloodletting. Gradually, over time, the details of the heinous massacre became known.

When Reagan was sworn in as president of the United States in January 1981, he rejected President Carter's talk of "human rights" and began supporting an aggressively anticommunist policy toward El Salvador. Steep increases in military aid from the United States went hand in hand with support for the moderate politician Jose Napoleon Duarte, who ran for president in March 1982. When Duarte won the election, many international observers hoped that his victory would bring an end to the bloody war in the countryside and the death squad violence in the urban areas. Those hopes were dashed, however, when rightwing parties formed a powerful coalition in the government's national assembly. The coalition chose Roberto D'Aubuisson, head of the rightist ARENA party and a key force behind the Salvadoran death squads, as president of the Constituent Assembly, which weakened Duarte's influence over the government. Within a few months, D'Aubuisson would be succeeded by Alfredo Magana, who was also a rightist but decidedly more moderate than D'Aubuisson. Still, for the remainder of the decade, the bloody civil war dragged on, and human rights abuses remained pervasive. The death squads continued to dump corpses at El Playon, "the Place of the Disappeared," a stark, hilly black lava rock bed just outside of San Salvador. Recurring news reports of death squad killings, overcrowded refugee camps, and government corruption gave the outside world the impression that El Salvador was a surreal and nightmarish land. To make matters worse, Washington's foreign policies contributed to the spread of violence. In 1982 alone, the Salvadoran government received more than $82 million in military aid from the U.S. government. Often, the death squads turned out to be the direct beneficiary of massive shipments of guns and aid coming from the United States. While Reagan administration officials and members of Congress were outspoken about human rights violations in Nicaragua, most of them remained silent about much worse abuses occurring in neighboring El Salvador. In the mid-1980s, U.S. military advisors were quietly training Salvadoran soldiers while American aircraft covertly bombed rebel targets in rural areas.

The worst of the violence had passed by the early 1990s. More than 75,000 people had perished in the conflicts of the previous decade. A 1992 peace treaty brought an end to the long and bloody civil war in El Salvador, and government

Human Rights Activism in the 1980s

During the 1980s, human rights organizations such as Amnesty International and Human Rights Watch flourished in the United States, carefully monitoring abuses in all parts of the world. They attracted a small but intensely dedicated coterie of young activists, many of them university students who volunteered part-time. London-based Amnesty relied on the dues of members, who paid $25 per year to join the organization in the 1980s. The main London office was a bustling place, with about 300 activists researching reports of human rights violations each day. They coordinated their efforts with 46 "section offices" around the world. In 1988, there were approximately 300 different chapters of Amnesty across the United States, with many renting spaces in community centers and churches. There were also a thousand college and high school chapters of Amnesty located in all 50 states.

The smaller but equally robust Human Rights Watch employed a regular staff of 125, and it, too, had an army of volunteers supporting the organization at any given time. Human Rights Watch grew steadily throughout the 1980s, and in the last years of the decade it oversaw four committees: Helsinki Watch (which monitored human rights violations in the Soviet Union), Asia Watch, Americas Watch, and the Fund for Free Expression. Also, by decade's end, Human Rights Watch announced plans to establish Middle East Watch and Africa Watch.

Because they so closely monitored events in other countries, human rights activists were often called upon by the media to comment as experts on foreign affairs. During the Tiananmen Square protests in Beijing, China, from April to June 1989, observers around the world relied on updates and reports from human rights organizations to help remain abreast of events.

Torture, disappearances, the incarceration of prisoners of conscience, censorship of opposition newspapers, capital punishment, abuses by military forces, and excessive civilian deaths in war-torn nations were among the top concerns for human rights activists. It was, to be certain, a demanding line of work. The pay was low and the work was often thankless and ignored by the public and press. To make matters worse, some governments stubbornly refused to comply with human rights standards and, in particularly repressive countries, human rights workers went missing.

Not surprisingly, one of the regions most closely monitored by human rights groups in the '80s was Central America. Of all the countries in the area, only Costa Rica enjoyed a robust democratic tradition. In Honduras and Guatemala, military juntas or some combination of civilian and military leaders typically controlled the government, and their human rights records were ranked among the worst in Latin America. Moreover, strife between the military and leftist guerrillas inevitably resulted in numerous atrocities and disappearances. Amnesty International, Human Rights Watch, and other groups kept the pressure on these governments by sending delegations to the countries to investigate allegations of abuse.

Continued on next page

Human Rights Activism in the 1980s, Continued

In both Guatemala and Honduras, a mixture of tension and fear was constantly palpable throughout the 1980s. Mutual-support networks for families of the disappeared often received death threats, and some of their volunteers would end up among the missing. Local groups worked closely with Amnesty and Human Rights Watch in hopes of getting the word out about disappearances. The American delegations, in turn, would travel back to the United States and spread the word at churches and other public forums, and would write columns in newspapers and letters to policymakers. By its very nature, human rights work could often be discouraging. Yet committed volunteers took some solace in the very gradual changes that occurred over time. As Aryeh Neier, executive director of Human Rights Watch, noted, "most governments at least pretend they comply with internationally recognized standards. That's an advance. A decade ago, many fewer countries made that pretense" (Kristin Helmore, "The Politics of Human Rights," *Christian Science Monitor,* June 8, 1988, 16).

---

repression subsided. Most of the Salvadoran rebels laid down their arms, and death squad murders tapered off. But the legacies of the destructive war remained apparent for years after it ended. Even though El Salvador became a more democratic and open society, it remained marred by widespread gang violence, abject poverty, illiteracy, and homelessness decades after the gruesome events of the 1980s.

The Sanctuary Movement

The sanctuary movement in the 1980s began in response to growing numbers of Central American refugees who came to the United States seeking political asylum. The movement, which was largely the work of religious clergy and more than 200 churches and synagogues across the country, aided refugees by providing them with shelter, food, and, in some cases, financial support. It was founded in 1981 by James Corbett, an Arizona rancher and Harvard-educated philosopher, and Rev. John Fife of the Southside Presbyterian Church in Tucson.

The sanctuary movement was a well-organized network that operated in churches and out of the homes of supporters. What it lacked in finances and resources was compensated for by spirited young activists who dedicated countless hours of time and effort to sustain it. It became a modern-day "underground railroad" of sorts, where idealistic activists who were mostly Christians sought to assist impoverished Central Americans, many of whom were escaping persecution—sometimes death—in their homelands. In El Salvador alone, an estimated 1 million refugees fled the war-torn nation during the violent decade of the 1980s.

For the thousands of Americans who volunteered to help the refugees, the sanctuary movement proved to be an eye-opening and highly educational experience. As one former minister who was active in the movement recalled, "I was pretty much a plain-vanilla kind of guy before refugees started showing up on our church doorstep and telling us of these atrocities. In fact, I had even served as a member of the U.S. Department of Justice. Now, I realize that what I did back then had an effect on whether people lived or died—whether they got deported back to the living hell from which they came" (Julienne Gage, "Saints at the Border: A Salvadoran Refugee Shares Her Memories of the Sanctuary Movement," *Tucson Weekly,* March 21, 2002).

Typical of the refugees who trekked to the United States in the early 1980s was Carlos Amaya, a young Salvadoran who hastily departed his homeland a desperate and terrified man. Archbishop Oscar Romero had recently been assassinated, and the violence in the urban areas was spilling out into the countryside. Amaya and his wife, Patricia, fled El Salvador in the summer of 1980, first heading to Costa Rica, then north to Mexico, where the couple eventually waded across the Rio Grande River and entered the United States. Amaya explained his reasons for leaving El Salvador: "The government and military make a lot of repression. They kill people, women, children. They kill in the street and throw [bodies] in the river" (Alex Fryer, "Salvadoran looks back on 23-year journey," *The Seattle Times,* March 18, 2006, B1).

The couple made their way to Los Angeles and resided for a few years in an apartment connected to the University Baptist Church. The Amayas were assisted by the sanctuary movement, which furnished them with food, clothing, job training, and shelter. A 1985 sweep of Salvadoran communities across the United States by the INS resulted in numerous arrests and deportations, including a few key sanctuary movement activists. That year, the Amayas moved into their own apartment, and using a fraudulent Social Security card, Carlos found a job washing dishes. When the Reagan administration offered amnesty to illegal aliens in 1987, the young Salvadoran couple became permanent residents. Five years later, Carlos received his U.S. citizenship while Patricia became a permanent resident. They eventually settled in Seattle, where their sons, who were born in the sanctuary churches of Southern California, went on to become the first university-educated members of their family.

Not all stories had such happy endings, however. Some foreign-born sanctuary activists were deported back to their homelands while others endured jail time and trials for helping refugees evade capture. In 1985, eight sanctuary workers in Arizona were convicted of smuggling illegal aliens across the border, harboring the aliens, and conspiracy. They were given suspended sentences, and each received between three to five year's probation. In New Mexico in 1988, Glen Thamert and Demetria Martinez were put on trial for violating immigration laws, and both faced long prison terms (Thamert 35 years, Martinez 25 years) if convicted. The two activists were eventually acquitted, but their trial proved long and costly. Ultimately, though, the trial was considered a victory for the sanctuary movement, and activists felt vindicated. As Martinez explained, "People can say what they want about faith and politics, but the fact is the court came down on the side of the sanctuary movement" (Paul Logan, "N.M. Sanctuary Defendants Say They Did the Right Thing," *Albuquerque Journal,* August 2, 1998, B1).

Even though refugees continued to pour into the United States from Central America long after the 1980s, the sanctuary movement had run its course by decade's end. Nevertheless, small, localized efforts have continued to assist refugees entering the country well into the new millennium. In 2006, huge protests across the country (including a march of 500,000 people in Los Angeles) provoked debates over immigration in the United States. Cardinal Roger M. Mahony of Los Angeles stirred controversy when he called on the 288 parishes in the Los Angeles Archdiocese to assist impoverished refugees entering the country. Indeed, in these contentious debates that stirred once again in the new millennium, echoes of the 1980s' Sanctuary Movement could be heard.

DRUG WARS AND THE WAR ON DRUGS

A subject of intense controversy and debate in the United States, the so-called War on Drugs was a costly and heavily publicized campaign that was supported by the Reagan administration and numerous members of Congress, Republicans and Democrats alike. It commenced in October 1982, when President Ronald Reagan announced the War on Drugs to the American public. Although the impetus behind the War on Drugs originated at the highest levels of government, it received widespread and enthusiastic support from all levels of society and helped initiate grassroots antidrug movements in cities and small towns across the nation.

A small, vocal minority of Americans condemned the War on Drugs; there were some people who thought it was a good idea in theory but that it emphasized law enforcement solutions too heavily. Like President Lyndon Johnson's War on Poverty in the 1960s, the War on Drugs in the 1980s gave observers the impression that the federal government was acting decisively to solve one of the most acute crises of the time. By the closing years of the decade, however, even the most committed defenders of the War on Drugs questioned its effectiveness. The crusade ended up costing billions of dollars, but its results were, at best, difficult to gauge. While certain types of drug abuse plunged in some communities, elsewhere the picture was not as promising. In other locales, there were instances in which drug sales actually increased, and the War on Drugs seemed to have little effect. In the end, neither side claimed victory or defeat after the war on drugs. This section will explore the following themes:

- Illegal drug use in the 1980s
- Crack
- "Just say no"

Illegal Drug Use in the 1980s

By 1982, drug dealing in the United States had become a $90 billion-a-year industry. "Only Exxon is bigger than the illegal drug trade in this country," declared billionaire H. Ross Perot, who at the time headed a Texas task group to combat drug abuse (Hilary DeVries, "Americans face up to drug problem—at home, on job, in school," *Christian Science Monitor,* May 3, 1982, 12). Cocaine sales in 1980 alone surpassed $30 billion, making it a more profitable drug than marijuana. The FBI estimated in 1986 that 20 million Americans had used cocaine at least once, and that 4 million used it regularly. In 1985, three years into the War on Drugs, the Drug Enforcement Agency (DEA) estimated that between 12,600 and 15,000 metric tons of marijuana were used by an estimated 22 million people across the United States. The same year, the National Organization for the Reform of Marijuana Laws (NORML) found that 200,000 Americans were involved in the cultivation of marijuana. By 1986, so-called black tar heroin, a less-expensive yet highly potent form of heroin from Mexico that was not available in the United States at the beginning of the decade, was being sold in 27 states. And in the 1980s, a powerful new form of cocaine made its debut in the nation's thriving drug markets: crack. As Newark's Police Director, Louis E. Greenleaf, announced in 1986, "Crack is the biggest seller on the drug market today" (Andrew H. Malcolm, "Worried Citizens are Joining Officials Around U.S. to Fight Spread of Crack, *New York Times,* September 14, 1986, 26).

Both within the United States and abroad, powerful drug empires rose and fell in the 1980s. In the town of Medellín, Colombia, a powerful cartel dominated the community and relied on the work of a well-armed and efficient network of producers, traffickers, distributors, and—most importantly—security forces. Americans in the 1980s were alarmed by daily headlines and nightly network news reports about the spread of drugs. Parents feared that drugs were more easily available in the nation's public schools than they had been in previous years. Newspapers routinely ran stories about teenagers overdosing and drug dealers peddling dope near playgrounds. Drugs that utilized needles, such as heroin, also heightened anxieties about the spread of AIDS.

The word "crisis" was frequently used to describe the drug problem in America during the 1980s. At the time, it was not easy to discern whether there

Bricks of cocaine confiscated by the U.S. Drug Enforcement Agency in 2003. Drug trafficking is one of the many areas of both domestic and international organized crime. (U.S. Drug Enforcement Agency)

genuinely was a crisis unfolding, or if people were succumbing to fear due to the intense publicity surrounding the War on Drugs. Throughout the history of the United States, drug abuse of one form or another had always existed, and it often cut across race, class, and gender lines. But in the past, the use of drugs occurred largely in secrecy while in the 1980s the problem was much more out in the open than it had ever been before.

It would be a mistake to dismiss anxieties about drugs as groundless products of nationwide hysteria. People had compelling reasons to be nervous about drugs. Not only were more kinds of drugs becoming increasingly accessible and cheaper but the drugs that were being sold in the 1980s were also more powerful than ever. Some of them were new generations of "hybrid" drugs that often contained powerful, sometimes harmful chemicals that were supposed to enhance the experience of using them. But they could also be incredibly deadly when abused. The sudden death of University of Maryland basketball superstar Len Bias in June 1986, following an early-morning cocaine binge, shocked the nation. Tragically, Bias died two days after his selection in the first-round draft picks by the Boston Celtics.

Drug abuse also took a serious toll on impoverished neighborhoods in cities across the nation. A homeless, drug-addicted single mother from Houston looked back on the decade and remarked, "It's hard to get a job. There is no work. . . . Somebody told me that Mr. Reagan had a war on drugs. . . . Well, he hasn't been to my neighborhood. That's why I'm here in the shelter and not at home" (Tony Freemantle, "Viewpoints of the Reagan Era," *Houston Chronicle,* August 16, 1992, 9). When Washington officials spoke of the War on Drugs, they typically ignored such vexing issues as poverty and the lack of economic opportunities that existed in some communities. Class analysis was typically absent in the rhetoric of the antidrug crusades. What could have been a valuable opportunity to explore systematically the connections between poverty and drug addiction was largely squandered by politicians. Such a dialogue might have pointed to unpleasant realities in American society that people in high places were trying to ignore. Like countless other reformers in America's past, most apologists for the war on drugs sought to remedy the symptoms of the problem without carefully exploring the deeper roots.

Crack

Despite the nationwide war on drugs, cocaine use increased sharply across the United States in the 1980s. A derivative of cocaine, crack first appeared in New York City around 1984 or 1985, and within a few years, the powerful drug was "sweeping not only the big cities but small towns," noted the *Christian Science Monitor* (John Hughes, "War on Drugs," *Christian Science Monitor,* August 1, 1986, 14). Crack frightened authorities because it was highly addictive and cheaper than regular cocaine. Prices ranged from $5 to $40 for two hits of crack. The off-white pellets were usually sold in a plastic vial or tinfoil and were typically smoked in pipes and made a crackling noise while burning (hence, the name "crack"). Nicknames for the substance included "Rock," "Readyrock," "Baserock" and "Roxanne."

The poor were particularly vulnerable as the use of crack spread, and dealers frequently made their biggest profits in impoverished, inner-city neighborhoods. Law-enforcement authorities took note of the rapid expansion of the crack market in the mid-1980s. In 1986, police in Detroit estimated that 60 percent of their cocaine-related arrests involved crack, and police in Chicago guessed that 25 percent of cocaine arrests were crack related. That same year, Los Angeles police noted a rise in the number of crack arrests that occurred in their city as well. In hospitals across the country, the number of emergency room cases related to cocaine use jumped from 5,223 in 1983 to 21,543 in 1986, and crack played no small role in that sharp increase.

Crack could be very deadly, and stories of overdoses were common. In January 1988, for example, Gerald Clark, a 17-year-old high school dropout living in Tampa, Florida, with his girlfriend and young son, overdosed after he swallowed three pieces of crack cocaine to avoid being arrested when the police pulled over the vehicle he was driving. Forty-five minutes later, Clark experienced painful seizures and his tongue became swollen. His mother Gwendolyn recalled, "His eyes rolled up into his head, he gagged twice and then his heart stopped. He died right in front of me. He was dead by the time the paramedics came" (John Burr, "Teen dies after swallowing pieces of crack," *St. Petersburg Times,* January 8, 1988, 1).

Curbing the sale of crack became a high priority for the DEA and local police forces throughout the 1980s. In several cities, authorities launched anti-crack sting operations that resulted in numerous drug busts. Some crack busts attracted a great deal of media attention, such as the May 1987 arrest of 52-year-old Nancy Capurso, the so-called Crack Queen of Washington Square, who oversaw an army of teenage crack sellers in New York City. Netting Capurso turned out to be a real coup for the police, and their raid received national attention. But the repeated efforts of authorities to break the crack market did not halt the proliferation of the sinister drug into large cities such as San Diego, Los Angeles, San Francisco, Dallas, Boston, Philadelphia, Miami, and Atlanta. The media reported extensively about the growth of the crack industry in the United States, but the biggest crack story by far was the arrest of Washington, D.C., mayor Marion Barry in January 1990. Grainy images of the former civil rights activist smoking crack cocaine with his ex-girlfriend were captured on surveillance cameras right before police and FBI agents arrested him, and then later beamed onto television sets across the nation.

Crack proved to be a constant source of frustration for law-enforcement officials across the country. According to one police detective, young people who were enlisted by dealers to help sell crack "are living a *Miami Vice* fantasy, heavy gold chains, $200 sweat suits, 500 SEC Mercedeses, and $160 Porsche sunglasses. Their aspiration is to be a successful supplier with a string of drug concessions and a string of condos" (Troy 2005, 288).

Crack did not disappear because of the War on Drugs. On the contrary, it became even more potent and easier to obtain during the second half of the 1980s. Moreover, the deleterious effects of crack sometimes went hand in hand with racism, and the result was particularly devastating for African Americans, even after the War on Drugs ended. In 2006, the Sentencing Project, a Washington, D.C.-based nonprofit organization, cited statistics from the U.S. Department of Health and Human Services and the U.S. Sentencing Commission when it reported, "Despite the fact that less than half of crack cocaine users in the general population are African American, more than 80 percent of persons convicted in federal court for crack cocaine offenses are African American" (Lee Hammel, "Crack vs. cocaine: Caught between a rock and a powder," *Worcester Sunday Telegram,* February 19, 2006, A1). This was but one of the many devastating legacies of crack culture in the United States.

Miami Vice (1984–1989)

Each Friday night beginning in 1984, millions of Americans tuned in to the enormously popular NBC television show *Miami Vice,* or they set their VCRs to record it. The opening theme, a mix of synthesizer, guitar, and thudding percussion (the only television theme song to make it to No. 1 on the Billboard singles charts), set the stage for an exotic mixture of action, violence, humor, and drama that was the *Miami Vice* experience. The show's creator, Michael Mann, insisted that every episode contain a mixture of hit music and lesser-known songs from the time. Many songs featured on the show became radio hits, including Glenn Frey's "You Belong to the City," and the show revived interest in Phil Collins's dark ballad "In the Air Tonight." The show was highly stylized, as Mann explained: "We want to feel electric, and whenever we can, we use pastels that vibrate. . . . It was no accident that one of our characters appeared in a pale turquoise shirt against the pink ocher walls" (Sally Bedell Smith, "'Miami Vice': Action TV With Some New Twists," *New York Times,* January 3, 1985, C20). With its fast cars, police detectives dressed in pastel linen jackets, gunfights, explosions, and edgy portrayals of rich drug dealers, *Miami Vice* instantly became an era-defining, pop-culture event that tapped into the zeitgeist of the period. *Miami Vice* influenced fashion, music, and even popular slang. Other networks raced to air their own *Miami Vice* rip-off programs, which all turned out to be forgettable and short-lived. Without question, it was an American original.

Detective James "Sonny" Crockett (Don Johnson), the main character, was a tough-talking Vietnam veteran with a five o'clock shadow who lived on a sailboat, owned a pet alligator named Elvis, and drove various Ferraris (one of which was destroyed on an episode). His partner, Rico Tubbs (Philip Michael Thomas), a cop from New York, dressed in fancy suits, always kept his cool, and allowed Sonny to hog the spotlight most of the time. The show featured numerous guest stars who later gained fame in films, including John Turturro, Julia Roberts, Bruce Willis, Wesley Snipes, and Benicio Del Torro.

Most episodes in the first season were action-packed, and contained contrived dialogue, and little character development. The typical early episode played out like a cross between an MTV video and Brian De Palma's 1983 hit film *Scarface.* But as the series progressed, its tone grew darker, its content became increasingly politicized, and it boldly tackled a series of complex social issues, such as Vietnam veterans suffering from post-traumatic stress disorder, covert CIA operations in Nicaragua, inner-city drug addiction, and bloodshed in Ireland. Sonny Crockett evolved from being a garden-variety, cliché-spouting TV cop to a genuinely complex and brooding figure, and the lives of other regulars on the show, such as Lt. Martin Castillo (Edward James Olmos), were also explored in more depth.

The show enjoyed an intense cult following, and in its second season, it was one of the top-10 rated television programs in the United States. Most importantly, the influence of *Miami Vice* extended far beyond its ever-fluctuating ratings.

Continued on next page

Miami Vice *(1984–1989)*, *Continued*

Interest in the show gradually waned, though. *Miami Vice* was well suited to the sensibilities of the mid-1980s, but the final years of the decade were less hospitable, and some viewers began to find the show passé. In its final season, 1988–1989, its ratings plunged to number 34, and it no longer shaped fashions and popular music the way it did four years earlier. Nevertheless, the show's creator, Michael Mann, later went on to become a widely respected director; he remade *Miami Vice* in 2006 as a motion picture, starring Colin Farrell as Sonny Crockett and Oscar-winner Jamie Foxx as Rico Tubbs. The popularity of the remake, coupled with the rerelease of *Miami Vice* seasons on DVD, ensured continued interest in the 1980s phenomenon.

"Just Say No": The War on Drugs

During a decade that was free of large-scale, catastrophic conflicts, the War on Drugs captured the attention of the American public and stirred debates across the country. Among ordinary Americans, there was never a consensus about whether the War on Drugs was productive or even necessary. It won the applause of men and women who saw it as a welcome and long overdue crusade by the government to confront one of the most vexing crises in American history. Other observers were more skeptical, though, criticizing the War on Drugs for what they perceived to be its excessive reliance on law enforcement solutions and the lack of funding for rehabilitation and counseling programs. Not surprisingly, critics tended to dismiss it as a lot of empty ballyhoo while supporters claimed that it was having a largely positive influence by helping to reduce accessibility to harmful substances.

The reason for such deep divisions had to do with the uneven results of the War on Drugs. In some communities, it really did have a lasting impact, cutting off the flow of certain types of drugs and reducing the efficiency of the drug trade. DEA agents intercepted drug shipments on planes and boats, police arrested dealers as part of organized sting operations, and public school students listened to lectures about the harmful effects of drugs. Moreover, in the 1980s, moviegoers were inundated by movies with drug-related themes, including *Scarface, River's Edge, Less Than Zero, Drugstore Cowboy,* and *Colors.* Television also got in on the act, with news shows such as *60 Minutes, 20/20,* and *West 57th* regularly featuring stories on vice cops, drug dealers, and addicts. In 1986, the CBS news show *48 Hours* devoted an entire episode to crack, sending camera crews into some of the roughest inner-city neighborhoods across the United States to film sellers, users, and the devastated relatives of overdose victims. Almost every popular television show of the day, from comedies such as *Family*

Nancy and Ronald Reagan at their California ranch. Nancy brandishes a sign bearing the antidrug campaign slogan "just say no," September 6, 1986. (Library of Congress)

Ties and *The Cosby Show* to police shows like *Miami Vice, Cagney and Lacey,* and *Hill Street Blues,* tackled the drug issue. Songs such as the Thompson Twins' "Don't Mess With Dr. Dream," Grandmaster Flash's "White Lines," and Glen Frey's "Smuggler's Blues" were but a few songs that reflected the antidrug sensibilities of the time.

The federal government assumed a central role in the War on Drugs with the passage of the Anti-Drug Abuse Act of 1986, a sweeping new law that stepped up funding for enforcement, education, treatment, and border interdiction. The War on Drugs was having an impact. It raised awareness across the country about the dangers of substance abuse. In 1985, a mere 1 percent of Americans polled believed drugs were a serious threat to the United States; four years later, more than half of Americans categorized drug use as a major threat to the country. By 1988, authorities at the federal, state, and local levels were spending $15 billion annually in the War on Drugs. First Lady Nancy Reagan turned the

War on Drugs into her own personal crusade. She crisscrossed the nation delivering speeches, visiting rehabilitation centers, and touring inner cities, meeting
with former addicts and municipal officials. "The things I've seen would make
the strongest hearts break," she lamented at a press conference (Schaller 1992,
87). When a little girl at an elementary school asked Mrs. Reagan what to say if
someone offered her drugs, the First Lady replied, "Just say no." It instantly became the slogan of the nationwide struggle, and it resonated deeply with millions of people.

The War on Drugs suffered, however, due to an excessive emphasis on law
enforcement. The focus on distribution resulted in untold thousands of sellers
and purchasers going to prison in the 1980s, but policymakers largely failed to
formulate coherent strategies that addressed the problem in the production and
addiction stages. Cocaine sales in the 1980s actually increased because of the
government's inadequate response to the production of the drug in South America. A 1989 State Department report warned, "We will have only limited success
in battling cocaine until we forge a comprehensive, multifaceted strategy which
recognizes that cocaine is not simply a law enforcement issue but is also a complex foreign policy matter, requiring a long-term approach" (Elaine Sciolino,
"Drug Production Rising Worldwide, State Dept. Says," *New York Times,* March 2,
1989, 1). Moreover, in states across the country, rehabilitation programs struggled due to poor funding, and there were even stories of rehab centers closing
their doors in various communities. In Boston, the Department of Public Health
Commissioner David Mulligan noted, "The myth is that addicts don't want
treatment. It's only a myth. They want the treatment but the state doesn't have
enough programs for them" (*Boston Globe* 1990). Prisons became increasingly
overcrowded with street dealers and addicts, and some of the sentences were
harsh. In 1989, Melanie Green, a drug-addicted pregnant woman from Rockford,
Illinois, was charged with manslaughter and delivery of a controlled substance
to a minor as a result of her newborn daughter's death from drug-related com-
plications two days after her birth. Many indignant observers believed she
should have received treatment, not imprisonment. Her case gained nationwide
attention, and angry critics pointed to her as an indication that the War on Drugs
was punishing ordinary people and failing to interfere with high-level drug lords
and powerful cartels.

To make matters worse, American foreign policy in the 1980s often proved
to be contradictory and sometimes compromised the success of the War on Drugs.
President Reagan's efforts to topple Nicaragua's Sandinista government and buttress autocratic regimes in El Salvador, Guatemala, and Honduras occasionally
resulted in Washington forming alliances with known drug sellers. The Pana-
manian strongman Manuel Noriega, for example, remained on good terms
with the CIA throughout much of the 1980s, and high-level U.S. officials in
Washington often looked the other way when he worked closely with the thriving drug trade. In Nicaragua, the Contras formed ties to Noriega and the leaders

of Colombia's Medellin Cartel, and some Contras were actively involved in an extensive drug-trading network that extended into America's inner cities. At the time, the Senate Foreign Relations Narcotics Subcommittee issued a report that found that "individuals who provided support for the contras were involved in drug trafficking, the supply network of the Contras was used by drug trafficking organizations, and elements of the Contras themselves knowingly received financial and material assistance from drug traffickers. In each case, one or another agency of the U.S. government had information regarding the involvement either while it was occurring, or immediately thereafter" (Johnson 1991, 268).

Was the War on Drugs a success story, a dismal failure, or something in between? In this case, a verdict is difficult to reach. One set of statistics often contradicts another, and the numbers were frequently manipulated by critics and apologists alike to support their arguments. A safe answer is that the War on Drugs—like the War on Poverty in the 1960s and the War on Terror after September 11, 2001—did not completely purge the ills it sought to address; in some parts of the country, it had no tangible effects or, worse, actually exacerbated the problem. The nationwide campaign did, however, raise awareness about drug-related issues and undoubtedly deterred untold numbers of people from casually sampling different types of illegal substances. The War on Drugs also resulted in thousands of people joining the nation's prison population, including many African Americans, Latinos, and poor people. And, alas, some of the new inmates undoubtedly would have benefited more from humane rehabilitation than grim incarceration.

LEGACIES OF VIETNAM

When the last helicopter lifted off the rooftop of the U.S. Embassy in Saigon at the end of April 1975, America's longest war came to an end. But an even longer conflict—the struggle over how to remember the Vietnam War—would soon begin. For much of the rest of the 1970s, there was little debate about Vietnam, as the devastating events in Indochina were still too fresh and raw in the nation's collective memory. Few people wanted to discuss it, and even fewer sought to make sense of it. Most Americans regarded the Vietnam War as a dark blemish that they would just as soon forget, and they were prepared to move on with their lives. Indeed, part of Ronald Reagan's appeal to ordinary Americans in 1980 was that he promised renewal and regeneration for the traumatized nation. Yet the ghosts of Vietnam could not be so easily exorcised. The passage of time gradually enabled people to look back and reflect. Early Vietnam War films, such as Michael Cimino's 1978 epic *The Deer Hunter* and Francis Ford Coppola's surreal 1979 *Apocalypse Now*, left indelible impressions on the minds of moviegoers in the United States. Moreover, pioneering histories of the war like George Herring's *America's Longest War* and Stanley Karnow's *Vietnam: A History,* appeared in bookstores in the early 1980s. In 1983, the Public Broadcasting System aired a nine-part documentary on the Vietnam War based on Karnow's book, and the series gave public television ratings a much-needed boost. Gradually, poets, politicians, veterans, artists, filmmakers, writers, and ordinary people began to weigh in and offer their thoughts and reflections on the Vietnam War. The war, however, remained contested terrain, just as it did when it was going on, and no clear consensus about its meaning ever emerged.

The themes explored in this segment include:

- The Vietnam Veterans Memorial ("the Wall")
- Vietnam veterans in the 1980s
- Oliver Stone, Vietnam, and popular culture

The Vietnam Veterans Memorial

During the 1980s, an estimated 15,000 people per day visited the Vietnam Veterans Memorial, a long, black granite wall bearing the names of almost 58,000 men and women who died in the Vietnam War. (Later, as more deaths were verified from the Vietnam War or as direct results from the war, more names have been added to the wall, bringing the number to over 58,000.) Located on the National Mall in Washington, D.C., the memorial—also known simply as "the Wall"—was dedicated on the cold and rainy day of November 12, 1982.

The memorial was an overdue tribute to the nation's Vietnam veterans, and with stark simplicity, it conveyed the price that America paid for the war in human lives. Over 150,000 people attended either the dedication or one of the many ceremonies leading up to it, according to the National Park Police in Washington, D.C. Countless Vietnam veterans trekked to the nation's capital from as far away as Alaska and Hawaii to witness the dedication. Some veterans wore green fatigues and dog tags while others navigated through the Mall in wheelchairs. Many visitors were visibly shaken as they made "rubbings" of names or ran their fingers over the engraved letters, and some openly broke down and wept.

The memorial was designed by Maya Linn, a 21-year-old senior at Yale majoring in architecture who submitted her entry to a national contest along with 1,400 others. When the design was revealed to the public, it triggered a small but vocal barrage of criticism. It was described as "Orwellian glop" by *National Review* magazine, "a tribute to Jane Fonda," by author Tom Wolfe and activist Phyllis Schlafly, "something for New York intellectuals" by Texas billionaire H. Ross Perot, and "a black gash of shame" by Vietnam veteran Tom Carhart (Louis Menand, "The Reluctant Memorialist: Maya Lin tried to put the business

Visitors at the Vietnam Veterans Memorial on the day before its official dedication, November 12, 1982. Located in Washington, D.C., and today the capital's most visited monument, the Vietnam Memorial is inscribed with the names of the more than 58,000 American men and women killed or missing in the Vietnam War. (U.S. Department of Defense)

of monuments behind her. Then came September 11th," *New Yorker,* July 8, 2002, 55). But most visitors to the Wall were overwhelmed by the emotional intensity and the heartbreaking pathos of the memorial. Indeed, Vietnam veteran John Ketwig's recollection of leaving the dedication ceremonies was indicative of how most people responded to the Wall. "Behind us, there were no proud sabers or dancing horses. There was only a black wall with 57,939 terrible reminders of the American blood shed in The Nam. Every morning, members of Congress would see it, feel it. It stood out, black and somber, and it couldn't be ignored. I was fine" (Ketwig 2002, 367).

What made the Vietnam Veterans Memorial particularly unique were the many "offerings" that visitors left on the ground near the names of the dead. "From the first day," wrote scholar Kristin Ann Hass, "the [National Park Service] volunteers were faced with a growing collection of photographs, medals, letters, clothing, and teddy bears. They anticipated that people would take rubbings of names important to them. They did not expect people to leave things" (Hass

1998, 21). The "offerings" were regularly collected, catalogued, boxed, and stored for posterity in a warehouse belonging to the National Parks Service. Often, Parks Service officials will allow selected items to be displayed at museums.

The Wall also inspired numerous imitators. In 1984, veterans created a so-called Moving Wall, a half-size replica of the memorial that was transported to cities and towns across the country so Americans could share the experience of viewing and touching the names of the dead. Smaller variations of the Wall featuring the names of local soldiers killed in the war were dedicated in Mobile, Alabama; Long Beach, California; Pensacola, Florida; Springfield, Illinois; Billings, Montana; and Cody, Wyoming.

In the years that followed, other types of Vietnam memorials and monuments were created across the country. Heated debates over whether Maya Lin's design was sufficiently patriotic prompted the National Parks Service to commission the so-called Three Servicemen Statue, which is located near the Wall in Washington, D.C. Created by sculptor Frederick Hart and unveiled on November 11, 1984, the bronze statue features three soldiers, each about 7 feet tall, standing side by side and gazing ahead, with one carrying a machine gun on his shoulder.

Elsewhere, almost every major city and many smaller towns across America featured Vietnam memorials of some sort. Omaha led the way with the dedication of its Vietnam memorial in 1976, which was nestled inside of the city's serene Memorial Park. In 1985, New Yorkers held a ticker-tape parade for 25,000 Vietnam veterans to mark the dedication of a new Vietnam War monument between South Street and Water Street in lower Manhattan. The memorial, funded by Donald Trump, was a 16-foot high glass wall that contained original letters written by or to New Yorkers who served in the Vietnam War. In Salt Lake City, Utahns dedicated a Vietnam memorial in October 1989. Historian Allan Kent Powell describes it: "Located on the west side of the State Capitol Grounds, the memorial includes an eight-foot-high statue of a soldier returning from battle with his buddy's rifle, flanked by a curved, gray granite wall with polished black granite panels on which are inscribed the names of the 388 men and one woman who died or were listed as missing in action in Vietnam between August 13, 1963 and April 4, 1975" (http://historytogo.utah.gov, March 14, 2006).

On November 11, 1993, the Vietnam Women's Memorial Project sponsored a ceremony in Washington, D.C., to dedicate a bronze statue of three nurses helping a wounded soldier in Vietnam to honor the 11,500 women who served in the war. The statue, designed by Santa Fe sculptor Glenna Goodacre, was made possible by donations raised by groups and individuals from all parts of the country. Male Vietnam veterans proved to be especially generous contributors. Statues, sculptures featuring war artifacts, paintings of battle scenes, walls bearing the names of the dead—these were but a few of the ways ordinary people have sought to remember and connect with America's longest war in the 1980s.

Vietnam Veterans in the 1980s

Vietnam veterans faced a host of formidable challenges at the beginning of the decade. It was not until the late 1970s and early 1980s that the Veterans Administration in Washington, D.C., launched extensive counseling and rehabilitation programs to meet the needs of the men who served in Vietnam (programs for women who served as nurses in Vietnam were still unheard of). In addition to an appalling lack of services, veterans also had negative stereotypes with which to contend. The myth of the "psychotic Vietnam vet" perpetuated by films such as Martin Scorsese's gritty 1976 film *Taxi Driver* and many other movies and television shows, as well as in media portrayals of homeless and mentally ill vets, created a largely negative image of Vietnam veterans. The stereotypical Hollywood "vet" of the late 1970s and early 1980s was volatile, unhinged, and easily susceptible to violent, mind-altering flashbacks. The image was, to some extent, at least partly anchored in reality, even though it was grossly distorted and overblown. While most Vietnam veterans successfully readjusted to life back in the United States, hundreds of thousands of veterans suffered from severe Post-Traumatic Stress Disorder (PTSD). A delayed reaction to the experience of combat in Vietnam, the symptoms of PTSD included recurring nightmares, sleep disruption, depression, anxiety, suicidal feelings, sudden bursts of rage, and intense feelings of loneliness. Veterans groups in the 1980s estimated that more than 500,000 Vietnam veterans suffered from PTSD (Kim Heron, "The Long Road Back," *New York Times Magazine,* March 6, 1988, 33).

For those who served in Vietnam, the agony of war was still fresh in their minds in the early 1980s. It is important to remember that at the beginning of the decade, the average Vietnam veteran was only in his early 30s and was often trying to move on with his life. As Michael Cohen, a Vietnam veteran and psychologist in San Francisco, observed, "The war really tore this country apart. I don't think people can step back and look at it objectively. . . . Many of the issues surrounding the war are unresolved for Vietnam veterans and those who opposed it" (Michael Oricchio, "Is

A disabled veteran in a wheelchair participates in the dedication day parade for the Vietnam Veterans Memorial on November 13, 1982. (U.S. Department of Defense)

Vietnam War a Laughing Matter?" *St. Louis Post-Dispatch,* January 31, 1988, 7C). Many veterans "dropped out" of American society, distancing themselves from a world they believed had rejected and shunned them.

In the 1980s, a community of 60 or so veterans built a village of shacks in the dense woods near Pompano Beach, Florida, which they called "the Jungle." The residents of "the Jungle" shared food and marijuana, built homes out of plywood, collected battered old furniture from nearby dumps, and created a "Honeymoon Suite" for men to entertain female visitors.

For other alienated veterans, a less extreme option than dropping out was to take advantage of the many so-called vet centers that opened their doors in the 1980s throughout the United States. By 1988, more than 200 vet centers existed nationwide, the result of legislation passed by Congress in 1979. The vet centers typically offered outreach programs, counseling, legal advice, community gatherings such as picnics, and—most important—a place to get together with other veterans from the community. In Baltimore, Maryland, the Patapsco Avenue Vet Center provided marriage counseling for veterans and their spouses. The Los Angeles vet center conducted weekly rap sessions in which groups of men pulled their chairs up into a large circle and discussed their past and present experiences. In Little Rock, Arkansas, the Vet Center created programs to assist the thousand or so homeless Vietnam veterans in the city. "We see perhaps fifty homeless veterans a month at our hospital," remarked a social worker at Little Rock's VA hospital (Jerry Dean, "VA hospital seeking to help homeless veterans —Pilot program affects 26 states," *Arkansas Democrat-Gazette,* April 27, 1987).

Of course, not all Vietnam veterans suffered equally after returning home. Most of the veterans who served in the massive rear echelon during the war and who saw little or no fighting obviously did not face the same debilitating problems of PTSD as combat vets. Moreover, many high-profile Vietnam veterans experienced great success in post-1975 America. Some veterans entered the world of politics and saw their careers take off in the 1980s, including senators John Kerry of Massachusetts, John McCain of Arizona, Bob Kerrey of Nebraska, and Al Gore of Tennessee. Others found lucrative jobs in the private sector or discovered a niche in academe or law.

But even the more financially successful Vietnam veterans still faced problems rooted in their service overseas, particularly if they experienced combat. Worsening matters still, many Vietnam veterans refused to seek help for the psychological problems during the 1980s. In 1986, Albert Singerman of Vietnam Veterans of America observed, "Of the 15 percent to 20 percent [of Vietnam veterans] who have readjustment problems, the vast majority are combat vets who for the most part can't be persuaded to seek treatment. Even veterans who are financially successful and appear well adjusted often need some type of counseling, but will not seek it because they won't openly identify themselves as Vietnam vets" (Albert B. Singerman, "Yes, It Is Worse for Vietnam Combat Vets" (letter to the editor), *New York Times,* March 25, 1986, 30). It was estimated that of the 43,000 Vietnam veterans living in New Hampshire in the late 1980s, only about 10 percent sought help at the state's Vet Center located in Manchester. "Many of them wouldn't go to established veterans' programs because they felt some of those people didn't understand. It was a different kind of war and if you feel nobody understands, maybe you don't want to talk to them," said a therapist at the center (Shawne K. Wickham, "Outreach Center Helps Viet Vets," *Union Leader* [Manchester, N.H.], October 30, 1989, 5).

Countless veterans were eager to put the war behind them in the 1980s. But, unlike earlier wars in American history, there were also many veterans who pushed for a national dialogue about the war and its varied meanings. This increased openness led to a flowering of cultural expression among Vietnam veterans. A vocal and active segment of Vietnam veterans began writing memoirs, novels, and poetry; speaking at high schools and allowing historians to interview them; making movies; creating art; and using a variety of other means to bring their memories of the conflict to the fore. Authors such as Larry Heinemann and Tim O'Brien; memoirists Ron Kovic, John Ketwig, and Philip Caputo; poets W. D. Ehrhart, Bruce Weigl, John Balaban, and David Connolly; and filmmaker Oliver Stone were among the key contributors to the new Vietnam veterans' renaissance. In 1981, a group of veterans and volunteers in Chicago opened the National Vietnam Veterans Art Museum, which eventually found a home on Indiana Avenue in the city's South Loop. Soon, the museum would boast an impressive collection of 1,500 works of art, including paintings, sculptures, photographs, poetry, and music. Like the rest of the nation, Vietnam veterans tended to be deeply divided in their views about the Vietnam War and its legacies. The more artistic veterans—the poets, novelists, and filmmakers—tended to be on the left politically. Their words served as scathing critiques of the war, and they often presented their experiences as cautionary tales to challenge the arguments of the war's apologists. The key figures of the Vietnam veterans' renaissance saw no reason to celebrate the war. Instead, they condemned it as misguided at best, wantonly destructive and brutal at worst.

By contrast, a community of right-wing veterans and their supporters attempted to rehabilitate the war in the 1980s. They agreed with Ronald Reagan that the Vietnam War was fundamentally a "noble cause" but that it was lost by cautious politicians in Washington, D.C., who forced soldiers to fight without sufficient support. A small yet vocal group of these fiercely anticommunist veterans believed that the Vietnamese were still imprisoning untold numbers of American prisoners of war in squalid camps. They created the POW/MIA (prisoner of war/missing in action) lobby to campaign to free POWs they believed were still being held captive all these years later in Vietnam. Even though the POW/MIA advocates were few in number, their cultural influence was enormous. A spate of popular movies in the 1980s, including *Uncommon Valor* with Gene Hackman, *Rambo: First Blood Part II*, with Sylvester Stallone, and the *Missing in Action* films, which featured Chuck Norris as the hard-nosed Col.

James Braddock, all featured Vietnam veterans returning to Southeast Asia to rescue American POWs from their sinister Vietnamese captors. Meanwhile, the familiar black-and-white POW/MIA logo, featuring the white silhouette of a prisoner of a war, became ubiquitous at this time.

POW/MIA lobbying groups were very active and frequently held press conferences to reveal new evidence verifying that prisoners of war were being held in Vietnam. The "proof" was often sketchy, and some critics of the POW/MIA advocates accused them of exploiting the anguish of families of men who were still listed as "missing in action." The POW/MIA supporters thought they scored a major coup in July 1990 when they revealed a haunting, grainy, black-and-white photograph purported to be of three American servicemen—Col. John L. Robertson, Lt. Larry Stevens, and Maj. Albro Lundy—all believed to be alive in Vietnamese POW camps. The image proved to be an elaborate hoax. In 1992, Defense Department officials revealed that the photograph, along with six others, was created by a network of Cambodian entrepreneurs who saw an opportunity to cash in on the POW/MIA craze. The photograph of the three veterans, it turned out, was taken directly from an old Soviet magazine and slightly altered. In the mid-1990s, when the U.S. and Vietnamese governments normalized relations, official American fact-finding delegations issued statements refuting the myth that POWs were still being held in Vietnam. For the most part, the POW/MIA myth faded, although the coming of the Internet in the late 1990s offered a new bully pulpit to its dwindling number of defenders.

In the 1980s, a consensus about the nature and legacies of the Vietnam War remained elusive. But the most important achievement of the outspoken Vietnam veterans in the 1980s—whether they were on the right, center, or left side of the political spectrum—was their willingness to discuss the varied meanings of the war, which emboldened people from all walks of life to learn more about the conflict and add their voices to the nationwide dialogue. For years after the Vietnam War ended, much of the public sought to ignore it and its lessons, yet the 1980s represented a time when the contested legacies of the war became fair game for robust inquiry, discussion, and debate.

Oliver Stone, Vietnam, and Popular Culture

In the 1980s, a variety of different types of artistic expression about America's longest war assumed a central place in the nation's popular culture. It took time for authors, filmmakers, poets, and artists to formulate art and narratives that helped ordinary American people understand the complex experience of the Vietnam War.

The earliest films about the war, *Coming Home, The Deer Hunter,* and *Apocalypse Now,* appeared in theaters in the late 1970s, and helped pave the way for later films. For several years in the early 1980s, there was a lull in high-quality, dramatic films about the Vietnam War. Instead, Hollywood generated a rash of films about American rescue teams returning to Vietnam to free prisoners of war who were still being held in the battered and war-torn nation. Films such as *Uncommon Valor* (1983), *Missing in Action* (1984), and *Rambo: First Blood Part II* (1985) presented the war as revisionist fantasy, with the United States successfully accomplishing its decidedly more limited goals in Vietnam.

Eventually, Oliver Stone would emerge as one of Hollywood's most successful and controversial film directors, ultimately winning several Academy Awards and stirring debate across the country. But in the mid-1980s, he was still relatively unknown. He was born in New York City in 1946, grew up in a comfortable middle-class home, served in the Army in Vietnam, and went to film school at New York University. An intensely creative man who could often be prone toward excesses in both his artistic and personal life, Stone wandered the world of cinema for several years in the 1970s as an aspiring screenwriter. His main ambition was to direct, and at any given time, he had several projects that he envisioned turning into films. But he was also radical politically and very iconoclastic—not necessarily a recipe for success in cautious Hollywood. He worked for several years on low-budget, independent projects, but his first big break in Hollywood was as the screenwriter for the 1978 Alan Parker film *Midnight Express,* a controversial movie about an American accused of drug smuggling and locked inside of a nightmarish Turkish prison. Even though Stone did not direct *Midnight Express,* his polemic style was evident throughout the film. The same was true of Brian De Palma's *Scarface* (1983), a remake of Howard Hawks' 1932 classic film of the same title. The film had all of Stone's touches: the excesses in behavior and language, the elements of the cautionary tale, and edgy characters with a dark side whose ambitions prove to be their undoing.

Stone's directorial debut was *Salvador* (1986), a gritty and extremely low budget film about events in war-torn El Salvador in the late 1970s and early 1980s. The film, based on the experiences of journalist Richard Boyle and his ordeals reporting events in the Central American nation, was almost not made because no major Hollywood studio dared to finance it. *Salvador* was a damning indictment of U.S. policy in El Salvador, and the final product was, like most of Stone's other films, an uncompromising film that was bold yet lacked subtlety.

His second directorial effort, about his personal experiences in Vietnam, was also almost not made. Stone wrote the original script for the film in 1976, working long, 12-hour days for more than a month until his screenplay was completed. Once again, Stone could not find a major Hollywood studio to back the film, so he accepted $6 million from the British company Hemdale and $2 million from Orion in the United States. With a small film crew and a cast of mostly unknown actors (the most famous was Tom Berenger, who starred in the 1983 hit *The Big Chill*), Stone traveled to the Philippines to shoot the movie, which doubled as the jungles of Vietnam. The film, *Platoon,* depicted a young GI named Chris Taylor who was torn between two father-like sergeants: the compassionate yet battle-weary Elias and the patriotic but savage Barnes. Chris finds himself thrust into a nightmarish world of relentless jungle combat, where he is forced to choose which of the two men he will emulate. *Platoon* was released in 1986 to widespread critical acclaim. Vietnam veterans across the country celebrated it as an authentic masterpiece, and film reviewers gushed over it for the most part. Made for less than $10 million, *Platoon* took in more than $136 million at U.S. box offices and millions more around the world. Stone received a Best Director award from the Director's Guild of America, and *Platoon* was nominated for eight Academy Awards. It ultimately netted four Oscars, including the coveted Best Picture award of 1986. And it helped usher in a long-overdue nationwide dialogue about the varied meanings of the Vietnam War.

After *Platoon,* Stone no longer had to struggle so vigorously to secure funding for his movies. Major studios now readily financed his films, and the Vietnam War became a central theme in many of his motion pictures. In fact, after *Platoon,* Stone indicated in interviews that he planned to direct a trilogy of Vietnam War films. The second, *Born on the Fourth of July* (1989), was based on the real-life experiences of Ron Kovic, a paraplegic Vietnam veteran who became an antiwar activist. The third was *Heaven and Earth* (1993), the true story of Le Ly Hayslip, a young Vietnamese woman who joined the Viet Cong guerrillas during the war but eventually married an American serviceman and settled in the United States. In addition, Stone made several other films in which the Vietnam War era served as a backdrop or war-related themes were central, including *The Doors* (1991), *JFK* (1991), and *Nixon* (1995).

For the remainder of his career, Stone fearlessly tackled controversial topics and made films that were consistently jarring and intense. *Wall Street* (1987), like *Scarface,* was a rise-and-fall cautionary tale about a young stockbroker who falls under the spell of a charismatic corporate raider; *Natural Born Killers* (1994) focused on the sensationalism of violence in the media; *Commandante* (2003) and *Looking for Fidel* (2004) celebrated the accomplishments of the Cuban revolution; and *World Trade Center* (2006) was one of the first major Hollywood films made about the September 11, 2001, terrorist attacks. But it was Stone's *Platoon* that finally offered the American public a realistic portrayal of the Vietnam War from the perspective of ordinary GIs in the war. After *Platoon,* the Vietnam War no longer seemed like a taboo or inscrutable subject in the minds of millions of Americans.

BIOGRAPHIES

Elvia Alvarado, 1940–

Honduran Human Rights Activist

Elvia Alvarado worked tirelessly through the 1980s for an end to repression in her native land and to change the Reagan administration's Central America policies.

She grew up in the impoverished village of Lejamani, one of seven children in a poor peasant family. Her father worked for a large landowner in the area while her mother raised the children and sold various farm goods grown on the Alvarado's patch of land to support the family. Like so many women in impoverished rural Honduras, Elvia Alvarado got pregnant early, at age 15, and eventually raised her six children almost single-handedly.

Alvarado's first taste of activism came in the mid-1970s, when she joined a Catholic organization of mothers seeking to improve the nutrition of children in local villages. This proved to be Alvarado's introduction to organizing on behalf of human rights, and in the 1980s she would emerge as one of the most vocal and visible critics of government repression in Honduras. She campaigned

Honduran civil rights activist Elvia Alvarado. (Courtesy Speakoutnow.org)

for agrarian reform, women's rights, and democratic reforms, and against domestic abuse. Predictably, Alvarado repeatedly put her life at risk by struggling to make Honduras a more open society, and she became an outspoken critic of American foreign policy. She ended up spending long periods in Honduran jails, and she was tortured repeatedly.

In 1986, she told her story in a memoir titled *Don't Be Afraid, Gringo,* with the help of author and activist Medea Benjamin. She went on a speaking tour of the United States in 1990, which she used to draw attention to human rights abuses in Honduras. In 1998, she threw herself into around-the-clock fundraising after Honduras was hit by a devastating hurricane. She was also the subject of an award-winning 1998 PBS documentary titled *Elvia: The Fight for Land and Liberty.* She lives in Honduras.

Maude DeVictor, 1940–

African American Counselor at the Veterans Administration's (VA) Chicago Regional Office

Maude DeVictor, an African American counselor at the Veterans Administration's (VA) Chicago Regional Office, was instrumental in drawing national attention to the devastating effects of Agent Orange, a chemical used extensively during the

Vietnam War. From 1962 to 1971, the U.S. government sprayed around 19 million gallons of the herbicide over Vietnam in an effort to destroy the foliage used by the communists as protective cover. The chemical contained an impurity called dioxin, and Vietnamese and Americans who were exposed to it during the war experienced various illnesses, including higher than usual rates of leukemia, respiratory cancers, and other diseases, and their offspring were often born with severe birth defects.

In 1977, DeVictor, a hardworking VA counselor and single mother, filed a claim on behalf of a Vietnam veteran who had terminal cancer, insisting that his illness was due to exposure to Agent Orange. Years earlier, DeVictor had been a nurse in the United States Navy, and she had reason to believe that she and other Navy nurses had been exposed to potentially dangerous levels of radiation on the job. By the early 1980s, DeVictor had become an advocate for other Vietnam veterans suffering from the ongoing effects of Agent Orange. Thanks to her efforts, other veterans stepped forward claiming they had been exposed to Agent Orange during the Vietnam War. By the early 1980s, a class-action lawsuit filed by a group of Agent Orange victims led to an out-of-court settlement in 1984 of $180 million for the veterans.

Due to a long and bureaucratic appeals process, Vietnam veterans exposed to Agent Orange ultimately did not receive the compensation they originally sought. Moreover, DeVictor faced a number of challenges within the VA. Because she dedicated countless hours to researching the effects of Agent Orange on Vietnamese and Americans who had been exposed to it during the war, VA officials began exerting intense pressure on her to either quit her job as a counselor or else abandon her Agent Orange activism. Ultimately, DeVictor refused to abandon her work, and she soon became the subject of widespread media attention. In 1978, a local CBS affiliate in Chicago aired a documentary about the use of Agent Orange in Vietnam, which profiled DeVictor's activist struggles. The 1986 made-for-TV movie *Unnatural Causes* starred actress Alfre Woodard as DeVictor and depicted the counselor's efforts to aid a decorated Vietnam veteran who had been exposed to Agent Orange and was struggling for compensation.

Throughout the 1980s, DeVictor remained an ardent champion of government compensation for veterans plagued by Agent Orange–related illnesses, even though her struggle was constantly an uphill one. She watched helplessly as numerous veterans who were friends died of Agent Orange–induced diseases. She earned only a modest salary in the 1980s, which proved a challenge for her as a single mother. And, much to her frustration, most of the lawsuits she helped initiate that demanded compensation for Agent Orange victims were unsuccessful. Despite these discouraging setbacks, DeVictor remained committed to her cause. Thanks to her efforts, greater numbers of Americans became aware of the devastating effects of Agent Orange and the lengths the federal government was willing to go to in order to destroy its enemies in wartime and shun its ethical responsibilities to its veterans in times of peace. Long after the

1980s, a series of Agent Orange lawsuits continued to move slowly through the nation's legal system.

James Gordon "Bo" Gritz, 1939–

Flamboyant Speaker, Radio Host, Author, Vietnam Veteran, and Soldier of Fortune

Bo Gritz gained a following in the 1980s for his militant anticommunism and conspiratorial distrust of the federal government. During the 1980s, rumors circulated that Gritz was the inspiration for Sylvester Stallone's legendary cinematic character Rambo. Born in Enid, Oklahoma, and a graduate of the University of Nebraska, Gritz was a highly decorated member of the U.S. Army's elite Green Berets during the Vietnam War. He gained nationwide fame during the early 1980s when he led an unsuccessful mission into Southeast Asia to rescue American POWs that he believed were still being held in Vietnam. Upon returning home, Gritz emerged as a symbol of the flourishing POW-MIA movement, and his efforts to lobby the government to take a more aggressive role in finding POWs and MIAs received a great deal of media attention.

Gritz could be counted on to speak his mind and make colorful quotes, yet his anticommunism, anti-Semitism, and identification with white supremacist movements made many traditional conservatives uneasy. Gritz was also a master of self-promotion, and his articles promoting soldier of fortune activities and mercenary lifestyles appeared in marginal, right-wing publications across the country. A syndicated radio show merely buttressed his fame.

The end of the Cold War in the early 1990s took the wind out of the sails of Gritz's anticommunism, as it did for an entire generation of Cold Warriors in the United States. Accordingly, Gritz focused more on his antigovernment conspiracy theories, insisting during the Gulf War (1990–1991) that the Bush administration was aggressively seeking to establish a "New World Order" headed by the United States. The end of the Cold War did not derail Gritz's career. Even though anticommunism and the POW-MIA movement fell by the wayside, Gritz continued to focus on survivalist movements, third-party presidential campaigns, and the radio airwaves to get his message across. Even into the new millennium, he continues to have a following of antigovernment populists and extremists across the country.

Robert O. "Bobby" Muller, 1946–

Paraplegic Ex-Marine

Bobby Muller, a paraplegic ex-Marine whose spinal cord was severed by a bullet in Vietnam in 1969, became the foremost spokesman for the rights of Vietnam veterans across America in the 1980s. Muller grew up in a working-class neighborhood of Long Island; in the 1960s, the intensely patriotic young man enlisted in the Marines. Before shipping off to Vietnam in 1968, he finished his bachelor's degree in business administration at Hofstra University in Hempstead, Long Island.

In South Vietnam, Muller served as combat lieutenant in charge of an infantry platoon. The wound that turned him into a paraplegic also prompted young Muller to engage in soul searching, and after he returned to the United States, he became an ardent peace activist. He joined Vietnam Veterans Against the War, spoke at antiwar demonstrations, and allowed filmmaker Peter Davis to interview him for the Academy Award–winning 1974 documentary *Hearts and Minds*. He founded Vietnam Veterans of America (VVA) in 1980. VVA is an advocacy group that lobbied for increased federal funding to programs for Vietnam veterans, such as drug abuse counseling, psychiatric care, and other benefits. In 1981, Muller was one of the first Vietnam veterans to journey back to Vietnam, where he laid a wreath of reconciliation at the tomb of Ho Chi Minh. This caused an enormous backlash in the Vietnam veteran community back home. Thousands of veterans reviled Muller for his actions, and rightwing groups vilified him as a traitor. But by the end of the 1980s, a growing number of Vietnam veterans followed Muller's lead and returned to Vietnam in an effort to heal and come to terms with their past. Muller remained a determined critic of U.S. intervention in Central America and continued to speak out on issues of militarism and peace. After the 1980s, he spent years crusading for a ban on landmines. His group—the Vietnam Veterans of America Foundation (VVAF)—was part of the International Campaign to Ban Landmines, which received the Nobel Peace Prize in 1997. Muller continues to speak across America and around the world in support of peace and global reconciliation.

Daniel Ortega Saavedra 1945–

Sandinista Leader

Daniel Ortega Saavedra, a leader in Nicaragua's Sandinista revolutionary movement, was born in La Libertad to parents who strongly opposed the dictatorship of Anastasio Somoza. In his youth, Ortega's two heroes were Jesus Christ and Nicaraguan patriot and independence leader Augusto Sandino (1895–1934). He was educated at the University of Central America in Managua. While still a teenager in the early 1960s, Ortega joined the Sandinista National Liberation Front (FSLN), proved himself to be a capable guerrilla fighter, and eventually rose to a position of leadership in the organization. By the mid-1970s, Ortega was widely respected for his insights, diplomatic skills, and moderate leadership.

The 1979 revolution elevated Ortega to a key figure within the Junta for National Reconstruction. He and other Sandinista leaders governed Nicaragua during a very troubling time in the nation's history. By 1982, the U.S.-backed Contra war began taking a toll on the country, as bombings, random killings, and other acts of Contra terrorism became routine. Eventually, the CIA mined Nicaragua's harbors, and despite a congressional ban on aid to the Contras, the anti-Sandinista guerrillas continued to receive U.S. aid surreptitiously. The Sandinistas responded to the bloodshed by tightening restrictions and curbing certain freedoms, including imposing bans on criticisms of the government in the press.

Ortega was elected president in the 1984 elections, which many impartial observers from other countries found to be fair. He remained a firm social democrat committed to increasing literacy rates and bringing health care to the poor. In the 1990 Nicaraguan elections, Ortega was defeated by his longtime political foe, Violeta Chamorro. He withdrew from politics for a time, returning in 1996 and again in 2001 to run for office as leader of the Sandinistas. In both elections, the Sandinistas lost, but they remained a powerful force in Nicaraguan politics. In 1998, Ortega's stepdaughter accused him of sexually abusing her, which left many observers doubting his political future. Nevertheless, he refused to leave politics, and his stepdaughter's potentially damaging allegations failed to discredit him. In 2006, Ortega was once again elected president of Nicaragua.

Samantha Smith, 1972–1985

A Fifth-Grade Student Living in Manchester, Maine

In 1982, as the United States reached the depths of the Cold War, 10-year-old Samantha Smith, a fifth-grade student living in Manchester, Maine, became concerned about the escalating arms race and decided to act. In November, the precocious Smith wrote a brief letter to Soviet Communist Party General Secretary Yuri Andropov asking him whether he intended to go to war. She suggested that if he had no intention of going to war, he should work for peace instead. Months later, in April 1983, she received a warm letter from Andropov claiming that Soviet leaders were working toward peace and Russia would never be the first country to use nuclear weapons in a global conflict. The exchange of letters turned the public spotlight on Smith, and she became a youthful symbol of deepening antinuclear sentiments in the United States. She journeyed with her family to the Soviet Union in July 1983 at Andropov's request, and upon her return home, she appeared as a guest on numerous talk shows and television programs, including *Nightline* and *The Tonight Show.*

She hosted a political program for kids on the Disney Channel, and ABC created a television show for her called *Lime Street,* co-starring Robert Wagner and Lew Ayres. On August 25, 1985, Smith and her father were killed when the airplane they were on missed the runway at an airport in Maine and crashed in a nearby field. She was only 13 years old. The nation mourned her loss, and the Soviets issued a stamp commemorating her. There were numerous tributes to Smith, both in the United States and around the world. As an emissary of peace, her legacy has outlasted her short life.

REFERENCES AND FURTHER READINGS

Alvarado, Elvia, and Media Benjamin. 1989. *Don't Be Afraid, Gringo: A Honduran Woman Speaks from The Heart: The Story of Elvia Alvarado.* New York: Harper Perennial.

Anderson, Thomas P. 1971. *Matanza: El Salvador's Communist Revolt of 1932.* Lincoln: University of Nebraska Press.

Baum, Dan. 1996. *Smoke and Mirrors: the War on Drugs and the Politics of Failure.* Boston: Little, Brown.

Beattie, Keith. 1998. *The Scar that Binds: American Culture and the Vietnam War.* New York: New York University Press.

Bonner, Raymond. 1984. *Weakness and Deceit: U.S. Policy and El Salvador.* New York: Times Books.

Borge, Tomás. 1982. *The Sandinistas Speak: Speeches and Writings of Nicaragua's Leaders.* New York: Pathfinder.

Brody, Reed. 1985. *Contra Terror in Nicaragua. Report of a Fact-finding Mission: September 1984–January 1985.* Boston: South End Press.

Burkett, B. G., and Glenna Whitley. 1998. *Stolen Valor: How the Vietnam Generation Was Robbed of its Heroes and its History.* Dallas: Verity Press.

Danner, Mark. 1994. *The Massacre at El Mozote.* New York: Vintage.

Dickey, Christopher. 1987. *With the Contras: A Reporter in the Wilds of Nicaragua.* New York: Simon & Schuster.

Hall, Mitchell K. 2005. *Crossroads: American Popular Culture and the Vietnam Generation.* Lanham, Md.: Rowman & Littlefield.

Hass, Kristin Ann. 1998. *Carried to the Wall: American Memory and the Vietnam Veterans Memorial.* Berkeley: University of California Press.

Hershberger, Mary. 2005. *Jane Fonda's War: A Political Biography of an Antiwar Icon.* New York: New Press.

Hunt, Andrew E. 1999. *The Turning: A History of Vietnam Veterans Against the War.* New York: New York University Press.

Isaacs, Arnold R. 1997. *Vietnam Shadows: The War, Its Ghosts, and Its Legacy.* Baltimore: Johns Hopkins University Press.

Johnson, Haynes. 1991. *Sleepwalking Through History: America in the Reagan Years*. New York: W. W. Norton & Company.

Kagan, Robert. 1996. *A Twilight Struggle: American Power and Nicaragua, 1977–1990*. New York: Free Press.

Ketwig, John. 2002. *And a Hard Rain Fell: A GI's True Story of the War in Vietnam*. Reprint, Naperville, Ill.: Sourcebooks.

Lembcke, Jerry. 1998. *The Spitting Image: Myth, Memory, and the Legacy of Vietnam*. New York: New York University Press.

MacPherson, Myra. 1984. *Long Time Passing: Vietnam and the Haunted Generation*. New York: Doubleday.

Marez, Curtis. 2004. *Drug Wars: The Political Economy of Narcotics*. Minneapolis: University of Minnesota Press.

McCoy, Alfred W. 2003. *The Politics of Heroin: CIA Complicity in the Global Drug Trade*. Chicago: Lawrence Hill Books.

McMahon, Robert J. 2002. "Contested Memory: The Vietnam War and American Society, 1975–2001." *Diplomatic History,* 26 (2): 159–184.

Nicosia, Gerald. 2001. *Home to War: A History of the Vietnam Veterans' Movement*. New York: Crown.

Paige, Jeffrey M. 1998. *Coffee and Power: Revolution and the Rise of Democracy in Central America*. Cambridge: Harvard University Press.

Prevost, Gary. 1999. *The Undermining of the Sandinista Revolution*. New York: Palgrave-McMillan.

Schaller, Michael. 1992. *Reckoning with Reagan: America and its President in the 1980s*. New York: Oxford University Press.

Scott, Peter Dale, and Jonathan Marshall. 1998. *Cocaine Politics: Drugs, Armies, and the CIA in Central America*. Berkeley: University of California Press.

Stacewicz, Richard. 1997. *Winter Soldiers: An Oral History of the Vietnam Veterans Against the War*. New York: Twayne.

Sterk, Claire E. 1999. *Fast Lives: Women Who Use Crack Cocaine*. Philadelphia: Temple University Press.

Streatfeild, Dominic. 2003. *Cocaine: An Unauthorized Biography*. New York: Picador.

Troy, Gil. 2005. *Morning in America: How Ronald Reagan Invented the 1980s*. Princeton: Princeton University Press.

Valentine, Douglas. 2004. *The Strength of the Wolf: The Secret History of America's War on Drugs*. New York: Verso.

Walker, Thomas W. 2003. *Nicaragua*. 4th ed. Boulder, Colo.: Westview Press.

Walker, Thomas W., ed. 1982. *Nicaragua in Revolution*. New York: Praeger.

Webb, Gary. 1999. *Dark Alliance: The CIA, the Contras, and the Crack Cocaine Explosion*. New York: Seven Stories Press.

Whiteside, Thomas. 1971. *The Withering Rain: America's Herbicidal Folly*. New York: Dutton.

Wilcox, Fred A. 1983. *Waiting for an Army to Die: The Tragedy of Agent Orange*. New York: Vintage.

Williams, Terry M. 1993. *Crackhouse: Notes from the End of the Line*. New York: Penguin Books.

Culture Wars, Dissent, and Other Conflicts

OVERVIEW

If the 1960s is widely regarded in the popular imagination as a decade of protest and upheaval, the 1980s is usually seen as a quieter period characterized by relatively little dissent. The Eighties, in many respects, have become the anti-Sixties in the minds of many observers. Yet both generalizations, it turns out, are problematic. Many parts of America in the 1960s were not racked with turmoil and street demonstrations, while the era widely known as the "Decade of Greed" and the "Reagan Era" actually witnessed a flurry of social movements across the nation. Unresolved tensions dating back to the 1960s and beyond continued to trigger debates, protests and polarized viewpoints in some parts of the country, while entirely new sets of tensions surfaced and posed unanticipated challenges to the nation.

A cursory glance at protest struggles in the 1980s indicates a breadth and scope of dissent wider and more sweeping, in many respects, than the movements of the 1960s. Gays and lesbians became emboldened in the Eighties and challenged their marginalized status in society using methods more militant than anything ever seen in the 1960s. Protesters on both sides of the political spectrum took to the streets in the 1980s to air their grievances. Feminists continued a tradition of resistance that dated back decades. Pro-life and pro-choice demonstrators screamed at one another outside of abortion clinics. Labor unions remained in a state of decline, losing tens of thousands of members in the 1980s, yet dramatic strikes occurred throughout the decade. The ten-month strike of employees at the Hormel meat factory in Austin, Minnesota, in 1985–1986, and the Pittston Coal strike in Pennsylvania from 1989 to 1990, rivaled the most dramatic labor showdowns of earlier eras in American history.

Liberals were on the defensive in the 1980s, usually resisting President Ronald Reagan's domestic agenda and foreign policies. Yet the forces of the left remained potent. These years saw countless protests against nuclear weapons, U.S. intervention in Central America, the apartheid regime in South Africa and high levels of homelessness in some parts of the country. While President Reagan's approval ratings typically hovered high in the 1980s, many of his policies triggered acts of resistance. Civil rights leader Reverend Jesse Jackson's races for the presidency under the banner of the Rainbow Coalition in 1984 and 1988 motivated liberals and leftists across the country to act. Many joined local Rainbow Coalition campaigns in their communities. Meantime, scholars and participant-observers began to sort out the meaning of the 1960s during the 1980s. While the successful Hollywood film *The Big Chill* portrayed ex-Sixties activists as cynics who no longer cared about politics, the reality was that many former politicos, such as Abbie Hoffman and Tom Hayden, remained dedicated to progressive politics in the 1980s.

At the heart of many of the debates across America in the 1980s were social and cultural matters that lacked easy resolutions. Such issues as religion, gun control, affirmative action, feminism, race, sexual orientation, diversity, family life, and the environment provided the ammunition for the culture wars that engulfed the nation in the 1980s. Central in these issues was the question of America's future. Far from petering out in the Reagan years, dissent thrived. In most cases, America proved to be a fertile ground for open disagreements and the free exchange of ideas.

TIMELINE

1980   Gay and lesbian liberation movement protests discrimination.

The Democratic National Convention adopts the first gay rights platform plank.

U.S. Steel closes 13 plants.

Fundamentalists hold Washington for Jesus rally; 200,000 attend.

The Moral Majority exerts political power.

The Sagebrush Rebellion grows in western states.

The Moonies movement begins.

1981   The Reagan Recession begins.

June 5: the AIDS epidemic is first reported in United States.

The Moral Majority begins antigay crusade.

The first woman is appointed to the U.S. Supreme Court, Justice Sandra Day O'Connor.

The Supreme Court rules that the exclusion of women from the draft is legal.

The Supreme Court rules that husbands do not control a wife's property.

The first test tube baby is born.

Renault purchases AMC.

The unemployment rate rises to 8 percent.

The first Solidarity Day march on Washington, D.C., is held.

President Reagan breaks the PATCO strike.

Generation X attracts media attention.

One million in New York City protest nuclear winter.

1982   Wisconsin is first state to pass an antigay discrimination law.

The Equal Rights Amendment (ERA) fails ratification.

Major league baseball players strike for seven weeks, the longest baseball strike in history.

The first Japanese auto plant opens in the United States.

The United Mine Workers of America (UMWA) abandons militant traditions.

Economic recovery begins.

The working-out fad gains popularity.

Reagan announces the War on Drugs.

1983   Gerry Studds of Massachusetts is the first openly gay member of Congress.

HIV is identified as the virus causing AIDS in 250,000 Americans.

Jane Fonda's Workout is the best-selling home video.

The first African American Miss America is crowned, Vanessa Williams.

Sally Ride is the first American woman in space.

The Supreme Court affirms *Roe v. Wade.*

Silkwood is nominated for three Oscars.

Fifty-one percent of American women work outside the home.

The Supreme Court upholds the right of scabs to retain jobs.

Reagan's approval rating falls to 37 percent.

1984   More than 21,000 Americans have died from AIDS.

The *Wall Street Journal* substitutes the word gay for homosexual.

The first woman is nominated for vice president, Geraldine Ferraro.

The Supreme Court rules all-male organizations are illegal sex discrimination.

Nike transfers sewing work off shore to Indonesia.

Video became a home entertainment format.

Louisiana World Exposition declares bankruptcy.

1985   President Reagan acknowledges the AIDS crisis after Rock Hudson dies in October.

The New York Times substitutes gay and lesbian for homosexual.

The first international conference on AIDS is held in Atlanta.

Hormel meatpackers strike.

The Supreme Court rules union members may resign in a strike without union penalties.

The national problem of homelessness is recognized.

The Internet becomes popular.

The Indian Gambling Regulatory Act is passed, which allows reservation gambling.

Environmentalism becomes a leading public issue.

Congress promotes historic preservation with the Tax Reform Act.

1986   The Supreme Court upholds a Georgia sodomy law.

The Surgeon General releases a report on AIDS.

New York City bans discrimination by sexual orientation.

The Reagan administration says treatment of AIDS is a state, not federal, issue.

Five million U.S. children, or 55 percent, are in daycare.

The Supreme Court rules sexual harassment is job discrimination.

United Airlines flight attendants win lawsuit over fired married workers.

Operation Rescue is founded.

1987   ACT UP organizes the first AIDS awareness demonstration in New York City.

Barney Frank of Massachusetts is the second openly gay congressman.

The AIDS Memorial Quilt is first displayed in Washington, D.C.

The first condom commercials air on television.

The march on Washington for lesbian and gay rights is attended by 500,000 people.

The judge in Baby M case denies parental rights to the surrogate mother.

The AFL-CIO is readmitted to the Teamsters Union.

Reagan appoints Alan Greenspan as chairman of the Federal Reserve System.

Chrysler purchases AMC.

Democrats regain control of Congress.

A Seabrook, New Hampshire, nuclear power plant opens.

Pope John Paul II makes a second visit to the United States.

1988   The Episcopal diocese of Newark first condones blessing gay and lesbian couples.

Fashion model Gia Carangi dies of AIDS.

The Surgeon General mails AIDS brochure to 107 million families.

Studies report women are the fastest growing group in the AIDS epidemic.

Working Girl is nominated for four Oscars.

The Supreme Court rules that workers crossing a picket line do not lose their jobs.

United States and Canada sign a free trade agreement.

Jesse Jackson campaigns for president.

Republicans nominate George H. W. Bush for president.

1989   The Kinsey Institute reports that the sexual revolution was exaggerated.

Women are 42.5 percent of the U.S. labor force.

Single mothers number 5.8 million.

The Supreme Court rules in the Webster case that states may deny funds for abortions.

Pittson Coal strikes in Virginia.

Eastern Airlines strikes.

TWA v. Flight Attendants case goes to the Supreme Court.

Honda Accord is the bestselling car in the United States.

President Bush vetoes the minimum wage increase.

The Latino population in United States reaches 22 million.

GAY AND LESBIAN LIBERATION STRUGGLES AND THE SPECTER OF AIDS

"Coming out of the closet" was a common expression in the 1980s that meant living openly as gay or lesbian. Millions of men and women "came out of the closet" in this decade, moving into dwellings with their gay or lesbian companions and accepting their sexual orientation without apology or reluctance. These men and women lived on the cusp of a great social change; it had only been in the previous decade that the rest of the nation gradually—almost imperceptibly—began to accept that gays and lesbians were a part of American society.

Each passing year brought more tolerance, but change was still slow, and many gays and lesbians lived in larger cities that were more receptive to their alternative lifestyles. Not only did they face challenges from hostile forces outside their community but they sometimes found the new subculture in which they lived to be complex with difficult choices. Some gays and lesbians were monogamous while others were more experimental and, in some cases, promiscuous. In cities like San Francisco, Los Angeles, Chicago, and New York, bathhouses and gay bars had a dedicated clientele, even after the AIDS epidemic began. Gays were often much more flamboyant in public than lesbians, sometimes wearing leather outfits, sporting handlebar moustaches, or dressed in drag costumes. By contrast, there were many gays and lesbians who preferred to live quieter lives, content to remain far away from the spotlight. Some felt alienated living within the insular gay and lesbian milieu. As one lesbian commented, "It's hard to break into a new gay community. It's very closed and clique-ish. I had to go to the bars and dances a lot. Let's face it—you meet a lot of people you don't like. It's hard to make friends with people there" (Author unknown, "Double Lives: Gays in Syracuse," *The Post-Standard* [Syracuse, NY], June 4, 1989).

Protesters hold a red sign reading "Fighting for Our Lives" during a Gay Pride Day march along Manhattan's Fifth Avenue in July 1985. (Owen Franken/Corbis)

The gay and lesbian "community" in the United States was far from monolithic, because homosexuality transcended class, race, gender, and ethnic lines. Even the name "gay and lesbian community" was something of a misnomer because not all gays and lesbians interacted with one another. Some gays were quite sexist toward lesbians while many lesbian women felt that homosexual men were insensitive to their circumstances and needs. Often, the lifestyle differences between gays and lesbians could be quite striking. For one thing, women tended to be more restrained in their sexual practices. As lesbian Virginia Vida said, "I don't think our freedom translated into casual sex overall. Lesbians are less visible. We have very few bars. We prefer to meet other women through friends and informal situations. Lesbians are inclined to set up a home and build a nest. Our lifestyle is different from men in that respect" (Norman 1983).

Mutual support proved to be very important among gays and lesbians, as many men and women found themselves rejected by family members after making their sexual orientation known. "There is still a hesitancy to come out," noted one Massachusetts therapist in 1988. "The major issue with which I deal with clients who are lesbians has to do with their uncertainty about acceptance. That is very dependent on the nature of the workplace in which they find themselves. That still prevails, even in this day and age" (Longcope 1988). Indeed, social pressures resulted in many homosexuals concealing their sexual preferences, even choosing to marry heterosexual partners to keep their identity a secret. In 1981, the *Washington Post* estimated that of the 13 to 20 million practicing homosexual men in the United States, about two-thirds were also involved in relationships with women (Weiner 1981). So widespread was the trend that the New York author John Malone titled his 1981 book, *Straight Women/Gay Men: A Special Relationship*. By the mid-1980s, with the rapid spread of AIDS in the homosexual population, living a double life could be risky. There were instances of married women testing HIV-positive because they were unaware of their spouse's secret homosexuality.

Another segment of the population who struggled with issues of sexuality was the nation's gay and lesbian teenagers. To help teenage homosexuals come to grips with their sexuality in the 1980s, bookstore shelves featured parental self-help books aimed at parents of gay and lesbian teenagers. Raising a gay or lesbian teenager could be an enormous challenge, and some parents were not prepared for it. These especially vulnerable youths faced teasing, bullying, banishment, and violence in schools. Moreover, the rate of suicide attempts for gay and lesbian teens was higher than the national average: 30 to 40 percent for males and 20 percent for females (Murdock 1988). In 1986, a Washington, D.C., social worker who assisted gay teens noted, "Kids dealing with gay feelings go through adolescence in a skewed way. . . . What they learn is how to hide what they are really feeling" (Kantrowitz 1986).

Despite these issues, a robust tradition of activism emerged in many gay and lesbian communities by the 1980s. About seven out of ten politicized gays and lesbians were on the liberal to left-wing side of the political spectrum, although gay Republicans founded the Log Cabin Republicans in 1978 with grassroots chapters in 37 states. Both liberal and conservative groups promoted awareness, solidarity, and pride. One important tradition was the annual Gay Pride Parade, which was held in most major American cities. Gays and lesbians—some flamboyant, others restrained—marched, protested, danced, staffed information booths, registered people to vote, and sometimes accompanied "straight" loved ones or friends to show support for this public event. In many cases, the Gay Pride Parades represented deliberate shows of strength. As a gay Boston city councilor remarked, "Gay Pride Day sends a political message that's very clear. The gay community votes like a bloc, acts like a family, has financial resources, and there's a lot of political power there" (Howe 1989). Scores of new advocacy groups appeared throughout the 1980s, ranging in size from little more than a post office box to huge national organizations with chapters in every state.

The Specter of AIDS

In 1987, the New York City gay activist Larry Kramer founded the AIDS Coalition to Unleash Power (ACT UP). This anarchistic, direct-action organization adopted cutting-edge protest techniques to publicize the plight of people with AIDS. Many young radicals first cut their teeth by getting involved in local ACT UP demonstrations, and their level of commitment was often intense. ACT UP activist Jean Carlomusto, who was part of some early actions, remembered working "seventy or eighty hours a week, including weekends. That's what was happening then. A movement was growing" (ACT UP). Under the motto "Silence = Death," ACT UP organized the most dramatic political protests of the decade. The Wall Street protest on March 24, 1987, began when 250 activists chained themselves to the balcony of the New York Stock Exchange to draw attention to the prohibitively expensive drug AZT, an AIDS medication manufactured by Burroughs Wellcome. Equally compelling protests occurred at the White House in June and at the March on Washington for Lesbian and Gay Rights in October 1987. ACT UP had chapters in more than 60 cities by 1989, and New York City had the largest membership with a $300,000 budget. Although ACT UP meetings seldom attracted more than 100 to 200 members, their demonstrations were always newsworthy events with headline-grabbing civil disobedience.

While the militant ACT UP tactics generated news coverage across the country in the late 1980s, most gay and lesbian activists took a moderate approach emphasizing the need for assimilation and positive role models. They welcomed gay-theme films such as *Making Love* (1982) and *Personal Best* (1982) and the groundbreaking Showtime cable TV show *Brothers* (1984–1987). Other positive gay films included the HBO movie *What if I'm Gay?* (1987) and the sensitive treatment of AIDS victims in *Longtime Companion* (1990). These sympathetic portraits of gay characters bridged the gap between homosexual and "straight" culture and gave reason to hope for increased tolerance and acceptance in American society.

Although the government was slow to recognize the AIDS epidemic, in 1987 President Reagan appointed James D. Watkins, former chief of naval operations, as chairman of the Watkins Commission on AIDS. Advocates of AIDS-awareness were gratified when this conservative panel recommended antibias laws, more treatment for drug addicts, and more research on the disease. By 1990, gays and lesbians had made impressive gains in attracting attention to the crisis. Many discovered comfortable niches in urban centers where they could organize self-help groups and lobby for more treatment and research. AIDS remained a constant threat but increased awareness of this disease calmed public fears. Gradually, old stereotypes about gays as moral degenerates were replaced by new stereotypes about gays as sophisticated, fashionable, and witty individuals. But neither cliché helped the larger homosexual population make sense of the gay community. They could not marry until 1990, and then only in a few states. They still had to exercise caution in many parts of the country. They had a long way to go before they were fully accepted in the United States. Indeed, many struggles lay ahead.

Gay Community Activism

Inspired by the civil rights movement, the counterculture's sexual revolution, the women's liberation movement, the anti-Vietnam war protests, and the Black Power movement, the Gay and Lesbian Liberation was founded in 1969. This movement expanded rapidly in the 1980s. The first event to trigger this struggle may have been the Stonewall Riot on June 28, 1969, when the New York police arrested men and women at the Stonewall Inn, a gay bar on Christopher Street in Greenwich Village. An estimated 2,000 onlookers battled with 400 policemen in a riot that continued for three days. Gay men and women protested police brutality in making arrests at the tavern.

In response, Brenda Howard (1946–2005), a bisexual activist, organized annual Christopher Street Liberation Day marches beginning in 1970 to commemorate the Stonewall Riot. By the 1980s this march became an annual gay pride march in many cities. Howard also founded the Gay Liberation Front to lobby for local and state laws against homophobia, violence, and discrimination based on sexual orientation. In response, the American Psychiatric Association revoked its definition of homosexuality as a mental illness in 1973 because scientific evidence indicates that homosexuality occurs naturally before birth.

Gay community activism expanded when the Centers for Disease Control (CDC) recognized the AIDS epidemic, or Acquired Immune Deficiency Syndrome, in June 1981. This fatal disease so prevalent in gay populations became a focus for Gay Lib or Gay Power activists. The alarm about the "gay plague" increased when the *New England Journal of Medicine* reported in 1983 that AIDS can be transmitted from men to women.

Bella Abzug (1920–1998) and Edward Koch (1924–), Democratic members of Congress from New York City, won support from the gay community because of their advocacy of gay and lesbian liberation causes. In 1983 Gerry Studds, and Barney Frank in 1987, both Massachusetts Democrats, were the first openly gay congressmen. This practice of "coming out of the closet" to proudly acknowledge one's sexual preference did much to diminish hostility to homosexuals despite the antigay views of conservatives in the Moral Majority. At the Democratic National Convention in 1984 over 100,000 gay and lesbian protesters demanded increased federal funds for AIDS research. Although Secretary of Health and Human Services Margaret Heckler promised a new vaccine would soon be discovered, medical treatment offered little hope for AIDS victims. Gay organizations continued to demand more attention to this global pandemic.

Small Steps Forward

The gay and lesbian liberation struggles spread in the 1970s as college students formed campus gay organizations and others lobbied the 1972 Democratic presidential candidates to endorse laws prohibiting discrimination against homosexuals. In 1979 more than 75,000 gay rights supporters marched on Washington, D.C. Demands for a cure and improved medical care for AIDS victims began soon after the CDC report in 1981 that pneumocystis carninii pneumonia attacked gay men in disproportionately high numbers. Evidence proved that this disease, which was later confirmed as one of the opportunistic diseases related to AIDS, perhaps transmitted from chimpanzees to humans in Africa by 1959, was present in the United States as early as 1969. This was the first official recognition of the dangerous epidemic soon known as AIDS. By 1981, doctors in France, Belgium, and Haiti reported some cases, and New York City doctors found cases among drug addicts and children. In 1982, the CDC created a national task force to investigate what the media called the "gay plague." The CDC

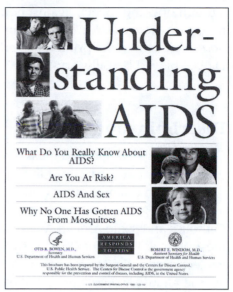

Cover of the federal government's AIDS information brochure Understanding AIDS *(1988). (U.S. Department of Health and Human Services)*

scientist Dr. James Curran acknowledged that AIDS was an unprecedented epidemic in American medicine with 413 cases and 155 deaths in one year. Federal scientists created a blood test and a clone of the AIDS virus in 1984, important steps in developing a vaccine. The CDC hosted the first international conference on AIDS in Atlanta in 1985. However, President Reagan's budget director, James Miller, announced in 1986 that the treatment of AIDS patients was a local or state government problem rather than a federal issue. The president was isolated from the subject of AIDS by his domestic policy staff. Nonetheless, Congress appropriated funds for AIDS research and treatment as the number of deaths reached 70,000 by the end of the 1980s. In 1986 the surgeon general, Dr. C. Everett Koop, called for AIDS education in schools and greater use of condoms. However, his AIDS brochure mailed to 107 million families in 1988 led to much conservative criticism and his resignation in 1989.

The struggle for gay and lesbian equal rights also expanded steadily in the 1980s. Wisconsin passed the first state law banning antigay discrimination (1981), followed later by New York City (1986) and other state and local governments. Religious denominations also expressed more toleration for gay and lesbian couples seeking marriage or some equivalent, first in the Episcopal diocese of Newark, New Jersey (1988). By 1990, the 101st American Conference of Rabbis accepted gay men and lesbians as rabbis. However, Pope John Paul II presided over a conference on AIDS at which Cardinal John O'Connor of New York made a tough opening speech against homosexuality and condoms as *Time* magazine noted on November 27, 1989. But television responded in a small way with *Soap,* one of the first primetime series to include a regular gay character, Jodie Dallas, played by Billy Crystal (1977–1981).

Discrimination

Gays and lesbians suffered gross discrimination in American society in the 1980s. Abandoning traditional hostility to Catholics and African Americans, the conservative Protestant groups who formed the Christian Right in the 1980s found a common ground in opposition to gay rights and feminism. Conservative Catholics and some African Americans became allied with the Christian Right on these issues. President Reagan still ignored the AIDS epidemic and found the subject distasteful. He feared any official sympathy for the victims would alienate the Moral Majority who saw the disease as God's punishment of sinful homosexuals and drug addicts. In her book *Talk: NPR's Susan Stamberg Considers All Things,* National Public Radio news anchor Susan Stamberg recalled that NPR, which regularly covered the first news stories about AIDS in 1981, reconsidered its frequent reporting on AIDS in 1984 (Stamberg 1993).

In press conferences, Reagan failed to reassure the public that AIDS was not transmitted by casual contact. White House lawyer John Roberts, later Chief Justice of the Supreme Court, advised the president to be cautious on the AIDS issue. Patrick Buchanan spoke for many in the Reagan administration when he remarked that homosexuals declared war on nature and now nature was exacting an awful retribution (Diggins 2007, 322). But state governments responded more quickly; in 1983, the New York State Department of Health established the AIDS Institute to improve prevention and health care for HIV-positive people. However, the death of Hollywood star Rock Hudson in 1985, a friend of Ronald and Nancy Reagan for many years, prompted dramatic and widespread attention for the first time. The president ordered Surgeon General C. Everett Koop to issue a report on AIDS in 1986. Koop's recommendation for abstinence, monogamy, and condoms outraged Phyllis Schlafly, Jerry Falwell, and Secretary of Education William Bennett, who said Koop encouraged immorality. Reagan made one speech on AIDS in 1987 to assure the public that blood donation was safe, but he did not support increased public funds for research. Although the Food and Drug Administration approved a blood test for AIDS in 1985, fear led to discrimination. In some cities bus drivers and police officers wore gloves to avoid AIDS.

One example of the homophobic reaction to gay liberation was the antigay campaign led by Anita Bryant, a conservative Southern Baptist singer and Florida orange juice spokeswoman. Aroused by a Dade County, Florida, referendum in 1977 to prohibit discrimination on grounds of sexual preference, Bryant led an

ACT UP

ACT UP, or the Aids Coalition to Unleash Power, began in 1987 in New York City with the aim to nonviolently protest social and government indifference to the AIDS epidemic. Since the first demonstration at Wall Street in 1987, this grass-roots organization adopted civil rights movement methods to achieve social change through unconventional politics with marches, boycotts, demonstrations, street theater, sit-ins, and political art. By 1989, ACT UP had organized 100 chapters in New York, Boston, Philadelphia, San Francisco, Chicago, and many other American cities. This commitment to gay and lesbian liberation by direct action and radical democracy, in contrast to the more conservative segments of the homosexual communities, reflected the lack of organization structure or official spokespeople. Targets of ACT UP were the Food and Drug Administration, the Department of Health and Human Services, the Catholic Church, mainstream media, the Department of Education, homophobic politicians, and drug companies. This dramatic movement achieved some success in raising public awareness of homophobia and the growing health crisis, and government responses increased in the 1980s.

antigay campaign, Save Our Children. Appearing on the evangelical TV programs *The 700 Club* and *PTL,* she focused on protection of children from predatory homosexuals. The Florida referendum was defeated by voters and spawned local activism against gay and lesbian people in Minnesota, Washington, California, Kansas, and Oregon. However, by the end of the 1980s, progress had been made. Gay rights advocates became more motivated. Attitudes were changing slowly, and William Hurt won an Oscar for best actor for his sympathetic role as a gay man in *Kiss of the Spider Woman* (1985). But some music critics attributed the backlash against disco music in 1980 to its supposedly gay community origins.

The California legislature proposal to guarantee confidentiality of human immunodeficiency virus (HIV) test results was adopted nationwide, and former first lady Betty Ford raised $1.3 million for HIV/AIDS research. Before his death, Rock Hudson donated $250,000 for AIDS research, and his friend Elizabeth Taylor became a spokesperson for AIDS funding. With 115,786 cases of AIDS and 70,313 victims dead by 1989, the scope of this public health crisis was clear. In 1990 Congress passed the Hate Crimes Statistics law; a student documentary, *Living with Aids,* won an Academy Award; and the Smithsonian Institution opened an exhibit on the Gay and Lesbian Rights movement. President Bush signed the Americans with Disabilities law, which banned discrimination for those with disabilities, including AIDS victims. When Magic Johnson, the Los Angeles Lakers star, announced he was HIV positive in 1991, some athletes and sportswriters questioned whether he should continue to play basketball if he might expose teammates to the disease. This controversy subsided when most athletes supported Johnson's decision to play.

Acquired Immune Deficiency Syndrome (AIDS)

The deadly Acquired Immune Deficiency Syndrome, or AIDS, was first reported in the United States in 1981. Its quiet, yet sinister debut sent tremors of fear through gay communities across the United States. A handful of staffers at the CDC in Atlanta were alarmed in the summer of 1981 when they discovered a new, mysterious disease that seemed to be sexually transmitted, and it spread quickly through the gay community. At first, information was difficult to come by, prompting some gays to panic. A story buried deep in the *New York Times* in 1981 announced, "Doctors in New York and California have diagnosed among homosexual men 41 cases of a rare and often rapidly fatal form of cancer. Eight of the victims died less than 24 months after the diagnosis was made" (Altman 1981). Before the CDC officially identified AIDS, the disease began ravaging gay men. At the Beth Israel Hospital on Manhattan's Lower East Side, the chief of infectious diseases at the facility, Donna Mildvan, began treating a German patient in June 1980. The man had worked as a chef in Haiti for several years and was admitted to the hospital with bloody diarrhea and a low white blood count. The patient's condition rapidly deteriorated over the next few months, and he was dead by December at the age of 33. As Mildvan recalled, "I can't even begin to tell you what an awful experience it was. You don't lose a 33-year-old patient. We agonized over it. Agonized over it all the time" (Bayer 2002, 12).

Rumors quickly spread throughout the gay community about a new disease: Gay Related Immune Deficiency, or GRID. In those confusing early months, nobody knew how the disease spread or why young gay males were particularly susceptible to it. By April 1982, 248 gay men were officially diagnosed with GRID, and that figure would escalate sharply over the years. Four thousand Americans were dead by 1984. That number climbed to 5,600 at the start of 1985. AIDS soon assumed epidemic proportions. CDC figures from January 1989 indicated that there were 82,764 AIDS cases and 46,344 deaths in the United States. The number continued to escalate sharply as the disease became a global pandemic.

With the passage of time, awareness of AIDS increased. Physicians discovered, for example, that it typically began as the Human Immunodeficiency Virus (HIV), which was transmitted by sex, blood transmission (such as blood transfusions and hypodermic needles), and from HIV-positive mothers to newborn babies. HIV attacked the immune system, eliminating CD4+ T cells, which helped the human immune system to function properly. Once the immune system was thoroughly devastated, full-blown AIDS soon developed.

Some AIDS activists lamented that it was difficult to convey the gravity of the disease to the heterosexual population. They had ample reasons to be discouraged. Once the general public discovered that AIDS could not be transmitted from kissing or sitting on a dirty toilet seat, anxieties diminished, but the stigma was replaced by indifference. The conservative Reagan administration seldom took the AIDS threat seriously. As presidential historian Richard Reeves observed in *President Reagan: The Triumph of Imagination* (2005), "the President himself never used the word 'AIDS' in public." Over time, too, it became apparent that AIDS did not discriminate based on sexual preference. By the late 1980s and early 1990s, heterosexual intravenous drug users were the fastest-growing group of AIDS victims, and they sometimes transmitted the disease to their companions and their children.

Many observers in the 1980s agreed that a more decisive response to the crisis by the federal government and medical community might have lessened the impact of the epidemic. Pessimists offered gloomy forecasts about the future of AIDS. When certain AIDS watchers predicted that the disease would one day kill hundreds of thousands, their dire warnings were largely dismissed by most Americans as excessively alarmist. But this bleak vision eventually came to pass. At the end of 1995, the CDC reported that nearly 320,000 people had perished from the disease, and estimated that as many as 1.5 million Americans might be infected by the virus. However, the dire predictions by the World Health Organization were well founded, 25 years after the CDC first reported the death of five gay men in Los Angeles from this lethal new virus in 1981, *Newsweek* magazine reported that more than 25 million men, women, and children had died and 40 million more were infected by HIV or AIDS.

Eventually, high-profile HIV and AIDS sufferers helped convince the American public that a crisis of enormous proportions was unfolding in the country. In the summer of 1985, a publicist for Rock Hudson, a Hollywood screen idol who starred in numerous films and the hit television series *Dynasty,* announced that the actor had been diagnosed with AIDS the previous year. The disease rapidly moved through Hudson's body and he died in October 1985. Most Americans had no idea that Hudson was gay, and his sudden death from AIDS came as a shock, even to those who knew him well, such as actress Doris Day. In 1987, the pianist Liberace and Connecticut congressman Stewart McKinney also died of AIDS.

Equally compelling was the plight of Ryan White, a soft-spoken and gentle teenager from Kokomo, Indiana, who developed AIDS through a blood-clotting agent used to treat his hemophilia. In 1985, White was expelled from his school after nervous school officials and parents learned that he had AIDS. Despite repeated statements by public health officials that White could not pass on AIDS through casual contact, fear prevailed, and White found himself ostracized in his own community. But he soon became a national symbol of quiet heroism in the face of discrimination against people with AIDS, and, like Rock Hudson, he helped put a human face on an enormous tragedy. *The Ryan White Story* (1989), a TV movie that dramatized his ordeal, portrayed him as dignified in the face of local hostility. When Ryan White died in April 1990, he was hailed as a hero in all parts of the country. Telegrams poured in from celebrities, President George H. W. Bush sent his condolences, and among his mourners were First Lady Barbara Bush, Michael Jackson, Elton John, the Rev. Jesse Jackson, real estate tycoon Donald Trump, and millions of TV viewers of the funeral. Congress passed the Ryan White Act in 1990 to provide funds for medical treatment of AIDS patients.

People who were not afflicted with AIDS, or who did not have loved ones suffering from it, often could not appreciate the excruciatingly painful ordeal it was to have the disease. AIDS often involved the rapid deterioration of one's body and mind. In some people, HIV and AIDS progressed slowly while in others it took a rapid toll. Some AIDS sufferers might live for years without any symptoms and then experience a sudden and brutal onslaught and a quick death. Some HIV-positive and AIDS patients lived normal lives for many years with the disease. One of the worst aspects of the disease was its very randomness. To have AIDS often meant living with purplish lesions on the skin, bleeding, numbness, loss of muscular control, dizziness, nausea, diarrhea, respiratory difficulties, hair loss, sweats, dementia, deteriorating eyesight and hearing, cancers, rapid weight loss, slurred speech, fatigue, glandular swelling, and shortness of breath.

Homophobia

When scientists confirmed that AIDS was transmitted by blood and semen or by intravenous drug use by hemophiliacs or drug addicts, the victims were shunned and stigmatized by many Americans fearful of contracting the disease. Others blamed the victims for immoral conduct that resulted in acquiring the dreaded disease. It was a serious medical and social problem, and at least 32,000 Americans had died of AIDS by 1990, but fear and bias continued.

Homophobia, the irrational fear of homosexuals, underlay much of the misunderstanding, ignorance, and hostility to the AIDS crisis in the 1980s. The American public was less concerned about AIDS when the disease was believed to be limited to Haitians, gay men, and illegal drug users. As it became known (in 1983) that AIDS was transmitted from men to women and was spreading rapidly, gay men faced discrimination and physical attack for infecting "innocent" victims. In 1985, blood centers began screening the nation's blood and plasma supply for HIV, and polls showed most Americans favored mandatory testing (72 percent), quarantine (51 percent), or tattoos (15 percent) for those infected with HIV. Vice President George H. W. Bush called for mandatory testing in 1987, but conservatives criticized public health education efforts that treated AIDS as a medical rather than a moral issue. President Reagan, at the request of actress Elizabeth Taylor, gave one speech on AIDS in 1987. Reagan had never discussed AIDS with Surgeon General Koop before this speech. He calmed public fears, asked for compassion, but proposed barring immigrants who were infected. It was Congress, not the White House, that took action when the World Health Organization in Geneva and the CIA reported in 1987 that the AIDS pandemic could become a threat to the United States. By 1990, one million Americans were infected out of 60 million AIDS cases worldwide.

Los Angeles gay and lesbian groups responded with a public education campaign and print and TV public service announcements titled *Fight the Fear with the Facts* in 1985. AIDS activists spoke out against AIDS-related prejudice. In 1987, ACT UP formed in New York to confront discrimination, and the AMA ruled that physicians were required to treat people with AIDS. But in 1987, Florida arsonists destroyed the home of the Ray brothers, three young hemophiliacs infected with AIDS through blood transfusions, to keep them out of the public school. North Carolina Republican senator Jesse Helms amended a federal appropriations bill to prevent funding AIDS education that encouraged or promoted homosexuality. The Immigration and Naturalization Service (INS) barred immigrants and travelers with HIV, and Delta Airlines attempted to ban passengers with HIV or AIDS until activists threatened a national boycott. Dinesh D'Souza, a conservative student at Dartmouth College, published the names of gay students in the *Dartmouth Review* in 1981, a bold attempt to embarrass homosexual classmates who were "in the closet."

However, 1988 reports that AIDS had spread most quickly to drug addicts, African Americans, and women raised new fears. California voters defeated a quarantine ballot initiative for a second time, but a New York City home for children with AIDS received bomb threats in 1989. Congress authorized $881 million for emergency relief to cities with high AIDS rates, but appropriated only $350 million for medical care, even though studies proved 85 percent of Americans with HIV did not receive early treatment. Like abortion and sex education issues, homophobia played an important part in the culture wars that divided Americans in the 1980s.

The Impact of AIDS

One impact of AIDS was to bring the issue of civil rights for gay people into mainstream political discourse. Despite irrational fears of this new epidemic, most Americans saw it as a disease, not a moral failing, and supported government research and treatment for AIDS victims. Among the American celebrities who died of AIDS-related diseases was actress Amanda Blake (1989), attorney Roy Cohn (1986), supermodel Gia Carangi (1986), choreographer Alvin Ailey (1989), and writer Isaac Asimov (1992). These deaths from blood transfusions, drug

The NAMES Project AIDS quilt, representing people who have died of AIDS, in front of the Washington Monument in 1996. (National Institutes of Health)

addiction, or homosexual activity aroused greater public attention to the AIDS epidemic. Madonna, the Queen of Pop, a gay icon in the 1980s, included aspects of gay culture in her concert and video performances. She was one of the first celebrities to raise funds for AIDS research.

Drug companies came under much criticism for the high cost of AIDS medicines and vaccines, AZT cost more than $10,000 for a year's supply in 1986. The Food and Drug Administration was also criticized in 1988 for its slow response to testing new drugs and its obsolete approval process, forcing the FDA to fast-track clinical trials of promising new drugs. Public pressure compelled the American Medical Association to remind physicians, hospitals, and health care workers of their responsibility to treat HIV and AIDS patients with confidentiality, dignity, and respect.

American attitudes also changed in 1987 when Cleve Jones created the AIDS Memorial Quilt with 6,000 panels in memory of the victims of this disease. Jones raised $500,000 for AIDS research by touring the country with the quilt, and he displayed the quilt on the National Mall in Washington, D.C., five times. National AIDS Awareness Day began in 1988, but it achieved new impact on December 1, 1989, when 600 art institutions marked the day by closing, or dimming their lights and shrouding the art exhibits for a "Day Without Art." By the decade's end, homophobia in all its forms was declining, but ABC encountered controversy in 1989 when one episode of the popular weekly dramatic series *Thirtysomething* showed two gay men in bed together although not engaged in sexual context. Some advertisers withdrew their commercials in fear of consumer boycotts (Shilts 2000).

President Bush experienced the wrath of irrational homophobia when he signed the Hate Crimes Act on April 23, 1990. The law mandated stiff penalties for crimes committed against people because they are members of a specific group, and supporters of the bill were invited to the White House ceremony. This routine event included representatives from Protestant, Catholic, Jewish, African American, Hispanic, gay, and lesbian groups that had supported the bill. Within days, the White House was flooded with letters and calls denouncing the president for destroying the moral fabric of the nation by supporting homosexuality. Jerry Falwell's Moral Majority and Pat Robertson's Christian Coalition and most Religious Right organizations condemned homosexuality.

Conservatives also opposed needle exchange programs that experts had proposed to decrease the risk of spreading AIDS. In this program, drug addicts could bring used hypodermic needles to be exchanged for sterile needles, thus reducing the number of needles shared among addicts. The allocation of federal AIDS prevention funds for abstinence and fidelity programs was also unrealistic and fostered a stigmatization of condom use to the dismay of AIDS prevention specialists. Although the president and Congress were committed to providing access to AIDS prevention and treatment services in the United States and other nations, moral or religious considerations interfered with this global health threat.

FEMINISM AND ITS CRITICS

Background

The women's movement, stimulated by the experience of many American women in the civil rights and anti–Vietnam War movements, and by the sexual liberation of the 1960s counterculture, prompted a negative reaction by conservative women who distrusted feminism. Many were attracted to Senator Barry Goldwater's campaign for president in 1964, and by Anita Bryant's antihomosexual Save Our Children crusade in 1977. Perhaps the leading event to arouse feminist critics and their leader, Phyllis Schlafly, was the Equal Rights Amendment (ERA). Conservatives and fundamentalist Christians worked tirelessly to defeat the ERA. One poster displayed at STOP ERA rallies warned "Women libbers, ERA Lesbians, Repent, Read the Bible while you're able." The Christian Right saw feminism as a left-wing secularist threat to the American family. Feminism may have been the victim of its own extremist rhetoric and the hostile media that repeated the myth of bra-burning radical women's libbers, as *Time* magazine noted on December 4, 1989.

Working-class women, who were 80 percent of employed women by 1980, had little contact with the women's liberation movement except through the media. Their issues were overshadowed by the more publicized agenda raised by middle-class professional women. In a study of female hospital workers, many women revealed fears that disturbing traditional sex roles would cause men to respect women less. Although the working women surveyed agreed that sex discrimination was a serious problem, that the women's movement helped women get better jobs and better pay, and that they supported the ERA, on the whole they saw feminism as a middle-class and young single woman's movement in the 1980s, according to Patricia Cayo Sexton in *The New Nightingales* (1982). Only indirectly did the women's movement have an impact on working-class women, largely by raising their consciousness and their expectations over time.

The middle-class homemakers who had long provided the moral and spiritual safeguards for capitalist American society were often working outside the home in the 1980s. Fearful of moral bankruptcy in their communities, many saw the new feminist superwoman as a convenient scapegoat. This backlash against feminism reflected the growing moral condemnation of America's materialistic consumer society and concerns about the decline of family values. In addition, the Generation X adolescents who came of age in the 1980s also rejected feminism, or more to the point, they took for granted the gains the women's movement had made but avoided the label feminist. Few young women admired Holly Hunter's role as a brilliant workaholic TV producer and unloved woman in the movie *Broadcast News* (1987), but the film was a warning about the dangers professional women faced. The issue of women's role in the military was also frequently cited by opponents of the ERA.

Seeds of Change

Until 1930, most American women worked at home or in domestic service, but experiences in World War I and World War II proved that women could contribute to society in other roles outside the home as wage earners. In the postwar 1950s, growing numbers of women found employment, especially in accounting, education, health care, management, office work, retail sales, and in many professions. Inspired by the civil rights movement and the anti–Vietnam War protests, young women demanded social changes that recognized their desires and talents. The introduction of the birth control pill in 1960 and the liberating counterculture revolution during the 1960s changed the lives of all American women. By the 1980s, it became clear that gender discrimination was inconsistent with modern life. More women attended college and found careers in law, medicine, and other professions. They delayed marriage and used contraception to plan their families. Lesbians were an important part of the gay liberation movement, and the economic crisis required more women to work outside the home. But social change frightened many Americans.

Defining Moments

As the women's liberation movement progressed from the 1960s sisterhood to the 1980s superwoman, more women believed they could have it all: education, career, sexual fulfillment, marriage, and motherhood. All seemed to be in their grasp. Increasing numbers of women attended colleges and universities and moved into nontraditional jobs. The rapid increase in working mothers, who numbered 42.5 percent of the U.S. labor force in 1980 and 60.5 percent in 1983, made day care more necessary and more common. By 1986, 55 percent of children, or 5 million, in the United States attended day care.

The public image of feminism, shaped by the media and therapeutic self-help movements, revolved around the selfish superwoman or the man-hating lesbian dressed in boots and overalls. Both became the symbols and scapegoats for problems and changes in society. Public protests by young radical feminists reinforced these stereotypes, but many events and social changes in the 1970s became landmarks of the women's movement's successes. These include legal remedies to gender discrimination like the Equal Employment Opportunities Commission in 1965 and affirmative action policies. The founding of the National Organization for Women (NOW) and *Ms. Magazine* in 1971, establishing Women's History Week in 1980, and the establishment of rape crisis centers in most cities were dismissed as radical steps at first but were widely accepted by 1990.

The Supreme Court decision in the *Roe v. Wade* (1973) case made abortion a constitutional right. Women's consciousness-raising groups were seen as a fad but, in retrospect, were quite influential in changing public perceptions. By 1977, many cities held annual Take Back the Night marches to protest urban violence against women. The 1972 presidential candidacy of Shirley Chisholm (1924–2005), the first African American woman elected to Congress (1968–1983), was another startling development that seemed much less unusual by the 1980s. The election of Ella Grasso as governor of Connecticut (1975–1980) and Madeleine Kunin as governor of Vermont (1985–1993) were landmark events. Jewish women, who were pioneers in the woman's movement, became rabbis by 1974. The successful participation of physicist Sally Ride in the 1983 and 1984 *Challenger* space shuttle flights was further confirmation that American women would contribute to every aspect of society. *Time* magazine's cover story on February 4, 1985, "Discord in the Church," noted that women were even challenging Pope John Paul II by demanding new roles in Catholicism. Despite assumptions that feminism was primarily a white middle-class movement, in 1982 Chicana feminists in California founded a national feminist organization called Mujeres Activas en Letras y Cambio Social (MALCS) to bridge the gap between academics and the Mexican-American community.

Decline of Feminism

Until 1980, feminism and the women's movement had been so successful that young American women took for granted the legal rights and social equality women had won. Women were commonly found in jobs not traditionally associated with women. The failure of ERA to be ratified in 1982 concerned younger women less than expected because state ERA laws and federal court decisions achieved some of the same goals. Single women, traditionally Democratic voters, did not vote as often as married women, who increasingly supported Republicans. In 1980, the gender gap was obvious when President Reagan won only 47 percent of the female vote compared with 56 percent of male voters. Despite the decline of feminism as a political movement, its effects were a permanent feature in American society.

Despite an overall decline in the number of women in high-level government positions, some notable women in the Reagan administration included Jeane Kirkpatrick, Elizabeth Hanford Dole, and Margaret Heckler. Kirkpatrick was the U.S. permanent representative to the United Nations (1981–1985). Dole served as secretary of transportation (1983–1989) and secretary of labor (1989–1991). She later married the 1996 Republican presidential nominee Sen. Robert Dole, and she ran for president in 1999 and was elected to the Senate from North Carolina in 2002. Hecker, a Republican member of Congress from Massachusetts (1967–83), was secretary of health and human services (1983–1985) and ambassador to Ireland (1985–1989). Feminism may have declined in the 1980s, but *Ms. Magazine* discussed third-wave feminism, which put less emphasis on the experience of white middle-class women and greater focus on working-class and minority women.

Newsweek magazine caused many antifeminists to gloat and other women to grimace with a 1986 cover story reporting on new demographic research. The study predicted that white female college graduates who did not marry by age 35 had only a 5 percent chance of ever marrying. This seemed to support the views of the older conservative women and the younger women who were opposed or merely uninterested in feminism. The uppity women's libbers who pursued higher education, careers, and a single lifestyle in preference to or before marriage might never find a husband. Although this study was flawed, it reflected society's concerns that in the 1960s about half of American women married by age 20 while only 14 percent of women born between 1955 and 1964 married after age 30. Traditionally, a woman unmarried by age 30 was con-

The ERA

The Equal Rights Amendment (ERA), first proposed in 1923, was approved by the U.S. Senate in 1972 but was ratified by only 35 of the 50 state legislatures by the 1982 deadline. Ratification by 38 states was required to add this amendment to the Constitution. The ERA proposed to invalidate federal and state laws that discriminated against women. It said that "equality of rights under the law shall not be denied or abridged by the United States or by any State on account of sex." The National Organization for Women (NOW) argued that many laws kept women in economic dependency, but Phyllis Schlafly and other conservative critics claimed that the ERA would cause women to lose protections and privileges, such as economic support by their husbands, or exemption from military service. NOW lobbied for state equal rights amendments, and the ERA has been reintroduced in Congress each term since 1982. Polls indicated that a majority of Americans (74 to 52 percent) supported the ERA.

ERA supporters remained confident that the amendment would be ratified even after the election of Ronald Reagan in 1980, but doubts increased as a backlash against feminism emerged and the electorate moved to the right. Reagan had supported the ERA but reversed his position during the presidential campaign. The press became hostile to NOW president Eleanor Smeal and other pro-ERA leaders, and more admiring of the skill of the influential Phyllis Schlafly and anti-ERA leaders who distrusted big government. When the time extension for the ERA expired on June 30, 1982, Schlafly held a dinner in Washington to celebrate. Speaker of the House Thomas P. O'Neill held a dramatic roll-call vote in the House on November 15, 1983, to reintroduce the ERA. It failed to pass by six votes, and the ERA campaign was over. But court decisions on the Civil Rights Act of 1964 and the 14th Amendment have achieved some ERA goals, so the issue faded from public debate, and 17 states passed their own ERA laws.

sidered an old maid who would never marry. But the researchers failed to take into account that times had changed. In the wake of the 1960s counterculture, feminism, and other social movements, delaying marriage no longer meant never marrying. The women's movement changed many things: sexual freedom; using birth control; choosing an abortion; having a career; being a single mother; cohabiting with a partner; marrying outside class, religion, or race; and, it is now clear, when to marry. In 2006, *Newsweek* reported that its controversial 1986 cover story was inaccurate.

But feminism was on the defensive in the Reagan era when the New Right controlled the Republican Party's position on women's rights. For the first time in American history, the Republicans opposed the women's movement, criticizing the key issues, the ERA, and a woman's right to an abortion. Feminists turned to state legislatures and state courts to expand day care, pay equity, and rape and domestic violence victims' rights. It may be more accurate to say that radical feminism declined in this decade, to be replaced by a broad deradicalized movement that moved away from social critiques, confrontation, and sex wars toward a reform of marriage and the family. Betty Friedan, an early leader of the women's movement in the 1960s, wrote *The Second Stage* (1981) advocating this broader social movement.

Abortion

Abortion had always been a controversial issue in American history, but the U.S. Supreme Court's decision in the landmark *Roe v. Wade* (1973) case aroused an antiabortion or pro-life lobby that contributed to the defeat of the ERA. Reagan had been elected with pro-life voter support, and he was personally opposed to abortion as well as creation of human embryos for stem cell medical research. This contributed to the Republicans' gender gap in which a majority of feminists and single women voted for Democrats in 1980. Reagan's nomination of Sandra Day O'Connor to the Supreme Court in 1981 also aroused the antiabortion lobby. But in 1985, Secretary of Health and Human Services Otis R. Bowen banned federal funding of organizations that counseled or performed abortions. In

Sandra Day O'Connor was the first woman to serve as an associate justice of the U.S. Supreme Court, 1981. (U.S. Supreme Court)

1987, Randall Terry, a born-again Christian conservative from Binghamton, New York, formed Operation Rescue, an antiabortion group that used civil disobedience and direct action to picket, protest, and block access to reproductive service medical clinics. Jerry Falwell, Pat Robertson, and other Religious Right leaders endorsed Terry's controversial demonstrations even after abortion clinics were firebombed and four doctors were murdered by antiabortion extremists.

The Supreme Court's decision in *Webster v. Reproductive Health Services* (1989) began a trend to limit women's rights to abortion. However, when Florida proposed limits, polls showed that 60 percent of Floridians opposed further restrictions; the state supreme court ruled the state constitution protected abortion under the right-to-privacy clause and overturned a state law requiring notification of parents when teenage daughters seek abortions. Congressmen began to defend abortion rights when membership in abortion-rights organizations skyrocketed following the Webster case. New York mayor Rudolph Giuliani promised he would defend the right to choose, prompting a rebuke from Cardinal John O'Connor according to *Time* magazine on October 23, 1989. Since then the pro-life lobby focused on presidential appointments that might change the membership of the Supreme Court and lead to repeal of the *Roe v. Wade* decision. Abortion quickly became a key issue defining conservatives and liberals in the 1980s.

Economic Opportunities

Economic opportunities for American women expanded dramatically in the 1980s. Women accounted for 34 percent of the new doctors and 42 percent of the new lawyers. Incomes for women ages 23 to 34 rose 62 percent by 1990. Union members, who earned as much as 30 percent more than their nonunion counterparts, were increasingly female, especially in the professions of education, health, accounting, food processing, garment trades, and office or retail jobs. The Equal Employment Opportunities Commission (EEOC) was criticized for its sluggish response to complaints of gender discrimination, but many state courts were more open to these arguments and the public approved of affirmative action. With more education, more women found jobs in a wider variety of industries, and by 2000, the national labor force participation rate for women peaked at 67.3 percent. However, as manufacturing jobs declined in the 1980s from 32 percent to less than 25 percent, fewer families had health insurance provided by their employer. More Americans, especially women, worked in small firms less likely to offer these fringe benefits. Many women also worked as temporary or contract workers or were self-employed, usually with no health insurance (Swartz 2006). Working mothers spent an average of $3,000 per child per year on day care, but conservatives opposed Congressional proposals to expand Head Start programs, increase tax credits for poor families with three or more children, and require states to set standards for child-care facilities as *Time* magazine noted on October 16, 1989.

The "F" Word: Making Feminism Relevant

American women made impressive progress by the 1980s, so much so that many young women took for granted equality in banking and credit; fairer treatment in divorce, rape, paternity, child support and gender discrimination court cases; and in equal employment opportunities. That all these gains were the result of the women's liberation movement in the 1960s and 1970s was overlooked. "Feminist" was a label young women shunned because, to many in the more conservative era of the 1980s, it evoked the image of the bra-burning angry radical

Women and the New Right

Since Barry Goldwater's presidential campaign in 1964, Republican candidates had benefited from thousands of grassroots conservative women meeting at coffee klatches, ringing doorbells, and gathering signatures. Phyllis Schlafly's book *A Choice Not an Echo* (1964) rallied many women to right-wing causes. This activism sprang from the conviction that America was in a moral and social decline. Alienated by the 1960s liberalism and what they considered the 1970s radical feminist movement, women of all ages by the 1980s turned to the Republican Party and to their churches. They would influence race relations, reproductive rights, homosexuality, the mass media, school curricula, the role of the family, and other spheres beyond electoral politics. Schlafly's STOP-ERA grassroots campaign against the Equal Rights Amendment in 1971 mobilized conservative women, especially in the fast-growing Sunbelt states of the South and the West. By 1980, these suburban warriors transformed the party of Lincoln from the moderate Republicanism of the northeastern Wall Street establishment into the ultraconservative party of Ronald Reagan. Concerned about permissiveness, welfare fraud, rising crime, and big government, millions of women were inspired by the resurgence of evangelical religion to confront new social and cultural issues. These included abortion, the environment, evolution, sex education, and prayer in schools.

Guided by Jerry Falwell's Moral Majority, Pat Robertson's Christian Coalition, televangelists, and right-wing radio commentators such as Rush Limbaugh, these Christian women formed the social base of the New Right. The Institute on Religion and Democracy, a conservative Washington think tank, was founded in 1981 to oppose the more liberal National Council of Churches, an alliance of 35 mainstream Protestant denominations. Two nonpartisan charitable organizations frequently clashed over the social and moral impact of these public issues.

Many women won local or state elected offices in places as diverse as Orange County, California; the middle-class suburbs of Scottsdale and Phoenix, Arizona; Fort Worth and Dallas, Texas; and Colorado Springs, Colorado. After the Cold War and the fading of anticommunism in the 1980s, they focused on big government, liberalism, feminism, and gay rights as barriers to creating a God-centered America. In 1984, Democrat Walter Mondale lost to President Ronald Reagan despite Mondale's historic choice of a female running mate, New York congresswoman Geraldine Ferraro. Reagan won only 47 percent of the female vote in 1980, but in Sunbelt states married women, unlike single women, continued to turn to Republican candidates. Despite much debate about the "gender gap" Republicans faced in winning the votes of women, the Roper poll in 1984 found 43 percent of women called themselves conservative and only 22 percent chose the label liberal. The election of vice president George Bush in 1988 to the presidency also suggested that the gender gap may have been more apparent than real.

women's libbers. Television responded to the new acceptance of feminism with successful women who were journalists on sitcoms (*Murphy Brown*) or lawyers and police officers on dramatic shows (*LA Law* and *Hill Street Blues*).

Taking advantage of new opportunities, women delayed marriage and child-birth to complete their educations and establish their careers. The baby boom-let of the late 1980s reflected daughters of the baby boom who had their first baby later in life, often in their early thirties while the "biological clock" was still ticking. They expected equal pay for equal work, legal abortion and birth control, affordable child care, and laws and workplace policies that protected them from sexual harassment and discrimination.

Since 1972, they had Title IX guarantees of equal funds for female school and college sports, and women could even compete in the staid Boston Marathon. This new view of women as athletes had a profound impact on society because the jogging craze took place in this context of feminist awareness. The physically fit woman was no longer seen as an exceptional or socially deviant super-woman but rather as an ordinary woman who was fit, healthy, and beautiful. Popular books like Gayle Barron's *The Beauty of Running* (1980), Liz Sloane and Ann Kramer's *Running: The Women's Handbook* (1985), and Manfred Steffny and Rosemary Breuer's *Running for Women: A Basic Guide for the New Runner* (1985) pointed the way to physical fitness and femininity for millions of recreational runners in the 1980s. Another offshoot of feminism in the 1980s was ecofeminism, a social movement linking environmentalism and feminist values. Its proponents linked the oppression of woman with the degradation of nature.

The long-term relevance of 1980s feminism to American society became clear in 2002 when the secretary of education formed a panel to assess the impact of Title IX. Its advocates maintained that this landmark law contributed greatly to creating opportunities for women. In 1971, 294,000 girls participated in high school sports, but 2.7 million did so in 2001, and the number of women on college teams increased by two-thirds. This change influenced higher education overall because, in 1972, only 44 percent of all bachelor's degrees went to women compared to 57 percent in 2000. Over this same period, women earning medical degrees rose from 9 percent to 41 percent; dental degrees rose from 1 percent to 40 percent; and law degrees rose from 7 percent to 46 percent. As Rita J. Simon claimed in *Sporting Equality: Title IX Thirty Years Later,* it was no longer unusual to see women in positions of power and leadership in all walks of life.

Transformations

The impact of feminism is difficult to overestimate. Its advocates transformed American society and made possible careers for women in almost every profession and occupation. However, its critics transformed American politics and helped the Republican Party to dominate all three branches of the government. Before the rise of the Christian Right, Phyllis Schlafly's hostility to feminism created a grassroots network, the Eagle Forum, in 1972, which provided an

STOP-ERA leader Phyllis Schlafly speaks at a rally in the Illinois State Capitol rotunda on June 19, 1978. (Bettmann/Corbis)

alternative to the liberal and moderate Eastern establishment wing of the Republican Party. By 1971, her STOP-ERA organization rallied opposition in the states to the ERA passed by Congress in 1972. Defending women's privileges and "pro-family" values, Schlafly led a women's crusade against "radical" feminists who she claimed would destroy the American family by support for secularism, abortion, and gay rights. With the decline of communism, social conservatives like Schlafly focused on traditional family values to form one important bloc in the Republican Party. At the same time, liberal activists and feminists erred in dismissing the largely Midwestern conservatives in the STOP-ERA lobby as irrelevant to the ratification process.

In many ways, feminism did win: women serve in the military and the NASA space program, abortion is still a legal right, homophobia is against the law, and women serve on the Supreme Court. Marriage was becoming more egalitarian and husbands were learning to be more sensitive. Despite the failure of ERA to win ratification, state laws and court decisions have achieved most of its goals. Since the 1980s, discrimination on the basis of gender is not only illegal but less common or tolerated. Ellen Willis, a noted feminist writer in New York City, founded the street theater group called No More Nice Girls to protest for pro-choice policies. But by the end of the decade antifeminist warnings proved groundless and radical feminism subsided as women turned from confrontation to reform of American society in what was called Second Wave feminism.

THE STATE OF AMERICAN LABOR

Background

In 1979 President Carter appointed Paul Volcker, former vice president of the Chase Manhattan Bank, as chairman of the Federal Reserve Board (1979–1987). Volcker's restrictive monetary policy to combat inflation imposed a sharp increase in interest rates, which led to a wave of bankruptcies and mass layoffs in basic industries. Employers used the threat of mass unemployment to weaken labor unions and reduce living standards for American workers. By 1982 President Reagan demonstrated that his administration would be hostile to labor unions in his handling of the Professional Air Traffic Controllers Organization (PATCO) strike, and the once-militant AFL-CIO did little to help PATCO air traffic controllers as their leaders were prosecuted and imprisoned. Even 25 years later, the effects of the PATCO strike mark the American labor movement. It was one of the most dramatic acts of union-busting in the 20th century.

The United Auto Workers, which had agreed in 1980 to wage concessions with the almost-bankrupt Chrysler Corporation in exchange for seating UAW president Douglas Fraser on the Chrysler board of directors, had lost its militancy. In 1982 attorney Richard Trumka was elected president of the United Mine Workers of America. Under his cautious leadership, coal miners lost strikes in 1984 and 1987; wages were lowered, working conditions were unsafe, strikers were fired and blacklisted, and West Virginia and Kentucky union miners were forced to work with strikebreakers. Supreme Court and National Labor Relations Board decisions in the 1980s often disappointed labor union members, whose numbers fell from 23.6 percent in 1980 to 19.4 percent in 1984 despite the sharp increase in female union members nationwide. Reagan's choice of a building contractor, Robert J. Donovan as secretary of labor (1981–1985), indicated that the administration would not be sympathetic to unions.

Another change in the state of American labor in the 1980s was the increase in self-employed, middle-class workers or nonpermanent and contract employees with few fringe benefits provided by their employers. This was especially common in the computer industry, accounting, engineering, publishing, and higher education. These service-sector employees often worked for smaller companies that provided less or no health insurance, vacations, or pension

Professional Air Traffic Controllers Organization (PATCO) strike at LaGuardia Airport on July 29, 1981. The walkout was part of a nationwide strike to demand wage increases from the federal government and was the largest strike by federal employees ever. Eleven thousand of the employees were fired on August 5 after failing to return to work under President Ronald Reagan's orders. (Bettmann-UPI/ Corbis)

programs. From 1979 to 2005 the U.S. workforce employed in firms with fewer than 50 employees rose from 37 percent to 44 percent. By 2005, one in four adults ages 25 to 34 and nearly one in five adult's ages 35 to 44 had no health insurance. Finally, by 1987 off-shore or overseas operations took many jobs from U.S. workers. American Airlines hired keypunch operators in Barbados for $2 an hour when American workers earned $8 and $10 an hour for this work. Pier I Imports was the first U.S. company to store inventory records in China, a practice American hospitals followed for storing medical records. Nevertheless, U.S. productivity rose by 3.5 percent in the 1980s and industry as a whole remained about 22 percent of the gross national product (GNP).

The causes for the problems American labor encountered in the 1980s may begin with high unemployment, the loss of high-wage union jobs, and the rise of lower-wage service-sector jobs. Globalization, computer technologies, immigration changes, and the deindustrialization of the nation combined to create an era of economic change and union decline in the 1980s. Labor union membership shrank to levels not seen since 1900. In the name of free market enterprise, conservatives weakened or removed federal regulations that protected workers' rights, health, and safety. President Reagan appointed new members of the National Labor Relations Board who were unsympathetic to unions and a director of the Occupational Health and Safety Administration (OSHA) who had been cited for OSHA violations. The U.S. Supreme Court ruled in three cases that union members may quit the union during a strike without any penalties imposed by the union.

James Earl Carter Jr., president of the United States (1977–1981). (Library of Congress)

As the wealthiest Americans grew richer, about 80 percent of workers saw real wages decline or stagnate, and the gap between the rich and the working class expanded. The steel, mining, rubber, and automotive industries suffered from foreign competition, and many U.S. manufacturers closed plants and moved production to Third World countries with low labor costs. The number of steel workers in the Pittsburgh area fell from 90,000 in 1980 to 44,000 in 1984. By 1982, Japanese auto makers outsold U.S. cars and trucks and opened non-union auto plants in southern states. The 1982 recession, when unemployment skyrocketed to its highest levels since the Great Depression, during Reagan's reduction in social programs, created a flood of out-of-work, homeless,

Jimmy Carter's Unpopularity

Elected in 1976 over President Gerald Ford, Jimmy Carter's administration ended when he was soundly defeated for reelection in 1980 by the conservative Republican governor Ronald W. Reagan of California. President Carter's unpopularity was a result of his humiliating failure to bring the 52 hostages home from the U.S. embassy in Iran, combined with popular resentment of the 1973–1974 gasoline shortages, his plans for energy conservation, inflation, and the declining economy called "stagflation." Turning the Panama Canal over to Panama and Carter's own admission of a malaise in American society outraged Ronald Reagan's conservative supporters and dismayed the public. Republicans criticized Carter's National Energy Plan because it regulated the economy and imposed restrictive environmental laws on business. The Carter administration was marked by vacillation, indecision, and confusion, and it lacked effective communication with the Democratic Congress. Even the loyal Speaker of House Tip O'Neill was offended and ignored by Carter, the most conservative Democrat since Grover Cleveland and whose deregulation and disinterest in labor law reform widened inequality.

Carter's approval rating in 1980 polls was the lowest of any modern president because the public was dissatisfied with his "era of limits" as interest rates soared to 20 percent and inflation reached 17 percent. His appointment of Paul Volcker in 1979 as Federal Reserve chairman resulted in the 1981–1982 recession and a postwar high unemployment rate of 10.8 percent. Volcker's policies lowered inflation from 13 percent in 1980 to 4 percent in 1982, and the U.S. economy was recovering gradually during Carter's 1980 reelection campaign. But Carter faced a strong challenge in the Democratic primaries by Senator Ted Kennedy, and the moderate Illinois Republican congressman John Anderson's independent campaign drew away 5.7 million (or 8 percent) of the popular votes. Political scientists believe more voters in 1980 voted against Carter (35.5 million votes, or 41 percent) than for Reagan (43.9 million votes, or 50.7 percent). In the Electoral College, Reagan had 489 votes, with 49 for Carter and none for Anderson. Carter was the first president since Herbert Hoover in 1932 to lose an election for a second term.

Although Carter was an evangelical Christian, the expanding Christian conservatives, or New Right, believed the American family was under attack by liberals. Along with conservative Catholics, the Moral Majority born-again Christians and many blue-collar Democrats supported the optimistic free market ideology of the folksy Ronald Reagan. Jimmy Carter's presidency seemed to end in failure, but his place in history is yet to be decided. Later Carter wrote books, promoted housing for the poor, human rights, and democratic elections around the world. He won the 2002 Nobel Peace Prize but aroused controversy when he wrote a book, *Palestine: Peace Not Apartheid* (2006), that suggested that the American-Israel Political Action Committee prevented criticism in the United States of Israel for its harsh treatment of the Palestinians.

and mentally ill people living on the streets. Although prosperity returned in 1984, unions never recovered their confidence or political clout.

The 1981 PATCO strike helped to shape labor relations during the decade. When federal air traffic controllers began a nationwide strike in August 1981, President Reagan fired most of the 11,345 controllers who defied a back-to-work order. This was a shock to organized labor because the Professional Air Traffic Controllers Organization, unlike most unions, had endorsed Reagan in the 1980 election, and Reagan was a former union president. Over the objections of a delegation of Republican former secretaries of labor, and congressional and airline industry leaders, Reagan fired the strikers, decertified PATCO, and replaced them with military personnel. The nation's air traffic control system did not recover until 1988, and the memory of this strike still haunts the union movement; nevertheless, the public approved Reagan's decisive action.

An optimistic trend during the decade was the increase in female union members in the 1980s, especially in health- and service-sector jobs. The trend, however, was for labor unions to surrender their militancy and for the union leaders to cooperate with corporate management with concessions and freezing wages and benefits. For example, the United Auto Workers (UAW) union leaders supported the bailout of Chrysler in 1980, which established a pattern of concessions and give-backs which continued in UAW contracts in 1984 with Ford, General Motors, and Caterpillar, the heavy equipment company. These contracts also gave union officials some management rights of union workers. The AFL and UMWA leaders followed this "corporatism" and concessions policy which gradually caused thousands of miners and auto workers to lose their jobs throughout the 1980s. Overall, about 32 million industrial workers lost their jobs from 1970 to 1990. At the same time, America's oldest industry, agriculture, also suffered foreign competition and a credit crisis as Midwest farms went into debt or bankruptcy.

Another significant change in the 1980s was the internationalization of the United States, not by the traditional expansion of American business and culture to other nations but by globalization inside the United States. Many European, Japanese, and Middle Eastern investors purchased American stocks, bonds, real estate, and corporations. The Firestone, Brooks Brothers, and 20th Century Fox companies were owned by foreign investors, and millions of American workers were paid by foreign companies. Consumers were accustomed to buying "American" products made all over the world. From Levi blue jeans and Nike athletic shoes to automobiles, customer service, and televisions, American jobs and products in the age of globalization were increasingly offshore and outsourced. At the same time, an enormous surge of immigration brought millions of people to the U.S. surpassing the peak years of European immigration in the early 20th century. This helped to increase the U.S. population from 226,542,399 in 1980 to 248,718,302 in 1990.

The nation changed in many ways from 1980 to 1984. The Reagan Revolution continued to the end of his term in 1989, but the first four years of the Reagan era was a transformation, the culmination of a decade-long ideological shift. This change in attitudes "embodied a deep suspicion of the public sphere, finding the public purpose of the old-style Rustbelt liberals both corrupt and counter-productive" (Schulman 2003, 220). Reagan hit organized labor hard, withdrawing government support in the unions' struggles with big business; weakening federal agency regulation of industry's health, safety, and environmental rules; and increasing deregulation overall. Businesses now had more responsibility for our economic life as well as our national social and cultural life. Free markets and internationalism were equated with economic growth, and protectionism was equated with isolationism and economic stagnation.

Tax cuts in 1981 gave corporations tax breaks and lower taxes on gifts, inheritances, and capital gains. More tax cuts in 1986 lowered the maximum rate on individual income to 28 percent but only 35 percent on business income. It was more difficult to reach and remain in the middle class because the distribution of wealth favored the wealthy. However, the severe recession of 1981 was followed by the economic recovery of 1983, a period of unprecedented growth. Many Americans believed Ronald Reagan's promise of prosperity would trickle down to even the poorest.

The Automotive Industry in Transition

In 1980, General Motors (GM) was the largest employer and largest corporation in the United States. However, by the mid-1980s GM and Detroit, the center of the American automotive industry, faced difficult times. Competition from Europe and Japan continued to lure American buyers away from the Big Three U.S. automakers: GM, Ford, and Chrysler. Smaller, safer, cheaper, more fuel-efficient imported cars out-performed American vehicles and dominated the domestic market. Globalization, based on the idea that the free market provided lower-priced imported products, translated into fewer industrial sector jobs, especially for Michigan auto workers. Postwar prosperity, interstate highways connecting new suburban communities, and cheap gas prices had created a boom in the U.S. automobile industry that permitted the UAW to win contracts from major automakers with high wages, improved benefits, and better conditions for union members. This ended in the 1980s.

Imported compact cars surpassed Detroit's gas-guzzling standard large cars in sales at a time when gas prices first rose over one dollar per gallon. The recalls of downsized American cars; the restructuring or closing of GM, Ford, and Chrysler plants; and layoffs of workers shook consumer and investor confidence. Even before 1980, UAW complacency and union members' loss of confidence in

Japanese Cars

In the 1980s, U.S. automakers' share of the domestic car market dropped from 83 percent to 67 percent. Japanese corporations built nonunion plants in America, first the Honda plant in Ohio in 1982, then Nissan in Tennessee in 1983, Toyota in Kentucky in 1988, and Subaru in Indiana in 1989. Hollywood depicted the culture clash of American workers and Japanese managers in the comedy *Gung Ho* (1986), but these problems were overcome. Japan produced cheaper, more popular cars and trucks that outperformed American cars in reliability, safety, and comfort.

By 1980, the top automakers in the world were GM, Toyota, and Nissan, with Ford and Chrysler dropping out of the Big Three. The Honda Accord became the best-selling passenger car in the United States in 1989, and by the decade's end, Japan surpassed the U.S. as the largest automaker in the world. Americans told themselves a Toyota assembled in Kentucky was almost an American car, but few were convinced. By 1987, about 30 percent of new cars sold in the United States were imported. As a result, some economists claimed that Japan could overtake the United States as an economic superpower.

their union leaders became apparent as Hollywood depicted in the comedy *Blue Collar* (1978). Detroit's dominance of the industry slipped away in the 1980s as President Reagan and Federal Reserve chairman Paul Volcker advocated mass consumption in a new free market global economy. By 1981, the French automaker Renault purchased AMC, and in 1982, German and Japanese automakers opened nonunion U.S. assembly plants outside of Michigan to produce the well-designed, innovative cars and small trucks that American motorists found irresistible.

In the 1980 campaign, Ronald Reagan promised to restrict Japanese auto imports, despite his free market ideology, and in 1981, Japan was persuaded to limit their exports to 1.68 million vehicles. The Reagan administration blamed the American loss in automobile production on unions and overregulation. They claimed Detroit vehicles were hampered by air bags, pollution control devices, and strict safety standards. However, this trend continued throughout the Reagan era, and under President George H. W. Bush (1989–1993), both the unemployment rate and the long-term unemployment rate increased, especially in the auto, steel, mining, and other heavy industries. In the 1980s, job creation also declined for the first time since 1933, and most new jobs were in retail or other service-sector employment rather than manufacturing or management.

The Hormel Strike

When workers at the Hormel meatpacking plant in Austin, Minnesota, faced drastic wage and benefits cuts in 1984, their local union went on strike for fair wages and safer conditions. The arduous, dangerous job of butchering hogs on a fast-moving assembly line caused many injuries to workers. As depicted in the film *American Dream,* which won an Academy award in 1990 for best documentary, the 1,500 families in this typical Midwestern town faced economic ruin. Although their national union, the United Food and Commercial Workers (UFCW), refused to support a strike, the local union workers walked out of the plant and designed a consumer boycott of Hormel Spam, chili, sausage, and other meat products. After 10 months of picketing, consumer boycotts, and civil disobedience, little was accomplished (Hage and Klauda 1989).

By 1986, the UFCW leaders declared the strike over and made important concessions to the Hormel Company on health, pension, vacation benefits, and work rules. With the protection of National Guard troops, 400 of the 800 strikers crossed the union picket line along with new replacement (or scab) workers to reopen the Hormel plant in Austin. The strike of the decade ended in total failure for the rank-and-file workers, and the bitterness still divides this Midwestern town. It was an example of the few gains and many losses American unions suffered in the 1980s as the new postindustrial economy demanded lower costs, increased productivity, and increasing automation by computerized equipment. In the 1980s, big business and big labor executives negotiated in their own best interests, and the workers paid the heavy costs.

Unions in Retreat

The American labor movement supported the New Deal and was a partner with big government and big business during World War II. But in 1947, the Republican assault on unions began with passage of the Taft–Hartley Act over President Truman's veto. Once-powerful unions were hit hard in the 1980s by antilabor legislation, economic turmoil, and the decline in morale and union membership due to deregulation of industries and government hostility. Union membership declined from 34 percent in 1954 to 16 percent in 1991. By 1989, the Supreme Court decided that the enforcement of immigration laws was more important than protecting the right of workers to organize a union. The Immigration Reform and Control Act of 1986 made it a crime to use fraudulent documents to get a job, but it was not a crime to fire a worker for advocating or organizing a union. This encouraged employers to hire the 8 million illegal immigrants in the United States who could not complain about low pay or unsafe conditions by appeal to the National Labor Relations Board.

Declining economic conditions and resistance to unions by government and private employers, especially after President Reagan fired unionized PATCO air traffic controllers in 1981, reduced strikes in the 1980s. This unexpected step against one of the few unions that had endorsed Reagan encouraged businesses to fire prounion and striking workers. Work stoppages fell steadily from 235 in 1979 to 51 in 1989. On the other hand, the penalties for unfair labor practices were so light and enforcement so lax that many employers violated these laws and fired or blacklisted employees. Right-to-work laws in the South and West hampered union organizing, and influential conservative Christian groups were generally hostile to labor unions and supported state right-to-work laws. Ironically, many Americans blamed liberals, unions, and bureaucrats for unemployment, inflation, and poverty. Labor historians have noted how the portrayal of unions in the media influenced American attitudes about unions. In the 1980s, labor unions were a subject Hollywood usually ignored or ridiculed, all of which created a very hostile atmosphere for U.S. labor unions (*Boston Globe,* July 31, 2006).

The heavily industrial states, once the pride of the nation, became known as the Rustbelt when factories closed in the 1980s, and the UAW smashed token Japanese and European compact cars in futile protests. In response, some labor unions attempted coalition-building with other progressive activists in the labor reform, women's rights, civil rights, and gay rights movements. More women entered the labor force to compensate for declining family incomes, and as a result more women became union members. This is reflected in the fact that the largest labor union in the United States was the National Education Association (NEA) with 2.8 million members, and the fastest growing union was the Service Employees International Union (SEIU) with 1.8 million members, many low-paid female or immigrant workers.

In September 1981, Lane Kirkland, the president of the AFL-CIO, told a Washington, D.C., Solidarity Day audience of 400,000 that President Reagan was wrong in claiming that he spoke for all working people in America. Tax cuts benefiting the wealthy, attacks on Social Security, monetary policies causing high interest rates, and indifference to social justice were not in the American tradition. Kirkland quoted the American Federation of Labor founder Samuel Gompers: "More school houses and less jails; more books and less arsenals; more learning and less vice; more constant work and less crime; more leisure and less greed; more justice and less revenge" (Livesay 1978). As labor's fortunes changed, union leaders and rank-and-file workers searched for new solutions. However, the liberal answers to these problems—progressive taxation on the wealthiest, higher minimum wage laws, enforcement of the Wagner Act recognizing the right to form unions, and increased federal reimbursements to states and cities—were out of fashion in the 1980s.

Labor's Last Hurrah: The Pittston Strike

In September 1989, 98 miners in the United Mine Workers of America (UMWA) occupied the Pittston Coal Company's preparation plant in Cardo, Virginia, beginning a 10-month strike. Soon the strike spread to other coal fields in southwestern Virginia, West Virginia, and eastern Kentucky. Wildcat strikes by union miners in sympathy with the strikers and mass civil disobedience against court injunctions broke out. Violent confrontations erupted between the miners and nonstriking workers, the U.S. Marshalls, and Virginia state police. The UMWA complained that the police, courts, and media were biased. The media ignored the strike or focused on only violent incidents rather than the substantive safety issues in the strike. The promanagement trend in labor law enforcement combined with national union leaders' loss of militancy and preference for concessions to retain union control offered little hope for the striking coal miners.

For 10 months thousands of the 10,000 strikers and their supporters were arrested and fined until the Bush administration pressured the participants to settle on a new contract. Eventually the Supreme Court in the 1994 *UMWA v. Bagwell* case relieved most strikers of the $64 million fines, although many lost their jobs and health and pension benefits. This strike was a clear lesson to people in those chronically impoverished mining communities that state and federal government supported the corporations, the National Labor Relations Board was impotent, and the employers were bolder, and these facts alienated many workers from their government.

Labor's Future

GM once made half the autos sold in America, but by 1990, it sold only one in four. What did this say about the future of U.S. manufacturing and labor unionism? To begin, GM and other major manufacturers did not learn how to compete globally because of poor management and poor public policy. Since 1973, total productivity of the U.S. economy increased 70 percent. Managers and executives received the benefits of this wealth rather than the average American workers, which resulted in the most unequal distribution of wages and opportunities since the late-19th century. Automation and relocation of plants meant manufacturing would no longer have as many well-paid jobs as it once did, but to stay viable, the United States needed a coherent industrial policy, such as the policies Germany, Japan, China, and Korea had created. Many economists believed a radical revision of management and government free-market ideology was required to revive American manufacturing. Labor unions like the SEIU grew stronger and increased wages in the expanding service sector, much of which could not be transferred offshore, but they could not restore American manufacturing. The service sector now accounts for two-thirds of the U.S. economy, and many Americans were diminished by this change. The film *Rising Son* (1990) depicts workers at a family-owned Pennsylvania factory in the 1980s who lose their jobs to downsizing when a multinational corporation buys the factory. This American tragedy was repeated in many industrial communities across the nation.

The United States was once a country where people made things in mill towns, factory towns, and mining towns. When America changed in the 1980s, once-proud towns had only vacant storefronts, empty streets, and wounded people in fragmented communities. The nature of work was transformed by deindustrialization, automation, and downsizing. The workplace became different as more workers tended machines rather than worked cooperatively with fellow workers on the assembly lines or in work shops. Intent on high profits with lower costs, management won concessions from union management and demanded higher productivity and reductions in health and pension benefits of union workers. Communities based on one industry, such as Detroit, Youngstown, or Homestead, suffered the most in the 1980s. Their unemployed workers retrained, found service jobs, or migrated to the Sunbelt states, but few prospered. Unions had driven out most radicals in the 1950s, and the new generation of union leaders, like Lane Kirkland, overlooked organizing new workers in new industries; as a result, union membership shrank.

Michael Moore used black humor in his devastating documentary *Roger & Me* (1989) to depict the aftermath in Flint, Michigan, when General Motors closed 11 auto plants in 1986. Moore, the son of a Flint autoworker, took his audience on a journey to the shattered American dream in a city filled with abandoned homes, boarded up stores, 25 percent unemployment, and record rates of suicide, alcoholism, spouse abuse, evictions, homelessness, and violent crime. Although car sales rose steadily since 1983 and GM enjoyed record profits, the company built new plants in Mexico and Asia, and invested in Isuzu and Toyota, and, as Moore repeatedly demonstrates, made 35,000 highly paid auto workers and their families in the Rustbelt poor. The movie title refers to Moore's futile quest from yacht club to country club to GM headquarters for an interview with GM's CEO Roger Smith.

SOCIAL MOVEMENTS OF THE 1980s

Something for Everyone

Social movements of various stripes emerged in the 1980s as Americans became more willing to cooperate with like-minded people to achieve some social change. Not since the 1960s did reformers find the public so eager to promote the civic goals they found desirable. Christians joined the Moral Majority or the Christian Coalition to find God and bring their own morality into the public sphere. Operation Rescue and other antiabortion organizations recruited many of these born-again Christians to protect the unborn. Others sought salvation in such cults as the Moonies and Scientology. Working out was much like a religion for increasing numbers of Americans seeking personal growth in physical fitness, health, and beauty.

For many people, protecting nature became a new faith as environmentalism and the anti-Nuke and animal rights crusades appeared and the ranks of the Sierra Club, Audubon Society, and Appalachian Mountain Club swelled. Some extreme defenders of Mother Nature engaged in ecoterrorism to impose their views, and the Unabomber was one example of how far a solitary fanatic could go. Those opposed to South Africa's apartheid system of racial segregation found a leader in the Rev. Jesse Jackson, who also founded the Rainbow Coalition to include progressive politics and social justice in politics. The emergence of the Gay and Lesbian Liberation movement precipitated the homophobic Save the Children movement, which led to a national witch hunt for sexual predators that evolved into the decade's most divisive controversy called the Culture Wars. More than ever before, Americans from all walks of life were willing to join organizations and volunteer for crusades to save their society or even the world. By 1989, membership in abortion-rights organizations dramatically increased, and public funding of day care services for working mothers became popular.

Environmental and Public Health Issues

The government environmental regulation that began in the 1960s resulted from broad public concerns about the deteriorating environment. In 1965, a scientific advisory board warned President Johnson that increasing atmospheric carbon dioxide could led to climate changes by the end of the century. The landmark bills President Nixon signed to promote clean air and water had bipartisan support in Congress. President Carter also had a pro-environment record and added millions of acres of wilderness land to federal control. Scientists warned that unrestrained industries were endangering the environment and must be halted. But in the 1980s, much opposition to federal regulation developed, and support grew for allowing free market forces to deal with environmental issues. In 1988, the United Nations created the Intergovernmental Panel on Climate Change, but many scoffed at this as alarmist or junk science.

This clash of views underlay the Reagan era debate and provoked resistance by many corporations and conservatives to the reality of climate change and environmental degradation. However, it precipitated a new and broader movement to protect nature. The basic issue was the role of government and whether cost-analysis should be applied to social values. Public concern about catastrophic disasters included the degrading environment, nuclear weapons, and nuclear energy. Congress responded to the growing interest in the preservation of architecturally or culturally significant buildings and historic sites with the Tax Reform Act of 1986. By 1988, the National Park Service reported that investment in historic properties amounted to $12 billion since 1976 and involved 19,000 properties.

In a similar way, the 1980s saw much contention over public health. Because poor people produce poor children, they required public funds for health services they could not afford. Lower socioeconomic groups were more likely to smoke; less likely to have good diet, exercise, and hygiene habits; and less likely to have preventive medical care or health insurance. Inequality in wealth, generated by the free market forces that conservatives valued, bred inequality in health. Since the New Deal, the government took steps to remedy this inequality, but President Reagan ended the New Deal era abruptly in 1980. This also led to much controversy over the proper role of government in the environment and in public health in the era of AIDS, sexually transmitted diseases, and other epidemics. Confidence declined in every form of authority—the government, universities, military, and business. Since the 1970s, whenever a nuclear reactor was proposed in the United States, local voters, students, environmentalists, politicians, and scientists organized protests. Massive civil disobedience protests by the Clamshell Alliance (1976–1989) opposed construction of a nuclear power plant in Seabrook, New Hampshire. Despite assurances by experts, the demonstrators cited the radioactivity leaking from even the best designed power plants and lack of safe evacuation plans in case of an accident or sabotage. The Seabrook Station was completed in 1989, but 10 years overdue and much over budget, at a cost of $7 billion by the bankrupt utility company. On Long Island, New York, Sound and Hudson against Atomic Development (SHAD) and the Abalone Alliance in California made similar efforts to protect the environment from nuclear radiation.

Another public issue in the 1980s was smog, the man-made degradation of air quality from auto emissions, power plants, refineries, chemical plants, and other industrial pollution. Public health agencies estimated that 700–1,500 people per year died prematurely in North American cities due to smog. Los Angeles, Houston, and Washington, D.C., suffered most from smog, which contains ozone, a pollutant harmful to health. In the summer, when warm upper air inhibits vertical circulation over high cities surrounded by hills, smog is trapped in the cities. Many times during the 1980s, air quality was so poor that local television weather forecasts included warnings about smog conditions. Asthma, emphysema, and bronchitis were identified in the 1980s as the most common health threats from smog. The Environmental Protection Agency suggested that reduction of coal-burning industrial plants was the most important remedy to eliminate smog, but little was accomplished until the 1990s. Although Ronald Reagan enjoyed the outdoors, he believed environmental laws hampered the economy. He and Secretary of the Interior James Watt called for deregulation rather than restrictions that would put the United States at an economic disadvantage to other nations.

Since the *New York Times* first used the words greenhouse effect in 1969, and after President Carter declared in 1977 that energy conservation was the moral equivalent of war, conservation became an important public issue in the 1980s.

Today, when the Sierra Club has 800,000 members, and 62 percent of those interviewed in a Gallup Poll in 2006 claimed they worry a great deal about the environment, the environmental movement no longer seems an odd or eccentric fringe group. By 1969, scientists in Boston organized the Union of Concerned Scientists (UCS) to express doubts that technology and science could improve or even save civilization without more democratic control. The large Clamshell Alliance protests in New Hampshire throughout the 1980s led to prolonged Atomic Energy Commission hearings on safety plans. Questions raised included the possible explosion of a nuclear power plant, and sabotage or theft of plutonium to make a bomb. Consumer advocate Ralph Nader, Barry Commoner, and the Sierra Club joined this expanding public debate. The American Society for Environmental History formed in 1975 would address this issue in the 1980s.

In 1980, nuclear power produced only 10 percent of the United States' and the world's electricity, although it was apparent that coal and oil were limited resources. Analysis suggested that radioactive waste from nuclear power plants was the chief health risk, perhaps less than the cancer and lung disease resulting from mining and burning coal or oil. But the Three Mile Island reactor accident in Pennsylvania (1979) and the Chernobyl accident in Ukraine (1986) persuaded government officials to focus on nuclear reactor safety as depicted in the movies *China Syndrome* (1979) and *Silkwood* (1983). Fiction writers and the media also emphasized the problems and dangers of nukes, conflating bombs and reactors, which made the nontechnical public worried but still hopeful that nuclear energy could be produced safely, as President Reagan promised. New fears emerged when scientists coined the term nuclear winter in 1983 to describe the smoke from burning forests or cities after a nuclear war. The bombs and smoke, blocking the sun, could destroy civilization, as Hollywood depicted in the three *Mad Max* movies (1979, 1981, 1985).

Opponents of the environmental movement included the Sagebrush Revolution, a coalition of conservatives; ranchers; hunters; and lumber, gas, and oil industry lobbyists in the western states. By 1979, they persuaded the Nevada legislature to pass a law for state oversight of all public lands and to promote transfer of land from the federal government to the state. Several other western states passed similar laws in the 1980s. President Reagan declared "I am a Sagebrush Rebel" in an August 1980 campaign speech in Utah, joining the backlash against the pro-environment policies of the Carter administration. Utah senator Orrin Hatch introduced a bill in 1980 authorizing states to select any federal or wilderness land for transfer to state ownership, but it failed to pass. The Reagan administration included Secretary James B. Edwards of the Department of Energy (1981–82), who advocated nuclear power rather than solar, wind, or water power and supported plans to sell civilian nuclear reactor wastes for use as military weapons. Other members of the administration doubted the evidence of climate scientists who warned that global warming caused reduction of habitat for polar bears, for example, which foreshadowed catastrophic changes for humans.

No Nukes

On June 12, 1982, 750,000 people rallied in New York's Central Park to protest against nuclear weapons, with appearances by Bruce Springsteen, James Taylor, Linda Ronstadt, and other celebrities. The debate on nuclear proliferation and the threat of nuclear war revolved around the idea that more may be better, and the contention that nations acquiring nuclear weapons will use them to deter threats and maintain peace. In contrast, many argued more may be worse, contending that risk of nuclear war increased because new nuclear states lack organizational control of the weapons. The opponents of nuclear weapons and nuclear energy faced an uphill battle in the 1980s. Even in the wake of the Three Mile Island accident in March 1979, Republican congressman David Stockman, who was soon to become President Reagan's Office of Management and Budget director, denounced a proposed moratorium on building new nuclear reactors.

Demonstrators march to Central Park in New York City on June 12, 1982, to join with 750,000 other advocates of the nuclear freeze movement. (Lee Frey/Authenticated News/Getty Images)

Underground Test Protests

Since the United States used the first atomic weapons on Japan to end World War II in 1945, the public had been concerned about this devastating technology. Hydrogen bombs in the 1950s only increased concerns. More than 2,000 nuclear tests were conducted worldwide since the first nuclear bomb was designed in World War II. Later radioactive fallout from aboveground tests was a cause for much concern in the 1980s, but the U.S. government did not formulate a public health response. Since 1963, the long-term health hazards of testing nuclear weapons underground also had been a focus of political protests after the Limited Test Ban Treaty (1963) and when more limits were accepted by the United States and Russia in 1976. However, France continued atmospheric tests until 1974, and China until 1980. Nuclear radiation fallout spread by winds remained a serious issue, and underground tests were not considered much safer. Eight countries (United States, Russia, Great Britain, France, China, Pakistan, India, and Israel) possessed about 30,000 nuclear weapons, most of them (over 90 percent) in the United States and Russia. At least 44 other nations could build nuclear bombs, and the main dangers were accidental launching, false alarms, malfunction, and theft of weapons by terrorists.

In a March 1983 speech, President Reagan described Russia as an "Evil Empire" and advocated the use of nuclear weapons for American defense. He promoted his Strategic Defense Initiative (known as Star Wars), but for political and technical reasons his controversial program was not funded in full. The National Academy of Sciences and the American Physical Society doubted Stars Wars could work, and antinuclear activists increased their protests. In June 1982, 750,000 protestors gathered in New York's Central Park while the United Nations held a special session on ending the arms race, and 2.3 million Americans signed antinuke petitions. *Time* magazine's cover story on June 3, 1985, posed the question on many American minds, "Who Has the Bomb, the Nuclear Threat is Spreading." But Stars Wars advocates appropriated the no nukes and nuclear freeze language for their own purposes, and the movement gradually faded despite films like *The Day After* (1983) and *Amerika* (1987) that raised public awareness. Still the arms control advocates formed the U.S. Comprehensive Test Ban Coalition in 1985 with peace, labor, environmental and other groups. The Physicians for Social Responsibility lobbied Congress in 1986 for a moratorium on testing if the Soviet Union agreed to on-site inspection. Annual demonstrations at the Nevada Test Site attracted 14,000 people in 1988 when 4,000 nonviolent protestors were arrested for civil disobedience.

The end of the Cold War in 1990 and the dissolution of the Soviet Union in 1991 resulted in curtailment of nuclear testing, the end of production of new nuclear weapons, and reduced stockpiled weapons by half in the 1990s. The problem that Secretary of Defense Richard Cheney noted was environmental protection of former nuclear sites and the security of aging nuclear weapons in the United States

Continued on next page

Underground Test Protests, Continued

and former Soviet states. In 1992, President Bush approved a moratorium on testing as part of a broad arms control program. Stockpile stewardship was used to
ensure the reliability of the U.S. arsenal without testing, and U.S. intelligence
agencies monitored nuclear weapons in other nations. However, the effectiveness
of these methods was unknown and the increased rate of cancer and other diseases from all nuclear fallout had not been studied in the 1980s.

He claimed it would legitimize "half-baked and unsubstantiated conclusions being shamelessly propagated by the windmill and woodstove people" (Greenya
and Urban 1986, 46).

The No Nukes movement was dismissed by conservative groups such as the
College Republicans as an eccentric lobby of communists and unrealistic paci-

*During his national security speech on March 23, 1983, President Ronald Reagan
speaks to the nation regarding the Strategic Defense Initiative, proposing intensive
research on a space-based antiballistic missile defense system (popularly known as
"Star Wars") that would destroy Soviet missiles before they reached their target.
(Ronald Reagan Library)*

fists, but a 1983 FBI investigation found the No Nukes groups had no link with the Soviet Union. Beginning in New England town meetings, local governments called for an immediate bilateral halt to testing, production, and deployment of American and Soviet weapons. Polls found more than half of Americans supported a freeze as the Reagan administration revealed a militant anticommunist foreign policy. This movement gained greater credibility in May 1983 when the U.S. Catholic bishops condemned the nuclear arms race as immoral. Even Hollywood proved to be timely in its representation of social history. *Testament* (1983) depicted a small town dealing with a nuclear holocaust, and *Silkwood* (1983) revealed workaday life in an Oklahoma nuclear energy plant. The gas leak in Bhopal, India, that killed 3,400 people in 1984 shocked many Americans and was the cover story for *Time* magazine on December 17, 1984, "India's Disaster, the Night of Death, a Global Worry." The Chernobyl nuclear plant disaster in 1986 also made thoughtful people reconsider the dangers of nuclear power. Public pressure had some effect; by 1989, Secretary of Energy James D. Watkins (1989–1993) announced plans to improve environmental protection and waste management facilities and created the Office of Environmental Restoration. He also reported to Congress in 1992 that for the first time since 1945 the United States was not building any nuclear weapons. But doubts about an accidental nuclear war remained, as seen in the movie *War Games* (1983), when a teenage hacker and a sophisticated computer almost start World War III.

Animal Rights Movement

The animal rights movement, a grassroots campaign for humane treatment and protection of all animals, took many forms in the 1980s. Originating in the Society for the Prevention of Cruelty to Animals (SPCA) in London (1824), Philadelphia (1867), and Boston (1868), and with the American Humane Association (1892), this worldwide crusade of concerned people lobbied Congress to pass the Animal Welfare Act (1966). In 1982 the International Whaling Commission banned commercial whaling by 1986, and mistreatment of animals in the rodeo, zoo, and circus also came under more criticism. The Revlon Company responded to consumer pressure in 1987 by ending its cosmetics tests on research animals. Colorado State University introduced the first ethics course at a U.S. veterinary school in 1982.

Peter Singer, author of *Animal Liberation* (1975), was considered the father of the modern animal rights movement, especially for apes and monkeys. He and author Tom Regan argued against commercial hunting and breeding animals for food or experimentation, and proposed a vegetarian diet as more ethical because at least 10 billion animals were killed each year in the United States for food. Leather clothing was also condemned by the most ardent members of People for the Ethical Treatment of Animals (PETA), an animal rights organization founded in Virginia in 1980. PETA attracted headlines by undercover investigations of National Institutes of Health (NIH) primate laboratories in 1981, and for public demonstrations against Kentucky Fried Chicken, McDonald's, Procter & Gamble, General Motors, and university labs. PETA was best known for its "I'd Rather Go Naked Than Wear Fur" campaigns in which celebrities appeared partially nude to protest against fur clothing. Some members joined the Animal Liberation Front to engage in ecoterrorism to free or protect animals in the United States and other nations. A sentimental account of the cruelty chimps faced in military research was seen in the movie *Project X* (1987).

Efforts to protect wild animals and their natural habitat were recognized by Congress in the Endangered Species Act (1974), but this law was frustrated by Secretary of the Environment James Watt, who refused to add any animals to the list of endangered species. Ranchers, hunters, and members of the Sagebrush Rebellion also opposed these efforts. However, the grey wolf was reintroduced successfully to Yellowstone National Park, and the California condor and the bald eagle populations recovered by 1990 due to federal and state protection programs. California voters approved a 1990 law protecting mountain lions, which numbered 6,000 in the state by 1988. Other groups attempted to protect grizzly bears, mustangs, and burros on federal land. One indication of the environmental impact on wildlife was in 1985 when the U.S. Fish and Wildlife Service reported only 62 million among the major duck species, a decrease by half from 1960.

Antiapartheid Movement

By 1900, European nations divided 90 percent of Africa into colonies, and in 1948, the white-dominated South African government began a policy of racial segregation known as apartheid (apartness) in the Afrikaans language. Black leaders, such as the lawyer Nelson Mandela, who protested this policy in 1962, were imprisoned. In 1976 more than 600 black students were killed in the Soweto and Sharpeville massacres. Violence continued in the 1980s when the South African government allowed white farmers to use arms to protect themselves against the black dissidents. Concern in the United States about this issue had increased since Sen. Robert F. Kennedy visited South Africa in 1966, and President Carter made human rights a focus of his administration. By 1980, apartheid, which L. Ron Hubbard, founder of the Scientology cult, had supported in the 1960s, was a daily topic in the American media. However, Congressman Richard Cheney and other New Right leaders opposed the use of sanctions against apartheid and opposed releasing Nelson Mandela from prison.

In the 1984 presidential campaign, Walter Mondale criticized President Reagan for his opposition to sanctioning South Africa to end apartheid. Under pressure from Congress in 1986, Reagan reversed his position. College students, consumers, and churches in the U.S. called for divestment, or boycotting and withdrawing foreign investments in South Africa. In 1985, the United Nations adopted an international convention against apartheid in sports, a symbolic but effective protest. By 1988, many major American corporations, cities, states, and 155 colleges agreed to divest. The Rev. Jesse Jackson became a leader of this antiapartheid movement in America. The music industry responded in 1985 by forming Artists United Against Apartheid and releasing an album to promote a boycott against South Africa. Paul Simon recorded his album *Graceland* (1986) in South Africa to help end apartheid.

Prime Minister F. W. de Klerk, responding to this international boycott against South Africa's apartheid policy, lifted the ban on the dissident African National Congress and freed Mandela from prison in 1990. Mandela and de Klerk won the Nobel Peace prize in 1993, and Mandela was elected president of South Africa (1994–1999). But the antiapartheid movement in the United States is also significant because it was an example of acting locally and thinking globally, a popular slogan for social movements in the 1980s.

Radical Right and Social Movements

Save the Children was a rallying cry for American conservatives in the late 1970s and 1980s that united parents and bigots against perceived threats to children and teenagers. These threats included predatory pedophiles, pornographers, drug peddlers, terrorists, cultists, and even nursery school teachers. With little evidence that any crimes were committed, anxious parents and conservative Christians urged the local police and government to respond to these dangers. Consequently, politics was often involved in moral and social policy issues in the 1980s. The media and a flood of books based on flawed research warned of the threat to children by gay pedophiles, pornographers, and pimps, and a new federal agency, the National Center on Child Abuse and Neglect (1975), sponsored local and state agencies. The movie *Hardcore* (1979) depicted an anguished father rescuing his daughter from a Los Angeles sex ring.

Following the Save Our Children movement, several high-profile cases of sexual abuse in day care centers captured public attention in the 1980s. Teachers at the McMartin preschool in Manhattan Beach, California, were accused in 1983 of sexually abusing a 2-year-old boy. Under questioning by parents and therapists, other young children described bizarre satanic rituals, mutilating animals, and sex games. Police arrested seven teachers in the longest and most expensive criminal trial in U.S. history. The trial introduced controversial videotapes of the children's testimony, but by 1990 all the teachers were released. This was followed by a similar case in Malden, Massachusetts, in 1984. Three day care teachers were imprisoned but eventually released in 1999 and 2002. Other cases in Maplewood, New Jersey, in 1988 and Edenton, North Carolina, in 1989 discredited these prosecutions due to the lack of physical evidence, prosecutorial misconduct, and questions over whether the children's testimony (called recovered memory) had been tainted by suggestive questioning by psychologists, police, and prosecutors. The charges were later dropped as totally unfounded and were attributed to the hysterical concern about pedophilia, child protection, and homophobia.

Operation Rescue, a radical antiabortion organization founded in 1987 by Randall Terry, was a similar Religious Right–response to social issues in the 1980s. This group used civil disobedience, picketing, and sidewalk counseling to close medical abortion clinics. Like Ralph E. Reed Jr.'s Christian Coalition, Operation Rescue relied on direct mail and adroit manipulation of the media to recruit members and donations.

The appearance of cults also aroused conservatives' fears in the 1980s. The Unification Church made news on July 1, 1982, when their leader, the Rev. Sun Myung Moon, a charismatic Christian from Korea, married 4,150 of his followers at Madison Square Garden in New York City. Two weeks later he was sent to prison for tax fraud. But the Moonies, as his young disciples were known, seemed to be unaffected as they sold flowers at airports and on city streets, and recruited young vulnerable teens and naïve college students into the secretive cult. Similarly, officials of L. Ron Hubbard's (1911–1986) Church of Scientology were convicted of conspiracy for brainwashing teenage recruits in 1979.

With the U.S. economy increasingly dependent on military expenditures in the electronics and aerospace industries in the 1980s, the irrational fear of technology increased. This was responsible for terrorist bombings that began in 1978 when a professor at Northwestern University received a suspicious package that contained a bomb. While opening the package, a campus policeman was injured. This incident was followed in 1979 by a bomb placed on an American Airline plane in Chicago; this bomb failed to explode. The first serious injury was in 1985, when a University of California graduate student in Berkeley lost four fingers and an eye opening a mail package. A California computer store owner was killed by a similar hand-crafted wooden bomb in 1985, and another terrorist bombing occurred in a Salt Lake City computer store in 1987. More bombs followed in 1993 at Yale University until a total of 16 bombs injured 29 and killed 3 people. In 1995, the Unabomber, as the media and police called the ecoterrorist bomber, promised to stop his campaign if his long statement was published. The *New York Times* and *Washington Post* published the Unabomber Manifesto in 1995. It argued that technology was dominating society and enslaving humanity. Acting on information from the bomber's brother, the FBI arrested Theodore Kaczynski in 1996 at his isolated cabin in Montana. He was a former University of California, Berkeley, mathematics professor. Born in Chicago, Ted Kaczynski was a shy, precocious boy who graduated from Harvard (1962) and earned a Ph.D. from the University of Michigan. He had acted alone in the bombings, and he never explained his random antitechnology terrorism when sentenced to life in prison.

Culture Wars

By the 1980s many Americans were afraid of a variety of threats and dissatisfied with liberal policies supported by the Democratic Party. These alienated, socially conservative or middle-of-the-road people believed abortion, affirmative action, civil rights, environmentalism, feminism, gun control, homosexuality, multiculturalism, sex education, and other liberal issues had received too much attention or had gone too far. Agribusiness and manufacturers needed cheap labor and the wealthy wanted gardeners, maids, and nannies, but workers and unions felt threatened by undocumented aliens. Libertarian secularists opposed government controls of the market economy, and the Religious Right feared immigration threatened the family and the community. The Reagan administration was clearly divided. Many doubted the wisdom of admitting so many new immigrants from Asia and Latin America, and worried about crime and drug problems in their communities. Since George Wallace's law and order campaign for president in 1968, the discontented white ethnic working-class voters had been switching to the Republican Party, and some moderate Republicans became Democrats. Social conservatives and even some liberal Republicans from the northeast (called "gypsy moths") were charmed by Ronald Reagan in 1980 and became convinced it was time for a change from the liberal New Deal welfare state. This unraveling of the New Deal coalition was polarizing, especially in cities where racial conflicts destroyed the old alliance of ethnic blocs, labor unions, women, blacks, Catholics, Jews, liberals, and intellectuals.

As chair of the National Endowment for the Humanities (1986–1993), Lynne Cheney was a public critic of trends in education in some of the books she wrote, such as *American Memory* (1987) and *50 Hours* (1989). William J. Bennett, the Secretary of Education, was also critical of multiculturalism in higher education in 1988 and refused to criticize teaching creationism in public schools. Patrick Buchanan used the term culture war in his speech at the 1992 Republican National Convention. These members of the Reagan administration were his spokespersons in the culture wars, but the president remained aloof. However, the culture wars of the 1980s may have been exaggerated by highly visible activist groups on both sides of the cultural divide, and most people were not polarized into liberal and conservative camps. Polls showed, for example, that a majority of Americans wanted abortion to be available in some form, and fewer than 10 percent wanted to ban abortion altogether. American Christians were increasingly divided, and moderates and liberals generally looked to the National Council of Churches for leadership on social and moral issues. But in 1981,

Affirmative Action

Affirmative action, which promoted women and minorities who had been excluded from jobs and education, was a divisive issue in the culture wars. Many conservatives felt betrayed when the Reagan administration did not oppose affirmative action. President Nixon authorized it by executive order in 1969, and President Ford and President Carter each supported this policy. U.S. Supreme Court decisions in 1980, 1986, 1987, and 1989 supported affirmative action. But Reagan's cabinet was divided on this issue; Secretary of Education William J. Bennett opposed it, but the secretaries of labor (Brock), state (Schultz), treasury (Baker), transportation (Dole), health and human services (Heckler), and housing and urban development (Pierce) supported it. The National Association of Manufacturers and corporate leaders favored it, fearing lawsuits for discrimination or reverse discrimination by white employees. University administrators and faculties generally supported it, although many college students feared it would harm their ambitions. Clarence Thomas, the assistant secretary for civil rights in the Education Department, and later head of the Equal Employment Opportunity Commission and a U.S. Supreme Court justice, had benefited from affirmative action, but he now opposed it. In the end, the campaign to end affirmative action had little support in Congress, and the pragmatic Reagan allowed it to fade away.

the Institute for Religion and Democracy, funded by conservative foundations and corporate executives, criticized mainstream Protestant clergy for their liberal or left-wing views.

James A. Baker, Reagan's chief of staff and one of the president's few close friends, persuaded Reagan to focus on reducing domestic spending and expanding the military rather than divisive social issues. Nancy Reagan persuaded Reagan to take a softer line, and by leading her campaign against illegal drugs, she gained public approval and avoided the divisive culture wars. However, many conservatives continued to denounce National Endowment for the Arts funding of objectionable art such as photographer Robert Mapplethorpe's museum exhibitions in 1988 depicting the sadomasochistic aspects of gay culture, even after he died of AIDS in 1989. Fueled by Wall Street profits, prices for art soared in the 1980s despite, or perhaps because of, the culture wars.

Distrust, Disaffection, and Disillusionment

Many of the 248 million Americans by the end of the 1980s had lost confidence in authority and established institutions. Only half of those eligible to vote cast a ballot, even in presidential elections. Many states and cities had much lower rates of voter participation, often around 30 percent, and the number of independent or unenrolled voters grew each year, disavowing both parties. Political scientists warned this voter apathy was unprecedented, at least since the 1920s, and a dangerous symptom. They wondered if this alienation was a consequence of the 1960s countercultural revolution, or the Vietnam War and Watergate, or because of inept government control of the economy and the environment. The antinuclear movement, for example, doubted the government's ability to protect people and criticized the scientific basis for nuclear weapons and energy. The environmental and animal rights movements blamed the government and greedy corporations for real or anticipated disasters. Despite the Reagan administration antipathy to environmental laws that "over-regulated" industry and hindered economic growth, public opinion favored some restrictions and prevented most deregulation. The environmental movement was not a political issue; it had become entrenched in the public consciousness as commonsensical.

In the 1980s many Americans wanted a less hierarchical society and looked to alternative sources of energy (windmills and solar power) and food (organic and vegetarian diets) as solutions. Some sought answers or relief in religion, cults, or drugs as deindustrialization, globalization, recession, and the threat of environmental degradation and nuclear war loomed over the nation. However, the culture wars alienated many working-class Americans from the liberal policies of the Democratic Party or from their government. Disillusioned liberal Jewish intellectuals like Irving Krsitol, a New York University professor, also led the neoconservative movement in the 1980s.

In higher education, the culture wars emerged in debates over politically correct or free speech and diversity on the campus or curriculum reform. Federal government restrictions on academic freedom in the name of national security began with the Supreme Court's decision in *Snepp v. United States* (1980), and censorship by tighter security classification continued in 1982 by a Reagan administration executive order that aroused many objections from academic researchers. In 1986, Reagan also limited the Freedom of Information Act by federal agency regulations (Curry 1988). Other campus issues included the place of feminism and postmodernism in the curriculum, academic freedom, affirmative action in admissions, and charges that the traditional curriculum was ethnocentric, or too Eurocentric by focusing on literature by "dead white males." Despite the end of the draft and banishment of ROTC from many campuses, the military issues concerning homosexuality and the role of women in combat were very divisive in the late 1980s. Many social issues became political issues in the 1980s, leading liberal and moderate Republicans into the Democratic Party and conservative Democrats to become Republicans. Globalization, deindustrialization, the waning union movement, the fear of AIDS, homosexuality, and the changing roles of women combined to politicize and divide American society into hostile factions. College students blithely told pollsters that making money was their primary ambition.

THE AMERICAN LEFT

Searching for New Directions

The liberalism of the American Left became the "L-word" in the 1980s, although it is difficult to pinpoint why or when. *Time* magazine said the 96th Congress that adjourned on December 16, 1980 "was the Congress in which liberals and Democrats finally ran out of gas." As Robert Brent Toplin argued in *Radical Conservatism,* by employing the label liberal as a pejorative and by dominating moral and political discourse, the radical conservatives dislodged traditional conservatives to seize control of the Republican Party. Talented neoconservative writers such as Irving Kristol, William Kristol, Milton Friedman, Allan Bloom, and William J. Bennett persuaded many Americans to see liberals as too solemn and gloomy, obsessed with environmental disasters, violations of human rights, and injustice to minorities around the nation and the world. On the other hand, the election of Ronald Reagan in 1980 did not indicate a swing to the right because most American still looked to government as the great problem solver. In polls only one in three voters claimed to be a conservative, and even fewer identified as Republicans. The Democratic Party was so ideologically diverse in 1981 that it included the boll weevils or conservative Southerners and the moderate centrist Democrats, as well as the liberal Black Caucus and the left wing Democratic Study Group. Conservatives claimed the left wingers or bleeding-heart liberals were too soft on communism and too socialist for most Americans. This helped the more focused and disciplined Republicans in the well-organized New Right to win the 1980 election and put liberals on the defensive by promising lower taxes and less regulation.

Reagan's 1981 inaugural address proclaimed, "government is not the solution to our problem: government is the problem," which appealed to many taxpayers who forgot or never understood the important role of the liberal New Deal, New Frontier, and Great Society in transforming the nation. His promises of law and order especially appealed to northern and Midwestern white ethnic Democrats who were dissatisfied with the liberals' racial, immigration, and crime policies. In an era of affluence, the liberal message of compassion for the poor and the needy articulated by Speaker of the House Tip O'Neill sounded old-fashioned, but O'Neill challenged Reagan as no Speaker had done in a century. When the administration proposed reducing Social Security benefits in 1981, O'Neill denounced this on television as callous and despicable, forcing Reagan to withdraw his proposals.

The attack on the Left included a vigorous Christian Right who became a cornerstone of the Republican Party by politicizing religion. They repeated simple words and phrases and told a clear narrative about how life in America should be. Pat Robertson organized the Washington for Jesus rally of 200,000 fundamentalists on April 29, 1980, and identified liberals as unpatriotic, fiscally irresponsible secular humanists in the Democratic Party, NAACP, ACLU, and NOW who threatened traditional American family values and national security. In an effective attempt to intimidate the media and escape its scrutiny, conservatives made the alleged liberal bias in the media a public issue but with little foundation. Jerry Falwell, Pat Robertson, and other "Christian Zionists" supported Israel to the consternation of many liberal American Jews. In the media, liberal TV and radio talk show hosts were outnumbered on the airwaves by those with a conservative or New Right agenda. Although not a member of the Christian Right, Ronald Reagan adopted an evangelical lexicon in 1980 and told a large Christian Right rally in Dallas, "I know you can't endorse me, but I want you to know that I endorse you." He often invited Jerry Falwell to the White House and endorsed a school prayer amendment to the Constitution. Falwell's Moral Morality criticized abortion, pornography, gay rights, feminism, secularism, and bans on school prayer, which suited the conservative agenda.

Most liberals underestimated the threat from conservatives and failed to respond quickly or adequately. The religious left, who had led the civil rights and anti–Vietnam War movements, was strangely silent in the 1980s. Led by the National Council of Churches since 1950, their ecumenical faith-based agenda to end global warming, combat poverty, raise minimum wages, revamp immigration laws, prevent immoral cuts in federal social programs, and protect gay rights made little progress. Like labor unions, the religious left seemed unimportant and obsolete to many liberals who were more concerned with human rights, the environment, and a wide variety of social issues. Consequently, the conservative Republicans focused on a simple, clear message to win control of the Senate from 1981 to 1987 and the White House from 1981 to 1989. Despite protests from labor unions and doubts about globalization, many liberals accepted the idea that the economy could achieve sustained growth only if markets were allowed to operate unfettered and globally. Only a minority dubbed economic populists argued that the national income flowed disproportionately into corporate coffers and to the wealthiest families. They proposed rethinking the U.S. role in the global economy to protect labor and the environment and to regulate markets more carefully.

New Problems

The unsuccessful assassination attack on President Reagan in 1981, and his plucky recovery, boosted his public approval by 10 points and won enough votes in

Congress to pass his first budget bill with tax cuts, more defense spending, and cuts in social programs. But in doing so, all the economic problems Americans faced became part of the Reagan agenda, and the optimistic promises made by the president and his budget director, David Stockman, failed to materialize. Federal Reserve Chairman Paul Volcker embarked on a tight-money course to wring inflation out of the economy, and the Wall Street bull market Stockman had predicted never appeared. Stagflation continued, unemployment rose to 8 percent, and interest to 20 percent in what the media dubbed Reagan's recession of 1981–1982.

Reagan unified disparate and often fractious groups of the New Right, but big business and religious conservatives proved difficult to manage. At the same time social issues that had not been considered very important suddenly became defining hallmarks. Opponents of abortion, for example, saw the 1973 Supreme Court decision legalizing abortion as an assault on the American family. They mobilized to defend the innocent unborn and found other issues around sex education, homosexuality, and feminism to identify allies in a new moral crusade. In response, these conservative grassroots activities reenergized existing liberal organizations such as Planned Parenthood and the National Education Association to defend their agenda. Also in scientific matters, the Reagan administration had a disturbing record. As Chris Mooney noted in *The Republican War on Science,* not only did Reagan fail to acknowledge the AIDS epidemic until 1987, his presidential adviser on science was George Keyworth, who was not well regarded as a physicist. Reagan's views on science were reflected in his position as governor to promote teaching creationism in public schools along with evolution. This apathy toward science contributed to the culture wars dividing Americans (and no doubt people in many other countries) and creating greater social and political conflict in the 1980s.

Immigration in the 1980s

Latin Americans have always lived in the United States; in fact, they predate the founding of the United States. The 1849 Gold Rush attracted many Latinos to California from Latin America, but the border between Mexico and the United States was always more a bridge than a barrier. By 1930, 1.5 million Mexicans had immigrated to America, as well as uncounted Cubans, Puerto Ricans, and other Latinos from Central America and the Caribbean. But by the late 1980s, exiles from Castro's Cuba gave Miami the second-largest Cuban population in the world, and Florida had ten Spanish-language radio stations. By 1989, the Hispanic population in the nation numbered 22 million, or 8.2 percent of the U.S. population, centered in California (34 percent), Texas (21 percent), New York (10 percent), and Florida (8 percent) (Andersen 1989). New York City was 28 percent Hispanic, Miami, 50 percent, and Los Angeles, over 40 percent by 1989. In the 1980s, for example, Florida fermented an ethnic brew of Cuban, Hispanic, and Asian immigrants that transformed the Sunshine State. Many Americans worried about this, as well as about the increasing number of immigrants from the Middle East and Asia. By 1989, about six million new immigrants had arrived from Asia and Latin America. For the first time, the Senate considered a bill in 1981 to declare English as the nation's official language, and many states and cities considered or enacted similar legislation.

This influx of immigrants forced the redistribution of federal funding and the relative clout of states in Congress. Thoughtful people wondered if this was wise, and if ethnocentrism, xenophobia, and racism would increase. Others doubted that this was a serious problem but questioned how officials applied the Refugee Act of 1980 to favor immigrants from Cuba, Vietnam, and El Salvador. The Reagan administration increased funding for the Border Patrol 130 percent with more law enforcement, detention centers, and militarized checkpoints. Hysteria about immigration and drug smuggling, especially from Mexico, led to the Immigration Reform and Control Act of 1986. Some even proposed building a wall or fence along the Mexican border to prevent undocumented immigrants from crossing into Arizona, California, or Texas. Still uncounted numbers of immigrants crossed the freezing Otay Mountains in California or the scorching Arizona deserts each day, and many died en route to the United States.

When Were the 1960s?

When we talk about the 1960s, we often mean the period of countercultural and social change in the years 1964–1974, not merely the decade 1960–1969. This was a period of profound permanent change in American society, summed up for many in the phrase "sex, drugs, and rock and roll." But the 1960s also featured much progress and deep conflicts on race, war, education, and economics. The 1960s may be seen most clearly by contrasting and comparing it to the 1950s and the 1980s, two eras that seemed conventional and conformist.

President Lyndon Johnson predicted that passage of the Civil Rights Act of 1964 would irreparably harm the Democratic Party and give the Republicans a foothold in the South for the first time since the end of the Civil War; Johnson was correct. The resignation of President Nixon in 1974 was the symbolic end of the 1960s. This was followed by a period of widespread fears and anxieties about economics, the environment, child abuse, ethnicity, pornography, communism, crime, drugs, and other social issues. Some Americans retreated to an absolutist morality, creating the atmosphere that brought Ronald Reagan to the presidency in 1980. Despite his confident, cheerful leadership and the support of the conservative and neoconservative New Right, the country had been transformed by the events of the 1960s, and there was no going back, not for adolescents, African Americans, women, gays and lesbians, or ethnic minorities. This liberalization in American society accounts for the ultimate failure of the Reagan Revolution. He promised to restore the nation, but at heart Reagan had little interest in retreating to the past.

The Yippie and the Yuppie

The Yippies were followers of colorful hippie celebrities Abbie Hoffman (1936–1989) and Jerry Rubin (1938–1994) in the Youth International Party, founded (1967) to satirize the 1968 presidential candidates. Hoffman and Rubin were members of the Chicago Seven, the seven antiwar protest leaders indicted for conspiracy and inciting a riot at the 1968 Democratic National Convention in Chicago. Hoffman and Rubin used the trial as a forum for Yippie protests. The Chicago Seven convictions were overturned by an appeals court. In 1973, Hoffman went underground while on bail for a drug charge, and he later became an environmentalist in a small New York town. Rubin became a businessman and entrepreneur in 1975. From their New York City headquarters, the Yippies still held on to the hippie counterculture values with an annual march to legalize marijuana and a tradition of throwing cream pies in the faces of prominent figures.

In contrast, Yuppie was a term coined in 1983 by Jerry Rubin for young urban professionals, the children or grandchildren of the baby boomers. They were mostly white well-educated, upwardly mobile materialists in their 20s and 30s, stereotypically selfish and superficial consumers of upper-middle-class culture. Yuppies could be found dressed for success in their fast-track careers drinking coffee at espresso bars, or driving a BMW or SUV while talking on a cell phone. *Chicago Tribune* columnist Bob Greene popularized the term yuppie, but it was also used in the novel *East Bay Express* (1982) by Alice Kahn. Yuppies were blamed for "gentrification" of low-rent city neighborhoods, which contributed to homelessness by driving up real estate prices when old housing was converted into condominiums in the new "yuppie slums." Married yuppies with no children were called DINKs, an acronym for dual income, no kids. The novel *Bright Lights, Big City* (1984) by Jay McInerney, and the movie *Bonfire of the Vanities* (1990) explored yuppie materialism, and the comedy *Baby Boom* (1987) depicted how children changed the self-indulgent yuppie life. The yuppie was frequently a former preppy. Michael J. Fox may have depicted the classic preppy and future yuppie in the popular NBC sitcom *Family Ties* (1982–1989). Much of the show's humor derived from the tension between two former 1960s flower children and their conservative Republican son, Alex Keaton. *Thirtysomething,* a popular ABC dramatic series (1987–1991), also depicted the plight of the baby boomers on reaching age 30 and living the yuppie good life of lavish consumption in a trendy Philadelphia urban neighborhood. As Gil Troy

American Socialism and Michael Harrington

Socialism has never made much headway in America, despite its appeal in many other nations. But this does not mean that socialism has made no contributions to American society. It is a valid intellectual viewpoint, and its leading spokesman in the United States in the 1980s was Michael Harrington. Born in St. Louis in 1928, Harrington graduated from the College of the Holy Cross and studied at the University of Chicago and Yale University Law School. He was editor of the radical *The Catholic Worker* (1951–1953) but left the Catholic Church and became a lifelong socialist. He is best known as the author of *The Other America: Poverty in the United States* (1962), an extremely influential book that led President Kennedy to launch the War on Poverty and President Johnson to support the Civil Rights movement.

Harrington, the most well-known socialist in the United States, was a bridge between the Old Left and the New Left. As a mentor in the 1960s to the young people of the New Left and the radical Students for a Democratic Society (SDS), he failed to convert them to socialism. But he was a successful lecturer and writer, and he worked for President Johnson's new Office of Economic Opportunity in 1969. By 1970, Harrington opposed the Vietnam War, and in 1972, he identified the emerging neoconservatives, many of them his former socialist allies, as a new threat to democracy, freedom, and the federal programs for the poor. In 1980, Harrington formed the Democratic Socialist Organizing Committee with New Left activists to cooperate with liberal leaders in the Democratic Party. He continued his high-minded struggle to bring democracy and socialist principles to his country until his death in 1989.

noted in *Morning in America,* conservatives dismissed yuppies "as Chardonnay-sipping, NPR-listening, *New York Times*–reading, Reagan-hating" liberals.

The good life for yuppies included fancy vacations, clothing, and cars, and expensive dinners in new restaurants with international cuisine. They read newspaper food critics like Craig Claiborne, the influential *New York Times* restaurant critic and editor. He introduced Americans in the 1980s to new foods: quiche Lorraine, guacamole, pesto, and bouillabaisse. Another yuppie favorite was Julia Child, the PBS chef whose cookbooks and TV programs brought more sophisticated continental cuisine to American kitchens. Although an elite minority, the yuppies popularized new fashions that many Americans emulated. By the late-1980s, many older yuppies built a McMansion, a new large house on a small urban or suburban lot. In another example of overconsumption, yuppies sometimes demolished a small house to build their new oversized home on the lot.

Yuppie women scoffed at feminism but expected a career as well as marriage and children, with a sensitive husband, equal pay, and the right to choose an abortion. They were the new female professionals; the number of female lawyers and judges increased from 7,500 in 1960 to 180,000 in 1989, female doctors increased from 15,672 to 108,000, and female engineers from 7,404 to 174,000. The number of women in elected office more than tripled from 1975 to 1989. They no longer looked for leadership to feminist leaders like Gloria Steinem or Molly Yard, president of the National Organization for Women. Yet they resented the fact that 90 percent of male executives under 40 were fathers but only 35 percent of their female colleagues had children, as *Time* magazine noted on December 4, 1989.

Rainbow Coalition

The Rainbow Coalition, founded in 1984, was one of the most dynamic and creative social movements of the 1980s. It was the idea of Jesse Jackson (1941–), a leading African American spokesman. Born poor and illegitimate in Greensboro, North Carolina, Jesse Louis Burns adopted his stepfather's name. He attended the University of Illinois on a football scholarship and graduated from North Carolina Agricultural and Technical College in Greensboro in 1964. He led Council on Racial Equality (CORE) desegregation sit-ins and marches in Greensboro in 1963, and left the Chicago Theological Seminary in 1965 to join Martin Luther King Jr.'s Southern Christian Leadership Conference (SCLC) civil rights demonstrations in Selma, Alabama. Thereafter, Jackson was a close disciple of King, became director of the SCLC's Operation Breadbasket in Chicago, and in 1966 he led Illinois demonstrations against hunger and poverty.

Ordained a Baptist minister in 1968, Reverend Jackson ran for mayor of Chicago in 1971 to protest Mayor Richard Daley's Democratic machine. He resigned from the SCLC in 1971 to found People United to Save Humanity (PUSH), which pursued economic advancement for African American people across the nation. A forceful critic of President Reagan, he ran for the Democratic nomination for president in 1984, winning 3.5 million votes. That year he founded the Rainbow Coalition. This nonprofit grassroots national organization combined progressive whites, women, homosexuals, Latinos, African Americans, and environmentalists fighting for social change. The primary issues were economic, social, and racial justice; voter registration; affirmative action; equal rights; labor dispute mediation; jobs for minorities; and antiapartheid in South Africa.

Jackson, again a candidate for the Democratic presidential nomination in 1988, was called the "conscience of the nation" and the "great unifier," but he was also an outspoken critic of President Reagan's policies. His multiracial, multi-issue Rainbow Coalition agenda was an ambitious effort to educate, organize, and mobilize farmers, unions, minorities, women, and the working poor

Jesse Jackson, Baptist minister and candidate for the Democratic presidential nomination in 1988, gives the thumbs up at the end of a campaign speech. (Jacques M. Chenet/Corbis)

from regional bureaus in Atlanta, Chicago, Cleveland, Detroit, Houston, Los Angeles, New Orleans, New York City, and Washington, D.C. A passionate preacher and the nation's leading African American spokesman, Jackson was best known for his slogan "keep hope alive."

In 1988, Jackson won the Michigan presidential primary and 6.9 million votes. He moved to Washington, D.C., in 1989 and was elected the District of Columbia's "statehood senator" (1991–1996). Jackson became a recognized Democratic leader of African Americans, traveling to South Africa (1979) to oppose apartheid, and to the Middle East, Cuba, and Central America (1984) and Iraq (1990) on personal diplomatic and peace missions. His multicultural Rainbow Coalition remains active in many American communities.

Economic Recovery and Technological Change

Economic recovery in 1983 and technological change had a profound impact on American society. The electronic revolution and new high-tech industries in

The Homeless

In 1981, homelessness became an issue in the media, and by 1984 it was a common newspaper feature story. Precise numbers were impossible to obtain, but in the U.S., the Department of Housing and Urban Development (HUD) estimated there were three million homeless people, and about one-third were women with children. In Washington, D.C., social welfare agencies counted 20,000 people living on the streets in 1982 but had only 3,000 beds for them in emergency shelters. Many slept at night in Lafayette Park across from the White House and panhandled for spare change or lined up to eat in church soup kitchens. This created serious problems for city governments, especially in San Francisco, New York City, and Chicago, when the safety net disappeared as federal funds for city budgets declined from 22 percent in 1980 to 6 percent in 1989.

Although there have always been poor people with no fixed home in American cities, modern homelessness became a major public issue in the 1980s. One study found homelessness tripled between 1981 and 1989. In 1984, HUD estimated 350,000 people lived on U.S. streets because shelters were full or unavailable and affordable housing had disappeared. This was due to drastic budget reductions for public welfare and federal low-income housing programs, the deinstitutionalization of mental hospitals, low minimum wages, lack of health insurance, rising housing costs, alcoholism, drug addiction, and an inadequate supply of urban housing. Public and private homeless shelters, soup kitchens, food pantries, medical and counseling services, and free clothing shops proved inadequate. Congress finally responded with the McKinney–Vento Homeless Assistance Act (1987), the only federal law allocating funds for direct services for homeless people.

Still the problem persisted and increased to more than 600,000 people living on the streets in 1987. Many cities criminalized homelessness by enacting laws against begging or sleeping in public places. President Reagan was criticized for his apparent indifference to the poor, but he remained convinced free markets would eventually bring prosperity to all hard-working Americans. In his 1989 inaugural address, President George H. W. Bush repeated his Thousand Points of Light proposal, urging each community organization and individual citizen to reach out to aid the homeless.

Private rehabilitation of urban slums by the yuppies inadvertently contributed to homelessness. Apartment buildings and industrial sites that became trendy lofts and condominiums for the affluent displaced many poor people. Nevertheless, the growing gap between the rich and poor led to more homelessness and a shocking increase in hate crimes against the homeless "street people" (Burt 1992).

computing, biotechnology, genetic engineering, pharmaceuticals, and financial services expanded both consumer purchasing power and the number of two-income households. The expanded economy and growth of technology demanded an educated labor force; young men and women such as those who were dubbed "yuppies" filled the need. University researchers contributed new products and developed partnerships with new research centers located near the campus. Congress approved this marriage of academia and industry by increasing military budgets for technology and passing the Bayh–Dole Patent Act in 1980, which made scientific discoveries in university labs proprietary. Government funding for this and innovative medical research also expanded, and the first in vitro fertilization—or test tube baby—was born in the United States in 1981. All of these factors supported President Reagan's optimistic vision of an expanding entrepreneurial America.

Stung by conservative charges that Democrats were captive to special interests (women, unions, minorities) and shocked by Reagan's popularity and the economic recovery, liberals, who had set the social and political agenda for 50 years, were in disarray. Deindustrialization and globalization weakened organized labor, and blue-collar families needed two incomes to maintain their middle-class lifestyle. By 1989 almost 60 percent of married women with children worked outside the home. The 20 percent of families headed by women sank into poverty. Conservative philosophy offered the promise of economic expansion that would benefit everyone, but government programs to help the poor, disabled, and aspiring college students were shrinking. Personal income for the poor dropped by 9.8 percent from 1980 to 1987. The U.S. poverty rate increased in 1980–1988 from 11.7 to 13.5 percent, the highest in the industrialized world. The growth of inequality in the 1980s meant that one child in every five lived in poverty in the United States.

BIOGRAPHIES

Gia Carangi, 1960–1986

Fashion Model

Born in Philadelphia, Gia Carangi became the first of American supermodels by 1978. Her photographs were often on the cover of *Vogue, Cosmopolitan,* and other popular fashion magazines. When Gia worked in New York City, she was frequently seen at the fashionable disco Studio 54, where she became addicted to drugs. When she died in 1986 of AIDS, she was the first female celebrity known to succumb to the epidemic. After her death, her mother appeared on television to promote public awareness of AIDS, and a 1993 biography and a 1998 movie, *Gia,* based on her career, made a further impact with the public.

Cesar Chavez, 1927–1993

Labor Leader

Born in Arizona, Cesar Chavez became a migrant farm worker as a young child when his parents lost their farm in 1938. Chavez served in the Navy during World War II and worked as a ranch hand and with a lumber company before becoming an organizer for the Community Services Organization that Dolores Huerta founded in 1955. In 1962, Chavez and Huerta founded the National Farm Workers Association (NFWA) to lobby for a minimum wage and collective bargaining for migrant farm workers. Chavez and Huerta then joined an AFL-CIO farm workers' strike in California in 1965, winning widespread support from students, consumers, and union longshoremen and truck drivers. Merging the two groups in 1966, the United Farm Workers (UFW) signed contracts with the major wine makers in 1967 and declared a consumer boycott on other grape growers. To the surprise of traditional union leaders, Chavez won the grape pickers' strike in 1969 and persuaded California to pass a new labor relations law in 1975. His charismatic leadership won support from many liberals, notably Sen. Robert F. Kennedy in 1968. Despite this success, the corporate growers contested UFW contracts in Texas, Florida, and California courts in the 1980s, and the UFW was beset with internal staff conflicts and an unstable membership. When Chavez died in Arizona in 1993, he was a hero to union members and Latinos everywhere.

Geraldine Ferraro makes her acceptance speech for her vice presidential nomination during the 1984 Democratic National Convention in July 1984. (Bettmann/Corbis)

Geraldine A. Ferraro, 1935–

Politician

Born in New York, Geraldine Ferraro graduated from Marymount College (1956) and Fordham University School of Law (1960). She served as a Democrat to the House of Representatives (1979–1985) and was the first woman nominated for vice president by a major party. As Walter F. Mondale's running mate in 1984, many expected she would win a plurality of the female vote for the Democratic ticket. But Reagan–Bush won 58 percent to 40 percent, and surprisingly women chose Reagan by 55 percent to 45 percent. Ferraro remained active in politics and became a hero-ine to millions of American women.

Rock Hudson, 1925–1985

Actor

Rock Hudson was a celebrated American actor who played a ruggedly handsome leading man in more than 50 films and television shows. His death in October 1985 from an AIDS-related illness and the announcement a few months before his death that he was a homosexual aroused wide attention to the disease. Hudson was the first celebrity—and a conservative Republican and Hollywood icon—to die from AIDS. His long friendship with Ronald and Nancy Reagan made the gay plague an important American and international public health issue. This led President Reagan to order a factual report by Surgeon General C. Everett Koop in 1986 on the AIDS crisis. Koop called for more sex education and reassured the public that the disease was not easily transmitted except by sexual contact, IV drug abuse, pregnancy, or blood transfusions.

Lee Iacocca, 1924–

Businessman

Lee Iacocca was chairman of the Chrysler Corporation (1978–1992) and one of the most well-known American businessmen in the 1980s. Born to Italian immigrant parents in Allentown, Pennsylvania, Lido A. Iacocca graduated from Lehigh University and studied at Princeton University. By 1946, Lee Iacocca worked as an engineer at Ford Motor Company and later became its president (1970–1978). He was known as the father of the popular Ford Mustang (in 1964), and the accident-prone Ford Pinto, both cars that were designed to compete with imports.

Recruited by Chrysler Corporation as chairman, he turned the nearly bank-rupt automaker around by substituting the popular Dodge Omni and Plymouth Horizon subcompact cars for the large gas-guzzler models that the public avoided during the oil crisis of the late 1970s. In 1981, he produced the popular Dodge Aries and Plymouth Reliant, both efficient compact cars, and he introduced the successful minivan in 1983.

In 1980 Iacocca lobbied Congress for loan guarantees, similar to the bailouts given airlines and railroads. Despite plant closings, job layoffs, and massive restructuring, Chrysler repaid its government-backed loans in 1983 ahead of schedule. In 1987, he directed Chrysler's purchase of AMC and had similar success with the Jeep Grand Cherokee. He was noted for motivating Chrysler's 140,000 employees and was the first CEO to appear as a pitchman in television commercials for his own cars.

President Reagan appointed Iacocca chairman of the committee to renovate and preserve the Statue of Liberty in 1982. This work and his best-selling autobiography, *Iacocca* (1984), made him an international celebrity. *Time* magazine celebrated Iacocca's star status in its April 1, 1985, cover story, "I Gotta Tell Ya, America Loves Listening to Lee." He was even considered as a Republican candidate for the presidential nomination in 1988. Retiring in 1992, he worked for several philanthropic causes but is still remembered for his television commercials in the 1980s when he declared, "If you can find a better car, buy it." Iacocca later appeared in memorable Chrysler commercials with the hip hop star Snoop Dog.

Lane Kirkland, 1922–1999

Labor Leader

Born in South Carolina, Lane Kirkland served in the Merchant Marine in World War II and later graduated from Georgetown University. He spent his career in the American Federation of Labor-Congress of Industrial Organizations (AFL-CIO), succeeding his mentor George Meany as president (1979–1995). In 1981 he organized a massive Solidarity Day demonstration in Washington, D.C., to dramatize labor union opposition to President Reagan's policies. He was a centrist, nonconfrontational Democrat and an early supporter of Walter Mondale in the 1984 election. Kirkland increased the role of women, African Americans, and Latinos in the AFL leadership. However, he and his big labor colleagues could do little to halt the precipitous decline of union membership in the 1980s. In 1995, Kirkland was forced to retire by dissenting union leaders led by SEIU president John Sweeney, who succeeded him.

Larry Kramer, 1935–

Writer, Gay Rights Activist

Born in Connecticut, Larry Kramer graduated from Yale University in 1957. He became a successful screenwriter in London and Hollywood and wrote *Faggots* (1978), one of the first best-selling novels on contemporary homosexuality. In 1981, Kramer became a gay rights activist and founded the Gay Men's Health Crisis, the world's largest service organization for AIDS. He wrote a hit play, *The Normal Heart* (1985), and was a founder of ACT-UP (1987). His play *Jut Say No* (1988) was critical of President Reagan. His book *Reports from the Holocaust: The Making of an AIDS Activist* (1989) is an important collection of writing on AIDS activism in the 1980s. Kramer, who is HIV-positive, was honored by Common Cause for his public service leadership.

Robert Mapplethorpe, 1946–1989

Photographer

Born in an English and Irish Catholic family in Floral Park, Long Island, New York, Robert Mapplethorpe graduated from the Pratt Institute in Brooklyn. He was best known for large-scale black-and-white portraits and male nudes. Among his subjects were the celebrities Richard Gere, Grace Jones, Patti Smith, and Andy Warhol. He aroused much controversy in 1988 when the National Endowment for the Arts funded his sadomasochistic exhibition with nude African American men that was considered by conservatives as obscene and racist. Mapplethorpe admitted using his considerable skill as an artist to depict the beauty of homosexual love by challenging the construction of sex and gender in American society. Partly as a result of the boom in contemporary art in the late 1980s, fueled by the Wall Street cash culture and speculation in art, prices for his work reached record levels, especially after he died of AIDS in Boston on March 9, 1989. His art was personal, political, shocking, and humorous, it was intended to open up art to everyone, for good or bad. Mapplethorpe was a genius who did much to arouse the culture wars and create demands to abolish the NEA.

Thomas P. "Tip" O'Neill Jr., 1912–1994

Speaker of the House

Tip O'Neill was the leader of his party and President Reagan's major opponent. Born in Cambridge, Massachusetts, to a pious and politically active Irish Catholic Democratic family, O'Neill graduated from Boston College in 1936. He served in the state legislature (1936–1952) and became the first Catholic and first Democratic speaker of the house (1949–1952) in Massachusetts. Elected to Congress (1953–1987), he epitomized the urban New Deal Democrat shaped by the moderate ideology of his party. O'Neill broke with President Johnson over the Vietnam War (1967), and as Speaker of the House (1977–1987), he adroitly resisted the neoconservatives during the Reagan era. Although appalled by Reagan's lax management, forgetfulness, and New Right policies, he remained on good personal terms with the president, and they had much in common. Conservatives who were determined to reverse the Great Society and repeal the New Deal demonized O'Neill as a big-spending liberal in 1981 caustic television commercials. But when he retired in 1987, Tip O'Neill was respected by Republicans and Democrats in Congress as the most popular, effective, and accomplished Speaker in 40 years. His autobiography, *Man of the House* (1987), recalls a lifetime in the political arena and reveals the inner workings of the Reagan era from a unique perspective.

Ralph E. Reed Jr., 1961–

Lobbyist

Ralph Reed Jr. represented the younger conservatives who supported the Reagan Revolution. Born in Virginia, Reed grew up in Florida and Georgia. He graduated from the University of Georgia (1985) and earned a Ph.D. in History at Emory University (1991). He spent most of his college years as a leader of the College Republicans' organization, and in 1981, he worked with lobbyist Jack Abramoff, the chairman of the College Republican National Committee (CRNC), in Washington, D.C. In 1983, Reed was reprimanded by the CRNC for rigging the election of the College Republicans at the University of Georgia, but he later became executive secretary of the CRNC.

Reed had a religious conversion in 1983 and became a born-again Christian. He moved to North Carolina in 1984 to found Students for America, a conservative group that supported the reelection of Republican senator Jesse Helms and organized abortion clinic protests. He boasted he was doing guerrilla warfare for the New Right Christians. Arson at abortion clinics in Illinois (1982), Florida (1982, 1984), Virginia (1983), and Washington, D.C. (1985), and the kidnapping and murder of staff members aroused much criticism, but FBI director William Webster refused to consider abortion clinic fire bombings as terrorism.

After Pat Robertson's unsuccessful 1988 campaign for president, Robertson hired Reed as executive director of the newly established Christian Coalition (1989–1997). Reed attracted members and donations by using direct mail that criticized the National Endowment for the Arts, which funded some disrespectful or sadomasochistic art by Andres Serrano and Robert Mapplethorpe. Reed made major gains in organizing the Religious Right until a federal investigation of financial irregularities led him to resign and move to Georgia. He was credited with mobilizing Christian conservatives by sophisticated direct mailing to support Republicans in Congressional elections. Later, the Federal Elections Commission charged violations of campaign finance laws, and the Christian Coalition lost its tax-exempt status. Reed remained active but unsuccessful in Georgia Republican Party politics.

Sally Kristen Ride, 1951–

Astronaut

Born in Encino, California, Sally Ride graduated from Stanford University (1973) and earned a Ph.D. in physics at Stanford (1978). Selected for astronaut training in 1978, she trained at the NASA center in Florida and was the first American woman in space. Her first flight was for six days on the shuttle *Challenger* in 1983, and again on the *Challenger* in 1984 for eight days. After the *Challenger* tragedy in 1986, she served on a presidential commission investigating the accident and as a NASA administrator in Washington, D.C. In 1987, Dr. Ride returned

Sally Ride, America's first woman astronaut, communicates with ground controllers from the flight deck during the six-day mission of the Challenger *in June, 1983. (National Archives)*

to Stanford University's California Space Institute, and she became a professor of physics at the University of California in San Diego in 1989. Since 1987, she has led organizations to encourage girls to study mathematics, science, and technology.

Steve Rubell, 1943–1989

Entrepreneur

Born in Brooklyn, New York, Steve Rubell was an avid tennis player. He considered playing professionally but instead attended Syracuse University where he earned a B.A. and an M.A. in finance. After his service in the National Guard, he worked in a New York City stock brokerage and operated some restaurants. In 1977, he and his college classmate, Ian Schrager, opened a disco in an old Manhattan television studio on West 54th Street. From the beginning, Studio 54 was a success. Celebrities arrived each night to be greeted by Rubell and presented with lavish gifts; ordinary customers who did not meet his standards of elegance were often turned away at the door. The club earned $7 million during its first year, but the disco nightclub was raided by the police in December 1978, and in June 1979, Rubell and Schrager were charged with tax evasion, conspiracy, and obstruction of justice. In 1980 they went to prison and sold Studio 54 for $4.75 million. When released from prison in 1981, they opened two other Manhattan clubs, but the disco fad ended in 1986. The mood changed shortly after Gia Carangi, a supermodel and 54 habitué, died of AIDS. Rubell also died of AIDS on July 25, 1989. Hollywood depicted the hedonistic Studio 54 nightly celebrities' drugs and sex scene in *54* (1998).

Randall Terry, 1959–

Lobbyist

Born in Binghamton, New York, Terry Randall became a born-again Christian in a summer Bible school. In 1987 he founded Operation Rescue in New York, an extremist antiabortion group that used civil disobedience, picketing, and direct mail to organize, protest, and close family-planning clinics where abortions were performed. By blocking driveways and doors, singing and preaching, and doing sidewalk counseling with those entering the clinic, they hoped to dissuade women from having an abortion. Randall, who was raised by feminists but described Planned Parenthood founder Margaret Sanger as a whore and adulteress, was arrested 30 times by 1990, at abortion clinic demonstrations in seven cities, along with 40,000 of his followers. Despite endorsements from Jerry Falwell, Pat Robertson, and other Religious Right leaders, Randall left Operation Rescue in 1990, but continued his antiabortion mission. He accosted President Bush on the golf course in Kennebunk, Maine, in 1991 and urged him to support the cause. But Bush only made a lukewarm statement to reporters and criticized lawbreaking. Later Randall hosted a radio show, wrote *The Judgment of God* (1995), which expressed his homophobic and anti-Muslim views, and ran for Congress in 1998. The murder of four doctors and two clinic staff members and fire bombings at abortion clinics discredited Randall and Operation Rescue.

REFERENCES AND FURTHER READINGS

Abzug, Bella. 1984. *Gender Gap: Abzug's Guide to Political Power for Women.* Boston: Houghton Mifflin.

ACT UP Oral History Project. A Program of the New York Lesbian and Gay Experimental Film Festival. Interview of Jean Carlomusto, December 19, 2002. http://www.actuporalhistory.org/interviews/images/carlomusto.pdf.

The Age of Aids, PBS *Frontline,* 2006. http://www.pbs.org/wgbh/pages/frontline/aids/.

Altman, Lawrence K. 1981. "Rare Cancer Seen in 41 Homosexuals," *New York Times,* July 3, 20.

Andersen, Kurt. 1989. "The New Ellis Island," *Time,* June 13, 15–18.

Atomic Veterans History Project, 1997. www.aracnet.com/~pdxavets/.

Baird-Windle, Patricia, and Eleanor J. Bader. 2001. *Targets of Hatred: Anti-Abortion Terrorism.* New York: Palgrave.

Barron, Gayle. 1980. *The Beauty of Running.* New York: Harcourt Brace Jovanovich.

Bayer, Ronald. 2002. *AIDS Doctors: Voices from the Epidemic: An Oral History.* New York: Oxford University Press.

Brisbin, Richard A., Jr. 2002. *A Strike Like No Other Strike: Law and Resistance During the Pittson Coal Strike of 1989–1990.* Baltimore: Johns Hopkins University Press.

Brower, David R., and Steve Chapple. 1995. *Let the Mountains Talk, Let the Rivers Run.* New York: HarperCollins.

Brownstein, Ronald, and Nina Easton. 1983. *Reagan's Ruling Class: Portraits of the President's Top One Hundred Officials.* New York: Pantheon Books.

Burt, Martha R. 1992. *Over the Edge: The Growth of Homelessness in the 1980s.* New York: Russell Sage Foundation.

Carter, Jimmy. 2006. *Palestine: Peace Not Apartheid.* New York: Simon and Schuster.

Chacon, Justin Akers, and Mike Davis. 2006. *No One Is Illegal: Fighting Racism and State Violence on the U.S.-Mexico Border.* Chicago: Haymarket Books.

Chase, Alston. 2003. *Harvard and the Unabomber: The Education of an American Terrorist.* New York: W. W. Norton.

Cheney, Lynne V. 1987. American Memory: A Report on the Humanities in the Nation's Public Schools. Washington, D.C.: National Endowment for the Humanities.

Cheney, Lynne V. 1989. 50 Hours: A Core Curriculum for College Students. Washington, D.C.: National Endowment for the Humanities.

Cockburn, Alexander. 1987. *Corruptions of Empire: Life Studies and the Reagan Era.* New York: Verso.

Critchlow, Donald T. 2005. *Phyllis Schlafly and Grassroots Conservatism: A Woman's Crusade.* Princeton: Princeton University Press.

Curry, Richard O., ed. 1988. *Freedom at Risk: Secrecy, Censorship, and Repression in the 1980s.* Philadelphia: Temple University Press.

Davis, Mike. 1996. *Prisoners of the American Dream: Politics and Economy in the History of the U.S. Working Class.* New York: Verso.

Diggins, John Patrick. 2007. *Ronald Reagan: Fate, Freedom, and the Making of History.* New York: W. W. Norton.

Dinnerstein, Leonard, Roger L. Nichols, and David M. Reimers. 2003. *Natives and Strangers: A Multicultural History of Americans.* New York: Oxford University Press.

"Double Lives: Gays in Syracuse," *The Post-Standard,* Syracuse, N.Y., June 4, 1989.

Dubofsky, Melvin, and Joseph McCartin, eds. 2004. *American Labor: A Documentary Collection.* New York: Palgrave Macmillan.

Early, Steve. 2006. "An Old Lesson Still Holds for Unions," *Boston Globe,* July 31, A11.

Farrell, John A. 2001. *Tip O'Neill and the Democratic Century.* Boston: Little, Brown.

Ferraro, Geraldine A. 1985. *Ferraro: My Story.* New York: Bantam Books.

Frady, Marshall. 1996. *Jesse: The Life and Pilgrimage of Jesse Jackson.* New York: Random House.

Garcia, Maria Cristina. 1996. *Havana USA: Cuban Exiles and Cuban Americans in South Florida, 1959–1994.* Berkeley: University of California Press.

Greene, John Robert. 2006. *Presidential Profiles: The George H. W. Bush Years.* New York: Facts on File.

Greenya, John and Anne Urban. 1986. *The Real David Stockman.* New York: St. Martin's Press.

Grinspoon, Lester, ed. 1986. *The Long Darkness: Psychological and Moral Perspectives on Nuclear Winter.* New Haven, Conn.: Yale University Press.

Gutierrez, David G., ed. 1996. *Between Two Worlds: Mexican Immigrants in the United States.* Wilmington, Del.: Scholarly Resources.

Hage, Dave, and Paul Klauda. 1989. *No Retreat, No Surrender: Labor's War at Hormel.* New York: William Morrow.

Harrington, Michael. 1962. *The Other America: Poverty in the United States.* New York: Macmillan.

Howe, Peter J. 1989. "Thousands Rally for Gay Pride; Festivities Blend with AIDS Concern," *Boston Globe,* June 11, 33.

Hunter, James Davison. 1991. *Culture Wars: The Struggle to Define America.* New York: Basic Books.

Iacocca, Lee A. 1984. *Iacocca: An Autobiography.* New York: Bantam Books.

Jeansonne, Glen. 2007. *A Time of Paradox: America from the Cold War to the Third Millennium, 1945–Present.* Lanham, Md.: Rowman & Littlefield.

Jenkins, Philip. 2006. *Decade of Nightmares: The End of the Sixties and the Making of Eighties America.* New York: Oxford University Press.

Kantrowitz, Barbara. 1986. "Growing up Gay," *Newsweek,* January 24, 50.

Karla, Jay. 1999. *Tales of the Lavender Menace: A Memoir of Liberation.* New York: Basic Books.

Kramer, Larry. 1989. *Reports from the Holocaust: The Making of an AIDS Activist.* New York: St. Martin's Press.

Kuttner, Robert. 1997. *Everything for Sale: The Virtues and Limits of Markets.* New York: Knopf.

Linkon, Sherry Lee, and John Russo. 2002. *Steeltown U.S.A.: Work and Memory in Youngstown.* Lawrence: University Press of Kansas.

Livesay, Harold C. 1978. *Samuel Gompers and Organized Labor in America.* Boston: Little, Brown and Company.

Longcope, Kay. 1988. "Area Lesbians Share Sadness, Fear After Couple's Slaying," *Boston Globe,* December 4, 1.

Love, Janice. 1985. *The U.S. Anti-Apartheid Movement: Local Activism in Global Politics.* New York: Praeger.

Malone, John Williams. 1980. *Straight Women/Gay Men: A Special Relationship.* New York: Dial Press.

Marcus, Eric. 2002. *Making Gay History: The Half-Century Fight for Lesbian and Gay Equal Rights.* New York: Perennial.

Martin, William. 1996. *With God on Our Side: The Rise of the Religious Right in America.* New York: Broadway Books.

Mathews, Donald G., and Jane Sherron De Hart. 1990. *Sex, Gender, and the Politics of ERA: A State and the Nation.* New York: Oxford University Press.

Mills, Nicolaus, ed. 1990. *Culture in an Age of Money: The Legacy of the 1980s in America.* Chicago: Ivan R. Dee.

Mooney, Chris. 2005. *The Republican War on Science.* New York: Basic Books.

Mormino, Gary R. 2005. *Land of Sunshine, State of Dreams: A Social History of Modern Florida.* Gainesville: University Press of Florida.

Morris, Edmund. 1999. *Dutch: A Memoir of Ronald Reagan.* New York: Random House.

Muir, William K. 1992. *The Bully Pulpit: The Presidential Leadership of Ronald Reagan.* San Francisco: Institute for Contemporary Studies Press.

Murdoch, Joyce. 1988. "Gay Youths' Deadly Despair; High Rate of Suicide Attempts Tracked," *Washington Post,* October 24, A1.

Murtagh, William J. 1997. *Keeping Time: The History and Theory of Preservation in America*. New York: John Wiley & Sons.

National Pollutant Inventory, Particulate Matter (PM$_{10}$ and PM $_{2.5}$) Substance Fact Sheet, September 2007. http://www.npi.gov.au/database/substance-info/ profiles/69.html.

Newsweek. 2006a. "Aids: 25 Years Later," May 15, 27–33.

Newsweek. 2006b. "Playing the Numbers," June 5, 40–49.

Ngai, Mae M. 2004. *Impossible Subjects: Illegal Aliens and the Making of Modern America*. Princeton: Princeton University Press.

Norman, Michael. 1983. "Homosexuals Confronting a Time of Change," *New York Times,* June 16, A1.

O'Neill, Thomas P. and William Novak. 1987. *Man of the House: The Life and Political Memoirs of Speaker Tip O'Neill*. New York: Random House.

Puddington, Arch. 2005. *Lane Kirkland: Champion of American Labor*. New York: Wiley.

Puette, William J. 1992. *Through Jaundiced Eyes: How the Media View Organized Labor*. Ithaca, N.Y.: ILR Press.

Rainbow/Push Coalition, http://www.rainbowpush.org/.

Reeves, Richard. 2005. *President Reagan: The Triumph of Imagination*. New York: Simon and Schuster.

Regan, Tom. 1983. *The Case for Animal Rights*. Berkeley: University of California Press.

Risen, Jim, and Judy L. Thomas. 1998. *Wrath of Angels: The American Abortion War*. New York: Basic Books.

Roberts, James C. 1980. *The Conservative Decade: Emerging Leaders of the 1980s*. Westport, Conn.: Arlington House.

Rosen, Ruth. 2000. *The World Split Open: How the Modern Women's Movement Changed America*. New York: Viking.

Schlafly, Phyllis. 1964. A Choice Not an Echo. Alton, Ill.: Pere Marquette Press.

Schulman, Bruce J. 2003. *The Seventies: The Great Shift in American Culture, Society, and Politics*. New York: The Free Press.

Sexton, Patricia Cayo. 1982. *The New Nightingales: Hospital Workers, Unions, New Women's Issues*. New York: Enquiry Press.

Shilts, Randy. 2000. *And the Band Played On: Politics, People, and the AIDS Epidemic*. New York: St. Martin's Press.

Simon, Rita J., ed. 2005. *Sporting Equality: Title IX Thirty Years Later*. New Brunswick, N.J.: Transaction Publishers.

Singer, Peter. 1975. *Animal Liberation: A New Ethics for our Treatment of Animals*. New York: Random House.

Sloane, Liz, and Ann Kramer. 1985. *Running: The Women's Handbook*. London: Pandora Press.

Stamberg, Susan. 1993. *Talk: NPR's Susan Stamberg Considers All Things*. New York: Random House.

Steffny, Manfred, and Rosemary Breuer. 1985. *Running for Women: A Basic Guide for the New Runner*. New York: Collier Books.

Swartz, Katherine. 2006. *Reinsuring Health: Why More Middle-Class People Are Uninsured and What Government Can Do*. New York: Russell Sage.

Terry, Randall. 1995. *Judgment of God*. New York: Reformer Library.

Tolpin, Robert Brent. 2006. *Radical Conservatism: The Right's Political Religion*. Lawrence: University Press of Kansas.

Troy, Gil. 2005. *Morning in America: How Ronald Reagan Invented the 1980s*. Princeton: Princeton University Press.

Tyrrell, R. Emmett. 1984. *The Liberal Crack-Up*. New York: Simon and Schuster.

Waltz, Kenneth. 2002. *The Spread of Nuclear Weapons: A Debate Renewed*. New York: W. W. Norton.

Weart, Spencer R. 1988. *Nuclear Fear: A History of Images*. Cambridge: Harvard University Press.

Weiner, Janet Ochs. 1981. "Private Lives: Gay Men, Straight Women," *Washington Post,* June 24, B5.

Worster, Donald. 1993. *The Wealth of Nature: Environmental History and the Ecological Imagination*. New York: Oxford University Press.

Popular Culture, Leisure, and Amusement

Overview

The 1980s was a decade characterized by consumerist values that reflected the Reagan era nostalgia for the past and the tastes of the young and the trendy from fashion and films to music and morality. Late-20th century American popular culture became very pervasive around the world. Since 1945, social scientists have studied popular culture and the youth cultures more carefully than ever before. This is due in part to new electronic information and media technologies and to the more open and egalitarian parent–child relationships. Postmodern youths simply created and consumed their own fascinating popular culture, leisure activities, and amusements.

In the 1980s, the distinction between elite culture and popular culture blurred. At first glance, this decade seems like an Age of Excess, populated by the self-absorbed Me Generation, when young Americans became conservative preppies and yuppies or vain disco dancers in contrast to the social consciousness of the 1960s and 1970s. Popular culture provides one method of understanding American youth culture in the 1980s because its commercial, repetitive nature often reflects social changes, values, and styles more quickly and accurately than other aspects of cultural history. Television and movies may be the most accurate barometers of culture in the 1980s, and music, sports, fashion, and fads have much to tell us about this dynamic decade (Barry and Derevlany 1987).

Children and adolescents, the greatest creators and consumers of popular culture music, fashion, and media, experienced such profound changes in the

1960–1970s era that there seemed to be little new that American youth might encounter in the 1980s. But each generation finds ways to identify and assert itself, and this was certainly true of American youth in the 1980s. The transition from adolescence to adulthood has never been easy, and American society provided few rituals or customs that clearly defined maturity. Adolescence is a struggle to find a sense of self and create identities in a confusing media blitz of popular culture. Despite economic and social problems in the 1980s, most teens emulated the cool, consensus, middle-class lifestyles American pop culture promoted.

One of the most striking changes in the 1980s was that the nuclear family often included grandparents. As life expectancy increased from 70 in 1970 to 75 in 1990, more adults became grandparents, and intergenerational relationships with their grandsons and granddaughters were more common. Adults who married in their mid-20s often became grandparents in their 50s, and great-grandparents in their 70s. Contrary to the popular culture stereotype, most Americans became grandparents in middle age in the 1980s, while still healthy, physically active, and financially secure. The average retirement age fell from 70 in 1950 to 63 in 1983, and the elderly population increased 24 percent from 1970 to 1980. Life expectancy was 54 for men and 55 for women in 1920, but this rose from 70 for men and 77 for women in 1980 to 72 and 79 in 1990. This was a stabilizing factor in most families because the grandparents' role was often more informal, friendly, and indulgent than the teenager–parent roles. Visits, telephone calls, vacations, and holiday events were common occasions to interact with grandchildren. Many grandparents became computer literate to communicate more easily with their grandchildren. Divorce, which ended over 40 percent of marriages in 1990, and the increase in working mothers, made grandparents a source of child care, especially in African American families. In any case, modern grandparents and grandchildren had more years in which to enjoy close relationships than previous generations (Barol 1988).

One reason Americans lived longer, more healthy lives in the 1980s was the development of new forms of medical care, such as the first coronary angioplasty; spinal cord injury treatment; surgery on fetuses in utero; bone marrow, liver, heart and lung transplants; artificial skin; lithotripsy for gallstones; and improvements in pediatric and geriatric medicine. In 1982 a Seattle dentist, Barney Clark, received the first artificial heart, which Dr. Robert Jarvik invented at the University of Utah. The U.S. medical schools and hospitals became the research engines of the nation's health system, and health insurance to pay for medical care was available to more people than ever before. One new issue was the incidence of Alzheimer's disease, which Harvard Medical School reported had afflicted 2.5 million to 4 million senior citizens (Purvis 1989). However, the popularity of healthy diets and exercise, and the decline in smoking contributed to the improved health and longevity of Americans. However, by 1983 there were more than 122,500 fast-food outlets in the United States, three times the number in 1963, and many nutritionists warned Americans about the health risks of the popular fast food diet.

TIMELINE

1980   The teen horror movie genre began with *Friday the 13th*.

Toxic shock syndrome is linked to women's tampons.

The VCR is introduced.

Rock 'n' roll fans backlash against disco.

Break dancing spreads to the suburbs.

John Lennon is killed in New York City.

The Sony Walkman fad spreads.

The number of U.S. daily newspapers begins to decrease.

U.S. boycotts the Olympics in Moscow.

U.S. hockey team wins the gold medal in Winter Olympics in New York.

The multiplex theater boom begins.

1981   MTV is founded.

ABC *20/20* program offered first national coverage of rap music.

MTV cable network is founded, which popularizes music videos.

A *Washington Post* reporter surrenders her Pulitzer Prize.

The mountain bike fad begins.

The IBM Personal Computer is introduced.

Muhammad Ali retires from boxing.

John MacEnroe wins his third straight Wimbledon title.

Seven-week baseball strike is the longest in history.

1982   The tattoo fad begins.

The national chain of Victoria's Secret lingerie shops begins.

Reagan's War on Drugs is announced.

Sony introduces compact discs.

USA Today gains popularity.

The NCAA loses college football TV monopoly.

1983   The Internet is introduced.

The first cellular phones are sold in the United States.

Michael Jackson introduces the "moonwalk" on TV.

Secretary of Interior James Watt bans the Beach Boys concert.

The camcorder is introduced.

Audio music cassettes outsell LP records.

U.S. Football League is founded.

The cult movie trend begins.

1984   NBC begins the hit TV series *Miami Vice*.

Madonna's *Like a Virgin* is the hit album.

Crack cocaine is popular in New York City.

Radio host Alan Berg is murdered in Denver in June.

President Reagan opens the Olympics in Los Angeles.

PG-13 movie rating is introduced.

Sony v. Universal City Studio case is heard.

1985   The term Generation X becomes popular.

The first Blockbuster Video store opens.

Reed Irvine founds Accuracy in Academia.

Pete Rose breaks Ty Cobb's record with his 4,192 hits.

Independent movies dominate Hollywood.

1986   Congress passes the Anti-Drug Abuse Act.

Fox TV begins the fourth network.

The Meese Commission condemns pornography.

National Football League (NFL) players strike.

The first personal computer virus is discovered.

Ted Turner creates the Goodwill Games.

Greg LeMond is the first American to win the Tour de France bicycle race.

Mike Tyson becomes the youngest heavyweight champ.

1987   *Wall Street* movie features greedy yuppie stockbrokers.

Soul Train Music Awards lists rap as a category.

The Vatican condemns Madonna's album *Who's That Girl*.

Allan Bloom publishes *The Closing of the American Mind*.

The 24-day NFL players strike fails.

Sports-talk radio format becomes popular.

Teens drive box-office receipts to a record $4.3 billion.

1988   Michael Jackson moves to Neverland Ranch.

Rap music featured for the first time on MTV.

Grunge music spreads from Seattle.

Federal regulation of the tanning salon fad begins.

Talk radio boom begins.

Skateboarding becomes an Olympic sport.

Nolan Ryan, age 42, sets the record with his 5,000 strike outs.

1989   The World Wide Web is introduced.

The Grammy Awards and MTV Awards begin a rap category.

CDs outsell vinyl records.

Manhattan's Studio 54 discotheque is closed.

Bart Giamatti is appointed commissioner of Major League Baseball.

President Bush orders the Panama invasion as part of the War on Drugs.

Paul Tagliabue succeeds Pete Rozelle as NFL commissioner.

Pete Rose is banned from baseball for gambling on games.

Roger and Me documentary excoriates General Motors.

YOUTH CULTURES

The baby bust generation, born between 1965 and 1975, received much less media attention than the baby boom generation born between 1946 and 1964. In the 1980s, they were dubbed Generation X or the "twentysomethings" who avoided the label of feminist but, whether male or female, took for granted the gains the women's movement had achieved—in child care, parental leave, birth control, and equal access to educational, professional, legal, and financial opportunities for men and women. Society had changed, and adolescents in the 1980s enjoyed unprecedented freedom. Music, movie, and television icons redefined style, and male rock groups like Bon Jovi challenged gender roles. As men became more feminine, and women's fashions became more masculine, materialism was celebrated (with Gucci shoes and Rolex watches) or satirized (with mismatched outfits) to make fashion statements. Many men took fashion and music hints from the NBC hit detective series *Miami Vice* (1984–1989), based on MTV to a large extent, which popularized Armani linen jackets and pastel T-shirts.

MTV

The 1980s youth culture was often derived from music and movie celebrities. In 1981, Music Television (MTV) was founded as a new cable television network in New York City; it featured short music videos and, later, news, documentaries, rock concerts, and irreverent commentary by hip young VJs (video jockeys). After several corporate reorganizations and mergers, by 1986 MTV was the leading promoter of rock music in the United States and Europe. Modeled on Top 40 radio, MTV was recognized by record companies as an ideal outlet for marketing rock music. Many successful MTV video directors became Hollywood movie directors. It removed the walls between sound and appearance as the first cable channel intended for teens. Major rock stars like Michael Jackson, Bon Jovi, Duran Duran, Madonna, and Culture Club became established stars on MTV. Later cartoon shows (*Beavis and Butt-head*) and reality shows (*The Real World*) were introduced to broaden the audience. Michael Jackson was the first African American artist heavily promoted on MTV, making his *Thriller* (1982) album and video best sellers. This reflects the impact African Americans have had on popular music and how popular culture mirrored the baby boomer cool and lucrative values—freedom, consumption, and celebration of youth. By 1989, the MTV Awards and Grammy Awards began a new category for rap, which found fans in suburban white teenagers and spawned rich hybrids in Puerto Rican New York and in Mexican neighborhoods in Los Angeles as well as in Hong Kong, Tokyo, Paris, Berlin, and Brazil (Campbell 2004).

Teenage America

American teenagers had fun in the 1980s, despite serious problems with the economy, the environment, and other world disasters. For example, streaking, which had been a fad in the 1970s, made a comeback in the late 1980s. Streakers ran naked, alone or in a group, through public places or events such sports stadiums, college campuses, or commencement ceremonies. Streaking became an annual event at Harvard University on the night before final exams, and at the University of Michigan in 1986 on the last day of classes. Thousands of students participated in this retro fad at high schools, colleges, and universities in the 1980s.

Skateboarding, which was a spin-off from surfing in the 1960s, grew from a California fad to a national phenomenon by 1980. In two years, 40 million commercially manufactured skateboards were sold, and hundreds of parks designed for skateboards opened in the United States. The National Skateboarding Association held competitions in 1981, and the video *Bones Brigade* (1984) revitalized the sport with vertical riding and a focus on technical tricks in street skating and from launch ramps. Magazines such as *Poweredge* and *Thrasher* popularized the sport until this fad declined during the 1991 recession. Always more popular with boys than girls, skateboarding was associated with rebellious youths and punk rock outlaws, who often encountered police harassment. This fad spun off snowboarding in 1965, which became an Olympic sport at Nagano, Japan, in 1998.

Teens rapidly accepted the IBM personal computer (1981) and the Apple PC (1982), and used the Internet as a playground (1983) much more often than adults did. President George H. W. Bush joked in a 1991 speech that he wanted to be "computer literate" like the kids were. *Time* magazine declared

The cover of Time *magazine's special "Machine of the Year" issue, January 3, 1983. (Time Inc./Time Life Pictures/ Getty Images)*

the computer was the "Man of the Year" in 1981 because young computer users were the pioneers on the Information Superhighway. America Online and CompuServe (1985) provided email and bulletin board communication to a fast-growing and young market, especially after the Federal Communication Commission (FCC) prohibited higher telephone fees for data rather than voice messages in 1983. Parents hoped the PC was an educational toy, and computer companies saw children and adolescents as a gateway into more homes. New technology for consumers included the Walkman, CDs, camcorders, VCRs, video game consoles, cable TV, answering machines, cell phones, and portable phone and fax machines.

Schools and colleges found a growing demand by students for computer facilities. The campus computer center quickly became a more popular hangout than the library, student center, or gym. But Robert Tappan Morris Jr., a Cornell University student, invented the first computer worm in 1986. For this prank, in 1989 Morris became the first person to be indicted under the Computer Abuse and Fraud Act of 1986. This was a warning to computer nerds and campus hackers everywhere, as was the disaster movie *War Games* (1983). When the FCC permitted cell phone service in 1983, adolescents also were the first to see its social possibilities beyond business uses. The first laptop computer was the Epson HX-20 (1981), followed by Radio Shack's 4-pound battery-operated TRS-80

Video Games

The development of personal computers in 1975 led to the video game fever that mushroomed in the 1980s. A minor offshoot of the high-technology electronics industry, these games—first as arcade games, then on a video console—made TV sets and the PC a new form of play for teenagers. Some critics worried about the violent nature of many games and compared them to the aggressive and unimaginative tone of Saturday morning TV cartoons. Defenders of Pac-Man (1981) and other video games claimed they taught hand-eye coordination and were educational, interactive, and promoted intellectual skills in deciphering clues as part of the fun. *Pac-Man Fever* and *Do the Donkey Kong* were hit songs that swept the United States in 1982. Based on Japanese folk tales or cartoons, Pac-Man was an alternative to the space invader games. The Atari Company obtained the first copyright for video games (1980), and Nintendo Company introduced the Donkey Kong arcade game (1981) with $3.2 billion in sales by 1983. The Super Mario Brothers game proved even more popular in 1985 and became a TV cartoon program in 1989.

Despite a monopoly lawsuit by Atari against Nintendo in 1988, video games were played in one-third of U.S. homes, largely by preteen boys. Hollywood responded with a popular movie, *The Wizard* (1989), based on the Nintendo World Championship tournament, which made the new Super Mario Brothers 3 game enormously popular, selling 18 million copies worldwide. Nintendo also released Mike Tyson's Punch Out! in 1987 and its very popular handheld video game player, Game Boy, in 1989. Conservatives expressed more doubts about the gratuitous sex and fantasy violence in many interactive electronic video adventure games and inserted language condemning this new entertainment media in the 1984 Republican Party platform. Others complained about the addictive nature of video games to which many adolescents succumbed.

(1983). By 1991, the rapidly expanding chain of 116 Starbucks coffee bars attracted students and yuppies who lingered over exotic coffee drinks with their laptops and cell phones.

Teen Culture

Clothing probably expressed teen culture best. Taking clues from the popular movies *Flashdance* (1983) or *Sixteen Candles* (1984), girls in the mid-80s wore leg warmers, artistically torn workout tops, and slogan T-shirts with headbands or pony tails on the side of the head. *Fame* (1980), a popular movie about students at New York City's high school for performing arts, influenced teen fashions, especially when it became a television series and a hit Broadway musical.

Fashions changed rapidly but included spandex pants with shorts worn over them or colorful surfer shorts called jams. Pricey brand-name sneakers by Reebok, Adidas, or PUMA and plastic sandals called jellies were popular. Brand-name clothes by Benetton, Laura Ashley, Ralph Lauren, Polo, and Armani were cool, as were pierced ears and Ray Ban sunglasses. Teen culture was difficult to define but unmistakable when seen. Cool teens dismissed most adult fashions as bourgeois, but American popular culture reflected a middle-class mentality. Teenagers dressed in a variety of trendy "uniforms" that concealed most social-class differences and promoted equality.

Teens enjoyed a variety of leisure fads and trends in this decade, including the Pac-Man and Donkey Kong video games, the Rubik's Cube puzzle, and the Trivial Pursuit game. Teens wore Swatch watches or calculator wristwatches and acid-washed jeans and had fade haircuts. For some teens the neo-hippie look was popular, but others adopted the punk or preppy styles. The backlash against feminism was seen in the number of teens and women who shopped for feminine lingerie at the national chain of Victoria's Secret shops founded in 1982. Teens patronized the rapidly growing number of fast food chains, although McDonald's made efforts to prevent its outlets from becoming hangouts by banning jukeboxes, telephones, and vending machines. Fast-food chains preferred families with young children to adolescent customers. Teens also enjoyed TV comedies like *M*A*S*H, Taxi, Soap, The Jeffersons, The Cosby Show,* and *Cheers,* or dramas like *Hill Street Blues* and *Cagney & Lacey.*

Youth Fashions

It is difficult to explain adolescent fashions of the rapidly changing 1980s. The fashions worn by young Americans in this decade reflected the great diversity of the era. After Gloria Vanderbilt introduced the first designer jeans in 1978, these versatile pants by a variety of designers became part of the teenage uniform. Brooke Shields, the teen model and actor, appeared in sexy ads for Calvin Klein jeans in 1980. But mainstream American advertisers in the 1980s appropriated feminism to sell youthful fashions and cosmetic products to women of all ages. Madison Avenue converted women's liberation into female narcissism and the ability to have

Popular fashion in the 1980s. (Renee Lee)

it all and do anything you wanted. Spending time and money on personal appearance demonstrated personal success and freedom according to ads for Christian Dior, Ralph Lauren, and Elizabeth Arden products in chic *Mademoiselle, Cosmopolitan,* and *Vogue* magazines. Prolonging youthful beauty and health was a new promise for every woman. The most popular magazines published for teenage readers, *Seventeen, Cosmogirl, Young Miss, Vibe,* and *Maxim,* told readers how to appear more attractive, successful, and popular, and how to define themselves apart from the dominant culture fashions. The hip New York City newspaper *The Village Voice* debuted *Vue,* a 30-page fashion supplement distributed in clothing shops and clubs in 1986. Females and, for the first time, males indulged in a constant effort to appear hip and cool. By 1985 hip teens and young adults also patronized the new tanning salons to maintain a beautiful bronze complexion in the winter and the fad prompted federal safety regulation of this new industry by 1988 (Zoglin 1985).

Partly in reaction to media fashion advice, many teenagers in the 1980s adopted the punk culture fashions of punk music artists with ripped clothes held together by safety pins or tape. They wore leather, rubber or vinyl clothing, and black leather jackets. Punk teens favored sneakers, combat boots, or Doc Martens shoes, and had spiked or Mohawk hair dyed in vibrant colors, and tattoos or body piercing. Satirizing femininity, punk girls wore ballerina skirts with black leather jackets and clunky boots, or parts of school uniforms. This clothing was most common among a punk subculture of working-class or middle-class high school and college students, and more white males than females identified as punks. However, the punk fashion transcended social class, race, and ethnicity.

The Goth subculture, an offshoot of British punk, had its own fashions with black clothing, black hair, stark makeup, torn fishnet stockings, and black motorcycle jackets with icons from Gothic literature and art. At first handmade or altered by hand, both punk and Goth clothing was commercially available by the late 1980s in North America, Europe, and Japan. Punk and Goth fashions were not very common on college campuses but were frequently seen among music and art school students in the 1980s. When *Tattoo Times* magazine began publishing in 1982, few middle-class Americans had a tattoo, but this type of body art became very popular with teens and young adults by 1990. Punks were among the first to wear tattoos, and by 1990, about one in eight Americans had a tattoo or body piercing.

The Valley girl was a teenage cultural phenomenon that began in the late 1970s and reached full force in the 1980s, partly due to movies like *Valley Girl* (1983) or later in *L.A. Story* (1991) and *Buffy the Vampire Slayer* (1992). She was a self-confident, spoiled young woman who lived in the affluent suburbs of the San Fernando Valley near Los Angeles. Frank Zappa's daughter Moon Unit may have been the prototype for Valley girls in his 1982 song "Valley Girl." Her slang ("as-if," "fer shur," "totally," "barf me out") and preference for pastel and neon colors with bodysuits, leggings, lace, ruffles, and blonde hair defined the airhead personality of the Valley girl in California and her sisters in Europe and Japan.

The traditional preppy style of the Northeast and Mid-Atlantic elite boarding schools and Ivy League colleges made a comeback in the 1980s. Southern preppies were quite similar, stereotypically with shaggy blonde hair and elegant, classic, and understated clothing, speech, and manner. Lisa Birnbach's *Official Preppy Handbook* (1980) was a witty guide to this subculture, and the movies *Dead Poets Society* (1989) and *Metropolitan* (1990) depicted the preppy type. Preppy women wore well-tailored and stylish clothes best described as traditional and conservative. For young men, the standard preppy look included a navy blue blazer, button-down Oxford-cloth shirt, khakis, and loafers, or any conservative clothing brands from Brooks Brothers, Patagonia, Abercrombie & Fitch, or Lacoste. Rugby, lacrosse, crew sports clothing, and L. L. Bean outdoor gear were also worn. Inspired by the classic look of Hollywood stars Cary Grant and Fred Astaire, the New York fashion designer Ralph Lauren produced a timeless Polo line of menswear derived from the elegant man-about-town or the country squire of a bygone age in English tweeds that appealed to preppies and yuppies in the 1980s. President George H. W. Bush may have been the prototypical aging preppy. Many preppies grew up to become yuppies, but both groups favored sophisticated Ralph Lauren clothing. Preppies, yuppies, and the noveau rich who hoped to polish their manners read Judith Martin's etiquette books, including *Miss Manners' Guide to Excruciatingly Correct Behavior* (1982).

One universal feature of teen fashions in the 1980s was the tendency to wear athletic clothing on all occasions. This was especially obvious in high school and college classrooms, when, for the first time, most students wore sneakers, T-shirts, sweat shirts, baseball caps, or gym shorts on campus. This new adolescent uniform reflected the popularity of physical fitness and sports, and a new informality and relaxed attitude toward fashion. John Hughes' film *The Breakfast Club* (1985) offers a realistic portrait of the variety of styles worn by high school students.

Donna Karan designed a popular sportswear line by 1985 that flattered women even if they were not runway-thin (Rudolph 1989). Nonetheless, dieting and exercise for weight loss became major trends. Nutra-Sweet (1981) and Diet Coke (1982) appeared in stores, and the Scarsdale Diet was popular during this time. However, the death of singer Karen Carpenter in 1983 from anorexia nervosa raised the issue of adolescents' emotional health and the high price many girls paid to look fashionably thin.

The hip-hop style became an international youth fashion in the 1980s, first as a new type of music, dress, and communication that enabled African American teens to survive ghetto life. Its popularity with white teens around the world is another example of African American's musicians' influence on pop music. However, by "keeping it real" and true to its gritty inner-city origins, hip hop became an object of aversion and contempt to the middle class. Its tough image warded off danger in the ghetto by aggressive body language, hooded coats, baggy pants, and slang phrases. Clothing lines such as Sean John offered hip-hop styles as did Adidas, Nike, and Reebok sneakers. Oversized flannel shirts and gold- or porcelain-capped teeth became cool. However, hip hop fashions were often a barrier to jobs, opportunities, and money when young people dressed in this style interacted with mainstream society. But rap music and styles survived radio bans and mockery; by 1987, new groups such as Public Enemy and LL Cool J emerged, and women rappers MC Lyte and Salt 'n' Pepa found commercial success. Ice-T made Los Angeles gangsta rap a national phenomenon as NWA, Ice Cube, and Too Short appeared.

Dating, Courtship, and Teen Sex

Adolescence required that all teens learn how to deal with romantic relationships and moving from asexual to sexual relationships. In most cases they were not told how or when to begin this transition, so they depended on their peers for advice and examples. In the 1980s, most teens started dating (although they avoided that term) in mixed-gender groups. There was greater emphasis on mutuality and sharing with more casual sexual relations and fewer committed relationships. Interracial dating became common on the college campus, but interracial marriage rates remained low, about one in ten. Computer or video dating and using personal ads to meet people were popular for college graduates.

Only one in five boys engaged in sexual intercourse by age 14, but by age 17 nearly 60 percent of boys had intercourse. Because the median age of first marriage for men rose to 27, and 24 for women, there was an extended period of adolescence and single adulthood for most young Americans in the 1980s. In their early 20s, dating became more serious and sexually active, merging into a short period of courtship before marriage. More effective birth control developed since the pill in 1960, especially the contraceptive sponge in 1983. Contraceptive use among all women aged 15 to 44 was 56 percent in 1982 and rose throughout the decade (Klein 2004). This change along with more liberal attitudes about sex permitted more sexual experimentation despite the danger of sexually transmitted diseases and AIDS. The abandonment of parietal rules (sex segregated dormitories, curfews for women) by most colleges by 1980 concerned some parents and university administrators who had acted in loco parentis, but in hindsight, this was an exaggerated fear. American culture became more explicitly sexual, and the typical teen engaged in sex at a younger age than in the 1960s, but safe sex practices were also more common.

The problem of teenage dating violence received more attention in the 1980s when research, intervention, education, and prevention services revealed a growing trend. The physical, emotional, and psychological battery many adolescent

Teen Pregnancy

Adolescents have always been sexually active, but the 1980s saw teenage pregnancy reach epidemic proportions. The number of single mothers rose from 5.8 million in 1980 to 7.7 million in 1990, largely due to adolescents' inability or decision not to use contraception and abortion. About one-third of the males involved in an adolescent pregnancy were teenagers, often poor and less educated. This trend was also attributed to the sexual revolution of the 1960s and 1970s. The supporters of women's liberation and abortion rights had made important gains in liberalizing abortion laws. For example, California had 5,018 legal abortions in 1968 and 100,000 in 1972 under a new therapeutic abortion law signed by Gov. Ronald Reagan. Other trends influencing teen pregnancy were the vigorous antiabortion movement, rising divorce rate, and the growing number of couples living together without marriage. This all resulted in a steady increase in out-of-wedlock births and an average of 1.3 million abortions a year in the 1980s. The number of female-headed households also rose 46 percent from 1980 to 1987. Fewer unmarried teen mothers placed their babies for adoption in the 1980s, and many women planned to have their first (and often only) baby whether married or not. Cooperative adoption, with the mother selecting her baby's adoptive parents, and international adoption also became more common.

girls suffered while dating boys increased their risk for eating disorders, substance abuse, risky sexual behaviors, pregnancy, and suicide. By 1997, the Massachusetts Youth Risk Behavior Study at the Harvard University School of Public Health estimated one in five high school girls experienced dating violence. Congress responded by including teenage dating violence in the Violence Against Women Act of 2000. Philip Jenkins reported that this was part of the rising concern about child abuse and child pornography in the late 1970s and continued in the 1980s as part of homophobia campaigns in Florida, Massachusetts, Idaho, and other states (Jenkins 2006, 114–125).

In 1978, a panic about teenage pregnancy swept the nation, leading Congress to pass the Adolescent Health Services and Prevention and Care Act. As a result, sex education in public schools, which had not been a very controversial subject, came under new scrutiny for teaching that a young man and a young woman could have a nonexploitive sexual relationship before or outside marriage and that contraception was prudent. This fear of teenage passion was based on the high rate of teen pregnancy in the United States compared to Western Europe. But it was unexpected because the birthrate for American women aged 15 to 19 had declined sharply from 1960 to 1975. Polling statistics also showed that in the late 1970s a majority of adults approved of premarital sex. However,

The John Hughes Movies

John Hughes (1950–) wrote, directed, and produced some of the best teen movies of the 1980s, including *Mr. Mom* (1983), *Sixteen Candles* (1984), *The Breakfast Club* (1985), *Ferris Bueller's Day Off* (1986), *Pretty in Pink* (1986), *She's Having a Baby* (1988), and *Uncle Buck* (1989). Hughes is a philosopher of adolescence in his sweet, warm-hearted comedies peopled with one-dimensional, dumb, distant adults who love but misunderstand teenagers. Most of these whimsical tragi-comedy films, set in the Chicago suburbs where Hughes grew up, have a serious undercurrent and offer insights on the universal human dilemma. Hughes, who wrote for *National Lampoon* magazine in the 1970s, inspired the Hollywood Brat Pack in the 1980s and was responsible for the three National Lampoon movies. Critics and audiences agreed that John Hughes movies never condescend to teenagers and the perils of coming-of-age, which may explain his popularity and success. His movie soundtracks, featuring new wave music and Beatles songs, were also quite popular.

the number of single mothers rose by 1980, and conservative Christian groups expressed grave concern about sexual promiscuity and urged teens to practice abstinence until marriage.

In 1981, the first federal funding for teaching sexual abstinence in public schools was included in President Reagan's budget, allocating $11 million in grants. Annual funding continued until 1995, when it increased dramatically. The Southern Baptist Convention urged high school students to make virginity pledges, although research indicated abstinence only programs had only mixed results in delaying unprotected adolescent sex. Partly due to the culture wars controversy over sex education, from 1970 to 1980 the number of Christian schools almost doubled. However, single motherhood became more common and more socially acceptable in the 1980s while adoption declined. Network television's comment on new American dating practices could be seen in a revived ABC television program *The New Dating Game* (1980–1989). One bachelorette questioned three bachelors, who were hidden from her view, and picked one for a date provided by the program.

Prostitution also attracted much new attention in the 1980s although it had always been one feature of impoverished communities that increased during an economic crisis. One surprising revelation was that researchers estimated 100,000 to 300,000 boys were sex workers in 1987, and many more girls were involved in commercial sex at a younger age. Most young sex workers were homeless high school dropouts and drug abusers with mental health problems who lived on city streets. Contrary to the stereotype, the boys were not always homosexual, but they engaged in prostitution as women and girls did to support themselves. Living on the streets, they were exposed to exploitation, violence, HIV, syphilis, hepatitis, and other diseases. In New York City, a Catholic priest, Father Bruce Ritter, established Covenant House as a ministry for homeless and runaway youths, an innovation many cities imitated in the 1980s. Unfortunately, films like *Pretty Woman* (1990) glamorized prostitution with an unlikely Cinderella story.

Youth Gangs in Los Angeles

Although teenage gangs have long been a part of American history, in the 1980s youth gangs in Los Angeles became a major crime problem as U.S. gangs doubled in number from 400 to 800 in a decade. These ethnic groups of boys and men (aged 12 to 25) organized in the ghettos and barrios of Los Angeles and engaged in robbery, extortion, gang rape, drug trafficking, and carjacking as well as violent confrontations with other gangs. The two largest street gangs were the Bloods and their rivals, the Crips, both African American gangs with affiliated gangs in 42 states. Ice Cube, Snoop Dogg, and many rappers and hip-hop artists claimed gang membership to obtain street credibility. Hispanic gangs like Surenos, Nortenos, and Mara Salvatrucha, or Southeast Asian gangs like Asian Boyz, often had distinctive graffiti, tattoos, and clothing. Central American refugees from that war-torn region also contributed to California's gang violence. The East L.A. barrio was home to the Mexican Mafia who took pride in *mi vida loca* (my crazy life) and the *pachuco* cross tattoo. Gangsta rap, like blaxploitation films in the 1970s, offered middle-class white listeners a view of ghetto violence, erotic fantasy, and an alternative to suburban boredom at a time when Los Angeles County had an unemployment rate of 45 percent for African Americans youths who turned to the crack drug economy. Ice Cube's song "A Bird in the Hand," from his album *Death Certificate,* describes a young African American drug peddler, just out of high school and unemployed, who supports his girlfriend and their baby.

Movies, gangsta rap songs, crack cocaine, and readily available guns contributed to the proliferation of gangs and their hallmark drive-by shootings. President Reagan launched his War on Drugs in 1982, and the death from cocaine of Len Bias, a young college basketball star drafted by the Boston Celtics, prompted Congress to pass laws in 1986 and 1988 to impose mandatory sentences for drug offenses. Because of these harsher penalties for drug pushers, gangs often hired young boys to transport or sell drugs on the streets, which expanded gang membership in the 1980s. Migrating inner-city gang members spread gang culture with female auxiliary membership to other cities, and more recently to middle-class suburbs. Spray-paint graffiti by gangs became a common feature in all public places and was often quite artistic in New York City. By 1990, subway cars,

Graffiti on a fire escape in New York City. (iStockPhoto.com)

bridges, and walls were covered with elaborate gang tags, and some of this art was exhibited in museums. Organizations such as United Graffiti Artists (UGA) and the Nation of Graffiti Artists (NOGA) formed to place aerosol art in mainstream galleries. They had some success in New York and Chicago, but art critics viewed it mainly as aggressive masculine street art rather than high art, and the UGA banned female members. By 1984, international tourists in New York City were eager to see graffiti painted subway trains as part of the local color, but this fad soon faded. Many observers of hip hop culture noted that rappers would often moonlight as graffiti artists.

Shocked by gangbang gunfights, the crack cocaine epidemic, soaring crime, random violence, daily murders, and the threatening presence of 2,000 youth gangs by 1990, Americans purchased guns and home security systems. The public demanded municipal curfews, or crime prevention programs, and treating adolescent lawbreakers as adults. The rise of the white supremacist Aryan Brotherhood in California prisons, and skinhead gangs in middle-class neighborhoods, was another feature of ethnic youth gang crime. Schools were no longer islands of safety in violent neighborhoods, and *Time Magazine* claimed 100,000 U.S. pupils carried guns to school in a 1989 report (Ostling 1989).

Selling illegal drugs was a common and profitable enterprise for youth gang members. By the 1980s, the DEA estimated that more than 60 percent of American teenagers had experimented with marijuana and 40 percent were regular users. Marijuana was smuggled across U.S. boarders or cultivated domestically and sold in small quantities by teenagers to other teenagers in most communities. Although illegal, it was so common that law enforcement officials did not consider smoking pot as serious an offense as the use of cocaine or heroin (Drug Enforcement Administration).

Generation X

In 1990 the U.S. Census reported 80 million Americans were born between 1965 and 1975, an age cohort accounting for 30 percent of the U.S. population, surpassing the Baby Boom generation (1946–1965) by 10 million people. As depicted by Hollywood in *Repo Man* (1984), *River's Edge* (1986), and *Slacker* (1991), this lost generation of disaffected college-educated "slackers" formed their own subculture, working in aimless, monotonous, temporary, or dead-end jobs. Living in the shadow of their middle-class parents' dominant Baby Boom generation, which hung on to its youth and popular culture, these "twentysomething" men and women were called Generation X. They saw a dim future of service-sector jobs, economic recession, downward mobility, AIDS, and environmental disasters. Young white males, having experienced higher education's false promise of rewarding careers, dropped out or never entered the mainstream society rat race.

On the other hand, by 1990, 34 percent of new American doctors and 42 percent of lawyers were women, and affirmative action laws saw the average income for women increase 62 percent in the 1980s. Douglas Coupland's novel *Generation X: Tales for an Accelerated Culture* (1991) popularized this ambiguous term for the nameless generation in Western society at the end of the Cold War. In part, GenXers rebelled against the routines of American life in the 1980s, as George Ritzer noted in his *The McDonaldization of Society*. Fast-food franchises, shopping malls, and similar commercial entities created dehumanized, rationalized environments maximizing corporate profits with low-paid, non-union temporary workers performing mindless service jobs. Employee turnover was high and morale was low. Even giving birth in hospital chains became popular, and birthing centers offer standardized service to parents on the fast-food restaurant model. One unusual response to Gen X was the Lotus Development Corporation that Mitch Kapor founded in Cambridge, Massachusetts, in 1982. Lotus created the popular 1-2-3 software that persuaded corporate American to use desktop computers. The company offered generous benefits and perks as well as worker-friendly policies (stock shares, day-care, and benefits for same-sex partners of employees). Creative Gen X workers found it a dynamic place to earn a living.

College Life

Postmodern society demanded an educated and highly trained work force. As a result, the number of U.S. college students in the 1980s increased dramatically, reaching 14 million by 1990. Increasingly they were female, African American, Latino, Asian, or international students. Women made gains in college faculties and administration, but 91 percent of college presidents were white males in 1986. The return to prosperity in 1982 expanded college and university endowments, which was reflected in larger enrollments, new campus facilities, and hiring new faculty. The Sunbelt states' population increase can be explained in part by the new trend for numerous out-of-state students to enroll in Colorado and California colleges. GenXers were too young to have protested the Vietnam War and faced dim prospects in the downsizing economy. Draft registration began in 1980, but military service was voluntary and became a less popular option for middle-class men or women. Because they often had to live with their empty-nester parents after college, they were dubbed the boomerang generation.

But not all was well on the nation's campuses because female and minority professors found the route to tenured professorship too slow and arbitrary, and the multiethnic students often found assimilation into mainstream academic life difficult. White students feared affirmative action would lower standards and the value of their diplomas. Consequently, racial and ethnic tension troubled some institutions of higher education. Also some university departments grew rapidly, attracting students to so-called practical subjects like accounting, business, communications, economics, engineering, mathematics, and the physical sciences while the social science and liberal arts departments shrank.

The downsizing, retrenchment, and budget cuts that resulted caused unrest at many universities as broader social changes occurred. The increasing number of international graduate students, reaching 190,000 by 1990, led many American college students to complain they could not understand their professors and teaching assistants because of their accents and poor language skills (Clayton 2001). By 1986, Missouri passed, and other states debated, laws requiring English proficiency for teaching assistants. Nonetheless, college enrollments grew steadily as Americans realized that college graduates earned higher lifetime incomes, and their real wages rose sharply in the 1980s.

In the Reagan era many intellectuals, professors, and college students retreated from political activism. As academia fragmented into new highly specialized research programs, professors in women's studies or postmodernist literary studies, for example, complained the traditional canon in literature was obsolete. They condemned the curriculum as an outmoded collection of books by "dead white male" Western European writers. Often they insisted on adding non-Western, minority, and female writers to eliminate racism and sexism, or they created their own departments and programs. William Bennett, a conservative educator who

Reagan appointed as chairman of the National Endowment for the Humanities in 1981, was quick to criticize these nontraditional academics on the left. He used NEH grants to support traditional teaching in the classics, literature, and history. When Bennett became Reagan's secretary of education (1985–1988), this educational debate became a national political issue. Conservative students at Dartmouth College in 1986, and liberal students at Stanford University in 1988, protested, and Bennett condemned the Stanford faculty for capitulation to pressure groups (Diggins 2007).

The College Republicans were very active on college campuses in the 1980s, led by the Washington lobbyist Jack Abramoff who hired the young Georgia conservative Ralph Reed as his executive director. They spent much time denouncing as communists the United States Student Association (USSA), a group of liberal or progressive student government leaders, because the USSA protested against Reagan's cuts in student loans. They also sued to prevent Ralph Nader's Public Interest Research Groups (PIRG) from receiving a portion of student fees because the liberal PIRG campus organizations advocated recycling and rent control. College students and professors who supported the nuclear freeze movement in 1982 were also labeled communists, but in general the college campus in the 1980s was quite apathetic about politics.

Nonetheless, the expansion of college and university campuses created a youth-oriented and rather comfortable world. The modern campus usually included a large student center, gymnasium, pool, and sports facilities, and the revised curriculum offered many new career preparation programs. Rising costs prompted an increasing number of students, as many as seven out of ten, to work off campus and live in dorms. Consequently, many students took more than the traditional four years to complete their education in the 1980s.

Despite overcrowded dormitories on some campuses, as the *Christian Science Monitor* noted on September 26, 1996, many students delayed graduation. Even after graduation, some continued to live near campus, lingering in the familiar collegiate world. The campus also attracted recruiters for cults, which college administrators and chaplains criticized as exploitation of young vulnerable students away from home for the first time. Attending graduate school was increasingly popular for recent graduates in the 1980s, which also prolonged adolescence and delayed entering the "real world." By 1989 about one in four college graduates earned a graduate degree, slightly more women than men (Coolidge 1996).

Tufts University responded to protests on the right and the left, and to campus racial incidents, by establishing a code of free speech in an effort to maintain civility but later rescinded it in the face of media criticism. Brown University and others imposed free speech rules but with little effect. In 1989, a federal court ruled the free speech code at the University of Michigan illegally violated freedom of expression. But the debate over the curriculum continued as liberal professors charged right-wing zealots with undermining academic integrity, and conservatives complained that American higher education had become an attack on traditional American values that brainwashed the young. The new emphasis on multiculturalism seemed to be a compromise, but one that conservatives dismissed as mere "political correctness." When President George H. W. Bush entered the White House, the media discovered what they called the "culture wars." One example is the substitution of African American for black, a change many American liberals proposed in the 1980s when more colleges introduced black studies courses to promote cultural pluralism. However, the public resisted this change, and a poll by the *Washington Post* in 1990 showed 66 percent preferred black to African American (Schlesinger 1992).

Even athletics became an issue in the culture wars when Congress passed Title IX of the Educational Amendments in 1972. This law guaranteed equal funding for school and college sports for female students. By the 1980s, women collegiate athletes routinely broke records and won championships as often as men did. Gradually most people accepted gender equality on campus as normal. The 1980s coed was found in every classroom, and almost every sport, preparing for every profession. Yet a vocal conservative minority complained this was unfair to male students and would undermine American society.

Another change in U.S. higher education was the increasing cost of a college education. Higher education held out the promise of a better life and higher lifetime earnings, but federal government financial support for college students dwindled while the cost of tuition, fees, and textbooks rose. This impacted students from lower-income families most, and their numbers declined from 15 percent in 1980 to 9.5 percent in 1990. At the same time, the number of bachelor's degrees awarded to students from high-income families increased from 44.3 percent to 52.8 percent (Burd 2006). The obsolete federal financial aid formulas reduced funding for less affluent students, who increasingly worked off campus or graduated with heavy debts. One in three college students worked part-time or full-time jobs, and 80 percent borrowed to cover college costs. The student loan debt of most graduating seniors doubled by 1990.

Students responded to the financial aid crunch in the 1980s by working longer hours, attending college part time, transferring from a private to a public college or to a community college. More students were taking five or more years to graduate, serving in the armed forces to obtain educational funding, or taking high-interest private loans in place of government funds. Although studies demonstrated that working more than 20 hours per week had a negative impact on a student's education, this trend became the most common solution for many college students in the 1980s.

At the same time, the cost of college prompted some to wonder if it was worth it. Despite Census Bureau statistics showing that college graduates earned much more in lifetime income than high school graduates or drop-outs, the cost was a deterrent. Also more Americans in the 1980s saw college as preprofessional training, and the Carnegie Foundation for the Advancement of Teaching reported in 1986 that only 28 percent of parents and 27 percent of high school students saw college as an intellectual experience where one became a more thoughtful citizen. On November 10, 1986, *Time* magazine observed that job prospects were limited for humanities majors but bountiful for business majors. Yielding to student complaints about costs and demands for career and professional education, American colleges and universities in the 1980s became more successful in credentialing (for future jobs) than in providing a quality education in the face of rising costs for a bachelor's degree (Bowen 1986).

Music

Youth Culture and Technology

Robert Pittman, the father of MTV in 1981, had the idea of blending new popular music with short films broadcast on cable television. Within months MTV was the most influential forum in music for teens, replacing radio as the avenue to stardom for singers and bands. Music companies spent lavishly to make short videos which were actually commercials that sold their albums. The British band Duran Duran suddenly became successful after their videos appeared on MTV in 1981, and Michael Jackson, Madonna, and George Michael had the same experience of instant stardom after appearing on MTV. Michael Jackson, who had unprecedented sales with crossover appeal in *Thriller* (1982), and Prince were the first of many African American artists to appear on MTV in 1983.

Just as the favorable economic climate affected rock and roll in the 1950s and permitted the excesses of hippies in the 1960s, the declining economy of the 1980s spawned the social protest and punk explosion. Punk rockers expressed their vehement left-wing rhetoric, anger, frustration, and rebellion in their music and culture. They also reacted to the giant corporations' slick commercial popular music that accounted for 80 percent of all record sales by 1978; Columbia, RCA, Decca, Capitol, MGM, and Mercury grossed $4 billion. Hip-hop culture, which soon surpassed punk music, was also inexpensive and very profitable for MTV and music companies to produce and showcase. Rap music, which emerged in the music industry by 1978, flourished in the 1980s with Grandmaster Flash and the first white rap group, the Beastie Boys in 1981, and the first international hip-hop tour, the Roxy Tour, in 1982.

Music, television, and film seemed to be everywhere and more compelling in the 1980s, largely because of rapidly changing technology. Suddenly it was easier to listen to music and to select the music each person preferred. Changing tastes in music were stimulated by the advent of MTV in 1981. The Sony Walkman was plugged into almost every ear, especially when the compact disc first appeared in 1982. Long-playing vinyl albums were outsold by audio cassettes for the first time in 1983, although we still called new recordings a record

Circa 1980s video cassette recorder that changed TV and movie viewers' habits.
(iStockphoto)

or an album. Personal computers were a new source of music by 1985. The introduction of the VCR in 1980 caused an increase in movie theater audiences especially when the first Blockbuster video store opened in 1985. *Time* magazine reported on this new home entertainment trend in its December 26, 1984 cover story, "VCRs, Santa's Hottest Gift, The Magic Box That is Creating a Video Revolution." Viewing old and new movies at home by renting a video cassette at a local store created a new generation of cinemaphiles who flocked to movie theaters in record numbers and rented movies to view again and again at home.

But the VCR also changed American television viewing habits because it was no longer necessary to be home to see a favorite TV program. More and more people viewed a tape of the program later, thus ending the custom of watching TV with family members or friends. Togetherness around the TV became less common. The Big Three TV networks, NBC, ABC, and CBS had a new competition when the Fox network began in 1986, and cable TV service expanded to 56 percent of homes by 1989. The three major broadcast networks had dominated U.S. TV programming, but they owned only 20 stations and lost audiences and advertising revenues. The other 620 local stations were affiliates who decided which network programs to carry. Satellites provided a new supply of programs for affiliates and 400 independent TV stations as new channels attracted more viewers for movies, syndicated reruns of popular shows, music, and sports (Castro 1989).

The angry punk rockers who emerged in the late 1970s became a dominant force in the 1980s rejecting the myth of the heroic, virtuoso performer who played with technical skill. Blurring the distinction between spectators and performers, they shouted angry sneering lyrics against apathy, intolerance, and racism and for anarchy. By 1982 hip hop began to overshadow punk rock, with pioneering rappers Grandmaster Flash and the Furious Five releasing *The Message.* Hip white groups like Blondie hopped on the bandwagon. Blondie had a hit single, *Rapture,* in 1980. Despite criticism and ridicule, in 1989 MTV recognized and promoted the hip-hop phenomenon with its new show *Yo! MTV Raps.*

The murder of John Lennon by Mark David Chapman, a deranged Beatles fan, in New York City shocked baby-boom Americans in 1980, but Music Television (MTV) had the greatest impact on American youth in the 1980s. It was a form that specifically addressed youth as consumers and producers of music. When MTV introduced the rap music art form on *Yo! MTV Raps,* which promoted rap and the hip-hop culture, suburban white teens expanded the rap market. MTV viewers grew from 1 million in 1981 to 350 million in 2000 as young men and woman around the world adopted this new music medium, and its dance, clothing, style, and language. As a result, the disco music fad faded quickly by the early 1980s.

The US Festival organized by Steve Wozniak of Apple Computer was held in a San Bernardino, California, park on Labor Day weekend in September 1982. Broadcast live on MTV, it was the first major music concert in America since 1969 that was not a benefit. This was a celebration of new technology with 400,000 people who gathered over three days in 105 degree weather to hear 20 rock stars and bands. A second US Festival was held on Memorial Day weekend in May 1983 with 670,000 fans, but, like the first concert, it lost money. Wozniak spent about $20 million for these two mammoth festivals. Pop music benefit concerts in the 1980s received more media attention, but the two US festivals were memorable events.

New Music Revolutions

New musical genres popular in the 1980s included heavy metal, New Wave, Jamaican reggae and ska, hardcore punk, alternative rock, dream pop, techno, acid house, and two-tone. Metallica's album *Kill 'em All* (1983), with muscular, hard-driving guitars, made this the most popular metal band in history and one of the top acts around the world. Deborah Harry and her band, Blondie, were the major New Wave or punk artists in the early 1980s. The MTV cable television network provided a new outlet for young adult entertainment and news. Country music remained popular in some areas, especially songs by Kenny Rogers, Ricky Skaggs, Dolly Parton, George Strait, and Randy Travis. But hip hop or rap music proved to be the most controversial music. Public officials, parents' groups, and many music critics condemned rap lyrics as racist, sexist, violent, and homophobic. They complained that much of the hip-hop culture

The Boss, Bruce Springsteen's America

Born in New Jersey in 1949, Bruce Springsteen ranked with Chuck Berry, Bob Dylan, and Elvis Presley as a pivotal figure in rock music by the 1980s. His energetic live shows, long concert tours, and evocative songwriting lifted pop music from the doldrums of the early 1970s disco, glam-rock, and heavy metal music. Since his 1973 debut album, *Greetings from Asbury Park,* and his more successful album *Born to Run* in 1975, the Boss and his E Street Band were, as music critic Jon Landau wrote after one concert, "rock and roll's future."

Springsteen released his even more popular acoustic folk song album *Nebraska* in 1982, chronicling the loneliness and troubles of blue-collar Americans. *Born in the U.S.A.,* his 1984 gutsy, passionate testimonial album to working-class heroes in America, and the globe-trotting tour to huge outdoor stadiums and arenas, like Michael Jackson's *Thriller* and Prince's *Purple Rain* (1983) was an all-time best seller and Top 10 hit. *Tunnel of Love* in 1987 was the Boss's fourth number one album in 10 years. Springsteen participated in the USA for Africa concert called We *Are the World* and the Artists United Against Apartheid campaigns. He won an Oscar for the title song *Streets of Philadelphia* in Jonathan Demme's AIDS movie, *Philadelphia* (1993). Since 1990, Bruce Springsteen remained just as popular and was inducted into the Rock and Roll Hall of Fame in 1999.

imitated prison inmate styles. The Vatican also condemned Madonna's erotic album *Who's That Girl* in 1987 as blasphemous. But thoughtful people remembered that rock and roll had been condemned in much the same way in the 1950s.

Punk music, the most important feature of the punk subculture, had simple, short songs and sarcastic lyrics espousing the anarchistic punk ideology, devoted to individual freedom, rejection of mainstream society, and direct action for political change. Punk, reinfusing rock with passion and social consciousness, began as an artistic rebellion against the corporate bland conformity the U.S. music industry foisted on consumers. Punks complained that major record companies emphasized musical proficiency and bland solo singers. Antimilitarism, antiauthoritarianism, gay liberation, environmentalism, and vegetarianism were common punk themes. The music, especially by the artists from working-class British backgrounds like Johnny Rotten and Clash, inspired hardcore dancing with stage diving, crowd surfing, and moshing and often caused damage to the sound equipment and arena. In the 1980s the major punk bands were the Sex Pistols, the Ramones, and the Dead Kennedys, and the most popular punk singers were Sid Vicious, Billy Idol, Joey Ramone, and Nancy Spungen. Punk embraced Jamaican reggae and ska music, and hip hop was in part a spin-off from punk music in New York City. By 1981, New Wave was also derived from punk but without the political rage. But the punk style caught the imagination of many teens and American business responded; by June 1980, *Mademoiselle* magazine had a four-page article offering readers a choice between punk or preppy fashions. Even the soft rock singer Linda Ronstadt flirted with the punk style, as did Billy Joel and Cher.

But some punk bands in California adopted right-wing politics, sporting Nazi armbands and shaved heads in the early 1980s. The movie *Sid and Nancy* (1986) is a harrowing look at the self-destructive relationship between punk artist Sid Vicious and groupie Nancy Spungen. In addition, Straight Edge Hardcore, an aggressive post-punk genre, appeared in the early 1980s with Ian McKaye as a dogmatic subculture free of drugs and alcohol. By 1986, there was some crossover from punk to rap; for example, the Beastie Boys released their first full album, *License to Ill,* the best-selling rap album of the decade and the first rap album to hit number one on the Billboard album charts.

Rap Music

Rap music began in the 1970s as New York City African American teens in Harlem, Brooklyn, and the Bronx created a new style of hip-hop popular music combining parts of the punk culture, break dancing, graffiti (spray-paint tagging), audio mixing (DJing), and rapping (MCing). Influenced by Jamaican music, the rapper tells an autobiographical story in very rapid, rhythmic, lyrical vocals to a beat performed by the DJ, usually from a rock, funk, or soul song's percussion. By 1980, hip-hop culture was closely associated with rap as a commercial genre in mainstream music in the United States and was spreading worldwide. Grandmaster Flash & the Furious Five released *The Message,* rated the best single by the Music Critics's poll in 1982. The documentary movie *Beat Street* (1984), with pioneer rap artists Afrika Bambaataa, Buck Four, and Doug E. Fresh, helped popularize rap as a cultural movement. Hip hop, which introduced break dancing in the late 1970s, separated from break dancing in the 1980s when the fad spread to teens in California, France, and Japan. Michael Jackson, MTV, and the movies *Wild Style* (1982) and *Flashdance* (1983) helped break dancing enter mainstream culture. Break dancing was even a cover story for *Newsweek* magazine in 1984. In 1989, the rap group N.W.A.'s *Straight Outta Compton* was the first hip-hop album to win mainstream success despite the outrage of law enforcement agencies and a warning from the FBI against gangsta rap. Public Enemy's *It Takes a Nation of Millions to Hold Us Back* (1988) was named the best album by *The Village Voice* music critics. In 1989, Public Enemy scored Spike Lee's film *Do the Right Thing,* and its song *Fight the Power* showed political rap at the center of urban culture.

Prison experience also shaped hip-hop fashions with baggy jeans slung low and gold chains, sneakers, bandanas, and high-top fade haircuts. Snoop Dogg and Tupac Shakur advertised hip-hop clothing that instantly became popular with teens. Gangsta rap was a later form with controversial lyrics, as in Ice Cube's performance in the movie *Boyz N the Hood* (1991), seen as profane, sexist, violent, homophobic, and misogynist. Rap had more problems with censorship than any other form of popular music on radio or MTV. Lynne Cheney, chair of the National Foundation for the Humanities, was a vocal critic of violent and sexually explicit lyrics, prompting the white rap star Eminem to ridicule her in his songs and music videos. On the other hand, as Tricia Rose noted in *Longing to Tell* (2003), African American women also protested the depiction of African American women as prostitutes in rap music and videos.

Eventually, the rap music of popular groups like Run-D.M.C or Ice-T and Body Count influenced white pop singers such as Aerosmith, the Backstreet Boys, Christina Aguilera, Jessica Simpson, and Britney Spears. Queen Latifah, M. C. Lyte, and Salt 'N' Pepa were the most prominent African American women in rap, although young African American men dominated this music. By 1990, rap generated more than $700 million in music sales, about 10 percent of the recording industry annual U.S. market, largely from young white male hip-hop consumers.

Music with a Message

The Reagan administration announced a War on Drugs in October 1982 and made some efforts to reach out to young Americans and their music. President Reagan, a veteran Hollywood and TV actor, quoted lyrics by Bruce Springsteen and John Mellencamp in some of his speeches, but this was seen as superficial and unsuccessful. In 1983, Secretary of the Interior James G. Watt may have spoken more candidly for the Reagan administration when he banned the Beach Boys from performing at a July 4 concert on the National Mall in Washington, D.C. Watt, a born-again Christian from Wyoming, claimed that rock concerts attracted "an undesirable element." Watt was not alone; Tipper Gore, the wife of Sen. Albert Gore, campaigned against rap music because it encouraged angry, unloved children to be violent. Many African American radio stations banned rap music from their playlists (Forman and Neal 2004).

By the end of the decade, the gangsta rap music emerging in Los Angeles and New York City was a ghettocentric response to the deindustrialization, right-wing politics, and economic changes that had removed productive resources and jobs from American cities. Chronically unemployed or underemployed young African Americans with frustrated ambitions and too much time on their hands took hip hop to a new level. Much gangsta rap was a critique of the criminalization of African American adolescents by police repression, the media's view of inner-city youth as gang members, and the misuse of prisons as dumping grounds for young African American and Latino males seen as a menace to society. In the 1980s, most African American Angelenos experienced police harassment and many knew firsthand the chokehold the Los Angeles Police Department made famous. As Robin D. G. Kelley notes in *Race Rebels* (1994), "Virtually all gangsta rappers write lyrics attacking law enforcement agencies, their denial of unfettered access to public space, and the media's complicity in equating black youth with criminals." By 1990, gangsta rap music first topped the pop album charts with its rich, dramatic, first-person storytelling. Robust criticism of public education, unemployment, punitive government policies, politicians, the police, and corporate greed as well as misogynistic narratives and pimp-inspired vitriol toward women was its trademark message. During an era when commercial success, profit, and materialism were regarded as the measures of worth, Snoop Dogg and Ice-T laid down potent social commentary. Hip hop had an activist basis from the first, and graffiti artists hoped to transform gang-infested urban slums into colorful, vibrant communities. New York City hip-hop artists organized the Stop the Violence Coalition in 1988. The profits from their song "Self-Destruction" supported antigang programs. Grandmaster Flash and Melle Mel released an anticocaine hit song "White Lines (Don't Do It)" in 1983. Punk rock music also continued to criticize racism and sexism, and Michael Jackson's hit single "Billie Jean" aroused controversy with its lyrics about illegitimacy in 1983. However, some media critics attributed the 1989 vicious rape of a young white woman jogging in Central Park by a gang of African American teenagers to the dangerous influence of rap music.

One result of the human rights organizations like Amnesty International and Human Rights Watch was to raise awareness of international problems. An unusual response in pop music was a worldwide series of benefit concerts raising funds for African famine relief. In 1984, Irish musician Bob Geldof organized Band Aid with a variety of pop performers to record the hit single *Do They Know It's Christmas,* which was also a popular MTV video. In 1985, Michael Jackson and Lionel Richie wrote the song *We Are the World* that raised $65 million for the USA for Africa fund. Recorded on the same night as the American Music Awards, it was sung by Bruce Springsteen, Paul Simon, Diana Ross, Stevie Wonder, Cyndi Lauper, Bob Dylan, Ray Charles, and many other stars. Later that year, Geldof organized the Live Aid concert for famine relief in Ethiopia. Broadcast simultaneously from London and Philadelphia, it included Led Zeppelin, Phil Collins, U2 with Bono, Cat Stevens, Kim Carnes, Bette Midler, Mick Jagger, David Bowie, The Who, Paul McCartney, Tina Turner, and Crosby, Stills, Nash & Young. This 16-hour concert raised $283 million for Africans facing drought, famine, starvation, and civil war.

Inspired by this effort, Willie Nelson and John Mellencamp held the first Farm Aid benefit concert in Illinois in 1985. The funds raised helped family farmers in the United States who were facing bankruptcy. Additional Farm Aid concerts raised $14 million in Texas (1986), Nebraska (1987), and Indiana (1990). *Time* magazine reported on the growing problem for farmers in its February 18, 1985, cover story, "Going Broke, Tangled Policies, Failing Farms." In response, Congress passed the Agricultural Credit Act (1987) to save family farms from

The first Farm Aid concert in Champaign, Illinois, September 1985. (Neal Preston/ Corbis)

foreclosure. Rock musicians and fans continued to raise funds for other phil-anthropic causes throughout the 1980s (Magnuson 1985). The Artists United Against Apartheid released an album in 1985 to promote a boycott against South Africa. The entertainment industry continued its activism to raise funds and pub-lic awareness of AIDS, poverty, and injustice.

Best known for humanitarian efforts was the Irish rock band called U2, founded in Dublin in 1976. Since the mid-1980s, U2 won 22 Grammy awards, and by 1985 *Rolling Stone* magazine called U2 the "Band of the '80s." The lead singer, Paul Hewson, known simply as Bono, was sensitive to the social responsibilities of a politically engaged international rock star. His appeal was based on the en-tertaining and poetic views he expressed in lyrics and interviews. This included pride in his Irish heritage, best heard in the band's thoughtful song *The Hands that Built America* in Martin Scorcese's film *Gangs of New York*. U2 played at the Live Aid concert for Ethiopian famine relief (1985), the Conspiracy of Hope tour for Amnesty International (1986), and Self Aid (1986), a benefit concert for the unemployed in Ireland. In fact, U2 was almost as well known for humani-tarian work as for music, including support for AIDS victims, Greenpeace, and children in Chernobyl.

Just Say No

Just Say No was a slogan for First Lady Nancy Reagan's antidrug campaign. To encourage American adolescents to reject illegal recreational drugs as part of the War on Drugs that President Reagan announced in October 1982, and to make an effort to reach teens, Mrs. Reagan appeared in 1983 as herself on the prime time TV soap opera *Dynasty* and on the popular sitcom *Diff'rent Strokes.* Singer LaToya Jackson became the spokesperson for this antidrug crusade, and she recorded the song *Just Say No* in 1987. Despite these efforts, illegal drug problems became an even more serious public issue, and the Just Say No campaign was criticized as a simplistic and ineffective appeal to teenagers. The federal war on drugs emphasized law enforcement but overlooked poverty and unemployment as causes of drug abuse. The illegal drug business reached $90 billion by 1982, and cocaine replaced marijuana as the most popular drug. Drug Enforcement Agency arrests grew from 19,884 in 1986 to 25,176 just three years later. Heroin users were also exposed to AIDS by sharing needles.

This issue and the violent drug trade in Latin America prompted *Time* magazine's February 25, 1985, cover story, "Cocaine Wars, South America's Bloody Business" (Iver 1985). On August 18, 1986, *Time* also reported that President Reagan declared a "national mobilization" on narcotics abuse and ordered key federal employees to take drug tests. The National Institute on Drug Abuse found 5 million Americans used cocaine, and cocaine-related deaths increased from 202 in 1982 to 600 in 1985. Polls showed that the public was more concerned about drugs than arms control or federal budget deficits. Still, Reagan did not increase federal funds for drug control, preferring to rely on state, local, and private sector funds. He met at the White House with major league sports executives to recruit athletes to the campaign (Thomas, 1986). First Lady Nancy Reagan regained some of her popularity by this campaign, part of the culture wars, but the AIDS activist Larry Kramer criticized the Reagan administration's efforts as hypocrisy in his play *Just Say No* (1988).

Impact of Popular Music

Just as rock music had been condemned by some American adults in the 1950s, pop music in the 1980s received more than its fair share of social criticism. Punk, heavy metal, and rap music and aerosol graffiti were especially alien or offensive to so many adults that its aesthetic value was often overlooked and its social significance underestimated. Each generation defines itself, in part, by its own music, art, and fashions. But in the conservative 1980s, American fears, anxieties, and hopes found new targets in this music and culture of the young. Antiauthoritarian punk and hip-hop lyrics often caused the greatest concern among conservative Christian adults like Lynne Cheney, the National Endowment for the Humanities chair. Some radio stations and record companies banned punk music, and local police carefully monitored or disrupted punk concerts.

LITERATURE, PRESS, AND MEDIA

Growing Illiteracy

Robert Penn Warren became the first U.S. Poet Laureate in 1986, and Richard Wilbur succeeded him in 1987. But this did not foreshadow a renaissance in American literature. In fact, the decade ended with a very different type of poetry, the slam. This was a hybrid of spoken word and performed poetry as an urgent emotional release on any topic, or as part of a slam poetry competition in a tavern or auditorium. Although traditional poets participated in slam readings or performances, it often attracted hip hop and punk rock artists.

Reading continued to decline as a leisure time activity throughout the 1980s. Competition from the electronic media made reading seem an old-fashioned activity for most teens. In the 1980s, college professors reported that many intelligent students admitted they had never read an entire book from cover to cover until they entered college. Plagiarism increased dramatically, partly because students were not accustomed to reading books, newspapers, and magazines for pleasure, and email made writing letters or essays seem quaint. Purchasing term papers from commercial firms was common on many campuses until some states made this practice illegal. A more compelling problem in American education was the U.S. Department of Education report that illiteracy was a growing problem, especially for adults who had been high school students in the 1980s. One study found that one in five Americans were functionally illiterate (Bowen 2005).

Libraries reported increased patronage, but this was due in large part to the circulation of recorded music and film cassettes rather than books, or because public libraries became community meeting places. Reduced government funding, however, forced many communities to curtail library hours or services. On the other hand, book stores proliferated in the 1980s as national chains opened book stores in most malls. Publishers established or expanded their paperback departments and began publishing paperback reprint editions soon after the release of hardcover editions. As a result, paperback books, once considered trashy, grew steadily in sales. By 1989, about 80 percent of the books purchased in the United States were lower-price mass market, trade, or textbook paperbacks from more than 80,000 stores.

The American Library Association established an Office for Intellectual Freedom due to protests in the 1980s about politically incorrect or offensive books assigned as required reading in schools and colleges. The U.S. Supreme Court

The Closing of the American Mind

Allan Bloom, a University of Chicago philosophy professor, wrote a best-selling book in 1987, *The Closing of the American Mind: How Higher Education Has Failed Democracy and Impoverished the Souls of Today's Students.* The book immediately provoked a controversy about college education in the United States when liberals claimed the book was elitist, and conservatives hailed it as vindication of their criticism of the counterculture's impact on modern education. Bloom recommended a return to teaching the classical authors and the Great Books to make young Americans capable of true self-examination and understanding based on philosophy. He claimed that the university should teach students how to lead a meaningful life by a deeper core curriculum rather than an endless choice of elective courses preaching moral and cultural relativism (Campbell 2004). Bloom's message resonated with many readers uncomfortable with materialism in the "greedy 1980s" or the "Me decade." But it conflicted with liberals and feminists who advocated the addition of more books by female and minority authors in the curriculum, although conservative partisans in the culture wars supported Bloom.

protected libraries and schools from most book banning, but conservatives objected to graphic language, violence, profanity, homosexuality, racism, explicit sex in books available to children. Conflicts with community values led to banning in public libraries and schools such classic books as *The Adventures of Huckleberry Finn, Of Mice and Men, Native Son, Moby Dick, The Naked Ape, Slaughterhouse Five, The Scarlet Letter, To Kill a Mockingbird,* and Shakespeare's *Twelfth Night* (De Vries 1982). However, a federal court in Mobile, Alabama banned 44 textbooks in 1987 because of secular humanist content.

Nonfiction

It is difficult to categorize the most popular nonfiction books in the 1980s; they include many pop science (*Cosmos,* 1980), and self-help books (*The One-Minute Manager,* 1982, and *Loving Each Other,* 1984). Autobiography was popular (*Iacocca,* 1984, *Trump,* 1987, and *Yeager,* 1985), as was humor (*Family: The Ties That Bind,* 1987, *Pieces of My Mind,* 1984, and *Time Flies,* 1987). Pop economics was another best-selling genre (*How to Prosper During the Coming Bad Years,* 1979, *Crisis Investing,* 1980, *Megatrends,* 1982, *Wealth Without Risk,* 1988, and *Liar's Poker,* 1989). Andrew Goodwin's *Dancing in the Distraction Factory* (1989) analyzed how the trend-setting MTV and popular culture overshadowed reading which declined as a leisure-time activity in this decade (Goodwin 1989).

The most popular nonfiction books in the 1980s reflected the physical fitness craze, including *The Pritiken Program for Diet and Exercise* (1979), *Beverly Hills Diet* (1981), *Jane Fonda's Workout Book* (1982), *Eat to Win* (1984), *Weight Watchers: Fast and Fabulous Cookbook* (1984), *Fit for Life* (1985), *The Rotation Diet* (1986), *The Eight-Week Cholesterol Diet* (1987), and *The T-Factor Diet* (1989). The death of James F. Fixx, author of the best-seller *The Complete Book of Running,* while jogging in 1984, did little to diminish the movement to look cool and to get healthier by working out and jogging.

Time magazine noted a new trend in its November 5, 1984, cover story, "Minding Our Manners Again" (Friedrich 1984). One solution was an unusually popular book, Judith Martin's *Miss Manners' Guide to Excruciatingly Correct Behavior* (1982), an etiquette book, and others in a series including *Miss Manners' Guide for the Turn-of-the-Millennium* (1989).

Fiction

Popular fiction in the 1980s included the novels of Robert Ludlum (*The Matarese Circle* and *The Bourne Identity*), Stephen King (*The Firestarter* and *Cujo*), James Clavell (*Noble House*), and John Irving (*Hotel New Hampshire*). Later, the works of Tom Clancy (*Red Storm Rising* and *The Cardinal of the Kremlin*), James Michener (*Texas* and *Alaska*), Amy Tan (*The Joy Luck Club*), and Scott Turow (*The Burden of Proof*) were best sellers. Nora Ephron's novel *Heartburn* (1983), a fictionalized account of her marriage to *Washington Post* reporter Carl Bernstein, was a hit and the basis for the movie *Heartburn* (1986).

Pulitzer Prizes for fiction were awarded to John Cheever (*The Stories of John Cheever*), Norman Mailer (*The Executioner's Song*), John Kennedy Toole (*A Confederacy of Dunces*), John Updike (*Rabbit is Rich*), Alice Walker (*The Color Purple*), William Kennedy (*Ironweed*), Alison Lurie (*Foreign Affairs*), Peter Taylor (*A Summons to Memphis*), Anne Tyler (*Breathing Lessons*), and Oscar Hijuelos (*The Mambo Kings*).

The Mainstream Press

American journalism enjoyed a golden age in the 1970s and 1980s, an era of crusading investigative reporters and modern muckraking typified by *Washington Post* reporters Bob Woodward and Carl Bernstein and their editor Ben Bradlee who broke the Watergate story in 1973. This period included the New Journalism, which continued in the 1980s with such popular chroniclers of the era of rapid cultural change as Tom Wolfe, Jimmy Breslin, John Sack, Joan Didion, Michael Herr, Norman Mailer, Gloria Steinem, Hunter S. Thompson, Truman Capote, and Gay Talese, and editor Clay Felker's *New York* magazine. Novelistic techniques and long-term research with vivid scenes and dialogue contributed to this innovative form of factual news reporting. Television, which covered stories faster than the old journalism, prompted the New Journalists to be more creative. Television also celebrated the crusading big-city newspaper editor with the Emmy-winning *Lou Grant* show (1977–1982), although lead actor Ed Asner's off-screen liberal politics may have led CBS to cancel the program.

Newspaper and television journalists became celebrities in the 1980s and often appeared on TV talk shows and made cameo appearances in sitcoms. The Emmy-winning CBS show *Murphy Brown* (1988–98) featured cameo appearances by Connie Chung, Walter Cronkite, Larry King, Charles Kuralt, John McLaughlin, Lesley Stahl, Mike Wallace, Paula Zahn, and other recognized journalists. However, in reality U.S. journalism experienced problems and a slow decline in the 1980s. The *Washington Post* published Janet Cooke's 1980 story of Jimmy, an 8-year-old drug addict, but when the articles proved to be fabricated, all newspaper reporters suffered much embarrassment and lost credibility. Ben Bradlee, her executive editor, publicly apologized for not verifying his reporter's story. Bradlee's wife, Sally Quinn, became more of a star than the Washington socialites she covered as a reporter. *Regrets Only* (1986), Quinn's first novel, "highlights a growing Washington phenomenon: reporters are no longer just ink-stained hacks who cover the capital's celebrities, they have become, in fiction, in fact, stars in their own right" (Stanley 1986).

Newspaper readership and circulation decreased sharply by 1990, when barely more than half of Americans (54 percent) read a newspaper during the week and only 62 percent on Sunday. The number of newspapers published in the United States declined steadily from 1,745 in 1980 to 1,457 in 2002. Readership was linked to age, income, and education, with better-educated, affluent, and older Americans reading papers more often. Most younger people aged 18 to 24 seldom read papers daily (40 percent) or on Sunday (48 percent), but in the 1980s readership dropped in all groups except for non-Hispanic whites and African Americans. The big city newspapers, national weekly news magazines, and the major three TV networks were the Old Media serving a broad but diminishing audience; by the late 1980s, they faced serious competition for their traditional audiences and readership from the New Media—the Internet and cable television.

An exception to the 20-year decrease in newspaper circulation was the national newspaper *USA Today,* introduced in 1981, and *The New York Times* and *The Wall Street Journal.* Industry executives and analysts also reported that suburban newspapers—more than 2,000 weeklies and small dailies outside of major cities—maintained circulation because they focused on local events, town meetings, and high school sports for a highly targeted readership. Investors recognized the profitability of suburban papers when Fidelity Investments purchased dozens of New England newspapers in 1986. These combinations of small-town newspapers sold advertising to large chain stores or to local merchants who could not afford city newspaper rates, and they reached large suburban consumer populations. In response, some big-city papers began publishing suburban sections distributed in specific regions (Rowland 2006).

Nonetheless, most Americans in the 1980s preferred radio and television news programs or online news reports to daily newspapers or weekly news magazines like *Time* or *Newsweek*. This was reflected in the closing or merging of many newspapers, creating an increasing number of one-paper cities. Network news programs also lost younger viewers, although older Americans remained loyal audiences for the Old Media—the ABC, CBS, and NBC nightly news shows —even after Walter Cronkite retired as CBS anchorman in 1981. Ironically, journalism and communications courses became very popular with college students in the 1980s, partly due to Hollywood movies like *All the President's Men* (1976), *Network News* (1976), *China Syndrome* (1979), *Broadcast News* (1987), and *Switching Channels* (1988), which glamorized careers in the media. Robert Redford depicted an aging TV news reporter who resisted the change to happy news in the 1980s in *Up Close and Personal* (1996). Local television news, however, sought increased ratings and revenue by employing glamorous overpaid news reporters and anchors without experience in the print media. Consequently, TV news reporting became slick and trivial in the 1980s, the so-called happy news, when profits were more important than in-depth information. The popular CBS situation comedy *Murphy Brown* (1988–1998) depicted an investigative television reporter and news anchor who struggled with the happy news format. Polls showed Americans who obtained their news from TV rather than newspapers or magazines were less informed.

The media came under fire during President Reagan's administration, which supported a revival of anticommunism that many journalists dismissed. Distrust of the media continued to be a conservative theme in the Bush era. The 1991 Republican Party platform declared that the media, entertainment industry, academics, and Democrats had waged "guerrilla war" against American values. One spokesman for this criticism was Reed Irvine (1921–2004), a conservative media critic who founded Accuracy in the Media in 1969 in Washington, D.C. This was a watchdog organization that identified alleged errors and omissions in the mainstream press. Reed expanded his oversight of purported liberal bias in 1985 with Accuracy in Academia. Like many conservatives, he believed liberal professors were a threat to American higher education and national values. Hollywood exposed the print media's excesses in *Absence of Malice* (1981) and *Bonfire of the Vanities* (1990).

One exception to the so-called liberal media was Rupert Murdoch, a conservative Australian media tycoon who owned 175 newspapers and television stations around the world by the 1980s. He bought the *New York Post* in 1976 and was a friend and firm supporter of Ronald Reagan, Pat Robertson, and George H. W. Bush. Murdoch was best known for introducing the sensational London tabloid-style of journalism to his U.S. newspapers, often revealing embarrassing details about the personal lives of public figures and celebrities. Another exception was the *Washington Times,* a conservative daily newspaper founded in 1982 and owned by the Rev. Sun Myung Moon. He said his purpose was to create a spiritual salvation in America, but the paper had an average daily circulation of only 103,000.

The Alternative Press

The alternative press popular in the 1980s included many underground newspapers and magazines founded by counterculture journalists. Each of the more than 120 non-daily free-circulation metropolitan papers had a distinct, local identity that set them apart from the mainstream press. Some survived by specializing in music, movies, and the arts to attract younger readers aged 18 to 34. Many, like the *Boston Phoenix,* featured irreverent reporting on local and national politics. Almost all papers included sexy escort service, massage, exotic dancer, and racy matchmaking classified ads to boost circulation. In fact, these salacious ads were a staple of alternative weeklies across the country, accounting for as much as 40 percent of the papers' revenues. Since 1978, the Association of Alternative Newspapers has been the trade organization representing these diverse alternative papers, whose circulation ranged from 16,000 to 130,000 per week in larger urban centers. A portrait of an underground paper in Boston was fictionalized in the movie *Between the Lines* (1977), and the gonzo journalism of Hunter S. Thompson was depicted in *Where the Buffalo Roam* (1980). The alternative media achieved some recognition in the 1980s; for example, *The Village Voice* cartoonist Jules Feiffer won a Pulitzer Prize for editorial cartooning in 1986, and in 1987, the *Voice's* columnist Andrew Sarris was a finalist for the Pulitzer Prize for criticism.

Attorney General Edwin Meese aroused public controversy when he appointed the Meese Commission to investigate pornography. The report issued in July 1986 was highly critical of pornography and its impact on American teenagers. Later *Time* magazine reported on July 21, 1986, that Meese Commission officials had persuaded 10,000 convenience stores, including mammoth chains 7-Eleven and Rite Aid, to ban dirty magazines, such as *Playboy* and *Penthouse,* from store shelves. The federal court in Washington, D.C., halted this ban as a violation of First Amendment rights, and the Reagan administration was widely criticized for this censorship. The Supreme Court also disappointed many conservatives in 1988 by ruling for *Hustler* magazine when Jerry Falwell sued publisher Larry Flynt. The court found that public figures could be ridiculed by the press. More revealing of the new moral militancy in the nation were the Court decisions to allow states to prohibit homosexual sodomy and to close adult bookstores.

The punk rock subculture generated much poetry and prose, often in the underground punk press known as fanzines or zines, which featured news, interviews, gossip, and comics. The Xerox machine and the personal computer

Edwin Meese was one of the most controversial and ideological aides to President Ronald Reagan during his presidency, pictured in 1982. (U.S. Department of Defense)

desktop publishing were most responsible for the growth of 20,000 fanzines in the United States by 1990. One leading punk writer was Jim Carroll, author of *The Basketball Diaries* (1978) and *The Book of Nods* (1986), who formed the Jim Carroll Band in 1980, a New Wave/punk rock group best known for the album *Catholic Boy* (1980). Patti Smith, punk rock's poet laureate, published poetry and rock journalism in *Creem* magazine. Her band, the Patti Smith Group, toured with her debut album *Horses* which was responsible for punk rock's increasing popularity in the 1980s. She was closely associated with Jim Carroll, and with the photographer Robert Mapplethorpe (1946–1989) before his death from AIDS.

The alternative media was not overlooked by conservative Republicans who turned to it after Sen. Barry Goldwater lost the 1964 election to Lyndon B. Johnson. Adopting the techniques of commercial direct mail, appeals were sent to the voters who supported Goldwater or subscribed to William F. Buckley Jr.'s conservative *National Review* magazine. Richard Viguerie, a young Houston Republican, was the pioneer in direct mail campaigns to raise funds for the Young Americans for Freedom (YAF) organization. Buckley founded the YAF to offer conservative college students an alternative to the predominantly liberal campus political organizations. Even before the advent of computers, Viguerie accumulated 150,000 names and addresses of people likely to support conservative social, economic, and political issues. Mailing these people information or requests for donations allowed conservative organizations to grow. This bypassed the liberal mass media magazines (*Time, Newsweek*), newspapers (*New York Times, Washington Post, Boston Globe, Los Angeles Times,* and most big-city papers) and network television (ABC, CBS, and NBC). By 1980, Viguerie and other conservative publicists had 2 million names of voters interested in the New Right or Christian Right agenda.

This simple inexpensive step created nationwide grassroots groups, the foot soldiers of the New Right, who donated funds, time, and energy for conservative social and political movements. Single-issue direct mail on abortion, handgun control, pornography, school prayer, or sex education proved very effective

Horror Movies

Horror movies were one of the 1980s most important genres both in popularity and in social impact. Americans were preoccupied with the apocalypse as President Reagan joked about bombing the USSR in a "winnable" nuclear war. Music featured nihilist punk and death metal, and newspaper headlines warned of the AIDS epidemic and the urgent need to quit cigarettes. If horror movies reflected the fears of the time period in which they were produced, then *The Final Conflict* (1981) and *The Seventh Sign* (1988), which depicted a Biblical end-of-the-world scenario familiar to millions in the Christian Right, were quite appropriate for this decade. Some of the most popular films conveyed an old conservative message: sinners must be punished, as seen in *Friday the 13th Part II* (1981) and *My Bloody Valentine* (1982). The dark side of the physical fitness fad was transforming the human body into a violent monster, as in *Cat People* (1982), *The Howling* (1981), and *An American Werewolf in London* (1981). Even the perfect American life in a new affluent suburban community proved dangerous in *Poltergeist* (1982). Yuppies leaving the city for the pastoral suburb in *Fatal Attraction* (1987) paid a frightening price for adultery. Horror films taught audiences that yuppie family values were good and then criticized these values in *The Stepfather* (1987) and *Parents* (1989). The novels of Stephen King were a rich source for horror movie scripts; in *Christine* (1983) even your automobile could become a monster, and a friendly dog proved lethal in *Cujo* (1983). These horror movies reflected the dichotomy of the Reagan era, the idea that prosperity and success at any price was possible, but the cost may be too much. Ordinary people could become perverted by evil, not only those under the curse of a mad scientist or vampire. One film critic suggested that the sexism common to horror movies made them a kind of pornography, as in *Dressed to Kill* (1980), for example. The extreme violence of this genre prompted the film critic Roger Ebert to dub the 1980s the "dead teenager decade." Nevertheless, these horror movies were often very successful at the box office—for instance, *Friday the 13th* cost $700,000 to make but earned more than $40 million—and they obviously appealed to millions of teenagers who went to the multiplex because they enjoyed being scared.

in coalition-building without the participation of corporate donors or political party leaders. Jerry Falwell's Moral Majority used direct mail as an educational and fundraising tool and employed other new low-cost technology (computers, fax machines, telemarketing, websites, video) as it appeared. Phyllis Schlafly did much the same to defeat the ERA. Richard Viguerie founded *Conservative Digest* magazine in 1975 and was its publisher until 1985. By 1990, he used the Internet to promote conservative social and political causes that he believed the liberal media ignored or misinterpreted.

Talk Radio

Talk radio, a format in which listeners telephoned a radio station to ask a question or make a comment on a specific topic, began in the 1940s but expanded dramatically in the 1980s. When many listeners switched from AM radio stations to the high-fidelity sound of FM stations, some all-music and all-news AM stations reversed slumping ratings by adopting an all-talk format. The repeal of the FCC fairness doctrine in 1987, which required free and equal air time for responses to controversial broadcasts, created new opportunities for partisan and often intentionally inflammatory programs. As LeRoy Ashby noted in *With Amusement for All,* under Reagan the FCC deregulation policy meant broadcasters were less interested in public service and could air more controversial programs (Ashby 2006). This immediate and emotional programming attracted large and loyal audiences, often middle-aged, educated, and conservative male listeners who were outraged about media news reports. James Dobson's daily *Focus on the Family* show began in 1981, but it attracted more women than men. The most successful of these right-wing shock jocks was Rush Limbaugh, who began in 1972 as a disc jockey in Pittsburgh. By 1988, *The Rush Limbaugh Show* in New York City was nationally syndicated; it became the largest radio talk show in the nation with 5 million listeners. President Reagan dubbed Limbaugh the voice of conservatism, but liberal critics named him one of the most dangerous men in America (Colford 1993).

Other conservative talk radio hosts included Oliver North, and President Reagan's son, Michael Reagan. Some cities featured liberal or left-wing commentators, including Jerry Brown, Mario Cuomo, and Alan Dershowitz. Conservatives argued that National Public Radio was a "little Havana on the Potomac" that provided a forum for liberal commentary, which NPR denied, pointing to the influence of the Republican leadership on the Corporation for Public Broadcasting. Other talk radio formats were limited to noncontroversial topics (relationships, science, comedy, automobiles, and personal finance), but Rush Limbaugh remained the most imitated and popular of the talk radio hosts in the late 1980s.

Talk radio programs devoted to sports, with fans phoning the host to discuss recent games and their favorite players and managers, or to vent their opinions and their outrage, began at New York City's WFAN in 1987. Sports-talk radio soon became a staple feature of AM radio in almost every city. This was narrowcasting, not broadcasting, in which the station tried to dominate one niche market in the general audience rather than appealing to the largest possible audience. FM radio had superior fidelity for music, but AM radio revived with the discovery of the sports-talk format or the all-news format.

However, talk radio was the most popular new format in the 1980s because cell phones and satellites provided the technology for inexpensive shows. Most of the 800 new programs on the air by 1989 were designed for angry conservative men, and only a few were outlets for liberals. The murder of the liberal

National Public Radio

The Public Broadcasting Act of 1967 created the Corporation for Public Broadcasting, which devoted its energies and funds to public television. In 1970, National Public Radio was incorporated, and *All Things Considered,* its flagship evening news magazine, began in May 1971. By the 1980s, this commercial-free drive-time news program known for its journalistic integrity was among the three most popular syndicated radio programs in the United States. Along with its earlier *Morning Edition* program and the *Weekend Edition,* NPR broadcast the programs to over 500 nonprofit stations reaching 12 million daily listeners. Susan Stamberg, *ATC's* original host, was the first woman to anchor a national nightly news broadcast in the United States (1971–1986). Renee Montagne was *ATC's* cohost (1987–1989), and she was later cohost of *Morning Edition.* Robert Siegel (1976–1992) was also a cohost and producer until he joined NPR's call-in talk show *Talk of the Nation.* Each of these innovative NPR award-winning shows developed a cult-like following in the 1980s, attracting a predominantly white middle-age educated audience who contributed approximately one-third of the NPR annual budget. Often quirky, with some stories lasting for 23 minutes, *ATC* and its spin-off shows made NPR the most trusted news source in the United States. Despite a financial crisis in 1983 and a congressional investigation, NPR noncommercial or educational (mostly university-based) member stations increased steadily. Government funds represent only 2 percent of the annual budget, and the remainder came from member station dues, foundation grants, corporate underwriting, and about one-third from on-air pledge drives. *Car Talk,* a humorous car advice show; *Only a Game,* on sports issues; and *Here and Now* and cultural programming added to NPR's popularity. Despite criticism from conservatives that NPR catered to a liberal elite and charges by liberals that NPR avoided controversial topics, this Great Society experiment grew to become the most popular and effective FM radio broadcast in the 1980s.

talk radio host Alan Berg in Denver in June 1984, allegedly by white supremacists, inspired Stephen Singular's book *Talked to Death: The Life and Murder of Alan Berg* (1987), and Oliver Stone's controversial film *Talk Radio* (1988). In any case, the format's reputation for rude and angry behavior and for taking its direction from entertainment rather than news programs was a new feature of radio in the 1980s.

Network Television

Television was the most controversial of all the mass media sources in the 1980s, and scholars debated the impact TV viewing had on audiences. The three major

TV networks reworked some established themes and broke new ground in other areas in an effort to capture more viewers for new programs. In the early 1980s a new type of docudrama transferred tabloid journalism to the small screen in programs like *Hard Copy, America's Most Wanted, Cops,* and *Unsolved Mysteries,* which combined the soap opera with the true crime story. As the economy declined and politics turned to the right, NBC introduced in 1986 the first of a new generation of lawyer programs, *L.A. Law,* which depicted the California yuppie lifestyle and traditional courtroom dramas. *Night Court* (1984) on NBC was a popular situation comedy featuring a young, unorthodox judge.

The American family was an important topic in the 1980s, and network television exploited this interest. *Dallas* was a successful prime-time CBS soap opera (1978–1991) about a wealthy Texas family in the oil and cattle businesses. NBC interpreted a modern substitute for family life in the hit sitcom *Cheers* (1982) where friendships revolved around a downtown Boston bar. The show was last in the ratings in 1982 but numbered in the top 10 for the next eight years. With *Golden Girls* (1985) NBC provided a novel view of three aging woman who shared a house in Miami in an unorthodox blended family. ABC offered more realism by depicting a working-class Illinois family in *Roseanne* (1988), a highly rated weekly sitcom for nine seasons. Workplace families were also popular on TV; *Hill Street Blues* (1981) was a successful police drama about the intricate relationships between the men and women in a big city precinct. Afternoon TV talk shows introduced in the 1980s, including *Sally* (1985) and *The Oprah Winfrey Show* (1986), frequently focused on family issues. The *David Letterman Show* was a live morning talk program in 1980, but his sharp comedy did not suit morning viewers. He found more success in 1982 with the *Late Night with David Letterman* program.

Televangelism Declines

Fundamentalist Christian evangelists such as Billy Graham moved from radio to television by 1960, and many developed national audiences by 1980. These born-again Protestant preachers joined traditional conservatives and disenchanted former liberals in the new conservative coalition of the late 1970s. Recognizing the significance of this trend, *Time* magazine called 1976 the "Year of the Evangelical." Ministers like Jerry Falwell (1933–2007), a Virginia Baptist televangelist who appeared on radio and television broadcasts, formed the Moral Majority in 1979 using sophisticated advertising, direct-mail solicitation, and television techniques. Falwell lobbied for prayer and teaching creationism in public schools, and he opposed abortion, the counterculture, divorce, the ERA, feminism, homosexuality, humanism, secularism, permissiveness, pornography, sex education in public schools, the U.S.-Soviet SALT treaties, and liberal Democrats. Presidents Nixon, Ford, and Carter benefited from this move to the right, as did the conservatives after the Supreme Court became more conservative under Chief Justice Burger (1969–1986) and Chief Justice Rehnquist (1986–2005).

The New Right, led by 6.5 million Moral Majority members, the neoconservative intellectuals, and traditional social conservatives, triumphed with the election of President Reagan in 1980. Evangelical groups, who numbered 45 million, or 20 percent of Americans, purchased many AM radio stations and reformatted them with right-wing and religious talk shows, and UHF or cable TV stations became the basis of a national Christian broadcasting network. When the Rev. Jerry Falwell reached 15 million viewers weekly with his *Old Time Gospel Hour,* and the Rev. Oral Roberts appeared on 170 TV stations in 1980, both preachers became show business celebrities. The Rev. Pat Robertson created the Christian Broadcasting Network, and by 1980, his *700 Club* talk show was on 120 cable and satellite stations. His key aid, Ralph Reed, used sophisticated direct mail techniques to mobilize the conservative Christian Coalition by 1989. *U.S. News & World Report* rated Falwell one of the 25 most influential Americans in 1983 (Ajemian 1985).

The Rev. Jim Bakker's *Praise the Lord* (PTL) show was on the Trinity Broadcasting Network, which also provided an outlet for many profitable television ministries. Later Bakker had his own PTL Network and 12 million viewers on 100 stations, and he built the Heritage USA theme park in North Carolina. Robert

Televangelist Jim Bakker and wife Tammy Faye sit with Edwin Louis Cole, a guest on their program, "People That Love," on April 28, 1986. Jim Bakker is founder of the PTL (Praise the Lord) television ministry. (Bettmann/Corbis)

Schuller, who began his Pentecostal ministry at a California drive-in movie theater, preached on his *Hour of Power* show on 150 TV stations by 1980. Business responded to this movement with the *Born Again Christian Catalogue,* which provided Christian music, and publishers offered Christian romance novels and books like Charles Colson's autobiography *Born Again* (1978).

But all was not well in televangelism. The internationally popular Rev. Billy Graham had been shocked by the Watergate scandal, but he offended both Republicans and Democrats by distancing himself from President Nixon. The American Christian College in Tulsa closed in 1977 when its founder and president, the Rev. Billy James Hargis, was accused of sexual improprieties with male and female students. In 1980, Hargis returned to evangelism, but his influence had peaked. Teaching creationism in public schools, a major issue for fundamentalists, was found unconstitutional by federal courts in Arkansas in 1981 and Louisiana in 1982. The Supreme Court disappointed fundamentalists in 1985 by ruling that an Alabama law for prayer in public schools was unconstitutional.

The Rev. Oral Roberts alienated many in 1987 when he claimed God would "call me home" if he failed to raise $8 million. He said God wanted the City of Faith medical center expanded in Tulsa despite community objections, but donations slowed and the hospital closed in 1989. Televangelist and faith healer Peter Popoff was revealed as a fraud in 1987 on the NBC *Tonight Show* by a magician who detected him using a hidden radio in his faith healing. The Rev. Jimmy Swaggart confessed to a sex scandal in 1988, and the Pentecostalist preacher Jim Bakker, exposed for adultery in 1987, served five years in prison for fraud. When Pat Robertson's military record proved to be exaggerated, his 1988 campaign for president failed, the Federal Election Commission later charged campaign finance violations, and the Internal Revenue Service denied tax exempt status for his Christian Coalition.

Robert Schuller provoked criticism from his own Reformed Church theologians for his unorthodox positive thinking sermons and constant appeals for donations to build his grand Crystal Cathedral, designed in 1980 by architect Philip Johnson. Each of these incidents embarrassed the evangelical movement and diminished their political influence, especially when Jerry Falwell left the Moral Majority in 1987, realizing his role in politics was no longer effective. When Falwell sued *Hustler* magazine publisher Larry Flynt for libel, the U.S. Supreme Court ruled against Falwell in 1988. The contributions to his *Old Time Gospel Hour* and Liberty University declined sharply and his once influential political action group dissolved in 1989.

Impact on Local Government

During the Reagan and Bush administrations, as federal revenue-sharing sharply decreased, local and state governments were forced to reduce public library

Personal Computers

Someday social historians may look at the 1980s as the Age of the Personal Computer. Recognizing its impact, *Time* magazine named the computer "Person of the Year" in 1982. The Apple PC, designed for the office or home, was introduced in 1980, but the Commodore VIC-20 was the first popular personal computer (1981). Costing less than $300, it sold one million units and introduced millions of Americans to personal computing. The mammoth IBM Corporation, famous for high-end mainframe computers, introduced the IBM PC in 1981, and with new spreadsheet software (1982) it attracted millions of users. It cost $3,000 and came with a floppy disk drive, monochrome graphics, and the DOS operating system licensed from the tiny Microsoft Company. In 1982, the Commodore 64 brought personal computers to the average consumer, selling 22 million units—more than any other PC—and used color graphics which made it useful for computer games.

COMPAQ soon introduced the first PC clone, a portable model that was completely compatible with the IBM PC. Apple's Macintosh computer, introduced in memorable TV commercials during the 1984 Super Bowl, had the first mouse and simple word processing but used the new 3.5" floppy disks that were smaller and sturdier than the 5.25" floppy but held more data. It was known as the Mac and was soon popular with artists, designers, and publishers for its PageMaker design software and the Apple laser printer. The popular WordPerfect software, for use with the IBM PC or Mac, soon was the dominant word processor for all PCs.

IBM produced the PC/XT in 1983, as well as the PC/AT with better performance, more capacity, and hard disk drives for $5,000. The Commodore Amiga (1985) was the first multimedia computer, but it was used mainly for games because few consumers understood the importance of its advanced color graphics, video, and stereo features. By 1987, the Color Mac, the Apple Macintosh II, was introduced as the first color Macintosh computer, with a larger 14" color monitor and Adobe's high-end photo editing software, Photoshop. Apple distributed the new interactive HyperCard with the Color Mac.

Personal computers changed radically when the first Microsoft Windows software was released in 1985, and later, the enhanced Windows 3 in 1990 with the Microsoft Word word processor and Microsoft Excel spreadsheet. This made a PC running Windows 3 as easy to use as an Apple Macintosh. Microsoft, cofounded by Bill Gates, went public in 1986. In a major event with longterm consequences, Microsoft won a copyright suit against Apple and was in a strong position to dominate the global PC market. Although portable or laptop computers appeared in 1981, they were bulky and heavy until Radio Shack's TRS-80 model in 1983, a four-pound battery-operated laptop. Another new innovative company was Lotus Development Corporation, founded by Mitch Kapor in Cambridge, Massachusetts, which introduced the popular Lotus 1-2-3 spreadsheet software in 1982.

The computer hardware and software industry, which became a main part of the New England economy in the 1980s, benefited from pioneering scientist-

Continued on next page

Personal Computers, Continued

businessmen like Dr. An Wang and Mitch Kapor of the Lotus Development Corporation in Massachusetts. However, by the late 1980s, the innovative center of the computer industry relocated to Silicon Valley in California where the job-hopping culture created an open exchange of information and learning. The new California companies had more flexibility and capacity for innovation than the older self-contained computer pioneer firms in Massachusetts.

---

budgets and to close branch libraries that often served as community centers, especially for teenagers. For example, by 1990, a third of the Massachusetts libraries had reduced hours to save money. Most cities and states reported similar fiscal crises. Despite protests by the American Library Association, the Bush administration recommended a 73 percent decrease in the annual federal appropriations for public libraries to $35 million. Consequently, the readers of fiction, nonfiction, newspapers, and magazines at public libraries suffered from the new mania for tax reduction and fiscal responsibility. Some critics noted library patronage rose as the new waves of the unemployed and homeless flocked to libraries in search of job information or to stay warm. Like public schools and colleges, which suffered similar reductions in federal aid to education, the nation's libraries tightened their belts in the 1980s or closed their doors to the reading public.

American newspapers recognized the success of the women's movement by renaming the Women's Pages as the Lifestyle or Style section. In the 1980s the society sections of most papers were smaller and were no longer limited to stories by female reporters covering weddings and debutantes. The rash of "first-woman" feature stories in the 1970s, which highlighted the first woman in a traditionally male occupation, also disappeared as feminism was generally accepted and no longer news. Gary Trudeau's popular comic strip *Doonesbury* introduced a no-nonsense feminist member of Congress, Lacey Davenport. Most television news broadcasts also included a female co-anchor who covered the hard news like her male counterparts. Traditional magazines such as *McCall's, Redbook,* and *Harper's Bazaar* continued to publish articles assumed to be of interest only to women, on cooking, diets, sex, and health, but in 1980, *Ladies Home Journal* dropped Letty Pogrebin's regular column on working women's issues. Dressing for success in the workplace became a common topic for the press in the postfeminist 1980s. In fact, most women outside the women's liberation movement learned about feminism from the mainstream press.

SPORTS

Broad Appeal

Games and sports have always appealed to Americans eager to assert their courage, skill, and teamwork by victory and prestige on the playing fields. In the 1960s, colleges and their alumni subsidized star players, and by the 1980s, intercollegiate athletics were commercialized spectacles on television. Championships on all levels brought fans, attention, and profit to teams, schools, universities, and communities. Despite insufficient funding for extracurricular programs in many schools and the rising costs, sports flourished because most people believed they promoted the competition, pride, and emphasis on winning that characterized American culture.

Americans recognized the wholesome aspects of sports, especially when talented, respected, and wealthy sports stars appeared on professional teams. New immigrants and poor families understood that playing sports could be an important part of their children's acculturation and might lead to college scholarships or professional careers. The baby boom generation embraced sports with a passion suggested by the lyrical movie *Field of Dreams* (1989), based on W. P. Kinsella's novel and in *Eight Men Out* (1988) by independent filmmaker John Sayles. The poet Donald Hall published an influential book of essays on sports, *Fathers Playing Catch with Sons* (1985).

The Evolution of American Sports

The American love of sports in the 1980s had come a long way. Early Americans were suspicious of sports, although traditional English games were common, and even Puritans recognized some lawful sports. By the 19th century, sports and athletic contests were widely popular, especially for the first time in cities. Transportation and communication changes abetted the growth of sports. The *National Police Gazette* (1845) and *Sporting News* (1896) became the first national specialized weekly sporting newspapers, and major dailies covered sporting events by the 1840s. Many saw sports as rational recreation promoting robust health, sometimes called muscular Christianity. Immigrants contributed their own games and sports to American society at saloons and all-male social clubs, and by 1900, some people found fame and fortune as professional athletes. Intercollegiate sports, the sporting fraternity, the expanding YMCA movement, and private athletic clubs stimulated the growing national obsession with sports. The new discipline of psychology endorsed the basic need for play and dedicated playgrounds and athletic fields at schools supervised by adults. This all combined to make sports an entrenched feature of American leisure culture in the 20th century, which offered a sense of community and identity. The media crowned sports champions as American celebrities in the consumer society. National Football League commissioner Pete Rozelle admitted that he was in show business but said he preferred the word entertainment (Oriard 2007). By the 1980s population growth in the Sunbelt encouraged professional leagues to expand the number of franchises or relocate teams, and the physical fitness crusade inspired more adults to enjoy more sports year round. African Americans, barred from professional baseball teams until 1947, outnumbered whites on many college and professional teams in the 1980s, and Latin American and Asian players became more common.

Americans are firmly committed to sports, but in the 1980s, high schools struggled with the increasing cost of extracurricular athletic programs. Players, parents, and educators extolled the teamwork, courage, physical skills, and character-building aspects of team sports, and most Americans saw sports promoting the competitive and civic pride that characterize American culture. Others questioned the expense of some team sports (football, hockey, basketball) on which only a few male students could play. They demanded more attention to and funds for sports teams (soccer, tennis, and track) that more male and female students could join. Physical education in lifelong sports seemed to be more egalitarian and practical. By 1987, dedicated sports fans on all levels discovered sports-talk radio on local AM stations. These shows were devoted to phone calls from fans who called to discuss games, players, managers, and coaching with knowledgeable radio hosts.

On the collegiate and professional levels, team sports remained very popular, although the television audiences for the games were much larger than the audiences in the stadium or arena. Some critics questioned the lack of spontaneity and a diminished love of the game once adult supervision became a major feature of school and college sports. The growing revenue from TV became a distorting influence on college and professional teams, and sports gambling scandals troubled many. In 1982 the National Collegiate Athletic Association lost its monopoly of college football on television when Notre Dame University, the University of Georgia, and the University of Oklahoma sued for home rule to gain more television revenue. The Supreme Court ruled against the NCAA in 1984. But college basketball was becoming even more popular than football, and the NCAA continued to prosper by controlling those broadcasting rights.

The death of the Boston Celtics' newest recruit, Len Bias, an All-American forward from the University of Maryland, from cocaine in 1986 was a shock to the National Basketball Association and prompted demands for testing of athletes for anabolic steroids and other drugs. He was Celtics President Red Auerbach's No. 1 draft pick, and Bias had signed a lucrative deal with Reebok shoes the day before his tragic death (Callahan 1986).

The decade began with an infamous sports hoax when Rosie Ruiz, an unknown 23-year-old New York woman, won the Boston Marathon on April 21, 1980. When race officials and photographers could find no evidence that she had run the 26 mile course, observers testified that Ms. Ruiz entered the race at the last half mile and merely sprinted to the finish line. She qualified for this race by running well in the New York City Marathon, but she had accomplished that only by riding the subway and then reentering the race. In any case, this unprecedented hoax highlighted the increasing presence of women in sports on all levels. Bicycling continued to attract young men and women, especially when Greg LeMond became the first American to win the Tour de France race in 1986 (Phillips 1986).

The U.S. Olympic team's unexpected victory over the Soviet Union hockey team, the "miracle on ice," in February 1980, was more in keeping with the mood of the nation in the 1980s. It created a national euphoria for hero-starved Americans by boosting national pride and patriotism and gave new popularity to college and National Hockey League ice hockey teams. The Most Valuable Player in the NHL in the 1980s was Wayne Gretzky of the Edmonton Oilers, and his dazzling play attracted more and more fans to the once obscure game. Gretzky shared a *Time* magazine cover story in 1985 with the Boston Celtics star Larry Bird (Callahan 1985).

It was the National Association for Stock Car Auto Racing (NASCAR), however, that claimed the highest paid attendance of any American sports events. By 1980, auto racing entered the modern era when the Daytona 500 was first nationally televised on CBS and the purses awarded for championships significantly increased.

Sports and Community

The National Basketball Association (NBA) outpaced baseball as America's favorite televised sport (after football) in the 1980s. Even in the 1960s, basketball had more participants and spectators than any organized sport. Los Angeles dominated the NBA with five championships; Boston had three; Detroit, two; and Philadelphia, one. Larry Bird of the Boston Celtics and Magic Johnson of the Los Angeles Lakers were the marquis players who revived the fierce Boston–Los Angeles rivalry in the 1980s. The contrast in styles between the rural white Bird of the hardnosed Celtics and the urban African American Johnson of the stylish Lakers attracted huge TV audiences to the moribund NBA. In keeping with the new racial harmony, the two players became good friends off court and they even appeared together on television and in commercials (Callahan 1985).

In the National Football League (NFL) no one team was dominant, but the San Francisco 49ers won four Super Bowl championships in the 1980s. The sport's popularity grew when the new U.S. Football League (USFL, 1983–1985) challenged the NFL for a few years. Real estate tycoon Donald Trump, owner of the New Jersey Generals team, made news by hiring veteran NFL players and coaches and Heisman Trophy winners Herschel Walker and Doug Flutie, but instability ended the USFL in 1985. When jurors awarded the USFL a mere $1 for damages in its antitrust suit against the NFL, the league cancelled the 1986 season. Trump spoke for most owners when he gave permission to Walker and

Los Angeles Lakers star Earvin "Magic" Johnson (right) moves in, attempting to block Larry Bird of the Celtics in an NBA Finals game at the Boston Garden on June 9, 1985. (Bettmann/ Corbis)

his other players to negotiate with the Dallas Cowboys. He told *Time* magazine, "While I have a legal right to their services, I don't think I have a moral right to stand in the way of their careers (*Time,* August 18, 1986, p. 20). By 1980, more sports fans (70 percent) followed football than baseball (54 percent), the sport once known as "America's national pastime."

In Major League Baseball (MLB) the Los Angeles Dodgers won the World Series in 1981 and 1988, but no single team dominated professional baseball in this decade. Fans introduced the new phenomenon known as the Wave on October 15, 1981, when the Oakland Athletics hosted the New York Yankees. This fad, in which fans stood and waved their arms in the stands section by section, soon spread to every baseball and football stadium. When the media mogul Ted Turner purchased the Atlanta Braves in 1976, he made news by micromanaging the team. The seven-week long MLB strike in 1981, the longest in

history, disrupted the summer for millions of fans. Some fans turned to minor league baseball for entertainment. But when Pete Rose surpassed Ty Cobb's record with his 4,192nd hit in 1985, Americans' passion for the game revived. However, Commissioner Bart Giammatti banned Rose from baseball for life in 1989 for gambling on sports games, and many fans were shocked. This kept Charlie Hustle, as Rose was known, out of the Hall of Fame in Cooperstown, even after Rose later admitted his guilt. Major League Baseball on television also changed; ABC broadcast every game of the 1985 World Series for the biggest audience ever, the first time all the games were night games. In 1989, NBC's Gayle Gardner became the first female MLB TV host.

The Boston Red Sox, who had not won the World Series since 1918, came close to winning in 1986 but lost to the New York Mets in a heart-breaking series. But some important changes occurred in baseball in the 1980s, especially the new adult hobby of collecting or trading baseball cards with formal organizations, exhibits, and the sale of the high-priced collectors' items in hobby shops. Traditionalists complained this distorted what had been a boys' hobby since the 1880s. Reports in 1989 of athletes on high school, college, and professional

Physical Fitness

By the 1980s, millions of American men and women embarked on a quest for improved health and self-fulfillment through regular rigorous physical exercise. This new fitness craze focused on the self, not on society. Teenagers and suburban middle-class professionals wanted to look and feel better and enjoy improved health and longer life. They heeded doctors' warnings about tobacco, alcohol, and obesity and became aware that cancer and cardiovascular diseases, the leading causes of death in the United States, were not controlled by medicine. By 1980, 20 million people reported they jogged or exercised regularly, YMCA memberships increased sharply, and the number of commercial health clubs rose to 7,000 in 1986. Colleges and universities used expanded sports and physical fitness facilities for men and women to attract new students.

Jogging became common, and the 26-mile New York City marathon had 20,000 official runners in 1985. The venerable Boston Marathon had similar gains each April, especially when women runners (1972) and corporate sponsors (1986) were permitted. The iron-man triathlon, a new invention in the running craze, attracted more than a million Americans from 1980 to 1986, who competed in a 2-mile swim, 112-mile bicycle ride, and a 26-mile road race. Weight lifting to reshape the body often accompanied running regimes, and dieting became a national obsession. One result was that 3 million people, especially young women, suffered from anorexia nervosa, bulimia, and other eating disorders by 1986, and cosmetic surgery became very common. Children, however, performed poorly on physical fitness tests and working-class Americans rarely engaged in any systematic exercise.

The sale of exercise clothing and equipment was highest among teens, but many middle-class adults considered jogging or running clothes and shoes with the brand names Adidas, Nike, Puma, and Reebok quite fashionable. College students wore sports clothing on campus every day. Many employers reimbursed workers for membership in fitness or wellness clubs. Housewives and senior citizens engaged in mall walking, a new form of exercise in suburban shopping malls. In a safe, secure, comfortable indoor environment, walkers gathered in small groups for low impact morning exercise through the long, uncrowded mall corridors. The influence of feminism was apparent, as the noncompetitive and social atmosphere of the fitness craze attracted more women than traditional sports. On the other hand, hockey became more popular in this decade and auto racing, especially NASCAR, attracted the largest paid attendance of any sport in the United States.

The term "couch potato" of the late 1980s was a term of reproach for men and women who rejected the physical fitness fad. Nutritionists recognized one obstacle to physical fitness was the popularity of fast-food restaurants, which increased from 70,000 in 1970 to 186,000 in 2001. As physical activity declined 13 percent among U.S. adolescents from 1980 to 2000, obesity became a serious health issue as Morgan Spurlock reported in *Don't Eat This Book* (2005).

teams using performance-enhancing steroids and other drugs also tarnished baseball and other sports. Traditionalists also fumed when Wrigley Field began its first night games in 1988. The appointment of Yale University president A. Bartlett Giamatti as president of the National League (1986–1989) was a surprising choice, and one expected to revive the game's prestige. Giamatti died shortly after he became the 7th commissioner of major league baseball in 1989.

Boxing experienced a revival in the decade. Marvin Hagler, one of the best middleweight boxers in history, defended his championship 12 times from 1981 to 1987. The welterweight champion Sugar Ray Leonard defeated Hagler in 1987 to become middleweight champion, and Leonard also won the title as light heavyweight champion in 1988. Michael Spinks, the brother of heavyweight champion Leon Spinks (1978), was light heavyweight champ in 1981–1988 and became heavyweight champ in 1985 until he lost to Mike Tyson in 1988. Iron Mike Tyson became the youngest heavyweight champion in 1986 but lost his title in 1990 and suffered a series of embarrassing personal problems.

Soccer had long been a popular recreational sport in the United States. The first soccer (or football) club was organized in Boston in 1862, and many cities had high school or ethnic community soccer teams by the 1960s. But this sport became much more popular in the 1980s as many budget-conscious schools and youth organizations saw soccer as more economical and egalitarian than football or hockey. As children played soccer in the schools, they grew to love the sport, and American college teams soon found more experienced players. Unlike the rest of the world, American soccer was more popular with women, who competed successfully at the Olympic and world championship levels. Stars like Mia Hamm, Julie Foudy, and Brandi Chastain were internationally celebrated long before American male soccer players emerged. In recognition, the first World Cup games were held in the United States in 1994 and United States Soccer League for professional teams formed. In 1990, the United States competed in the World Cup for the first time in 40 years. But the roots of American soccer in children's recreation are clear; in the 1980s, the term "soccer mom" was coined. It referred to suburban mothers who drove their children to soccer practice and attended their soccer games.

The Los Angeles Olympics, 1984

The 1984 Summer Olympics, the Games of the XXIII Olympiad, were held in Los Angeles from July 28 to August 12, 1984. For the first time an American president, Ronald Reagan, opened the games for 6,799 athletes from a record 140 nations. For the third consecutive time, a boycott prevented all member nations from participating. The Soviet Union and 13 Communist allies did not attend in retaliation for the U.S. boycott of the 1980 Olympics in Moscow. As a result, the level of competition was not what had been expected. The U.S. won a record

83 gold medals, 61 silver, 30 bronze, and ranked first in total medals with 174 medals. West Germany was second with 59 medals. However, 12 athletes were disqualified for use of anabolic steroids.

An American runner from Alabama, Carl Lewis, duplicated Jesse Owens' 1936 track and field success by winning four gold medals in the 100- and 200-meter race, the long jump, and in the 4 x 100 meter relay race. His teammate, Valerie Brisco-Hooks, also won three track events. The U.S. hurdler Edwin Moses won a gold medal too. However, the most popular American athlete was 16-year-old Mary Lou Retton, who won the women's All-Around gymnastic event. The American diver Greg Louganis, considered the greatest diver in Olympics history, won two gold medals. The American swimmers Mary T. Meagher, Tracy Caulkins, Nancy Hogshead, Rick Carey, Rowdy Gaines, and Mike Heath each won three gold medals. For the first time women competed in the marathon, and Joan Benoit of Maine won the race.

The 1984 Olympics were the first privately financed Games. The Games were so successful that *Time* magazine named the president of the organizing committee, Peter Ueberroth, as Man of the Year in its January 7, 1985, cover story. Corporate sponsorship and sale of the TV rights resulted in a surplus of $220 million and a worldwide revival of interest in hosting future Games. John Williams, who composed the theme for the Olympiad, won a Grammy Award for his *Olympic Fanfare and Theme*. Soccer games at the Olympics were surprisingly well attended, demonstrating soccer's new popularity in North America. But many were surprised when hip-hop culture was included in the closing ceremonies for the Summer Olympics, featuring 200 break dancers performing with Lionel Richie.

Race and Sports

By the 1980s, a new era of sophistication arrived in sports. CBS fired sports commentator Jimmy "the Greek" Snyder in 1988 a day after he said on air that African Americans had been bred to produce stronger children during slavery. The growing numbers and achievements of African Americans in sports and the universal acceptance they had won in society made such unwitting racism unacceptable. In the 1980s, African Americans counted for half the college and professional players, and Latino and Asian players added to the diverse racial composition of most teams. Stanford University named the first African American head coach of football, and the Oakland Raiders followed in 1989. By 1980, the new Entertainment and Sports Programming Network (ESPN) hired Greg Gumbel, and other African American sports commentators soon followed him on the air (Davies 2007).

Although Larry Bird of the Boston Celtics was dubbed the "Great White Hope," African American players dominated basketball in the 1980s. The friendship

Mike Tyson

The most successful and feared boxer of the 1980s was Mike Tyson, the world Heavyweight Champion (1986–1990). Born in 1996 in the Brownsville African American ghetto in Brooklyn, New York, Michael Tyson was raised in poverty and sent to juvenile detention centers for street gang crimes until he was trained by the legendary Cus D'Amato who became his foster father in 1980. Making his professional debut in 1985, Iron Mike was undefeated in 37 consecutive fights. He became the youngest Heavyweight Champion in 1986 at age 20 and added the WBA championship to his record in 1987. Often compared to the champion Jack Dempsey for his savagery, dazzling reflexes, and ability to galvanize the crowds, there was an unsettling air about him in the ring, an unglamorous, single-minded, and violent boxer. After the death of D'Amato in 1985, however, Tyson had a series of personal and professional troubles as his skills and training habits deteriorated. He lost the championships in 1990 but continued boxing until 2005 with a record of 50 wins, 6 losses, 2 no-contests, and 44 knockouts. Tyson earned $400 million in his career but later was bankrupt.

between Bird, a fierce competitor and key clutch player, and his on-court rival, Magic Johnson, blossomed when the two stars made a series of TV commercials for Converse sneakers in 1984. The Celtics and Lakers played in every NBA final series in the 1980s, which created a renaissance for professional basketball with Bird and Magic as the major stars. Even the Chicago Bulls star, Michael Jordan, who succeeded Bird as the league's most respected clutch player, did not hesitate to tell *Sports Illustrated* that Larry Bird was the only player he would want to take the last game-winning shot. The sportsmanship and racial harmony these and other athletes displayed did much to diminish racial tension in the United States.

Collegiate and professional sports provided other, if less striking, examples of racial harmony and mutual respect in the 1980s. Baseball, once the most segregated sport, recruited many outstanding African American, Asian, and Latino players, and football rivaled basketball as the African American athlete's route to fame and fortune. If fair play was a traditional American value, in this decade it found eloquent expression on school and professional playing fields. The United Nations' international convention against apartheid in sports (1985) also was a symbolic but eventually effective statement against racism.

Sports and Labor: The Football Strike of 1987

The National Football League Players' Association called a strike against the 28 NFL teams when their 1982 agreement expired at the start of the 1987 season.

This dispute dated from the founding of the union in 1956. Although five earlier strikes had failed, the players hoped to win a larger share of the NFL's TV revenues. Each team earned $17 million a year from TV, and the players, whose median salary was $170,000 per year, demanded salary increases, pensions, and other benefits. The 1,585 players argued that their football careers lasted only an average of 3.2 years and many veteran players suffered permanent injury and a shortened life span.

The AFL-CIO picketed some stadiums but the union had no strike fund to pay the strikers. Team owners prevented media coverage of the negotiations and used publicity more effectively than the union. Strikebreakers or replacement players hired at low salaries played the early games, and many TV viewers watched these broadcasts. Surprisingly, attendance at the games was as high as 28 percent of the usual numbers. A poll by the ESPN cable network showed fans favored the owners rather than the players by 3 to 1.

After 20 frustrating days, Gene Upshaw, the union's executive director, appeared on the *Monday Night Football* program to ask for an end to the strike. About 16 percent of the players had crossed the picket lines and more were prepared to do so. The strikers lost an average of $15,000 per game, or $80 million altogether. However, because the owners were in a strong position they delayed the players' return and rejected arbitration and most union demands. After discouraging rulings by the NLRB and a federal court, the season resumed with a much chastened union and the management in firm control of the NFL.

The Celebrity of Sports

College and professional sports became a very lucrative business in the 1980s. Television revenues, many critics complained, distorted athletics. But the popularity of AM radio sports-talk programs in every large city confirmed that the average sports fans were just as motivated by pure love of the game as they ever were. Sports stars had long been celebrities in America, but in the 1980s, many of them began acting like celebrities for which they were much criticized. Sports careers tend to be short-lived and many star athletes and even some ordinary players found new careers as television sports commentators (John McEnroe, Bill Walton, and Jerry Remy) or in the movies (O. J. Simpson and Jim Brown).

The owners and commissioners of professional sports leagues met with President Reagan in 1984 to support and participate in drug abuse prevention programs. The Drug Enforcement Administration sponsored a series of advertisements featuring the Washington Redskins players which augmented Nancy Reagan's Just Say No campaign. Nevertheless, drug scandals involving professional and collegiate athletes continued to prove embarrassing.

The Super Bowl

By the 1980s, more than half the U.S. population watched the Super Bowl on television. This annual faceoff was the national championship football game resulting from the merger of the American Football League with the National Football League in 1966. Surpassing the Kentucky Derby and baseball's World Series in viewership and attendance, each January the Super Bowl became a sort of national holiday with endless promotions, extravagant commercial ads, and elaborate halftime entertainment.

By 1960, professional football, an obscure game to most mid-century Americans, overshadowed all other sports. Its 32 teams created the most popular televised sport in the United States. Much credit is due to Alvin "Pete" Rozelle, the commissioner of the NFL from 1959 to 1989, who negotiated lucrative contracts with TV networks. In a 1982 battle among the networks for television rights to broadcast major league sports, the three networks annually paid $14.2 million to each football team. This permitted teams to recruit college stars, extend training and practice periods, hire sexy cheerleaders, increase advertising revenue, and attract wider and growing TV audiences.

The Super Bowl, an extravagant finale to the fall and winter football season in January, became the most popular single program of the year measured by attendance and the TV audiences in 150 countries. The Super Bowl had 35.3 million viewers in 1980, but an estimated 110 million by 1989. The introduction of the Apple Macintosh computer in a 1984 Super Bowl commercial was recognition of the game's impact on U.S. society and started a tradition of spectacular commercials and halftime performances at the Super Bowl.

CINEMA

A New Deal in Hollywood

Hollywood entered a new era in the 1970s and 1980s, comparable to the golden age of the 1930s and 1940s. One difference was that fewer movies were produced but with much bigger budgets. The blockbuster hit movies, like Francis Ford Coppola's *Apocalypse Now* (1979) or Robert Wise's *Star Trek* (1979), became financially necessary for the film studios, but this meant fewer low or moderate budget movies were made. Most U.S. movie studios had been purchased by major corporations in a merger mania. Rupert Murdoch, the international newspaper tycoon, bought 20th Century-Fox in 1985, and TV tycoon Ted Turner bought MGM in 1985. Consequently, the American film industry changed in fundamental ways. By limiting production and emphasizing the distribution and financing of movies produced by others, the new conglomerates or diversified

Scene still with Charlie Sheen and Michael Douglas from the movie Wall Street *(1987).* *(Richard Corman/Corbis)*

major studios dominated the U.S. and foreign markets. When the Supreme Court ruled in 1984 that television broadcasts could be recorded for home use, sales of VCRs and movies on videocassette soared. By 1980, 78 million households had a VCR, and by 1986, it was in more than 87 million U.S. households. This earned film studios more than $4.5 billion by 1985, not including the income from the growing video rental market. This trend was so popular and profitable that many movies were released in the video market rather than in movie theaters.

In contrast to most Hollywood movies in the 1980s, was the work of the controversial new director, Oliver Stone. His film *Salvador* (1986) was a critique of U.S. foreign policy in El Salvador. Next came *Platoon* (1986), a penetrating account of infantry life and death in the Vietnam War, which won four Oscars. He followed this with an exposé of greed in *Wall Street* (1987), and two other Vietnam movies—*Born on the Fourth of July* (1989) and *Heaven and Earth* (1993). Stone provoked more controversy with *Talk Radio* (1988), and with two films set in the 1960s—*The Doors* (1991) and *JFK* (1991). Other controversial independent filmmakers included John Sayles for *The Brother from Another Planet* (1984) and *Matewan* (1987) and Jim Jarmusch for *Permanent Vacation* (1980) and *Stranger Than Paradise* (1984).

By 1989, Warner Communications merged with Time Inc., owner of HBO and Cinemax, to form the world's largest communications company, Time-Warner, Inc. In 1987, Columbia merged with TriStar and was purchased by Japan's Sony Corporation in 1989. These mergers and conglomerations, reaching a peak in 1980, continued throughout the decade. In short, Hollywood made more money but fewer movies, and many serious critics wondered about the lack of creativity in the American cinema. Film buffs in big cities turned to art houses, small movie theaters that specialized in showing foreign or classic films, and film festivals devoted to one director or genre. Diverse movies for niche market audiences became more common.

Digital manipulation of color in movies began in 1985 and aroused much controversy. Ted Turner, who owned MGM/UA, planned to colorize classic black-and-white films by MGM, RKO, and Warner Brothers. Distribution of these films on television and videocassette was profitable but cinema aesthetes were offended by what they saw as violating film history and the original artistic intent. Computer-generated imagery (CGI), which appeared in the 1980s to create special effects for disaster and science-fiction movies such as *Star Trek II* (1982), soon became an industry staple.

A new category, the made-for-TV movies, began in the 1960s, and by the 1980s they attracted top talent and tackled controversial topics. Cable networks, in a challenge to the Big Three broadcast networks, employed experienced filmmakers like John Frankenheimer to cover adult subjects without interference or censorship. These movies and mini-series included dramatizations of Bruce Catton's *The Blue and the Gray* (1982), John Steinbeck's *The Winter of Our Discontent* (1983), James Michener's *Space* (1985), Agatha Christie's *Dead Man's Folly* (1986), and Larry McMurtry's *Lonesome Dove* (1989). About 1,400 of these films became the Movie of the Week on network television or cable networks. By 1982, some were dubbed the "disease of the week" or "celebrity of the week" because they focused on one major illness or major sports or entertainment figure after another on HBO, Showtime, or the Disney Channel. In any case, the made-for-TV movie added a new dimension to home entertainment in this decade.

Film Industry Changes

Motion pictures, thanks to Thomas Edison's invention in 1893, are America's major original art form. The golden age of movies in the 1930s and again in the 1970s proved to the world that Americans made the best movies. Hollywood, the headquarters of the international movie industry since 1915, underwent profound changes in the 1980s. The independent producers and filmmakers who emerged in the 1970s when the major studios downsized bloomed in the 1980s with many new independent films. Some independents produced R- or X-rated films for art houses and drive-in theaters, the so-called sexploitation or hard-core movies. At the same time as movie theater attendance declined, film became a new topic for writers, publishers, and university courses. Often low-budget movies in the 1980s were more popular than big-budget movies with top stars. In any case, independents offered the public a wider range of movies than the old Hollywood studio system, the so-called dream factory, produced. Cinema literacy became a necessity for yuppies to be cool.

Trends in Films of the 1980s

If the 1970s was a golden age of American movies, an influential era of creativity rivaling the 1930s, the 1980s was an era of more specialized movies focused on a narrow audience. Among the themes that captured moviegoers' attention was the plight of the thirtysomethings. These were the baby boomers as they reached age 30, seen in *The Big Chill* (1983), *Fatal Attraction* (1987), *Wall Street* (1987), *Baby Boom* (1987), and *Working Girl* (1988). This renaissance in movie-making featured young directors trained at university film schools such as Francis Ford Coppola and Paul Schrader (UCLA), George Lucas and John Milius (USC), and Oliver Stone, Spike Lee, Brian De Palma, and Martin Scorsese (NYU). Their academic training and technical brilliance is obvious in their films' cinematic effect and audience reaction. Although the movie industry was controlled by lawyers and accountants, some creative directors managed to remain productive. Hollywood searched for summer blockbuster hit movies like George Lucas's *The Empire Strikes Back* (1980) and Steven Spielberg's *Raiders of the Lost Ark* (1981). However, the major movie studios continued to produce a large number of expensive family films that flopped at the box office at a time when weekly movie audiences were shrinking and the number of movie theaters declined. Television and the VCR made movie theaters a secondary leisure activity in the 1980s.

Preferring to rely on movies with a proven profit record, Hollywood produced a stream of sequels with five *Star Wars,* four *Jaws,* five *Rockys,* three *Rambos,* and three *Aliens*. The psycho-slasher movie was another popular genre: *Prom Night* (1980), *Friday the 13th* (1980), *Hell Night* (1981), *The Slumber Party Massacre* (1982), and *A Nightmare on Elm Street* (1984). In 1981, half of the 50 top-grossing movies were slasher films, about 60 percent of all domestic movies released that year. Criticized for their gratuitous sex and violence, the gory slasher movie was joined by the mainstream horror film like *Poltergeist* (1982) and *Pet Sematary* (1989) and science fiction films like *Aliens* (1986), *RoboCop* (1987), and *Total Recall* (1990). These sinister movies reflected tensions in society regarding changing gender and family roles, increased technological dependence, the dissolution of community, and fear of environmental and nuclear disasters. Various evils and threats haunted children and their families in *The Shining* (1980), *Gloria* (1980), *Stand By Me* (1986), *Empire of the Sun* (1987), and *Home Alone* (1990).

Cult movies, a colloquial term for a film that failed at the box office but attracted a following of devoted fans, became popular in the 1980s. Danny Perry coined this term in his book *Cult Movies* (1981). Teenagers and college students sometimes perversely liked an offbeat film and even ridiculed it for its lack of artistic merit, but watched it many times. This trend began in the 1960s when Harvard University students patronized the Brattle Theater, a small art movie house in Cambridge, Massachusetts, to repeatedly view *Casablanca* (1942) and other Humphrey Bogart movies. *The Rocky Horror Picture Show* (1975) became the best-known cult film in the 1980s, most popular in special midnight campus screenings where audience members wore costumes from the film and shouted key lines in unison with the actors on screen. Madonna's role in her first movie, *Desperately Seeking Susan* (1985), inspired new fashions for teenage girls, and created a new cult film.

Other cult movies that maintained their popularity in the 1980s included independent films such as the Jamaican reggae movie *The Harder They Come* (1973) and the low-budget *Pink Flamingos* (1972), and major studio films such as *Blade Runner* (1982), or British comedies such as *Monty Python and the Holy Grail* (1975), and the punk rock film *Repo Man* (1984). The creative filmmakers of the 1970s were less welcomed in major studios in the 1980s, especially when Michael Cimino's $44 million film *Heaven's Gate* (1980) flopped at the box office. In the conservative 1980s, many talented filmmakers with dissenting political views were shut out or confined to making low-budget movies outside the Hollywood mainstream of conglomerated major studios.

Public television, established by Congress in 1978, was a key financier of the new breed of independent filmmakers in the 1980s. Some small films also enjoyed commercial success, like John Sayles' *Return of the Secaucus Seven* (1980), and Spike Lee's *She's Gotta Have It* (1986), or *My Dinner with Andre* (1981) and *El Norte* (1984). The home entertainment market benefited from the 1984 Supreme Court case *Sony v. Universal City Studios*. This made repeated viewing of classic, foreign, independent, or cult films at home on videocassette even more popular. New technologies such as cable and satellite television and home video created profitable markets for feature films beyond their theatrical run. In response, the conglomerates used takeovers and mergers to establish or acquire diversified entertainment corporations to meet these new audience demands.

The Decline of the Drive-In Theater

The drive-in movie theater combined two American passions, movies and cars, when Richard Hollingshead opened the first one in Camden, New Jersey, in 1933. By 1958, the United States had more than 4,000 drive-ins in every state, but the advent of television, the VCR, and cable TV slowly made this outdoor theater experience less popular, unprofitable, and obsolete. For example, Massachusetts had 58 drive-ins in 1958, 52 in 1982, and only 20 in 1987. Texas had 382 in 1958, 137 in 1982, and 56 in 1987. Most drive-ins offered a playground for children and a concession stand for snacks along with cartoons, previews, and double-feature movies. Because of the privacy offered by watching a movie at night in a car, the drive-in was sometimes decried as a teenage "passion pit" for back-seat love, but most were a popular form of inexpensive family entertainment. Many parents brought their young children dressed in pajamas. The sound was provided by individual speakers for each car or, later, by broadcasting the sound-track to the car radios.

In the 1980s, many drive-ins changed from family entertainment to horror, science fiction, or sexploitation films to attract an audience. By the late 1980s, cinema under the stars at the drive-in became a nostalgic or novelty experience until rising real estate prices made operating the drive-ins unprofitable. The opening of the Blockbuster chain of video rental stores in 1985 also contributed to the drive-in's decline. Some drive-ins survived by holding flea markets by day or because they operated in rural areas with few theaters. Long on the list of endangered roadside Americana, only 400 drive-ins operated in the United States in 2006.

The Birth of the Multiplex Theater

As shopping malls became popular in the 1980s and the old motion picture palaces closed in downtown areas, movie theater chains opened small, low-cost theaters with 2 to 20 screens in suburban shopping centers or malls. Stanley Durwood of American Multi-Cinema (AMC) opened the first multiplex in 1963 in Kansas City. By 1999, AMC was one of the largest movie theater chains in North America with 5,672 screens in 415 theater locations. Even larger was the Regal Entertainment Group, which had 6,273 screens in its 584 U.S. theaters. Regal began in Tennessee by combining several smaller chains that were built in the multiplex (or megaplex) building boom in 1980–1990.

The advantages of the multiplex included using the same staff to serve more patrons at ticket windows, concession counters, and projection booths by staggering movie start times. This attracted larger audiences and higher grosses to a theater with several choices of films. Disadvantages include smaller screens and theater hopping, a practice in which patrons buy one ticket and view two or more movies. Some multiplexes added paid advertising by slide shows before the feature film and previews of coming attractions. As movie theaters grew larger, crowd control became a problem until the hold-out line was created, which restricted ticketholders to the lobby until the theater was emptied and cleaned by the staff. Film critics also complained that the small screen and cramped theater with poor sound control detracted from the aesthetic cinema experience, but teenagers flocked to the multiplex theaters in the 1980s.

The Steven Spielberg Movies

The most successful and influential movie director in the 1980s was undoubtedly Steven Spielberg (1946–). Born in Cincinnati, Ohio, and raised in Arizona, he attended Long Beach University but dropped out to work as an editor on television programs. By 1974, he directed his first feature film, but came to critical notice with *Raiders of the Lost Ark* (1981) followed by the hit movie *Poltergeist* (1982) and the blockbuster *E.T.: The Extra-Terrestrial* (1982). *Indiana Jones and the Temple of Doom* (1984) was a commercial but not a critical success, but *Back to the Future* (1985) was another blockbuster hit. *Time* magazine's cover story on July 15, 1985, dubbed him the "Magician of the Movies." *The Color Purple* (1985) was a more serious drama, as was *Empire of the Sun* (1987). Known for his use of visual effects, in 1989 Spielberg returned with *Always, Indiana Jones and the Last Crusade,* and *Back to the Future Part II.* He later founded the production company Dreamworks and has continued to prove he is a brilliant and creative American filmmaker.

Box Office Hits and Escapism

Among the top 10 highest grossing films of the 1980s were many lighter movies that reflected escapism into science fiction, from *The Empire Strikes Back* and *Superman II* (1980) to *Raiders of the Lost Ark* and *Time Bandits* (1981) or *E. T.: The Extra-Terrestrial* and *Star Trek II: The Wrath of Khan* (1982). This trend continued with *Return of the Jedi* and *War Games* (1983), and *Starman* and *Star Trek III: The Search for Spock* (1984), then *Cocoon* and *Back to the Future* (1985). Other examples were *Stark Trek IV: The Voyage Home* and *Aliens* (1986). Science fiction and tales of the supernatural thrilled American moviegoers in *The Witches of Eastwick* (1987), *Big* (1988), *Indiana Jones and the Last Crusade* (1989), *Honey, I Shrunk the Kids, Back to the Future Part II,* and *Ghostbusters 2* (1989). Most of these movies were the PG-13 teenpix, a rating introduced in 1984.

Independent Cinema and Documentary Films

In 1985, independent film producers released more movies than the Hollywood studios. Consequently, independent or "indie" (not from a major studio) and documentary films had a renaissance in the 1980s. The variety and creativity of these films was unprecedented. In 1981, actor Robert Redford established the Sundance Institute to assist independent filmmakers who showcased their work at the prestigious Sundance Film Festivals throughout the 1980s. In addition, the PBS filmmakers produced original documentary films like *The World That Moses*

Built (1988), which explored the career of a New York bureaucrat who designed much of metropolitan New York City's urban space in the 20th century—beaches, bridges, parks, playgrounds, tunnels, and housing projects. It posed disturbing questions about the law of eminent domain and individual rights. In 1989, Bill Moyers made *Hate on Trial: Challenging the First Amendment* to explore the trial of Tom and John Metzger for inciting skinheads in Portland, Oregon, to kill an Ethiopian immigrant. This combination of investigative journalism and movie-making raised much debate on the relationship between violence and freedom of speech. But the public television audience, popular with the yuppies and elite audiences, was small and not a major rival to the major television networks or to the major Hollywood studios. The decade ended with Roger Moore's documentary *Roger & Me* (1989), which excoriated General Motors and its CEO Roger Smith with black humor for closing auto plants in Flint, Michigan, causing 40,000 people to lose their jobs. This low-budget film, financed in part by a mortgage on Moore's home, criticized the social attitudes and economic policies of the Reagan administration. It won numerous awards and had a successful box office run.

Not since the 1920s did so many small film companies produce outstanding independent movies as in the 1980s. These included movies like *Blood Simple* (1984), *Desperately Seeking Susan* (1985), *Raising Arizona* (1987), *Matewan* (1987), and niche-market films like Steven Soderbergh's *sex, lies and videotape* (1989). Many of these 1980s actors, directors, and producers became influential mainstream filmmakers by 1990. Oliver Stone may have been the best example of this. His uneven but compelling drama *Salvador* (1986) was critical of the Reagan policy in Central America and foreshadowed Stone's caustic view of the Vietnam War in *Platoon* (1986), which won four Oscars. In the very controversial *JFK* (1991), Stone mixed documentary and pseudo-documentary footage to rewrite, some critics claimed, American history. Other controversial movies on the Vietnam War included *Full Metal Jacket* (1987), *Good Morning, Vietnam* (1987), and Oliver Stone's *Born on the Fourth of July* (1989).

African Americans took understandable pride in the success of Spike Lee's *Do the Right Thing* (1989) and his later movies. Another innovative film was *Boyz n the Hood* (1991) by 23-year-old filmmaker John Singleton, which cost $6 million to make and earned $57.5 million. This work inspired other ghetto-centric youth films with crossover appeal to white audiences like *Straight Out of Brooklyn* (1991).

Americans' Habits Shape the Movie Industry

Americans in the 1980s spent more time at home watching cable television and movies or listening to music on their new home entertainment centers. The "nesting" phenomenon of more leisure activities at home may have been somewhat antisocial, or may have been merely a retreat from high-pressure lives. Youths were greatly impacted as consumers and producers of music by Music Television (MTV). As a result of new media and the VCR, the number of movie theaters declined, especially the ornate motion picture palaces downtown in big cities. The smaller multiplex theaters in suburban malls became the most common venue for movies. Hollywood and the independents struggled to create a wide variety of movies to attract more sophisticated and fragmented audiences. The corporate movie studio executives still controlled many "independent" films in editing and post-production, but the most creative new directors managed to produce many classic movies in the 1980s to reflect the profound changes of the more conservative and materialistic era.

BIOGRAPHIES

Larry Bird, 1956–

Athlete

Born in Indiana and raised in French Lick, Indiana, Larry Bird earned the nickname "the hick from French Lick" as an Indiana State University basketball star. As a forward with the Boston Celtics (1979–1992), Bird was rated the greatest forward in NBA history, the apex of basketball artistry, an original superstar. He was Rookie of the Year (1980), on the All-Star teams for 12 seasons, and won three national championships with the Celtics dynasty led by coach and general manager Arnold "Red" Auerbach. *Time* magazine recognized Bird's unique status with a March 18, 1985, cover story, "Simply the Best, Boston's Larry Bird." He and Magic Johnson led the U.S. "Dream Team" to a gold medal in the 1992 Olympics in Barcelona. After retiring in 1992, the man called "Larry Legend" was an assistant coach for the Celtics, and as coach of the Indiana Pacers was selected NBA Coach of the Year (1998). Bird was voted into the Basketball Hall of Fame (1998), and became president of the Indiana Pacers in 2003. He is remembered as one of the most admired and respected athletes of the 1980s.

Janet Cooke, 1954–

Journalist

Janet Cooke became an infamous *Washington Post* reporter in April 1981 when she won a Pulitzer Prize for her story about Jimmy, an African American 8-year-old heroin addict. This aroused considerable concern when it appeared on September 29, 1980. But Cooke refused to reveal more information about this boy or cooperate with Washington, D.C., police in locating him. Further investigation revealed that Cooke fabricated and exaggerated the facts, and she had earlier lied about her academic credentials in her resume. At a time when the *Washington*

Post's Ben Bradlee, Sally Quinn, Carl Bernstein, and Robert Woodward were celebrities more famous than the notables they covered, the *Post* was humiliated by this scandal and returned the Pulitzer Prize. Cooke resigned, and in January 1982 she appeared on the *Donahue* TV show, admitting Jimmy was a composite based on street talk about young drug addicts. She claimed that the pressure of writing for the *Washington Post* had forced her to lie to succeed. Although drug abuse in many American cities may have created children like Jimmy, this incident ended her career and damaged pubic confidence in the media.

Ice Cube, 1969–

Musician

Ice Cube was the most prominent rap artist to emerge from the hip-hop world in the 1980s. Born in Los Angeles, O'Shea Jackson (aka Ice Cube) began as a member of the controversial rap group CIA and wrote most of the songs for a mixtape called *My Posse* (1987). He formed the group N.W. A. in 1987 with a debut album *Straight Outta Compton* (1988) that earned notoriety for its violent and political lyrics. Ice Cube recorded his first solo album *AmeriKKKa's Most Wanted* (1989) in New York which brought rap into mainstream music despite charges by critics and conservatives that rap was sexist and homophobic. His role in John Singleton's movie *Boyz N the Hood* (1991) began Ice Cube's successful film and television career.

Dinesh D'Souza, 1961–

Writer

Dinesh D'Souza was born in Bombay, India, and came to the United States in 1978. He attended high school in Arizona and graduated from Dartmouth College in 1983. At Dartmouth he was leader of a group of conservative students who published the controversial *Dartmouth Review,* an unofficial campus newspaper. As editor he published the names of homosexual students in the Gay Student Alliance in 1981 as an effort to discredit and embarrass some of his liberal critics. After college D'Souza worked at Princeton University for the conservative organization Concerned Alumni of Princeton, who opposed affirmative action, birth control, and coeducation. He again became controversial for publishing the story of a female Princeton student who was in a sexual relationship with another student contrary to her parents' wishes. When the *New York Times* reported this scandal in 1984, D'Souza claimed his intentions were honorable. He later was an editor in Washington, D.C., for the influential conservative journal *Policy Review* published by the Hoover Institution. He investigated the U.S. Catholic Bishops organization, claiming they were manipulated by liberals to oppose the U.S. military expansion. He became a policy advisor in the Reagan administration (1987–1988) and then worked at the American Enterprise Institute and the Hoover Institution. D'Souza was a prominent example of the young neoconservatives who supported the Reagan Revolution as a television commentator and the author of *Falwell, Before the Millennium: A Critical Biography* (1984), *The Catholic Classics* (1986), *Illiberal Education* (1991), *Ronald Reagan: How an Ordinary Man Became an Extraordinary Leader* (1997), and several other books.

Michael Jackson, 1958–

Musician

Born in Indiana, Michael Jackson began his musical career as a child prodigy, age seven, singing with his brothers in the group The Jackson 5. In 1979 he began solo performances and left his brothers' group in 1984. His 1982 album *Thriller* was the best-selling album of all time and launched him into international stardom. He was twice inducted into the Rock and Roll Hall of Fame. After this enormously successful *Thriller* (1982) album and music video, Michael Jackson made popular commercials for Pepsi and introduced his signature "moonwalk" and hip-hop break-dancing moves in 1983. He won an unprecedented eight

Pop star and 1980s icon Michael Jackson. (PRNewsFoto/E! Entertainment Television)

Grammy awards and three MTV video music awards in 1984 and wrote his hit single, "We Are the World" in 1985 for African famine relief. His 1987 album *Bad* was followed by a world tour that led his friend Elizabeth Taylor to name him the King of Pop.

Jackson wrote and composed many of his best songs, but the songs also benefited from Quincy Jones's talent as a producer and guitar solos by Eddie Van Halen and vocals by Paul McCartney. One consequence of his success with *Thriller* was to return music by African American performers to mainstream radio programming. But Jackson also suffered much criticism for plastic surgery and skin lightening that drastically changed his appearance, for his brief marriage to Lisa Marie Presley, the daughter of Elvis Presley, and for hosting young children at the Neverland Ranch that he built in California in 1988. Nonetheless, Michael Jackson, the most successful crossover artist in the world, defined American pop music as a performer and producer of visionary music videos in the 1980s.

Earvin "Magic" Johnson, 1959–

Athlete

Earvin "Magic" Johnson was born in Lansing, Michigan, and was the star basketball point guard for Michigan State University. Playing for the Los Angeles Lakers (1979–1991, 1996), he won five National Basketball Association championships; played on 12 All-Star teams, and was the league MVP three times. The charismatic superstar revived the NBA and was inducted into the Basketball Hall of Fame in 2002. Johnson made off-court news in 1991 when he announced he was HIV-positive and retired. Although he played in the 1992 Olympics and briefly with the Lakers in 1992, 1994, and 1996, his brilliant career was over. He later entered several business and philanthropic ventures, was a spokesman for HIV/AIDS prevention, and wrote his autobiography *Magic Johnson: My Life* (1992).

Ralph Lauren 1939–

Fashion Designer

Born Ralph Lifschitz in New York City, Lauren attended the City College of New York and later served in the Army (1962–1964). He became a salesman and buyer at Bloomingdale's and Brooks Brothers in New York. In 1968, he founded his Polo Fashions company with his brother. His neckwear line was an immediate hit, and Polo created the "power suit" of the early 1980s along with stylish men's shirts. He followed this popular line with classic women's clothing, and in 1983 Lauren designed sheets, towels, and furniture and sold the new products in his own flagship store he opened in 1986. He was the first fashion designer to sell an entire lifestyle image of sophistication, class, and taste. His fashions were sold in 275 Ralph Lauren/Polo retail stores in the United States and more than 100 stores around the world. He was responsible for the revival of 1920s fashions after designing costumes for the movie *The Great Gatsby* (1974). He also is credited with the eclectic look for young women seen in Woody Allen's movie *Annie Hall* (1977). By 1981, he recognized the important Sunbelt with his Santa Fe collection, which created the fad for American Southwest clothing and cowboy styles for men and women. By 1989, Ralph Lauren had received many awards and honors for his influential fashions and philanthropic work.

Shelton Jackson "Spike" Lee, 1956–

Filmmaker

Born in Atlanta and raised in Brooklyn, Spike Lee graduated from Morehouse College (1979) and New York University's film school (1982). In the late 1980s he emerged as the most important African American filmmaker with *She's Gotta Have It* (1986), *School Daze* (1988), and his frank and realistic treatment of urban racial tensions in *Do the Right Thing* (1989). Following the 1986 Howard Beach riot and the highly publicized 1989 rape of a young white jogger in Central Park by African American teens, Lee focused this film on a Brooklyn pizza parlor. Revealing the complexity of a Bedford-Stuyvesant African American neighborhood to Public Enemy's rap music score, Lee depicted a violent riot in which the police valued a pizzeria more than an African American man's life. Although a box office and critical success, some pundits feared *Do the Right Thing* would spark urban riots despite Lee's insistence that his film merely exposed the reality of African American urban life. The film (and later Lee's *Malcolm X* in 1992) demonstrated that the hopes of the 1960s had evaporated and foreshadowed the police brutality and racial violence to come in the late 1980s. Nominated for two Oscars, Spike Lee and his Forty Acres and a Mule production company continue to be produce provocative and creative films.

Madonna, 1958–

Singer and Actress

Born in Michigan as Madonna Louise Veronica Ciccone, she studied at the University of Michigan (1976), and with dance teachers in New York (1978). She made her debut album, *Madonna* (1983), which earned critical acclaim for the single "Everybody." Madonna made her national television debut on the *American Bandstand* program in 1984 and quickly became the most famous female music and media star of the era. Her first movie, *Desperately Seeking Susan* (1985), was a hit that became a cult classic but she bombed in *Who's That Girl* (1987). Her second album, *Like a Virgin* (1985), which encapsulated the conservative materialism of the era, made her the Queen of Pop, and a *Time* magazine cover story on May 27, 1985, explained, "Madonna, Why She's Hot."

With a well-crafted punk and gay culture image, Madonna ridiculed the role of women as sex objects. Her songs and concerts preached that women should take control of their own sexuality and that it was liberating for young women to express sexual desire. Her shockingly suggestive performances at the first MTV Video Music Awards ceremony in New York at Radio City Music Hall (1984) and on her concert tours created the Madonna Wannabes—teenage girls who imitated the Madonna style and attitude by dressing in miniskirts, spandex, torn tee shirts, and lacy bras.

In 1985, when *Playboy* and *Penthouse* magazines published nude photographs of Madonna from the late 1970s, the publicity only increased her fame. *Rolling Stone* magazine said her internationally successful album *True Blue* (1986) made Madonna a pop poet who blurred the distinction between high and mass culture. Her elaborate 1987 concert tour *Who's That Girl* was also successful despite criticism by the Vatican. Catholic authorities also condemned her MTV music video *Like a Prayer* (1989) as blasphemous because she mixed erotic and religious symbols.

Expanding beyond music and movies, she made her Broadway debut in David Mamet's play *Speed the Plow* (1988). Although her music video *Justify My Love* (1990), which included bondage, lesbian, and nude scenes, was banned by MTV, it became the best-selling video single at that time. Madonna, the Me Decade's most Material Girl, symbolized excess, greed, and acquisitive capitalism as she continued her very successful singing and movie career.

Rupert Murdoch, 1931–

Publisher

Rupert Murdock was born in Australia and, in 1952, inherited a newspaper chain from his father. Aggressively expanding his media empire to newspapers, television stations, and recording, he became Australia's dominant and most politically conservative publisher. Murdock moved to England in 1966 where he repeated his success as publisher of *The Sun*, a London tabloid. In 1973, he expanded to the United States by purchasing the *San Antonio News* and founding a supermarket tabloid, the *National Star*, in 1975. By 1976, he owned the *New York Post*, 11 magazines and 84 newspapers, and he later purchased the HarperCollins publishing company. Murdoch became a naturalized citizen in 1985 to comply with the law that only a U.S. citizen could own American television stations. He sold *The Village Voice* in 1985 for $55 million because "it pandered to a homosexual community." As

Rupert Murdoch is an Australian-born media mogul known for his conservative political views. One of the wealthiest men in the world, Murdoch owns News Corporation, a conglomerate that includes television stations, film studios, newspapers, and books. (PRNewsFoto/Zack Seckler)

a conservative supporter of Ronald Reagan, this controversial media tycoon was often criticized for his ruthless business management and antiunion policies. All of Murdoch's media outlets were fiercely pro-American, anti-French, and pro-Israeli.

Pete Rose, 1941–

Athlete

Born in Cincinnati, Ohio, Pete Rose became the most famous baseball player for the Cincinnati Reds (1963–1986). He was a Rookie of the Year who won three World Series rings, one Most Valuable Player award, and two Gold Glove awards, he also played on 17 All-Star teams. He won the 1980 World Series with the Philadelphia Phillies and made his record-breaking 4,192nd hit in 1985 as player-manager with the Reds. He retired in 1986. In 1989, Rose agreed to a lifetime ban from baseball after he was investigated for gambling on baseball games. In 1990, he was imprisoned for tax evasion, then banned from the Hall of Fame. His later efforts for reinstatement were unsuccessful, and in his 2004 autobiography, Rose admitted betting on baseball games while playing and managing for the Reds.

Hunter S. Thompson, 1937–2005

Journalist and Author

Hunter Thompson was one of the founders of gonzo journalism. Born in Louisville, Kentucky, in 1937, Thompson served in the U.S. Air Force (1956–1958) and attended Columbia University, then worked briefly for *Time* magazine and as a journalist in Puerto Rico and South America. While working in San Francisco as a novelist, he received a doctorate in divinity from a mail-order church; thereafter he called himself Dr. Thompson. His book *Hells Angels: the Strange and Terrible Saga of the Outlaw Motorcycle Gang* (1966) established his reputation. Much of his best work was for *Rolling Stone* magazine and two of his books, *Fear and Loathing in Las Vegas: A Savage Journey to the Heart of the American Dream* (1971) and *Fear and Loathing on the Campaign Trail '72* (1973) were serialized in *Rolling Stone*.

Thompson, often fueled by alcohol and a variety of drugs, continued as a *Rolling Stone* correspondent in the 1980s. His novel *The Curse of Lono* (1983) recounted his bizarre vacation in Hawaii. Thereafter he concentrated on his four-volume book, *The Gonzo Papers* (1979, 1988, 1990, 1994), and his ESPN web sports column, *Hey, Rube*. The cartoonist Gary Trudeau based his *Doonesbury* character Uncle Duke on Thompson, who was an enthusiastic weapons collector and spent much time on the lecture circuit. Two movies were based on

Thompson's career, *Where the Buffalo Roam* (1980) and *Fear and Loathing in Las Vegas* (1998).

Thompson died at his home in Colorado in 2005 from a self-inflicted gunshot wound. He had planned his own elaborate funeral, during which his ashes were fired from cannon to a Bob Dylan song and fireworks; several prominent politicians and celebrities attended his funeral. But his legacy as a founder of the New Journalism, with a personal, novelistic, and nonobjective approach to reporting, may be his most significant legacy. Provocative, witty, and erratic, he broke free of the mainstream media objective style to cover politics and popular culture in the gonzo tradition of blurring fact and fiction to discover the artistic truth.

Garretson "Garry" Beekman Trudeau, 1948–

Cartoonist

A syndicated cartoonist best known for his *Doonesbury* comic strip, Garry Trudeau was born in New York City. After St. Paul's School, an elite prep school in New Hampshire, he graduated from Yale University and received an M.F.A. at the Yale School of Art (1973). *Doonesbury,* based on a comic strip he created at Yale, was syndicated in 1,400 newspapers. In 1975, Trudeau became the first cartoonist to win a Pulitzer Prize for editorial cartoons. He was nominated for an Oscar in 1977 for his animated short film *The Doonesbury Special,* and for a second Pulitzer Prize in 1989. He also wrote the plays *Rap Master Ronnie* (1988) and *Doonesbury: A Musical Comedy* (1983) and the HBO 1988 miniseries *Tanner '88.*

Trudeau, who married NBC news anchor Jane Pauley in 1980, was most controversial for satiric portraits of prominent politicians such as Ronald Reagan, George H. W. Bush, Condoleezza Rice, and George W. Bush. His comic strip character Uncle Duke was based on the journalist Hunter S. Thompson, and Lacey Davenport was modeled on New Jersey congresswoman Millicent Fenwick. Trudeau also created a series of comic strips in the *New Republic* magazine that satirized the antiabortion movement. For these reasons Trudeau was one of the most influential cartoonists in the 1980s, although many newspapers editors refused to publish some of his cartoon strips or printed them on the editorial pages.

References and Further Readings

Ajemian, Robert. 1985. "Jerry Falwell Spreads the Word," *Time,* September 2, 19–27.

Ashby, Leroy. 2006. *With Amusement for All: A History of American Popular Culture Since 1830.* Lexington: University Press of Kentucky.

Auletta, Ken. 2004. *Media Man: Ted Turner's Improbable Empire*. New York: W. W. Norton.

Austin, Joe. 2001. *Taking the Train: How Graffiti Art Became an Urban Crisis in New York City*. New York: Columbia University Press.

Barol, Bill. 1988. "The Eighties Are Over," *Newsweek*, January 4, 40–48.

Barry, Joseph, and John Derevlany, ed. 1987. *Yuppies Invade My Home at Dinnertime: A Tale of Brunch, Bombs, and Gentrification in an American City*. Hoboken, N.J.: Big River Publishers.

Biskind, Peter. 1998. *Easy Riders, Raging Bulls: How the Sex-Drugs-and-Rock 'n' Roll Generation Saved Hollywood*. New York: Simon and Schuster.

Bloom, Allan. 1987. *The Closing of the American Mind: How Higher Education Has Failed Democracy and Impoverished the Souls of Today's Students*. New York: Simon and Schuster.

Bowen, Ezra. 1986. "What Is College For?" *Time*, November 10, 24.

Bowen, Ezra. 2005. "Losing the War of Letters," *Time*, June 21, 17.

Bradlee, Benjamin C. 1996. *A Good Life: Newspapering and Other Adventures*. New York: Touchstone.

Brooke, Michael. 1999. *The Concrete Wave: The History of Skateboarding*. Toronto: Warwick Publishing.

Burd, Stephen. 2006. "Working-Class Students Feel the Pinch," *Chronicle of Higher Education*, June 9, A20.

Callahan, Tom. 1985. "Masters of Their Own Game," *Time*, March 18, 35.

Callahan, Tom. 1986. "An Empty Dream," *Time*, June 30, 23.

Campbell, Neil. ed. 2004. *American Youth Cultures*. New York: Routledge.

Carlisle, Rodney P., and J. Geoffrey Golson, eds. 2008. *The Reagan Era from the Iran Crisis to Kosovo*. Santa Barbara, Calif.: ABC-CLIO.

Castro, Janice. 1989. "The Sky's the Limit," *Time*, November 27, 14.

Clayton, Mark. 2001. "Open Doors?" *Christian Science Monitor*, December 18, 9.

Colford, Paul D. 1993. *The Rush Limbaugh Story: Talent on Loan from God: An Unauthorized Biography*. New York: St. Martin's Press.

Cook, David A. 2004. *A History of Narrative Film*. New York: W. W. Norton.

Cook, William A. 2004. *Pete Rose: Baseball's All-Time Hit King*. Jefferson, N.C.: McFarland & Company.

Coolidge, Shelley Donald. 1996. "This Fall, Students Find Cramped Quarters on Campus," *Christian Science Monitor*, September 26, 11.

Coupland, Douglas. 1991. *Generation X: Tales for an Accelerated Culture*. New York: St. Martin's Press.

Davies, Richard O. 2007. *Sports in American Life: A History*. Malden, Mass.: Blackwell Publishing.

Dempsey, John M., ed. 2006. *Sports-Talk Radio in America: Its Context and Culture*. New York: Haworth Press.

De Vries, Hilary. 1982. "Book Banning," *Christian Science Monitor,* June 29, 8.

Diggins, John Patrick. 2007. *Ronald Reagan: Fate, Freedom, and the Making of History*. New York: W. W. Norton.

Douglas, Susan J. 1994. *Where the Girls Are: Growing Up Female with the Mass Media*. New York: Random House.

Easton, Nina J. 2000. *Gang of Five: Leaders at the Center of the Conservative Crusade*. New York: Simon and Schuster.

Ehrman, John. 2005. *The Eighties: America in the Age of Reagan*. New Haven, Conn.: Yale University Press.

Eisenstock, Alan. 2001. *Sports Talk: A Journey Inside the World of Sports Talk Radio*. New York: Pocket Books.

Evans, Thomas W. 2006. *The Education of Ronald Reagan: The General Electric Years and the Untold Story of his Conversion to Conservatism*. New York: Columbia University Press.

Feinstein, Stephen. 2006. *The 1980s from Ronald Reagan to MTV*. Berkeley Heights, N.J.: Enslow.

Forman, Murray, and Mark Anthony Neal. 2004. *That's the Joint: The Hip-Hop Studies Reader*. New York: Routledge.

Friedrich, Otto. 1984. "Minding Our Manners Again," *Time,* November 5, 16.

Gems, Gerald R. 2000. *For Pride, Patriarchy, and Profit: Football and the Incorporation of American Cultural Values*. Metuchen, N.J.: Scarecrow Press.

George, Nelson. 2005. *Hip Hop America*. New York: Penguin.

Goldstein, Jeffrey, David Buckingham, and Gilles Brougere, eds. 2004. *Toys, Games and Media*. Mahwah, N.J.: Lawrence Erlbaum and Associates.

Goodwin, Andrew. 1989. *Dancing in the Distraction Factory: Music Television and Popular Culture*. Minneapolis: University of Minnesota Press.

Hack, Richard. 2003. *Clash of the Titans: How the Unbridled Ambition of Ted Turner and Rupert Murdoch Has Created Global Empires that Control What We Read and Watch Each Day*. New York: New Millennium Press.

Haenfler, Ross. 2006. *Straight Edge: Clean Living Youth, Hardcore Punk, and Social Change*. New Brunswick, N.J.: Rutgers University Press.

Hager, Steven. 1984. *Hip-Hop: The Illustrated History of Break Dancing, Rap Music, and Graffiti*. New York: St. Martin's.

Hareven, Tamara K., ed. 1996. *Aging and Generational Relations over the Life Course*. New York: Aldine de Gruyter.

Havill, Adrian. 1993. *Deep Truth: The Lives of Bob Woodward*. Secaucus, N.J.: Birch Lane Press.

Hunter, James Davison. 1991. *Culture Wars*. New York: Basic Books.

Iver, Pico. 1985. "Fighting the Cocaine Wars," *Time,* February 25, 19.

Jefferson, Margo. 2006. *On Michael Jackson*. New York: Pantheon Books.

Jenkins, Philip. 2006. *Decade of Nightmares: The End of the Sixties and the Making of Eighties America*. New York: Oxford University Press.

Johnson, Magic, and William Novak. 1992. *Magic Johnson: My Life*. New York: Random House.

Katz, Ephraim, ed. 2001. *The Film Encyclopedia*. New York: HarperCollins.

Kelley, Robin D. G. 1994. *Race Rebels: Culture, Politics, and the Black Working Class*. New York: The Free Press.

Kelley, Robin D. G. 1997. *Yo' Mama's DisFunktional!: Fighting the Culture Wars in Urban America*. Boston: Beacon Press.

Klein, Herbert S. 2004. *A Population History of the United States*. New York: Cambridge University Press.

Klein, Malcolm. 1995. *The American Street Gang*. New York: Oxford University Press.

Lee, Spike, and Kaleem Aftab. 2005. *That's My Story and I'm Sticking To It*. London: Faber and Faber.

Lever, Janet. 1983. *Soccer Madness*. Chicago: University of Chicago Press.

Levy, Barrie, ed. 1991. *Dating Violence: Young Women in Danger*. Seattle, Wash.: Seal Press.

Longley, Kyle. 2007. *Deconstructing Reagan*. New York: Sharpe.

Luker, Kristin. 2006. *When Sex Goes to School: Warring Views on Sex and Sex Education Since the Sixties*. New York: W. W. Norton.

Magnuson, Ed. 1985. "Clinging to the Land," *Time,* February 18, 13.

McIver, Joel. 2002. *Ice Cube: Attitude*. London: Sanctuary Books.

Modell, John. 1989. *Into One's Own: From Youth to Adulthood in the United States, 1920–1985*. Berkeley: University of California Press.

Morton, Andrew. 2001. *Madonna*. New York: St. Martin's Press.

Muir, John Kenneth. 2007. *Horror Films of the 1980s*. Jefferson, N.C.: McFarland & Company.

National Resource Center on Domestic Violence. Teenage Dating Violence, www.nrcdv.org.

Oriard, Michael. 2007. *Brand NFL: Making and Selling America's Favorite Sport*. Chapel Hill: University of North Carolina Press.

Ostling, Richard N. 1989. "Shootouts in the Schools," *Time,* November 20, 26.

Peary, Danny. 1981. *Cult Movies*. New York: Dell.

Phillips, B. J. 1986. "A Grand Tour for an American," *Time,* August 11, 28.

Price, Emmett G. 2006. *Hip Hop Culture*. Santa Barbara, Calif.: ABC-CLIO.

Purvis, Andrew. 1989. "Alzheimer's Rise," *Time,* November 20, 18.

Quinn, Eithne. 2004. *Nuthin' but a "G" Thang: The Culture and Commerce of Gangsta Rap*. New York: Columbia University Press.

Reagan, Ronald. 2004. *The Uncommon Wisdom of Ronald Reagan: A Portrait in His Own Words*. New York: Barnes and Noble.

Reeves, Richard. 2005. *President Reagan: The Triumph of Imagination*. New York: Simon and Schuster.

Ritzer, George. 2008. *The McDonaldization of Society*. Thousand Oaks, Calif.: Pine Forge Press.

Robinson, Bryan E. 1988. *Teenage Fathers*. Lexington, Mass.: Lexington Books.

Rollins, Peter C., ed. 2003. *The Columbia Companion to American History on Film*. New York: Columbia University Press.

Rose, Tricia. 1994. *Black Noise: Rap Music and Black Culture in Contemporary America*. Hanover, N.H.: University Press of New England.

Rose, Tricia. 2003. *Longing to Tell: Black Women Talk About Sexuality and Intimacy*. New York: Farrar, Straus and Giroux.

Rowland, Christopher. 2006. "Can Suburban Newspapers Survive?" *Boston Globe,* May 16, C-1, 6.

Rudolph, Barbara. 1989. "High," *Time,* October 23, 20.

Sanders, Don, and Susan Sanders. 1997. *The American Drive-In Movie Theater*. Osceola, Wisc.: Motorbooks International.

Schlesinger, Arthur M., Jr. 1992. *The Disuniting of America: Reflections on a Multicultural Society*. New York: W. W. Norton.

Sennott, Charles M. 1992. *Broken Covenant*. New York: Simon and Schuster.

Shapiro, Peter. 2005. *The Rough Guide to Hip-Hop*. New York: Penguin.

Simon, Rita J., ed. 2005. *Sporting Equality: Title IX Thirty Years Later*. New Brunswick, N.J.: Transaction Publishers.

Simon, Scott. 2002. *Jackie Robinson and the Integration of Baseball*. Hoboken, N.J.: John Wiley.

Singular, Stephen. 1987. *Talked to Death: The Life and Murder of Alan Berg*. New York: Beech Tree Books.

Spurlock, Morgan. 2005. *Don't Eat This Book: Fast Food and the Supersizing of America*. New York: Berkley Books.

Stanley, Alessandra. 1986. "Stars in Their Own Write," *Time,* August 11, 19.

Thomas, Evan. 1986. "Crack Down," *Time,* August 18, 13.

Thompson, Graham. 2007. *American Culture in the 1980s*. Edinburgh University Press.

Time. 1986. "American Notes Football," August 18, 20.

Tungate, Mark. 2005. *Fashion Brands: Branding Style from Armani to Zara*. London: Kogan Page.

Tzioumakis, Yannis. 2006. *American Independent Cinema*. New Brunswick, N.J.: Rutgers University Press.

Ullman, Owen. 1986. *Stockman: The Man, the Myth, the Future*. New York: Donald I. Fine.

Ulrich, John M., and Andrea L. Harris. 2003. *GenXegesis: Essays on "Alternative" Youth (Sub)Culture*. Madison: University of Wisconsin Press.

U.S. Drug Enforcement Administration History Book, 1980–1985. http://www .usdoj.gov/dea/pubs/history/1980-1985.html.

Viguerie, Richard A., and David Franke. 2004. *America's Right Turn: How Conservatives Used New and Alternative Media to Take Power*. Chicago: Bonus Books.

Weingarten, Marc. 2006. *The Gang That Wouldn't Write Straight*. New York: Crown Publishers.

Welcome to the Drive-In Theater! http://www.driveintheater.com/index.htm.

Wilentz, Sean. 2008. *The Age of Reagan: America from Watergate to the War on Terror*. New York: Harper.

Zoglin, Richard. 1985. "Going for the Bronze," *Time,* February 25, 31.

Transformations: From Rustbelt to Sunbelt and Demographic Shifts

OVERVIEW

The social history of the 1980s may be understood best by a focus on its economics. Ronald Reagan challenged President Carter in an October 1980 televised debate by asking the audience, "Are you better off than you were four years ago?" Most voters demonstrated their concern about economic security and their distaste for Carter's "malaise" by electing Reagan. Profound changes followed this election. Although the Free Trade Agreement signed by the United States and Canada in 1987 attracted little attention in the United States, it dramatically increased trade between the two North American countries. In 1980, exports accounted for 25 percent of Canada's gross domestic product, and by 1990 exports increased to 40 percent. This reflects more imports from Canada to the United States and an important global pattern of increasing international trade and accounts for economic changes and job losses in the United States.

The combined effects of a declining economy, automation, the movement of the middle class to suburbs and the Sunbelt, the energy crisis, and deindustrialization created financial problems for many Rustbelt cities. Congress bailed out New York City in 1975, and Cleveland in 1978 was the first major city to default since the Depression. The region from the Great Lakes to the Northeast, dubbed the Rustbelt or Frostbelt, was once the industrial heartland, attracting immigrants and migrants from the South. Since the 1960s, it lost businesses, jobs, and population, especially in the rubber, machinery, steel, and automobile industries. Plant closings from 1969 to 1984 ended millions of jobs. Daniel Bell predicted this in *The Coming of Post-Industrial Society* (1999) as the new knowledge-based economy of computers and telecommunications supplanted the old industrialized economy. John Cumbler, who studied Trenton, New Jersey, in *A Social History of Economic Decline* (1989), noted the city's decline paralleled the rise of national, not civic, capitalism.

The American labor force changed dramatically in the 1980s. The Bureau of Labor Statistics announced in 1984 that for the first time in American history, white males were no longer the majority of the nation's work force. They had been 50 percent in 1982 and declined to 48.8 percent in 1983. At the same time, the mothers of children under age 18 were over 50 percent of the work force. The Latino population in the United States reached 14.5 million in 1980 and 22 million by 1991, prompting demands for immigration restriction in some states. The porous border with Mexico made it easy for smugglers known as *coyotes* to bring illegal immigrants into Arizona, Texas, or California, placing an economic burden on the states for police, health, and educational services. When Democratic congresswoman Geraldine Ferraro of New York became the first woman nominated for vice president on a major party ticket, the media declared 1984 was the Year of the Woman. However, most women in the work force were in lower-paid service-sector jobs, and even the growing number of women in the professions earned less than their male counterparts, whether American citizens or immigrants.

Sunbelt growth in population was also due to a ready housing supply rather than a desire for a warm climate. Atlanta, Dallas, Houston, Las Vegas, Phoenix, and other Sunbelt cities were the nation's fasting growing metropolitan areas by 1980 while Boston, Cleveland, Detroit, Philadelphia, and other Rustbelt or Frostbelt cities lost population or saw modest increases. California, once attracting migrants to its Mediterranean climate and movie and aerospace industries, was surpassed in the 1970s by Texas and the Southwestern desert states. Strict environmental impact reviews for building and preservationist laws discouraged building in California in the 1980s, which resulted in an increased housing supply at lower prices in other Sunbelt cities like Austin, Boise, and Provo. However, development in low-density areas impacted the environment by increasing automobile traffic and energy use.

TIMELINE

1980   More than 14.5 million Americans are Hispanic.

The Mariel Boat Lift brings 125,000 Cubans to Miami.

The 1980 census shows a population shift to the Sunbelt states.

Retirees increase 50 percent since the 1970s.

The elderly population increases 24 percent since 1970.

Workers facing 10 percent unemployment move to the Sunbelt.

Mount St. Helens (Washington) erupts killing 34.

The EPA relocates 700 Love Canal families in Niagara Falls, New York.

The draft registration is reintroduced.

The Union of Concerned Scientists urges the use of solar power.

1981   President Reagan orders the removal all solar panels installed on the White House by President Carter.

The Reagan Recession hits; 11.5 million are unemployed.

Walter Cronkite retires from CBS News.

The EPA $1.6 billion Superfund list names 114 toxic sites slated for clean-up.

The Mediterranean fruit fly infests California crops.

John W. Hinckley Jr. shoots Reagan in Washington, D.C.

The Economic Tax Recovery Act is passed.

1982   Hawaii suffers its first hurricane in 23 years.

El Nino causes rain and mudslides in California.

Congress bans aid to the Contras.

White males are only 48.8 percent of the U.S. labor force.

Reagan appoints Clarence Thomas to the EEO Commission.

Best-selling *The Fate of the Earth* arouses arms race fears.

Los Angeles hosts the Summer Olympics.

1983   U.S. Catholic bishops condemn nuclear arms as immoral.

President Reagan fires Secretary of the Interior James Watt.

EPA director Anne Burford resigns under fire by Congress.

The *Nation at Risk* report focuses on school reform.

One out of three cars sold in the U.S. is imported.

Union of Concerned Scientists opposes Star Wars.

1984   Reagan and Bush are reelected.

Congress cuts off all aid by the CIA and defense department to Nicaraguan contras.

Walter Mondale and Geraldine Ferraro are nominated by the Democrats for president and vice president.

Seventy percent of Americans in service-sector jobs.

1985   U.S. bans leaded gasoline.

Seven hundred National Academy of Sciences members urge a ban on space weapons.

Congress passes the bill honoring Martin Luther King Jr. Day as a national holiday over President Reagan's objections.

Sierra Club membership grows from 165,000 to 350,000.

1986   Randell Terry founds Operation Rescue.

Rhode Island enacts the first state recycling law.

The Tax Reform Act is passed, decreasing tax rates for the rich and increasing tax rates for the poor.

Reagan and Canadian Prime Minister Brian Mulroney meet to plan acid rain reduction.

1987   Native American population increases to 1.7 million.

INF treaty bans nuclear missiles in Europe.

Congress passes the Clean Water Act.

The United States signs Montreal Protocol on ozone dangers.

The stock market crashes in October.

The United States and Canada sign the Free Trade Agreement.

1988   Medical waste closes Long Island beaches.

Congress passes a major war on drugs law.

Yellowstone National Park suffers fire.

Trans-Alaska pipeline reaches peak oil output.

1989   January 20, Bush says in inaugural "a new breeze is blowing."

The *Exxon Valdez* spills millions of gallons of oil into Prince William Sound, Alaska.

Colin Powell is named Chairman of the Joint Chiefs of Staff.

A San Francisco earthquake kills 63.

The U.S. trade deficit with Japan is $50 billion.

DEMOGRAPHIC TRANSFORMATION

Population Changes

The growth of the Sunbelt was reflected in its increasing political power from 161 electoral votes in 1948 to 184 in 1972, and the Northeast correspondingly declined in votes from 235 to 218. This means the previously unimportant Sunbelt states gained 22 new seats in the House of Representatives and the Northeast lost 17 seats due to population changes. Many of the new leaders in Congress, and the basic strength for the conservative wings of both political parties, were from the Sunbelt. The Nixon administration (1969–1974) marked the advent of the cowboy culture in Washington, D.C., years when President Nixon surrounded himself with conservative white males from the South or West appointed to the Cabinet, Supreme Court, White House staff, and federal agencies. Many of these men remained in place throughout the 1980s, gaining experience, power, and influence in the federal government. They prepared the way for Ronald Reagan to overthrow New Deal liberalism in the 1980s.

Sunbelt state growth also added to the U.S. Hispanic population, who numbered 14.5 million in 1980 and became the largest ethnic group in the nation by 1991. This made the Roman Catholic Church the largest denomination in America. The census revealed that the U.S. population increased 39 percent from 1960 to 1990, but the foreign-born population more than doubled to 19.7 million people. The proportion of foreign-born rose from 4.7 percent in 1970 to 7.9 percent in 1990. *Time* magazine's July 8, 1985, cover story, "Immigrants, the Changing Face of America," noted the impact of this "new immigration." Some states, especially Arizona, California, Florida, and Texas, had xenophobic movements to declare that English was the state's official language, which reflected the discomfort some conservative Americans felt in becoming a minority in their own communities. Others supported restrictions on Asian and Latin American immigration, denied public school education to the children of illegal immigrants, and demanded federal government tightening of the borders. One remedy considered was revival of the guest worker programs, such as the *bracero* system used in the 1940s and 1950s to recruit temporary migrant farm workers from Mexico for U.S. agriculture. Congress sought a balance between optimism about the nation's ability to absorb more immigrants and those who favored limits on immigration. The result was a compromise: the Immigration Act of 1990 (Friedrich 1985).

Deindustrialization

In the 1980s, changes in manufacturing profoundly transformed U.S. cities in the Rustbelt as automation, foreign competition, and the free market economy made a deep impact. The steel industry reacted first to these changes; Pittsburgh had 90,000 steel workers in 1980 but only 44,000 in 1984. Similar upheavals occurred in the auto industry centered in Detroit; GM's 600,000 workers in 1980 dropped to 125,000 by 2005. By 1982, 1.9 million auto and steel industry workers had been laid off, and 3.5 million other manufacturing workers were laid off. Despite tariffs and patriotic appeals to buy American products, the lower prices and higher quality of imported goods proved irresistible to consumers. The Reagan recession in 1981–1983 saw 11.5 million people lose their jobs, but the economy rebounded by 1983 although most new jobs were in the lower-paid service sector, not in heavy industry.

By the end of the decade, the term "globalization" was common, referring to the conservative economic policy of the Reagan administration, especially Federal Reserve chairman Alan Greenspan, that integrated the dominant U.S. economy to the world economy. It meant that goods, workers, and capital became more mobile in transnational world investments and commerce. Like the term multinational corporation, it was much debated. Manufacturing in developed nations, such as the United States, declined as it increased in the poor Third World nations due to new technology, communications, and transportation. Reagan's tax reduction on industry, deregulation, and free trade policies encouraged wealthy investors to close U.S. factories, such as steel and automakers, and invest in more profitable, cheaper production "off shore" or overseas. American workers and labor unions lost power to the wealthy investors and their corporations. Consumer goods were cheaper but still too costly for unemployed or underemployed blue-collar workers. The popularity of imported cars reflected this trend as did the 8 million new legal and illegal immigrants in the United States. The imported goods and workers did little to relieve the problems of the displaced U.S. workers. The new deindustrialized or postindustrial America was more diverse, but this multiculturalism or globalization troubled many Americans who lost jobs or high incomes in the 1980s. Anxiety increased as outsourcing, downsizing, and restructuring became part of the language in the new economy, especially in the Great Lakes region dubbed the Rustbelt.

For example, in Sparrows Point, a Bethlehem Steel company town outside Baltimore, a strong union allowed many steel workers to buy homes and live a comfortable working-class life until 1980. Deindustrialization reduced the number of mill employees and forced their wives back into the labor force. In white and African American families, the husband was no longer able to earn enough as the sole breadwinner to pay for home ownership and consumer purchases that brought their families into the middle class. Following ethnographic interviews with steelworker families, Karen Olson reported in *Wives of Steel: Voices of Women from the Sparrows Point Steelmaking Communities* that these economic changes had a profound social impact, making marriages more of a partnership despite the devastating damage done by deindustrialization in the 1980s (Olson 2005).

This General Motors auto manufacturing plant in Flint, Michigan, was closed in the 1980s. Pictured in 1988, it was part of the Rustbelt. (Bob Krist/Corbis)

The Decline of the Industrial Heartland

America's industrial heartland, the so-called Rustbelt states of Illinois, Indiana, Michigan, Ohio, Pennsylvania, New Jersey, New York, West Virginia, and Wisconsin, experienced substantial economic and population decline in the 1980s. After the 1971 recession, worldwide free trade agreements made it cheaper to import into the United States steel and heavy industrial goods from Third World nations. By 1982, the Rustbelt saw factories close, such as 13 U.S. Steel plants that closed in 1980, and 3.5 million manufacturing jobs disappear or be replaced by lower-wage service-sector jobs. By 2000, the gritty smokestack cities—Akron, Buffalo, Cleveland, Detroit, Flint, Gary, Kenosha, Lackawanna, Pittsburgh, Rochester, Syracuse, Toledo, and Youngstown—had lost jobs and population. Ontario, Windsor, Oshawa, Hamilton, Kitchener, and Cornwall also lost factories, mills, and jobs. The ethnic working-class or blue-collar workers felt the loss of jobs first, and by 1989, corporate retrenchment, automation, and downsizing affected middle-class managers and white-collar workers. Male breadwinners lost their jobs, their place in their community, and often their place as heads of families. Lower wage service- and public-sector jobs frequently were filled by women.

The industrialized northeast and upper Midwest area was also known as the Snowbelt or Frostbelt for its heavy snowfall and long winters. Rustbelt also refers to the abandoned, rusting machinery left behind and the automobiles and

The Buy American Movement

In response to deindustrialization and plant closings in the 1980s, and after exhausting available legal protests and strategies, angry American workers began Buy American movements. Combining economic and nationalist sentiments, unions like the International Ladies Garment Workers Union (ILGWU) and the United Auto Workers (UAW) urged U.S. consumers to purchase products made in America. Labor Day parades included protests and placards warning of the economic danger of importing consumer products. Catchy ILGWU television commercials featured union women singing "look for the union label." Posters reminded Americans that 300,000 UAW workers had been laid off, and they should park their Japanese car in Tokyo. Bumper stickers proclaimed "buy American, the job you save may be your own." In Minnesota, Alabama, and Pennsylvania unions sold lottery tickets for a chance to take a sledgehammer to a Toyota. In Detroit, a Chinese American man, Vincent Chin, was beaten to death in 1982 by two laid-off auto workers who thought he was Japanese. Other campaigns protested protectionist policies by Japan that barred U.S. products like fruit, beef, rice, and cars and denounced free trade or urged efforts to restore American competitiveness. None of these protests were effective because American consumers increasingly bought imported goods, which were usually cheaper, more popular, and better designed. Congress considered bills to compensate U.S. workers and their communities for lost wages and tax revenue, but no bill was passed until 1988 when the weak Worker Adjustment and Notification (WARN) act passed.

highway bridges rusting from salt used to de-ice roads in the snowy winters. Cities such as Detroit steadily lost population as white residents moved to suburbs or to other states and African Americans moved into the city. This was in contrast to the rapid growth in the Sunbelt states throughout the 1980s. However, some economists and demographers now believe the exodus from the northern states may be overstated because of the methods used by the census. It includes only domestic migration, not immigration, and does not properly account for college students or illegal immigrants. Errors in enumerating the northeast urban population were common (High 2003).

Another consequence of deindustrialization and the demand for greater profits was the reduction of fringe benefits for workers, especially in health insurance and pensions. In the 20th century, corporate America had provided a safety net for its employees. Under pressure from investors in the 1980s to produce bigger profits, U.S. firms shifted the pension burden to their workers. As executive pay and corporate profits rose, the old promise of lifetime employment and cradle-to-grave benefits in a social contract of employee loyalty and corporate paternalism was disappearing. Companies' pension and health insurance

Working-class Americans and Reagan

Much of Ronald Reagan's popularity derived from white ethnic working-class supporters who were convinced he understood them and was interested in solving their problems. Despite labor union endorsements of President Carter, an estimated 44 percent of union families voted for Reagan in 1980, those known as the Reagan Democrats. From 1954 to 1962, Reagan had been a spokesman for the General Electric Company and had much experience speaking to union employees and managers at 139 GE plants. As a former president of the Screen Actors Guild, he knew labor negotiations from personal experience. When he switched from a liberal to a conservative in 1964, he had been strongly influenced by friend Lemuel Boulware, the GE vice president and a very successful labor negotiator (Evans 2006).

Since Alabama governor George Wallace won 13.5 percent of the 1968 presidential vote, northern and midwestern white ethnic voters in cities and suburbs had supported new conservative candidates. Southern Democrats also switched to the Republican Party. Many blue-collar workers had grown dissatisfied with their union leaders, and in 1984, United Auto Workers union members told the New York congresswoman Geraldine Ferraro that they were Democrats but that Reagan made them proud to be Americans. Blue-collar workers liked the Great Communicator, as he was known, who beamed confidence, strength, and optimism and shared their hostility to big government and Washington insiders such as the Democratic Speaker of the House Tip O'Neill. Relying on supply-side economics, workers responded to promises of lower taxes that would stimulate the economy, business growth, and employment. Reagan quoted the popular songs of John Mellencamp and Bruce Springsteen to demonstrate his sympathy for farmers and workers, and he criticized welfare chiselers and free-spending liberals like Massachusetts senator Ted Kennedy. Most Hispanic, African American, and female voters did not vote for Reagan in 1980, but in 1984, Reagan won 56 percent of the female vote, especially married women in union households. Fewer than one in three voters claimed to be conservative, but Reagan had wider appeal with the working class than the beleaguered Carter did in October 1980, when most voters made their decisions at the end of the campaign (Evans 2006).

Ironically, Reagan, who seldom attended church, won broad support from conservative Christian voters in the south and west. This was the backlash against the 1960s counterculture of sexual liberation; violent antiwar demonstrations; liberation movements for women, African Americans, Latinos, and gay people; illegal immigration; and toleration of illegal drugs. Partly class warfare, it converted resentful blue-collar Democrats into Reagan supporters. The President's charisma, infectious optimism, self-deprecating humor, and sunny disposition did much to charm working-class supporters. As a result, the Democrats were the majority party in the House (1955–1995), but Republicans won control of the Senate

Continued on next page

Working-class Americans and Reagan, Continued

(1981–1987) for the first time since 1952. Led by the very popular Reagan, the motivated working-class and the innovative New Right put liberals on the defensive in the 1980s (Diggins 2007).

When Reaganomics failed, he assured voters this was due to the Carter administration and the spendthrift Democrats in Congress. In 1982, blue-collar voters and senior citizens, concerned about Republican plans to reduce Social Security benefits, returned to the Democratic Party, giving them a gain of 26 House seats in the mid-term election. But as the economy rebounded from the 1981–1983 recession, and after Reagan recovered from a 1981 assassination attempt, he assured the public in his 1984 campaign that it was once again "morning in America" (Levy 1996). Reagan won an overwhelming 58.8 percent of the popular vote in 1984 against Walter F. Mondale. He had the common touch; for example, in a 1983 visit to Boston, he dropped in at the Erie Pub, a working-class tavern in Dorchester, a Democratic neighborhood. Standing at the crowded bar, he ordered a beer and insisted on paying for it. While greeting every customer, one man told the president he didn't want to be seen on TV because he was supposed to be at work. Reagan quipped, "So am I."

He emerged unscathed from the Iran-Contra scandals in 1986, at first denying and then admitting his mistake in trading arms to Iran for hostages. His rating in polls fell from 67 percent to 46 percent in 1986, but he was known as the Teflon president because no blame clung to him very long. Colorado Congresswoman Patricia Schroeder coined this term, and veteran television news reporter Walter Cronkite adopted it. Lou Cannon, Reagan's biographer, admitted the term was accurate (Cannon 1991). Reagan endured and benefited from amicable relations with the USSR, the fall of Communism, and the quick wealth and extravagant spending by Wall Street investors and the new yuppies. Despite the sharp growth of poverty, homelessness, mental illness, drug addiction, and crime among the working class, Reagan left the White House on January 20, 1989, the most popular president since FDR and a hero to conservatives and the working class.

costs surged in this decade as the retirement age declined and life expectancy and the cost of medical care increased. Battered by fierce international competition and changing technology, many U.S. firms reduced pension benefits. Typically, the corporation converted pensions to cash-balance plans to which the company made annual contributions for individual employee retirement accounts tied to short-term Treasury bills. Because retirees lived longer, and the approaching retirement of 72 million baby boomers threatened to be a significant cost, corporations shifted the burden to employees to save employers millions of dollars. Executive pay was linked with the corporation's profits, and this led to erosion of traditional pension plans with guaranteed benefits. The advent of 401(k) plans tied to Wall Street performance was no solution for most workers, and executives received more generous pension benefits than workers. Many workers decided to delay retirement to improve their pension benefits.

The Ascendant Sunbelt

Stretching across the lower third of the United States, the Sunbelt states—Alabama, Arizona, Arkansas, California, Florida, Georgia, Louisiana, Mississippi, Nevada, New Mexico, North Carolina, Oklahoma, South Carolina, Tennessee, and Texas —saw significant economic and population growth in the 1980s. The Census Bureau reported in 1981 that the center of the U.S. population was west of the Mississippi River for the first time. One indication of the region's influence is that every American president elected since 1964 has been a Sunbelt resident, including Johnson (Texas), Nixon (California), Carter (Georgia), Reagan (California), Bush (Texas), Clinton (Arkansas), and George W. Bush (Texas). In contrast, between 1869 and 1945 only two presidents were born outside the Northeast. The declining influence of the Rustbelt reflected the power shift to the Sunbelt. This tend began by 1930 when 980,000 people migrated from the Northeast to the South, and 910,000 migrated from the Midwest to the West. Geographic mobility grew after World War II; for example, President George H. W. Bush joined many young World War II veterans in the postwar migration out of the cities and into the suburbs of the South and the West. The Bush family moved from Connecticut to Texas after Bush graduated from Yale in 1948. The baby boom these veterans created populated the Sunbelt, including future presidents Bill Clinton and George W. Bush. One indication of rising Sunbelt influence was the new cookbook from General Mills: *Betty Crocker's Southwest Cooking* (1989).

White migrants from the Rustbelt to Sunbelt states sometimes experienced culture shock from the large and growing Asian and Latino populations they encountered. By 1980, over 20 million African American and white southerners migrated from the South northward and westward. This Southern diaspora altered the social, political, and cultural fabric of the United States. For example, Baptist and Pentecostal churches were reinvigorated, and Southern blues, jazz, gospel, R&B, and country music spread nationwide. African Americans developed political power in expanding urban enclaves, and white working-class conservatives contributed to the New Right suburban movements. *Time* magazine reported on August 18, 1986, one unexpected change in Sunbelt cities such as Atlanta and Chattanooga, the emergence of gang violence. In a decade of tremendous growth, these and other Sunbelt cities attracted millions of people from depressed urban centers of the North, bringing violent youth gangs, robbery, rape, assault, and other crimes (Carney 1986).

Development in Atlanta surged in the 1980s as the Sunbelt population expanded. (Katherine Welles)

Atlanta of the Sunbelt

Atlanta, the capital of Georgia and the state's largest city, is the most important financial, commercial, and transportation center in the southeastern United States. By 1970, Atlanta had a majority African American population for the first time and elected its first African American congressman, Andrew Young, in 1972, and its first African American mayor, Maynard Jackson, in 1973. A new airport in 1980 promoted business and tourism, which helped to make Atlanta the nation's third most popular convention center. Suburban growth increased the metropolitan population from 2 million in 1980 to 4 million in the 1990s. Immigration from Central and South America, Asia, and the Caribbean in the 1980s also increased and diversified the population. The central-city population reached 389,760 by 1980 with more than 4 million in the suburbs by 1990, which reflected the population shift to the Sunbelt area. Only Phoenix had a larger metropolitan growth, and by 2000, Atlanta was the nation's 11th largest metropolitan area. The city has the largest concentration of federal agencies outside of Washington, D.C., making government and the military the area's largest employer and a stabilizing influence. Airport expansion and construction of three interstate highways to Atlanta created transportation connections that brought more business, jobs, people, tourists, and conventions in the 1980s. Race relations were improving despite white flight to the suburbs and neighborhood disputes over desegregating housing, and the local government promoted stable and orderly development.

Population Growth in the West

The 1980 census showed many Americans leaving the economically declining Rustbelt North and East for the Sunbelt states. Nevada (146 percent), Arizona (106 percent), Florida (91 percent), Utah (63 percent), Texas (52 percent), New Mexico (49 percent), Colorado (49 percent), California (49 percent), Wyoming (37 percent), Oregon (36 percent), and Georgia (41 percent) had the greatest increases in population as retirees and unemployed workers relocated. This trend began in the Great Depression (1929–1941), as New Deal hydroelectric projects like the TVA and Hoover Dam provided new sources of water and electricity for these states. Also, by 1950, air conditioners were more common. In the Sunbelt, air conditioners were as important as central heating was in other parts of the country.

The Dust Bowl migration of the 1930s, an exodus of rural white Protestants from the Great Plains, created an Okie subculture of two million people in California by the 1980s. This group shifted toward a cultural conservatism and suburban consumerism rooted in middle-class values and the Southern California military-industrial complex and became increasingly critical of liberal elites, minorities, and the poor. Many immigrants from Asia and Latin America also settled in the western states, which added diversity to Sunbelt society, especially in California, Texas, and Florida. After the Soviet Union permitted Jewish dissidents to emigrate, San Francisco had a new Russian Jewish population of 35,000 people in 1989.

The Political Impact of the Demographic Shift

The movement of affluent and retired Americans in the 1980s from the politically liberal Frostbelt states to the conservative Sunbelt states led to increased Republican control of Congress. Retirees from the Northeast or Midwest often vacationed in the Sunbelt as "snow birds" in the winter before eventually settling there in retirement communities. Ronald Reagan's election with 51 percent of the 1980 popular vote demonstrated the political consequences of this demographic change. Unemployed workers from the so-called Rustbelt states and immigrants from Latin America and Asia also swelled the Sunbelt state populations. By 1980, close to 8 million African American southerners, nearly 20 million white southerners, and more than 1 million Latinos migrated to the West and the North. In cities and suburbs they nationalized southern evangelical or fundamentalist religion and made conservative country music popular commercial entertainment (Gregory 2005).

Migration to the Sunbelt increased by 1950 and soon had significant political impact. This was obvious since 1968, when President Nixon rallied the silent majority against the elite Northeast establishment, and in 1972, when he revealed his southern strategy to lure conservative Democrats to the Republican Party.

Table 5.1. Asian-American Population Sources, 1970–1980

Year	China	Japan	Philippines	India	Korea	Vietnam	Total	Total % U.S. Population
1970	436,062	591,290	343,060	—	69,150	—	1,439,562	7%
1980	812,178	716,331	781,894	387,223	357,393	245,025	3,466,421	1.5%

Source: Daniel, Roger. 1991. *Coming to America: A History of Immigration and Ethnicity in American Life.* New York: HarperCollins. 351.

The influx of people from the heartland rekindled the lower-middle-class conservatism seen in Jerry Falwell's religious crusades and Ronald Reagan's anti-establishment movement. In popular culture, the *Beverly Hillbillies* TV series and the growth of country western and blues music are examples of the impact of the Southern diaspora on the nation. But the most striking feature of ethnic change in Sunbelt states in the 1980s was certainly the drastic increase in immigrants from Asia, as Table 5.1 indicates. California, Texas, New York, and Florida had the greatest increases in these new immigrants. Lower-cost housing proved to be a major factor in attracting population growth in the Sunbelt (La Chapelle 2007).

THE ENVIRONMENT

Background

Even before the counterculture of the 1960s had embraced environmentalism, the demographic shift from the North and the East to the South and the West raised issues of environmental impact and diminishing natural resources. As air-conditioning became common, energy demands rose, and existing power and water supplies could not support the new cities and suburbs of the Sunbelt states. By 1980, more than 43 percent of the 227.7 million Americans lived in suburban houses, usually with well-watered lawns and swimming pools, air conditioners, two-car garages, and a growing number of new electrical appliances, tools, and gadgets. The expanding suburban middle class expected to live a comfortable life, and this would conflict in the 1980s with the emerging environmental movement. From the first Earth Day (1970) and the establishment of the Greenpeace movement (1971), the influential suburban residents had expressed their concern about the environment and conservation of natural resources. Although suburbs, especially in the Sunbelt, consumed more energy, these residents would prove to be a potent lobby for environmentalism in the 1980s (Fisher 1990).

The New Immigrants, an Asset?

Perhaps more than any other social factor, immigration in the 1980s changed the United States. These "new immigrants" from Latin America and Asia created a profound demographic and cultural transformation of U.S. society. Abolition of the national origins quota system in 1965 together with the Refugee Act of 1980 and the Immigration Reform and Control Act of 1986 were intended to close the back door (of illegal immigration) and to open the front door (of legal entry) in the United States. Mexico represented the largest source of immigration to the United States, about 10 million (or 30 percent) of the 32 million foreign born. Almost 1 million Cuban exiles arrived since Fidel Castro came to power in Havana in 1959. The rest of Latin America accounted for 7 million (or 23 percent) and Asia accounted for 8 million (or 25 percent). While the Mexican-born population grew substantially in the 1980s, the undocumented (illegal) immigration grew even faster. As a result, half of the Latinos in the United States by the decade's end had entered illegally. Many of these immigrants settled in California, Texas, Florida, Arizona, New York, and Illinois.

The number of immigrants from Asia (China, Japan, India, Korea, Vietnam, Laos, and the Philippines) also significantly increased in the 1980s, proportionally much more than Hispanics. In *Arguing Immigration,* Linda Chavez, the former director of the U.S. Commission on Civil Rights, reported that studies in the 1980s showed both legal and illegal immigrants contributed much to the California economy, paying more in taxes than they received in services and creating jobs rather than taking jobs from American workers. Reducing immigration would cause labor shortages and drive up wages. Intangible benefits that immigrants provided the United States were their energy, creativity, and diversity. But in a national backlash against immigration in the 1980s, critics claimed the open-door policy of the past would overwhelm the United States and fragment our economy and culture. Some looked to the restrictive policy of Japan, which had only 2 million foreigners as guest workers, about 1.5 percent of the population, while the U.S. foreign-born population was almost 12 percent. Colorado governor Richard Lamm expressed his pessimistic views in a 1985 book titled *The Immigration Time Bomb.*

The growth of agriculture, industry, and transportation raised the temperature of the Earth's surface in a process known as the greenhouse effect. As the sun warms the Earth, heat is trapped by a layer of thermal gas. By the late-20th century the Earth's temperature rose, polar ice melted, glaciers shrank, the sea level rose, air and drinking water quality declined, coastal areas flooded, agriculture changed, the extinction of species occurred, severe tropical storms and diseases increased, and, in short, the global climate changed. Carbon dioxide increased ragweed pollen, which contributed to asthma and the growth and toxicity of poison ivy, and warmer air spread mosquito and tick-borne ills like Lyme and West Nile disease.

Contributing man-made factors included deforestation, coal and petroleum consumption, and increased cattle production. The U.S. chemical companies produced millions of pounds of methyl bromide and other pesticides each year that destroyed the ozone layer that protects the Earth from harmful ultraviolet radiation. Although scientists did not agree on the accuracy of these dire predictions, there was general agreement that global warming resulted from human activity and that it posed great danger. The White House Office of Science and Technology recommended immediate steps to reduce acid rain in 1983, but Reagan did not acknowledge until 1986 that humans caused acid rain. Secretary of Energy John Herrington, however, called for more research in 1986 rather than regulations for the "small" acid rain problem. However, within six years the United Nations Conference on Environment and Development issued a binding declaration on the need to reduce global warming, which was signed by 150 nations (Daniel 2005).

Because the United States produced about 25 percent of the Earth's greenhouse gases, its efforts to reduce deforestation and automobile mileage, improve energy efficiency in construction, recycle materials, and expand public transportation were considered essential. American cars and trucks produced about one-third of the nation's air pollution, so fuel-efficient cars were recommended. However, the Reagan and Bush administrations questioned the accuracy of these scientific warnings and opposed mandatory measures that had adverse economic consequences. In 1981, Reagan placed Bush in charge of a task force on regulatory relief and froze all new federal regulations. Despite the appeals of government scientists, independent experts, and environmental groups, the United States proposed only voluntary measures for reducing greenhouse gas and global warming. In addition, American agriculture used increasing amounts of chemicals on farms. Pesticide usage grew 75 percent from 1966 to 1999, and herbicide usage expanded 282 percent. Little toxicity research had been done on farm applications of chemicals that entered the U.S. food and water supply. Although the Department of Agriculture was responsible for approving pesticides, it had strong ties to agribusiness and was too willing to adopt the chemical industry's policies. Only when the Environmental Protection Agency assumed responsibility for investigating the health and ecological dangers of chemicals used in agriculture was this threat recognized. However, the United States had no farm-to-table government inspection of the food Americans consumed.

By 1980, an increasing number of Americans became devoted to protecting the environment as part of the quality of life. Since the 1970s, Gallup polls revealed that more than 53 percent of the public included pollution among the major public issues. This reflected a spiritual dimension of the 1960s counterculture, when many hippies reacting against mainstream corporate America found solace in nature, the outdoors, or wilderness. The back to the earth movement—

organic farming, vegetarianism, camping, hiking, gardening, antiauthoritarianism, antinuclear protests, the animal rights movement, an interest in Native Americans and conservation—contributed to the new environmental movement that bloomed in the 1980s. Familiar with mass movements and political protests, in the post-Vietnam War era Americans naturally turned to established and new nonprofit organizations to express their concern for nature and to protest threats to the environment. One example was the growth of the Sierra Club from 7,000 members in 1960 to 77,000 in 1980, and 480,000 in 1988, making it a potent lobby on legislation affecting the earth, ocean, and atmosphere.

In 1980, the Sierra Club conducted a major voter-registration drive for the first time, but Ronald Reagan was elected and the conservatives controlled the Senate Energy Committee and the Agriculture Committee, the Environmental Protection Agency, the Department of Energy, and the Department of the Interior. Federal environmental policy was under the control of the Sagebrush Rebels, and NBC News declared the end of the environmental movement. All was not lost, however; the public was determined to support the environmental movement. By 1984, Congress passed a strong Superfund law to clean up abandoned hazardous waste dumps. The media covered environmental issues more carefully than ever before. More acreage was added to the National Wilderness Preservation System, and new wildlife refuges were established.

Major Environmental Changes in the 1980s

In 1979, the Three Mile Island nuclear power plant in Pennsylvania became a near disaster. The Environmental Protection Agency (EPA) announced it would purchase the dioxin-contaminated town of Times Beach, Missouri, in 1983. These events shocked the American public and stimulated the environmental movement and related organizations. Completion of the Alaska pipeline in 1977 did little to mollify the concerns of environmentalists in the 1980s about the danger it posed to the fragile wilderness. Congress responded by designating millions of acres of land in the Western states and Alaska as protected wilderness by 1980. Congress passed the Endangered Species Act and the Federal Land Policy and Management Act to limit any economic development that might lead to extinction of plants and animals. Clearly the New Age view of spirituality embracing Mother Nature was influential. Hollywood responded with movies such as *Escape from New York* (1981) and *Blade Runner* (1982), which warned of environmental crisis if capitalist greed and public indifference were unchecked.

Ecological scientists, confronted by suburban sprawl, urban decay, pollution, and nuclear fallout in the 1980s, altered their research to study the degraded physical environment. This scientific movement and the popular conservation crusade prompted states to pass recycling laws. Rhode Island was the first state to pass a recycling law in 1986. Schools and colleges offered new courses on

The eruption of Mount St. Helens on May 18, 1980, lasted nine hours in Washington. (U.S. Geological Survey)

ecology and environmentalism. The five previous administrations had been more or less pro-environment, and throughout the 1980s, public concern grew over the antienvironmental policies of James Watt and others in the Reagan administration. All of this came to a resounding halt in the Reagan administration when petroleum corporations and economic and social conservatives expressed their doubts about the environmentalists they dismissed as radical "tree huggers." But natural disasters like the Mount St. Helens volcano eruption on May 18, 1980, the discovery of toxic medical waste on a New York beach in 1988, the Yellowstone National Park forest fire in 1988, the earthquakes in Mexico City in 1985, and the killer bee invasion in Texas in 1990 all convinced a growing segment of the public that protection of the natural environment was an important public issue. The earthquake in the San Francisco area in 1989 killed 63 people, cost $6 billion in damages, and was the costliest U.S. natural disaster at the time.

In 1982, the media began discussing El Nino, a periodic change in ocean temperatures in the Pacific that caused climate change. It reduced fish, bird, seal, and sea lion populations off California and brought red tides, torrential rains, mudslides, and floods. Hawaii had its first hurricane in 23 years on November 23, 1982. The northeastern states experienced milder winters, and the Southwest had abnormal cyclones, rainstorms, floods, and wind sheer. Other parts of the world had unusual rainstorms, hurricanes, typhoons, droughts, and famines. This ocean-temperate phenomenon reoccurred in the winter of 1986–1987. Some scientists claimed El Nino was related to global warming. Americans held a Live Aid concert on July 13, 1985, that raised $70 million for African drought and famine relief. Hurricane Hugo killed 70 people in the Carolinas in 1989 and caused $4 billion in damage and left thousands homeless; meteorologists predicted more devastating hurricanes and tornadoes would occur (Magnuson 1989).

The Reagan Revolution and the Environment

Led by Ronald Reagan to victory in the 1980s, conservatives dismissed government regulation that was said to thwart the nation's expansion, energy, and independence. Although Ronald Reagan was identified as a Westerner or cowboy who enjoyed the outdoors and working on his remote California ranch, his administration had a poor record on the environmental and scientific issues many Americans found important. Congress passed the Clean Water Act (1987) over

Reagan's veto because massive irrigation for farming on the Great Plains and in California was depleting the natural aquifer that stored drinking water for the western states. Logging companies in the Pacific Northwest had long exploited the land and polluted the water by clear cutting, or removing all the trees in a region. But even his staff was shocked when Reagan responded to a question about the environment with the quip, "A tree is a tree, how many do you need to look at?" While campaigning in 1980, he claimed the Mount St. Helens volcano released more sulfur dioxide than 10 years of automobile driving, and that decaying trees caused the most pollution (Tygiel 2006).

By executive order Reagan required federal regulations intended to reduce health and safety risks to be based on scientific risk assessment that were not remote or hypothetical. Another executive order required the Office of Budget and Management to review federal regulations for their economic impact, potential cost, potential benefit, and less costly alternatives. Environmental organizations saw this as an obstacle to progress. On the other hand, in 1982 Dale Corson, president of Cornell University, issued a National Academy of Science report that convinced Reagan to remove national security controls limiting basic scientific research. However, the administration was generally opposed to environmentalism, especially when it could interfere with U.S. business. For example, Vice President George H. W. Bush, a successful Houston oil executive who had invested in undersea oil drilling since 1958, was unsympathetic to the environmental movement. As president, Bush created the White House Council on Competitiveness to increase scrutiny of federal environmental regulations.

Reagan's secretary of the interior, a conservative born-again Christian from Wyoming, James G. Watt, insisted that less federal intervention in the economy was necessary for economic growth. He had founded the Mountain States Legal Foundation in 1976, an antienvironmental lobby, and in 1981 he fired Interior Department staff who he said were environmentalists who exaggerated the need for conservation of natural resources. He believed natural resources were waiting to be exploited by businessmen. Secretary Watt halted national park growth, refused to add to the lists of endangered species, sold millions of acres of wilderness land, and supported

The controversial secretary of the interior James G. Watt served in the first Reagan administration from 1981 to 1983 but was forced to resign. (Bettmann/Corbis)

using federal land for commercial business. He was reacting to the National Park Service (NPS) growth under his predecessor, Secretary Cecil Andrus, who had implemented the Alaska Native Lands Claims Settlement Act. This led to creation of 10 national parks by 1981 when the addition of 44 million acres doubled the size of the national park system. William J. Whalen, the NPS director (1977–1980) was a visionary who emphasized urban parks and created historical parks like the Martin Luther King Jr. National Historic Site in Atlanta. These scenic parks and historical sites attracted a growing number of 268 million visitors per year to 320 national parks, sites, and monuments.

Watt, who tirelessly promoted the administration's antienvironmentalist agenda, halted this expansion but resigned in 1983 due to public outrage over his controversial public statements. In 1996, Watt was found guilty in federal court for withholding documents from a federal grand jury (Diggins 2007).

In 1981, Reagan also appointed Anne M. Gorsuch Burford, a conservative Colorado legislator, as head of the Environmental Protection Agency (EPA), the first woman to hold this position. But Burford outraged environmentalists by cutting the EPA budget and staff. She resigned in 1983 when the House of Representatives cited her for contempt. Burford's husband, Colorado rancher Robert Burford, had a brief career as head of the Bureau of Land Management, but he too resigned after offending the public and Congress by opening western land for cattle ranchers. This demonstrated the growing influence of new and older environmental organizations and the increasing public concern about protecting natural resources and the environment.

A conscientious Seattle lumber company executive, William Ruckelshaus, replaced Burford (1983–1985), but he recalled that President Reagan never talked with him about the environment. Despite warnings by scientists that emission of the major global warming gas, carbon dioxide, was increasing, many denied these reports were accurate or derided them as too expensive, junk science, and alarmist or exaggerated. Environmental organizations and scientists warned that energy conservation and transportation changes were necessary, especially for power plants, cars, and trucks. State laws and regional cooperation to require increased energy efficiency for buildings and appliances could also reduce greenhouse gas emissions and would be more economical, but federal regulations were necessary.

The Union of Concerned Scientists (UCS) sued the Nuclear Regulatory Commission to improve safety standards at U.S. nuclear power plants in 1983. Seven hundred members of the National Academy of Sciences, including 57 Noble laureates, signed the UCS "Appeal to Ban Space Weapons" to avoid testing and deployment of nuclear weapons by the United States and Soviet Union in space in 1985, and they persuaded Congress to limit funds for Star Wars. Secretary of Defense Caspar W. Weinberger accused the *Washington Post* of giving aid and comfort to the enemy for publishing admissions by Robert Cooper, assistant

The Sagebrush Rebellion

By 1980, an influential coalition of western public-land users (ranchers, hunters, timber, oil and gas, and mining lobbyists) known as the Sagebrush Rebellion emerged in reaction to the success of the environmental movement. Enlisting the support of western state legislators and congressmen, they demanded that most federal land should be returned to the states. In a Salt Lake City campaign speech in August 1980, Ronald Reagan declared "I am a Sagebrush Rebel." Despite laws passed by Congress and overwhelming public opinion, the Reagan administration supported the Sagebrush Rebellion. Local concern about big government was a major issue because in Nevada, for example, 87 percent of all land was under federal control. The 700 million acres of public land under federal control comprised 96 percent of Alaska, 66 percent of Utah, 64 percent of Idaho, 53 percent of Oregon, 48 percent of Wyoming, and 36 percent of Colorado. Federal land policy and management was a mandate to keep this public land in perpetual trust, but since the 1970s, Congress and the executive branch restricted only 38 million acres for parks, wilderness areas, wildlife refuges, and other noncommercial uses. Tighter enforcement of federal environmental rules and laws protecting endangered wildlife and habitat rankled many westerners as the western populations grew rapidly. Preservation at the expense of economic development was the major issue.

The media romanticized the Sagebrush Rebellion in the 1980s as small ranchers and cowboys battling the monolithic federal government to regain local control of the wide open spaces. In fact, the Sagebrush Rebellion was a well-funded conservative backlash against increasing federal regulation and more careful scrutiny of natural resources. Corporations that had long benefited from operating subsidies by below-market rates for grazing, lumbering, and mining on public land, which often damaged public recreation, water, and air, found support in the Reagan administration. Secretary of the Interior Watt affirmed that he was part of the Sagebrush Rebellion but that he preferred changes in Bureau of Land Management policies to the conveyance of federal land to the states. Eventually, hunters and off-road vehicle enthusiasts joined environmental, recreation, and conservation groups to oppose privatization of public land. The cost of state management of vast tracts of wilderness land also deterred the Sagebrush Rebellion. Given opportunities to voice their complaints, and with the promise of more sympathetic views by the Department of the Interior, the rebellion faded away in defeat against the more influential environmental movement. They did influence the Reagan administration to slow environmentalism, and as R. McGreggor Cawley reported in *Federal Land, Western Anger,* this "produced a stalemate in the public land policy arena."

secretary of defense, that Star Wars was only a potential ground and space plan to protect the United States from strategic nuclear ballistic missiles but that no designs existed for this. Cooper claimed those who wanted to preserve space as a sanctuary from the Cold War were unrealistic, but he also called some of the Star Wars plan a disaster for its cost over-runs and missed deadlines.

However, defense, petroleum, and coal corporations continued to fund ideological groups to discredit the scientific warnings about Star Wars, global warming, greenhouse gases, melting sea ice, alpine glaciers, and disturbed animals and plants. These cautions by prominent scientists were derided as alarmist junk science (Mooney 2005).

Acid Rain

Acid rain is produced when sulfur dioxide combines with moisture and falls to Earth in rain, snow, sleet, or hail. It contaminates drinking water, aquatic life, and vegetation, and damages buildings and monuments. This had been recognized as a serious problem since the 1950s and became a major issue in the 1980s when Canada claimed acid rain from U.S. automobile exhaust and from factories and power plants that burned high-sulfur industrial fuel contaminated its air, forests, and water. Regulations in Europe and North America, including the Helsinki protocol (1985) and the U.S. Clean Air Act (1990) were not successful in reducing acid rain.

Much scientific evidence proved acid rain, holes in the ozone, and the greenhouse effect were due to globalization's plundering of the planet. Third World countries, in a rush to industrialize, ignored environmental damage. The loss of trade barriers and protective tariffs permitted importation of cheaper steel, lumber, rubber, and other products from these Third World nations without environmental protection laws. Nevertheless, the Reagan administration doubted the validity of scientific warnings and insisted that economic development was more important than protection of the environment.

When William Ruckelshaus replaced Anne Burford as the EPA administrator, he argued for a federal program to clean up acid rain, but the White House budget director, David Stockman, successfully argued that this was unnecessary and the cost was too high. Only after the abrasive Stockman left the Office of Management and Budget in 1985 did the Reagan administration recommend a multibillion dollar acid rain control program. The most satisfactory solutions to acid rain and air pollution may be eliminating fossil fuels and replacing the internal combustion engine with alternative sources of energy. The EPA ban on leaded gasoline (1985) offered some hope that the auto industry would produce electric or solar powered vehicles, but Detroit and the petroleum industry made little progress on this solution.

The *Exxon Valdez* Disaster

The American supertanker *Exxon Valdez* hit a reef in Prince William Sound on March 23, 1989, spilling 11 million gallons of crude oil on 500 miles of the pristine Alaskan coastline. Emergency cleanup efforts were unsuccessful due to weather conditions and the lack of proper equipment. Exxon, the world's leading petroleum corporation, admitted violating environmental laws and was fined $287 million by an Anchorage court in 1991, and $5 billion in punitive damages were imposed. Exxon spent $2 billion cleaning the oil on the sea and shoreline, and $1 billion to settle civil and criminal charges, but most damage claims had not been paid by 2006. The environmental impact was greater than the 1969 oil spill that fouled beaches and killed wildlife in Santa Barbara, California, or the 1988 oil tank spill at Pittsburgh. Uncounted numbers of Alaskan sea birds, otters, seals, eagles, shellfish, whales, and fish were killed. Native Americans and the fishing industry suffered much social and economic disruption from this environmental disaster, the most devastating to occur at sea in history. By 1999, only 2 of the 24 animal species had recovered from the persistently toxic oil spill and by 2008 Exxon was still appealing some court judgments against them.

Workers contain and remove oil from beaches along Prince William Sound, Alaska, in the aftermath of the Exxon Valdez *oil spill disaster of 1989. (Photo courtesy of the Exxon Valdez Oil Spill Trustee Council)*

In the aftermath of this environmental disaster, public concern led Congress to pass the Oil Pollution Act of 1990. Tankers shipping Alaska's crude oil to the West Coast were made safer and stronger with double hulls and redundant operating systems. Scientists warned the potential for oil spill disasters would continue as the newly built Trans-Alaska Pipeline from Prudhoe Bay in the North Slope to Valdez in Prince William Sound aged and deteriorated. Critics noted that the pipeline was built in 1977 for $8 billion with Japanese, not U.S., steel and in a great hurry under adverse weather conditions on unstable permafrost. The Department of Justice and the state of Alaska later asked Exxon for an additional $92 million to clean the oil spill. Twenty years after this disaster, the impact of the oil on marine species and fishing in the tidal zones was a continuing problem, as the *Boston Globe* reported on June 2, 2006.

The Environmentalist Movement

Even before President Theodore Roosevelt advocated wilderness conservation and professional management of the Forest Service in 1902, Americans had a long history of conservation of natural resources. The leaders were the Appalachian Mountain Club (established in 1876), Sierra Club (1892), National Audubon Society (1905), Izzak Walton League (1922), Wilderness Society (1935), National Wildlife Federation (1936), Nature Conservancy (1951), Union of Concerned Scientists (1969), and Greenpeace (1971), who advocated for preservation and conservation in many ways. Most of these elite lobbies and other new environmental organizations expanded membership and activities by the 1980s. The baby boom generation, so familiar with protesting against the government, energized the older, somewhat staid organizations, and the New Age wing of the 1960s counterculture added a grassroots spiritual dimension to concern for Mother Earth.

Since the first Earth Day celebration in 1970 and since the Greenpeace movement began in 1971, public awareness of pollution and environmental issues grew dramatically. Congress responded with the Environmental Protection Act (1970), the Clean Air Act (1970), the Clean Water Act (1972), and the Pesticide Control Act (1972). The Three Mile Island nuclear accident in 1979 renewed public fear of environmental disasters, as depicted in the movie *China Syndrome* (1979). By the 1980s, many schools and colleges taught ecology and environmentalism courses. Jonathan Schell's bestselling book *The Fate of the Earth* (1982) aroused public fears of a hydrogen bomb in New York City. The *Exxon Valdez* oil disaster in 1989 was only one incident that convinced many Americans that greater efforts were necessary to protect the fragile environment.

As more Americans supported the environmental movement, consumer pressure persuaded McDonald's to stop using Styrofoam packaging for their food in 1989. Similarly, Coca-Cola and Pepsi announced they would use recycled plastic for their soft drink bottles by 1990. In many cities Boy Scouts, college students, and local neighborhood groups volunteered for annual cleanup efforts in parks, vacant lots, and along rivers and lakes. Littering became a social gaffe in the 1980s. Perhaps the most obvious success for the environmental campaign was the pollution control device Congress imposed on the auto industry to provide cleaner air. The consumer impact was obvious when supermarkets stocked organic foods for customers concerned about the purity and quality of fruit, vegetables, milk, and other products, and the environmental or health dangers from agricultural pesticides. Vegetarians were also more common in the 1980s, avoiding meat to practice the philosophy of nonviolence toward animals and to respect nature or to improve health (Daniel 2005).

However, state and local government efforts to respond to the environmental organizations and to grassroots concerns about the environmental crisis were thwarted by federal government action. More than 25 percent of the federal laws preempting local and state laws since 1789 were passed between 1981 and 1989. These laws largely dealt with safety, health, and education, often with little awareness of the fiscal burdens they imposed during recession years. Mayors and governors complained that reduced revenue sharing and congressional or executive branch mandates required state and local government to meet new (and often lower) federal guidelines and with increased costs, especially in transportation, housing, medical care, safety, and education. This was compounded by a 64 percent decrease in federal aid in 1980–1990, shifting to U.S. cities, towns, counties, and states economic burdens that also impacted the environment. Air and water was dirtier, but in Washington the Reagan administration seemed not to care or understand as long as businessmen were content. As a congressman and as OMB director, David Stockman opposed the EPA Superfund and refused to accept the idea that there was any reason to conserve energy and natural resources. To the New Right and advocates of the influential Sagebrush Rebellion, conservation and environmentalism were effete lobbies of the northeastern establishment and the aging hippie radicals.

As the environmental movement grew in size, it grew in sophistication and focused on such invasive species as the Asian tiger mosquito found in Texas (1985) and the Zebra mussels in the Great Lakes (1988). The protection of such endangered species as bears, eagles, mountain lions, mustangs, seals, whales, and wolves became popular. The media reflected public interest as they celebrated the birth of the first California condor in captivity (1983). Scientific warnings of devastating earthquakes received more attention when 5,000 people died in Mexico (1985), 500 died in El Salvador (1986), 300 died in Ecuador (1987), and 7 died in Los Angeles (1987). The earthquake on October 17, 1989, during game three of the baseball World Series, killed 63 people and destroyed highways and bridges in San Francisco.

Environmental problems continued despite the Clean Air Act President Bush signed in 1990. It required the EPA to restrict sources of air pollution, especially benzene and chlorine emitted by vehicles, power plants, and factories, which caused asthma, cancer, and other ailments. This was an interstate and international problem; for example, air pollution produced in Boston affected the quality of air in Maine and Canada. However, the EPA lacked funds or leadership to meet its deadlines and responsibilities, and little progress was made.

The effects of nuclear fallout from earlier above-ground nuclear weapons testing were an increasing concern in the 1980s. Another issue was climate change due to global warming, which concerned scientists in the 1980s. As the ocean temperature increased, more intense hurricanes formed in the Atlantic and Pacific oceans and the Arctic and Antarctic ice melted. Meteorologists warned this could raise sea levels, make winters warmer, and have devastating impact on the earth. Throughout this decade environmentalists and scientists protested that the politicization of scientific debates and the manipulation of scientific information and government regulation undermined the quality and integrity of the political process (Mooney 2005).

THE REAGAN REVOLUTION EVALUATED

More and Less

The Reagan legacy of smaller government, fiscal restraint, and social conservatism would outlast his presidency. Reagan began his administration in 1981 convinced that Third World problems and revolutionary movements were caused by the Soviet Union. CIA reports overestimated the Soviet Union military power and supported Reagan's enormous military expansion, which was in contrast to his advocacy of fiscal restraint. Military budgets doubled from 1980 to 1985 to exceed $294 billion. He dubbed the USSR an "Evil Empire" in 1983, and the Reagan Doctrine in 1985 promised U.S. support for anticommunist movements and used covert means to interfere in foreign countries' domestic affairs.

Demonstrating American military power, Reagan sent the U.S. Marines to invade Grenada in October 1983 and bombed Libya in 1986. Despite antinuclear war protests around the world and at home in 1981–1983, Reagan claimed the United States could win a limited nuclear war. However, by 1986 he restored warmer relations with the new Soviet leader Mikhail Gorbachev but continued his controversial Star Wars project over the protests of many leading scientists.

Although President Reagan claimed victory with the fall of the Berlin Wall in 1989, the dismemberment of the Soviet Union in 1991, and the end of the Cold War (1947–1990), most historians agree these events had little to do with Reagan's policies. These turning points in history happened because the economic burden, with $17 trillion spent on U.S. military budgets, was too great for both sides to bear. Events in China, Cuba, Czechoslovakia, France, and Hungary re-

President Ronald Reagan delivers a speech at the Brandenburg Gate in West Berlin on June 12, 1987, calling upon Soviet leader Mikhail Gorbachev to tear down the Berlin Wall. (Ronald Reagan Library)

duced U.S. and Soviet Union power, and the Third World nations emerged in new international roles diffusing power. Finally, the global antinuclear movement demanded an end to bipolarism. Eventually, Soviet–American détente seemed practical to Gorbachev, Reagan, and Bush.

Costly military spending at the expense of the domestic economy was criticized by presidents Eisenhower and Kennedy, but Reagan and Bush dismissed this while their administrations benefited from the end of the Cold War and accepted a new world order by 1990. The half century of cold-war brinkmanship expanded the power of the executive branch as American government became less accountable. This was at the expense of neglecting injustice, inequality, and environmental damage. Reagan said in his farewell address in 1989 that "ours was the first revolution in the history of mankind that truly reversed the course of government." His administration did reduce federal government, but he did not achieve the social changes demanded by the New Right. One recent historian suggested that Reagan, the great communicator, was actually the great conciliator (Troy 2005).

The End of the New Deal

The Reagan Revolution ended the era of New Deal liberalism (1933–1980), dismantling many of the social welfare, economic, and regulatory structures that Democrats and moderate Republicans in Congress had created. It was more than a clash of ideas; it displaced one group of elites with another group of ethnic, economic, and regional constituencies. Reagan's supply-side economics, his Reaganomics, the culture wars, and increased military spending changed America. In one sense, he was a product of the Southern California Okie culture: conservative, hard-working, patriotic, and suspicious of liberal elites, minorities, and the poor. He identified with the singing cowboy and was a friend of Gene Autry, the cowboy singer-actor-businessman, and enjoyed country-and-western music and values (Reeves 2005).

But the Reagan Revolution ended with the signing of a Social Security bill in 1983, although the real revolution was probably a change in American attitudes on public policy. Distrust of the federal government's ability to solve national problems and a backlash against liberal reforms had led to his election in 1980. He had Christian Right support but was not part of that movement. He gave Americans new confidence, but he also increased fears of nuclear war as he expanded military spending and the federal deficit that justified reductions in social programs. When Reagan stepped down as president on January 20, 1989, he had served eight years. This was a feat only three presidents accomplished in the 20th century, Woodrow Wilson, Franklin D. Roosevelt, and Dwight D. Eisenhower.

Reagan's legacy, however, is difficult to estimate. His supporters tended to exaggerate conditions in 1981 when he entered the White House. The United States had been frustrated by its intervention in Vietnam, Cambodia, Laos, Angola, Ethiopia, Iran, and Nicaragua, and by the OPEC oil cartel. The Cold War, nuclear arms proliferation, inflation, gasoline shortages, drug abuse, crime, unemployment, and a stagnant economy troubled many Americans. Some of these issues resolved themselves during the Reagan era, and Republicans were quick to take credit for that good fortune. Other issues responded to Reagan's optimism, energy, and confident leadership style. As a leader, however, President Reagan's failure to reassure the public about the AIDS epidemic was a serious flaw. Unlike his close ally, Prime Minister Margaret Thatcher in Britain, Reagan did not assume leadership in combating this disease by advocating research for a cure and sympathy for its victims (Wilentz 2008).

U.S. Conservatism

In a sense, the Reagan Revolution never happened because Ronald Reagan was a consensus politician. His vision of a minimalist government resting on an ideal society of free men in free markets conflicted with the key constituencies on which Congress depended, the corporations, unions, farmers, veterans, educators, and state and local officials. The traditional conservatives were loyal but the neoconservatives, largely ex-radicals and former liberals from the Northeast who supported Reagan in his first term because they thought he shared their world-view, began to abandon him by 1987. The expanding College Republican radicals, led by Ralph Reed and coached by Jack Abramoff, Grover Norquist, Jack Kemp, and Newt Gingrich, were loyal to Reagan but had little interest in George H. W. Bush and his "squishy" moderate followers. This made the future of the Reagan Revolution rather doubtful.

To maintain harmony, Reagan avoided any direct contact with the College Republicans organization in Washington and fired David Stockman, James G. Watt, Anne M. Gorsuch Burford, and Donald Regan, and he quietly abandoned his traditional Midwestern and Southern conservative supporters. The Reagan Revolution was too radical even for Reagan. Perhaps his legacy depends on judicial appointments; he appointed 3 of the 9 Supreme Court justices, and 361 of the 743 federal judges who will have an impact on the nation for decades to come. He left office a very popular president succeeded by his loyal vice president who shared many of his values.

On the domestic front, however, the middle class felt squeezed in the 1980s. When Reagan took office, the economy seemed to be in desperate shape. Although President Carter's Federal Reserve policies started the recovery, the prime rate did not fall from 20 to 12 percent until 1982. Reagan offered a bold approach, one Vice President George Bush had earlier dismissed as voodoo economics. Cutting taxes and spending with deregulation and the transformation of traditional industries was Reagan's anti-New Deal program. It appeared to work. When he left office, inflation had dropped from 12 to 4.4 percent, the prime rate interest dropped from 21 to 9.3 percent, unemployment fell from 7 to 5.4 percent, personal income rose from $9,722 to $11,326, and the GNP had doubled.

However, public spending not private investment stimulated the economy. Economic studies showed that in 1977–1990, the tax bill for average taxpayers who earned $50,000 per year rose 7.75 percent, and the tax bill for those earning $200,000 per year fell 27.75 percent. Democrats noted that Reagan increased the federal deficit from $128 billion to over $200 billion and raised more regressive taxes than he cut to pay for Social Security and Medicare. He reduced taxes for the rich at the expense of the middle class, and economists confirmed that Reagan's supply-side economics was just another phrase for the discredited trickle down theory (Feinstein 2006).

Nevertheless, President Bush continued this trend in 1989 and vetoed the 1991 tax cuts passed by the Democratic-controlled Congress. Reaganomics had promised that lower tax rates for the rich and fewer economic disincentives would stimulate investment, entrepreneurs, a stock market boom, and a revived capitalism to benefit all. When corporate tax receipts and individual taxes on stock market profits and executive bonuses increased, this revenue would pay the federal deficit. But these promises that tax relief would unleash the nation's entrepreneurial spirit only benefited the rich at the expense of average American families. Surveys of economists in early 1989 offered little hope, some forecast a recession and some predicted the economy would continue to prosper, if the deficit was reduced, despite the October 1987 stock market crash and the summer 1988 drought (Rudolph 1989).

With fewer federal funds for state and city government, the states and cities enacted a variety of sales and excise taxes, fees, and local property tax increases to meet their budget needs. The Reagan tax reduction and tax code simplification was an illusion. The top 1 percent of Americans who held 50 percent of the privately owned stock in the United States were taxed at new, lower levels. The top tax rate on unearned income (dividends, interest, and rent) fell from 70 percent in 1980 to 28 percent in 1988 largely due to Reagan's Tax Reform Act of 1986. Calvin Coolidge, Reagan's favorite president, would have found familiar the conservative fiscal ideology of the 1980s when the richest Americans paid the lowest taxes (Diggins 2007).

For these reasons the Reagan legacy remains quite disputed. Interviews and books by his wife, children, and former members of his administration reveal his lax management style in unflattering terms. Critics and biographers questioned his economic policies, his role in ending the Cold War, and his leadership. In 1983, Democratic representative Patricia Schroeder of Colorado dubbed Reagan the "Teflon president," because luck and charm protected his reputation from the many errors, misdeeds, corruption, and abuse of power around him and in his Cabinet. Special Prosecutor Lawrence Walsh, the independent counsel investigating the Iran-Contra scandal, made 14 indictments resulting in 11 convictions. His final report in 1994 concluded that Reagan's conduct fell short of criminality to be prosecuted but created the conditions that made crimes possible by his appointees. Walsh pointed out Robert M. Gates, a member of the National Security Council and a CIA official, for his role in the Iran-Contra case, which was short of criminal. This criticism derailed Reagan's nomination of Gates as CIA Director in 1987.

Despite condemnation by the World Court in 1984 for the CIA mining of Nicaraguan harbors and illegal support of the anti-Marxist Contras in Nicaragua contrary to the 1982 Boland Amendment, the public forgave all this because Reagan presided over the longest era of peacetime prosperity in U.S. history. His foreign policy and often wasteful and inefficient military expansion, although overestimating the USSR, led to the toppling of the Soviet Union. Historians note that this change began in the 1970s and occurred after 1989 and can be attributed largely to Soviet leader Mikhail Gorbachev's *Glasnost* overhaul of the USSR to resolve domestic problems.

Nonetheless, the Reagan presidency (1981–1989) was a major event in the history of U.S. conservatism that transformed the Republican Party and American

President Ronald Reagan points to a chart during a televised speech from the Oval Office on July 27, 1981, promoting tax reduction legislation pending before Congress. The controversial Republican plan called for a reduction of income tax rates, the addition of deductions to encourage investment and savings, and adjusting tax rates for inflation. (Ronald Reagan Library)

society. Although he proved to be less committed to conservatives' favorite social issues, his supporters on the New Right were largely uncritical as he pursued his tax reduction and military expansion agenda toward the unrealistic goal of consensus. Unlike Carter, who emphasized restraint and sacrifice, Reagan stressed economic growth and freedom from governmental restraint, a message that appealed to business leaders.

When Reagan died in May 2004, many reassessed his role in the 1980s. Maligned by his critics more than most modern presidents, Reagan was loved by more Americans than most presidents. His experience as an actor prepared him for the modern media campaign and he brought to the White House an enthusiasm and style of popular rhetoric many underestimated. Not well-educated or experienced for the presidency, he picked a reliable staff and trusted their judgment. Known as the "Great Communicator," he sincerely believed in the inevitable triumph of freedom and liberty and assured the public all would be well. His speechwriters crafted a simple, confident, optimistic message that he delivered as only a professional actor could. Not everyone responded to the Reagan style and message, but most Americans did. His television commercials were equally well honed; in 1980, he promised it was "morning in America" and Americans everywhere responded to Ronald Reagan.

Reagan's Ruling Class

In *Reagan's Ruling Class: Portraits of the President's Top One Hundred Officials,* Ronald Brownstein and Nina Easton interviewed the men and women responsible for implementing the Reagan Revolution. From the lavish 1981 inaugural balls, it was obvious that the super-rich arrived in Washington on corporate jets and in limousines to celebrate a regal coronation. The surprising number of multimillionaires serving the new administration were the nouveau riche who earned rather than inherited their wealth. Selected by Reagan's Kitchen Cabinet of close-knit, wealthy friends who groomed him to become governor and president, these new officials were uniformly conservative, Republican, and loyal to Reagan. *Washington Post* columnist Mary McGrory called them the deserving rich, and the former Watergate special prosecutor Archibald Cox noted the oil executives' large tax deductible donations to redecorate the White House arrived after President Reagan decontrolled oil prices and allowed oil companies billions in profits. Times had changed from the frugal Carter era (Troy 2005).

Critics dismissed the Reagan economic program as the discredited trickle-down theory, the idea that as the rich became richer, their spending and investments transferred wealth down to the middle and lower classes. Liberals fumed and predicted economic disaster as the Reagan recession persisted into 1983, but gloom and doom was out of fashion and Reagan's optimism suited most Americans. The new version of the American dream was to make a personal fortune and retire early to a life of leisure.

Events in Education

College students in the 1980s often chose economics, finance, or accounting as their major subjects, and law school or an MBA degree was considered the road to personal wealth. Engineering and careers in manufacturing were less popular, except for the increasing number of international students at American universities. The law, banking, and Wall Street corporate careers rather than industry were the routes to success for most young Americans. Real wages for high school graduates declined in the 1980s but rose sharply for college graduates, which reflected deindustrialization and the rise of corporate culture. The result was a weakening of U.S. industrial power and innovation as the best and the brightest gravitated toward careers in Wall Street, banking, finance, and insurance. This was a short-sighted and short-term solution to globalization and the free market economy.

In the 1980s successful business executives were more widely admired than ever before, and many enjoyed new access and influence in the government. Young Americans who responded to this materialism were dubbed the yuppies —young urban professionals who sought and enjoyed a lavish lifestyle with expensive cars, new condominiums, exotic vacations, and a variety of pricey electronic gadgets. The tone of the decade was one of affluence, luxury, and personal satisfaction, but the working class, who had been living comfortable middle-class lives, faced economic stagnation or decline, and the number of Americans living in poverty increased. But *Time* magazine reported on August 11, 1986, that 37,000 law school graduates found entry-level salaries in large law firms higher than ever before (Lacayo 1986).

The Triumph of Corporate Culture

In 1980, President Reagan promised to reduce inflation, restore the U.S. international prestige, unleash economic energy, and improve the nation's moral climate. He turned to corporate leaders and appointed three conservative Westerners to key environmental posts on the recommendation of his friend, Joseph Coors, a wealthy Denver beer brewer. They were James G. Watt as Secretary of the Interior, Anne Gorsuch Burford as EPA director, and her husband Robert Burford as director of the Bureau of Land Management. They all represented corporate interests to the detriment of the public interest and their own agencies, and all left office under fire. When Reagan signed the 1982 bill deregulating the thrift industry he revealed his administration's corporate culture as he quipped, "All in all, I think we've hit the jackpot." The resulting savings and loan scandal, which engulfed President George H. W. Bush's son, Neil Bush, was symbolic of the influence big business had in the Reagan–Bush era. By 1989, 138 Reagan officials had been convicted, indicted, or investigated for misconduct or crimes. In addition, three other cabinet members—Secretary of Housing and Urban Development Samuel R. Pierce Jr., Secretary of Defense Caspar Weinberger, and Attorney General Edwin A. Meese III—and White House aides Lyn Nofziger, Donald Regan, and Michael Deaver left office in disgrace and scandal. Influence peddling, fraud, bribery, illegal lobbying, and other official abuses, including the Iran-Contra case, riddled the Pentagon, CIA, EPA, HUD, and Department of Justice (Diggins 2007).

Many members of the Reagan administration were his contemporaries from the World War II generation who made fortunes in the private sector before entering government service. They donated $110 million to the Republican Party in 1980, compared to $15 million the Democrats raised. These conservative older white men traveled in elite country club circles and brought to the White House wisdom, maturity, and pragmatism, but they lacked the radical ideology of young technocrats like David Stockman. For example, Secretary of the Treasury Donald

Regan was a Republican from Harvard and a combat Marine in World War II. He spent 34 years on Wall Street where he was head of Merrill Lynch and Company, the world's largest brokerage firm. When Regan became President Reagan's new chief of staff in 1985, it was clear the corporate Republicans would control the White House. *Time* magazine's cover story on January 21, 1985, reported on the "Shake-Up at the White House." Reagan's appointment of John Shad, a Wall Street executive, as head of the Securities and Exchange Commission, and Mark S. Fowler, a leading proponent of deregulation, as chair of the Federal Communications Commission, were other examples of the new corporate influence in this administration (Magnuson 1985).

Many examples of the influence business corporations exercised in the Reagan administration abound. His foreign policy in Central America reflected the tradition of supporting strong leaders who lacked popular support but were favorable to American business interests in that region. Secretary of Commerce Malcolm Baldrige supported the Reagan budget cuts in most cases, but he expected free-market ideology to take into account practical business experience. Baldrige favored lower taxes and less government interference in the economy, but he objected when David Stockman recommended elimination of the Commerce Department export subsidies. Secretary of Housing and Urban Development Samuel R. Pierce Jr. also struggled to retain funds for the Urban Development Actions Grants, a program of grants for distressed communities. Reagan's second chief of staff, Edwin Meese, agreed with Baldrige and Pierce, but in most cases the administration acted to protect big business from the federal regulation and oversight that had been customary. Reagan's second Secretary of Defense, Frank C. Carlucci (1987–1989), was committed to expanding military appropriations in new weapons and communications technology procured from private corporations for which he had worked. The OMB director, David Stockman, usurped the regulatory authority of the cabinet and federal agencies and often had off-the-record contacts with industry lobbyists and campaign contributors. Under President George H. W. Bush, a successful Texas oil businessman, this inclination to turn to big business for support and advice continued. Director Oliver Stone, the son of a New York City stockbroker, captured the new adulation in the 1980s for materialism and greed in the absorbing movie on insider trading, *Wall Street* (1987). However, the best-known American businessman in the 1980s may have been Lee Iacocca, the dynamic, popular and successful chairman of Chrysler Corporation, whose autobiography, *Iacocca* (1984), was a best seller.

It was these members of the Reagan administration that Democrats, led by House Speaker Tip O'Neill, castigated for leading the nation into the 1981 recession and for proposing a 1983 "Beverly Hills budget." John A. Farrell recalled in his biography *Tip O'Neill and the Democratic Century* that O'Neill said the president "has no concern, no regard, no care for the little man . . . because of his lifestyle, he never meets those people" and he "has forgotten his roots. He

Friendly but firm opponents President Reagan and House Speaker Tip O'Neill discuss the Budget in the Oval Office on January 31, 1983. (Ronald Reagan Library)

associates with that country-club style of people" (Farrell 2001, 586). When Congress passed the Boland amendment in 1982 to halt U.S. aid to the rebel Contras in Nicaragua, who Reagan compared to our founding fathers, his administration ignored the law. This secret illegal financing resulted in the Iran-Contra scandal. Neoconservatives like Irving Kristol, who did not support this tolerance of materialism and the corporate culture, also disagreed with military intervention to impose democratic government on other nations.

Life in the Military after the Cold War

David Stockman, the OMB director, shocked Ronald Reagan in 1981 by his briefing on the growing budget deficit, especially because Reagan hoped to balance the budget by 1984. Stockman proposed a massive reduction of the Defense Department budget. However, Secretary Caspar Weinberger persuaded Reagan that an ambitious military buildup was necessary to defeat the Soviet Union. As a result, military spending more than doubled from 1981 to 1986, from $162 billion to $343 billion. Weinberger was supported by conservatives like Secretary of State Alexander Haig, CIA Director William Casey, and National Security

Adviser Richard Allen. This was another indication that the Reagan administration was run much like a corporation, with Cabinet members like vice presidents and the President as the chairman of the board and his chief of staff as the chief operating officer (Magnuson 1985).

Reagan's policy of peace through strength had less to do with the fall of communism than he claimed, but his capacity to respond creatively to Mikhail Gorbechev's overtures and the 1989–1991 economic and political changes in the USSR left a new world order for President Bush. Without the Soviet Union as America's inveterate enemy in the Cold War, the mission of the U.S. armed forces was expected to change profoundly. Gen. Colin Powell, who served in the Army for 35 years and later in the Nixon, Reagan, Bush Sr., and Bush Jr. administrations, recalled his service in the Pentagon under Secretary of Defense Caspar Weinberger (1981–1987) with pleasure, and noted "the greatest contribution the Reagan-Weinberger team made was to end the long estrangement between the American people and their defenders. During this time, the rupture was healed, and America once more embraced its armed forces" (Powell 1995, 315).

When the draft ended in 1972, the Modern Volunteer Army was created, shrinking in size from 1.3 million men and women in 1973 to 780,000 in 1983. Despite military pay increases in 1981 and 1982 and an effective "Be All You Can Be" television advertising campaign in 1981, enlistments declined from 111,500 in 1989 to 74,200 in 1991. Female enlistments in the Army, however, rose from 2.1 percent in 1972 to 11 percent in 1992. African American men continued to join the Army in larger numbers, comprising 36 percent in 1980, and about 24 percent in 1990. Because more members of the armed forces were married and had children in the 1980s, military budgets for dependents also increased. Members of Congress and the Pentagon worried that these post–Cold War changes would diminish military service as an accepted feature in American society and that the all-volunteer Army would become a mercenary army. Blue-collar voters were mobilized with patriotic appeals when Reagan and Bush staged news events filled with patriotic symbols. Military force abroad in the 1984 Grenada invasion and the 1986 bombing of Libya demonstrated U.S. resolve and reinforced national pride at home.

The War Economy Endures

American military budgets were adjusted after the Cold War, but the expected peace dividend never appeared. After the Berlin Wall fell (1989) and the Soviet Union unraveled (1991), the United States celebrated its "victory" in the Cold War by treating Russia as a defeated enemy, not as a partner in nuclear disarmament and world peace. Since the U.S. containment policy in 1947, and détente in the 1960s, world peace and stability had been the goals. The Reagan and Bush administrations had not defeated the Soviet Union, but many in Washington acted as if they had done so. President George H. W. Bush declared the Cold War was over in his January 1990 address to Congress. Americans no longer had to fear that the country was on the brink of war or a nuclear bomb attack. However, rabid former Cold War hardliners were intent on destabilizing Russia under a Pax Americana in which the United States was the world's only superpower. This American position did not respect Russian sovereignty and focused on safeguarding the Soviet stockpile of nuclear, chemical, and biological weapons, ill-maintained nuclear reactors, and decommissioned nuclear submarines. Troubled by social and economic problems and conflicting ethnic and racial groups, the former Soviet Union seemed incapable of dealing with these issues.

To counter Soviet support for leftist guerrillas in Central America, the Bush administration funded the El Salvador right-wing military at the cost of $85 million a year. But in 1989, the 10-year civil war flamed up when peace talks broke down and a guerrilla offense led to a surge in civilian killings. The murder of Archbishop Oscar Romero in 1980 and the massacre by right-wing death squads in 1989 of six Jesuit priests who taught at the University of Central America aroused protests among U.S. Catholics. The planes and helicopters supplied by the United States created heavy guerrilla casualties and thousands of civilian refugees entered the United States. Secretary of State James Baker told the Organization of American States that the Soviet Union bears special responsibility for the violent war and for human rights violations in El Salvador (Smolowe 1989).

By 1990, Secretary of Defense Richard Cheney (1989–1993) cautiously reduced the military budget and downsized the military establishment from 2.2 million men and women in 1990 to 1.7 million by 1993. The Army shrank by 25 percent, the Navy by 14 percent, the Air Force by 22 percent, and the Marines by 9 percent. Congress also reduced the military budgets more than the Bush administration recommended. The problem remaining was how the reduced U.S. military forces could deal with small wars and regional conflicts around the world with its new and slimmer resources. The answer Secretary Cheney, General Powell, and Secretary Baker offered was a lean, mobile, and more technological military and greater reliance on diplomacy. President Bush nominated Robert M. Gates as the CIA director in 1991 to tackle post–Cold War threats.

The Reagan Revolution and American Families

Our only divorced president and a father estranged or aloof from his four children for many years, Ronald Reagan was the champion of family values for millions of Americans in the 1980s. Although he seldom attended church, Reagan had millions of devoted supporters among Jerry Falwell's Moral Majority and Pat Robertson's Christian Coalition. Yet Reagan may have been typical in his family and religious life. The ideal American nuclear conjugal family was probably never the norm. By 2000, only 20 percent of U.S. households were composed of married parents and their children. Single-parent households were increasingly common, and most mothers worked outside the home. Due to delayed marriage, divorce, birth control, and the gay liberation and feminist movements, about a third of adults lived alone. The divorce rate, increasing steadily since 1950, had tripled from 1960 to 1980. The mythical American family was cherished but rarely seen (Wallis 1989).

By 1980, Republican strategists mobilized evangelical Christians and grassroots conservatives by linking the profamily movement, opposition to abortion and gay rights, and support for prayer in schools to the support of free-market economics and military expansion. They claimed traditional values were under attack by liberals, social radicals, feminists, and political secularism, especially by Supreme Court decisions removing religion from public schools, banning state restriction of abortion, and protecting pornography as free speech. Although he was not a regular churchgoer, Reagan was a devout member of his mother's Disciples of Christ church by age 12 and graduated from Eureka College, which was under the auspices of the Disciples of Christ. Despite his Irish Catholic father's alcoholism and frequent unemployment, Reagan's boundless optimism and nostalgia idealized small-town Midwestern American family values and fundamentalist Protestant faith.

Reagan and the 1980 Republican Party platform called for a constitutional amendment banning abortion to reassure his right-wing supporters. Another plank promised a national family program on child care, schools, taxes, and Social Security. Leading the conservative backlash, Phyllis Schlafly claimed Reagan was elected by the rising profamily movement and the conservative movement working together, and election polls supported this view (Leo 1986).

However, when OMB director David Stockman could not persuade Reagan to reduce the federal deficit by cutting the military budget, he made drastic cuts in social welfare, health, housing, environmental, transportation, and education programs that harmed American families in the name of waste and fraud and inefficiency. The $110 billion that Reagan and David Stockman cut from the federal budget affected 325,000 families who lost welfare payments, 3 million students who lost school lunches, 1 million people who lost food stamps, and 700,000 college students who lost guaranteed federal loans. The safety net that protected the chronically unemployed, the working poor who could not live on a low minimum-wage income, and their children was unraveling because of federal government priorities.

Although the 1981–1982 recession and deficits forced Reagan to accept a $98.3 billion tax hike in 1982, the largest increase ever, the feminization of poverty was due to his federal budget cuts. This meant that 80 percent of working women—often mothers as the heads of households—were in lower paid jobs as clerks, waitresses, or teachers. From 1982 to 1985, 15 national studies concluded hunger was a serious problem. A Harvard University School of Public

Health report in 1986 estimated that half of the 20 million Americans going hungry were children as noted in *The Real David Stockman* (Greenya and Urban 1986). However, poverty was simply not an issue that excited Republicans, and few were surprised when President George H. W. Bush vetoed a bill in June 1989 that would have raised the minimum wage from $3.35 to $4.55. Liberals protested that raising the minimum wage gave some hope to the working poor, most of whom were mothers, but conservatives replied it would decrease employment and new business growth that benefited the poor.

The Impact of the Reagan Revolution

Average family income adjusted for inflation in 1990 dollars increased from $33,238 in 1970 to only $35,353 in 1990. But from 1977 to 1989, the wealthiest 1 percent of American families enjoyed a 77 percent increase in pretax income, and the wealthiest 20 percent an increase in income of 29 percent. In contrast, the middle 20 percent increased only 9 percent, and the poorest 20 percent of American families decreased 7 percent in average family income during the 1980s. One out of five children lived below the poverty level. In the 1980s, the rich got richer and the poor got poorer. The typical American family income rose only 4 percent, and the lower 40 percent of families had a decrease in income in an increasingly polarized society. By 1989, the top 1 percent—834,000 families— had $5.7 trillion in net worth while the lower 90 percent—84 million families —had only $4.8 trillion in net worth. Despite President Johnson's successful war on poverty in the 1960s, by 1988 about the same number of Americans (36 million) lived in poverty according to a report by the Social Science Research Council. The rate of children living in poverty increased 6 percent in the 1970s but increased 11 percent in the 1980s. One estimate found that 40 percent of the nation's poor in 1989 were children. Poverty was most common for African Americans, Hispanics, and Native Americans and for those who lived in the inner cities. Sociologists used the term the "working poor" to describe the 40 percent of Americans who could not find full-time, year-round employment (Wilson 1987).

Homelessness became a serious problem in the United States in the 1980s; rates tripled in 1981–1989, according to a survey by the Department of Housing and Urban Development of 182 cities. About 3.5 million Americans were homeless, but in addition to the mentally ill, the elderly, and those with addiction disorders, 39 percent of them were families with children. Although five states doubled or tripled shelter space, the increase in the homeless population remained a disturbing trend. Many reasons were suggested, but the National Coalition for the Homeless reported that this issue was viewed by the Reagan Administration as a problem that did not require federal intervention (Tygiel 2006). The first federal task force on homelessness was created in 1983 to provide

A homeless man lies under a clear plastic blanket in Lafayette Square across from the White House during the first snow of the season, November 11, 1987. (UPI/Bettmann/ Corbis)

information to local government and private agencies, but the task force did not implement federal government programs or policies. Congress disagreed, however, and passed laws in 1986 and 1987 to assist the homeless. However, the Department of Housing and Urban Development (HUD) funding cuts led to a decrease in homeownership rates and an increase in housing market discrimination. The declining availability of affordable housing had a devastating impact on millions of U.S. families as Lawrence L. Thompson reported in *A History of HUD*.

Workers paid the minimum wage in 1967 earned enough to raise a family of three, but in 1981–1990 the minimum wage was frozen at $3.35 per hour while the cost of living increased 48 percent and inflation reduced real wages. Combined with the drop in the number and bargaining power of unionized workers, a decline in manufacturing jobs, and the deterioration of older, cheaper housing, homeless families became more common in almost every state in the Reagan era (National Coalition).

Liberals insisted that the federal government should take action to assist the poor and the homeless. But since the end of World War II in 1945, conservatives had focused on resisting America's enemy, the Soviet Union, an evil empire intent on Communist domination of the world, rather than on domestic policy. With the end of the Cold War in 1990, these conservatives, who recently captured control of the Republican Party, searched for internal enemies. They portrayed liberals as weak-willed, cowardly Democrats who had long been soft on Communism and who now threatened the nation with humanist, secular, permissive, and radical social policies. Conservatives bewailed the feminization of America and blamed every threat or disaster on internal enemies who hated America. Ronald Reagan offered tough, practical, and traditional values to cure the nation's ills as we teetered on the brink of tragedy. Moral clarity rather than moral confusion was appealing to many insecure Americans resisting the winds of change, and every election became a moral drama in the 1980s. The conservative columnist Charles Krauthammer analyzed Ronald Reagan in *Time magazine* on June 14, 2004, attributing his effectiveness to luck and conviction. He quoted Sen. Edward Kennedy, a liberal critic of Reagan, "Whether we agreed with him or not, Ronald Reagan was a successful candidate and an effective president above all else because he stood for a set of ideas . . . and he wrote most of them not only into public law but into the national consciousness" (Krauthammer 2004).

THE BUSH ADMINISTRATION

The New Right

The $2.7 trillion budget deficit that Bush inherited from Reagan was a major reason the Bush administration (1989–1993) was stymied by gridlock government. Although Bush's inaugural address on January 20, 1989, promised "a new breeze is blowing," little could be accomplished because the Democrats had a 10-vote majority in the Senate and an 89-vote majority in the House. In his acceptance speech at the 1988 Republican National Convention in New Orleans, Bush pounded the podium and declared, "Read my lips. No new taxes." Essentially a social moderate from New England, Bush could not slash the budget as Reagan had done to move toward a balanced budget. As the recession returned in late 1989, inflation rose, the stock market plunged, and Bush proposed his 1991 budget to Congress. It included $14 billion in additional revenue from so-called user fees, but Congress demanded tax increases and a freeze on spending. Clearly, the Reagan era had ended, and many conservatives in Congress, like the Republican minority whip Newt Gingrich of Georgia, criticized Bush for raising taxes. The budget bill passed with $301 billion in spending cuts, and $134 billion in tax increases, but this was an embarrassing defeat for Bush. Republicans lost 10 Senate seats and 25 House seats in the 1990 election, despite Bush's popularity and the patriotic fever following the Persian Gulf War.

The Republican Party and the Reagan White House had some moderates, such as James Baker, Michael Deaver, George H. W. Bush and his followers, who the conservative hardliners disliked and dubbed "Bushyites" or "squishes." The New Right was disciplined and stayed "on message" by repeating key words and phrases that resonated well with many Americans who feared or resented elites and privileged classes. They blamed their own distress on groups that conservatives targeted as scapegoats, in contrast to liberals who embraced many causes and many constituencies. This difference was first apparent throughout the Reagan administration. It continued but with some changes in the Bush administration, first in foreign policy. Bush disagreed with Reagan's détente with the Soviet Union. He ordered a long policy review before consenting to reduction of conventional armed forces in Europe. With China, he also acted more deliberately, ignoring the June 4, 1989, Tiananmen Square massacre when the Red Army killed 3,000 demonstrators and wounded 10,000. Bush did not gloat when the Berlin Wall fell in October 1989 and nationalism rocked the Soviet Union, all of which further incensed conservative Republicans. He acted decisively in December 1989 by invading Panama to protect Americans and overthrow the dictator and drug lord Manuel Noriega.

Although conservatives never fully accepted President Bush as one of their own, he was elected with their support in 1989. One position he seemed to waffle on was abortion. In 1986, Randall Terry founded Operation Rescue, which used civil disobedience by conservative rights activists to protest against legal abortion. They blocked the entrances to abortion clinics, picketed them, and attempted to dissuade women from entering the clinics. As the group's leader, Terry was known for his fiery rhetoric, and he was supported by Jerry Falwell, Pat Robertson, and other conservative leaders. Bush, who was pro-life, was never comfortable with the extremist tone of the antiabortion (or pro-life) movement, and they distrusted him. First Lady Barbara Bush was also known to have pro-choice views. President Bush, although an active Episcopalian, was not an evangelical or fundamentalist, but the Christian Right's doubts about him were addressed by his born-again Methodist son, George W. Bush (Martin 1996).

However, the Bush campaign was managed by Lee Atwater, former political director for Reagan, and Atwater gave a hard-nosed approach to Bush's election efforts. John Sununu, former governor of New Hampshire, and Roger Ailes, a television producer who served as campaign director of advertising, were equally tough-minded. The chief weakness in the 1988 campaign was Bush's choice of Indiana senator Dan Quayle as his running mate, but after a few gaffes and misstatements to the press, Quayle was kept out of sight in the campaign. In November 1988, Bush defeated Massachusetts governor Michael Dukakis with 54 to 46 percent of the popular vote and carried 40 states. Although the Democrats won control of Congress, the New Right and the Moral Majority remained powerful. Liberal Protestant theologians like the Rev. Robert McAfee Brown, a prominent Presbyterian minister and professor of religion in New York, criticized the Moral Majority, but few Americans listened in 1988.

American Society in the Bush–Quayle Years

Having served eight years as Ronald Reagan's vice president, George Herbert Walker Bush claimed to be the rightful heir of the Reagan administration. Conservative hardliners were suspicious of Bush as a true conservative because he was a New England patrician from Yale who transplanted himself into the Texas oil business in 1948. Despite his devotion to the conservative movement, he had a chameleon-like record and only became a conservative in 1964. Bush was caricatured as a preppy wimp, but he was a bulldog in the 1988 campaign against Michael Dukakis. Bush was a down-to-earth man with a 67 percent approval rate for the first year of his term.

Bush entered the White House with an impressive record of government experience. He and Vice President J. Danforth Quayle pledged to carry on the Reagan Revolution with "no new taxes." But Bush soon faced economic stagnation, deepening poverty, high unemployment, increasing federal deficits, demands for education reform, a hostile Congress, and his own plummeting popularity. Globalization and the new economy soon confounded American business and workers—and the Bush administration.

Chief Justice William Rehnquist administers the oath of office to George H. W. Bush on the west front of the U.S. Capitol, with Dan Quayle and Barbara Bush looking on, January 20, 1989. (Library of Congress)

Despite the end of the Cold War, international crises in the 1990s that challenged American society and public confidence in the government included the Iraq invasion of Kuwait; the Persian Gulf War; civil unrest or war in Serbia, Bosnia, Kosovo, and Chechnya; genocide in Rwanda; the expanding drug trade in Colombia; a coup in Haiti; and the Palestinian *intifada* uprising. The HIV/AIDS epidemic killed over two million people each year, and the environmental crisis from greenhouse gas emission and global warming was a front-page story (Wicker 2004).

Many Americans lost confidence in government and in the liberalism they had supported since 1932. Reagan made the most of this 1980s skepticism by dismantling every federal program he could, except for defense. When his moral crusade against communism, which began for him in 1946, and the "evil empire" of the Soviet Union bent on world domination, was over, his administration floundered to find a new mission. He continued to enjoy the support of the Christian Right and the neoconservatives, many of whom staffed his administration, but the American public by 1984 was not interested in supporting the Contra army in Nicaragua or an activist foreign policy for freedom fighters in other countries. Even the Senate disagreed with President Reagan, voting 84 to 12 against further aid or intervention for the Contras.

Retiring to his ranch in California in 1989, Reagan left President George H. W. Bush a new world order and a massive federal deficit. The peace dividend many expected after the Cold War and the fall of Communism could have paid for military expansion debts. However, conservatives insisted on a strong military defense. Despite the success of the Gulf War, a recession in 1990 caused Bush's popularity to drop from 89 percent to 29 percent in 1992 polls. Although the American unemployment rate was lower than any industrialized country and the economy was fundamentally sound with the world's highest standard of living, still the American public was anxious. Deindustrialization had replaced well-paid blue-collar jobs with low-paid service jobs. Corporate reshuffling and downsizing displaced mid-level managers who were laid off in mid-career with few attractive options. At the same time, the polls indicated most Americans were skeptical of a return to liberal Democratic government. Voter dissatisfaction with Congress reached 70 percent in one 1991 poll, and the gender gap again showed female voters lacked confidence in Bush (Brands 2001).

A Weakened Economy

The $2.7 trillion federal deficit Bush inherited from the Reagan Administration was three times its 1980 level, and the erosion of the middle class in the 1980s and early 1990s reflected this and worldwide economic changes. Reagan redistributed the tax burden and reduced public services but without adequate public debate, planning, or awareness. Millions of well-paid, unionized blue-collar industrial workers lost manufacturing jobs by the mid-1980s. Midwest and Rocky

Mountain states lost farms, towns, and population according to the 1980 and 1990 U.S. censuses.

Divorced mothers and their children fell from the middle class so often that this was dubbed the feminization of poverty. Male high school graduates could no longer expect a middle-class life. White-collar workers in business and the professions lost jobs in the 1980s to downsizing and automation or outsourcing due to foreign or "off shore" competition with lower labor costs. This was difficult for middle managers, engineers, defense workers, and military personnel in Sunbelt states as U.S. military defense reorganized by 1989. Republican political analyst Kevin Phillips claimed in his book *Boiling Point* (1993) that despite unprecedented prosperity at the top, the middle class was 5 to 10 percent smaller in 1990 than it had been in 1980. In addition, living standards for most Americans were stagnant since 1975 because economic growth only benefited the wealthiest. Executive pay, relative to the typical worker's pay, increased tenfold in two decades. By 1990 the institutions that produced increasing opportunity and a broader middle class after World War II—trade unions, minimum wages, job security, improved health and retirement plans, Social Security rising with inflation, affordable college and housing, and economic regulation of Wall Street—had been weakened.

Economists observed that productivity and the per capita gross domestic product almost doubled in 1975–2005, but median wages increased little. Where did all this productivity go, they wondered? Most of it went to the wealthiest 10 percent of Americans. The upper 1 percent gained the most, and their share of the national income equaled that of the lowest 50 percent (Kuttner 2006, A15). Middle- and working-class Americans felt the pressures of a weakened economy but responded by taking even more conservative positions. They blamed unions, bureaucrats, and liberal Democrats for unemployment, rising taxes, and inflation—not Reagan, Bush, and the Republicans who had governed for the past decade. Kevin Phillips discusses historical parallels for this illogical assignment of blame in his book *The Politics of Rich and Poor* (1990).

Fewer than 4 percent of Americans were rural in the 1980s, but concern for the plight of the family farm was not reflected in President Reagan's veto of federal loan guarantees to debt-burdened farmers (Amy Wilentz 1985). Despite congressional speeches that praised the family farmer and in Hollywood films such as *Places in the Heart* (1984), *Country* (1984), and *The River* (1984), American agriculture was hard-pressed and often overlooked. However, the 1980s yuppie angst and economic turmoil of Reaganomics was explored more often by movies such as *The Big Chill* (1983), *Wall Street* (1987), *Bright Lights, Big City* (1988), and *Working Girl* (1989). The weaker economy President Bush faced had become a very troubling issue for most Americans whose anxiety and insecurity pervaded every aspect of society.

Constrained by the Federal Reserve System's tight money policy, the U.S. economy entered a recession in late 1989. Inflation rose to 4.8 percent, the stock market dropped sharply on October 13, 1989, and unemployment increased. Between 1989 and 1992, the economy grew slowly or not at all, and the GNP grew less than one percent per year. Median household income declined 3.5 percent. Many major corporations and 30 state governments faced serious financial difficulties, and Bush's popularity sank. The media reported that he seemed not to care, and, as Bush admitted once before, he had a problem with the "vision thing." Democrats who won elections were those who ran as pocketbook populists appealing to ordinary people suffering from outsourcing and the failure of the economy's gains to trickledown.

On the same day that Congress voted to fulfill Bush's campaign promise to reduce capital-gains taxes for the wealthy, President Bush hosted a meeting at the University of Virginia on education with his cabinet and the nation's governors. But the self-proclaimed education president cut federal education funds $400 million. White House officials noted that federal funds accounted for only 7 percent of education spending, and much of the money was spent inefficiently. Despite national evidence that public schools were failing to educate students, Bush only proposed school vouchers and alternative certification for people switching to teaching careers, as *Time* magazine reported on October 9, 1989 (Goodgame 1989).

RACE RELATIONS AND DISCRIMINATION

Culture Wars

The decade began with three days of race riots in Miami after an all-white jury acquitted four white policemen in the beating and murder of an African American businessman. This May 1980 violence, which left 14 dead, more than 300 injured, and 450 people arrested, was also attributed to widespread poverty and unemployment in the African American community. African American resentment of Cuban and Haitian immigrants was another factor in Miami riots later in June and July when President Carter's limousine was stoned by a African American mob in Miami's Liberty City. The crowd was angry about cuts in federal funds for urban programs. Chattanooga had similar race riots in 1980. Others cities experienced some racial conflict between African American, Latino, and Asian teenagers. But there were also some positive trends in racial relations. Vanessa Williams was the first African American woman to become Miss America, although she resigned within a year after *Penthouse* published nude photographs of her that had been taken years before.

In 1983, Congress honored the Rev. Martin Luther King Jr. by declaring the third Monday in January an annual federal holiday. This holiday was observed in more than 100 nations and many states, although conservatives in, for example, New Hampshire opposed honoring the assassinated civil rights leader

President Ronald Reagan signs legislation designating the third Monday of every January as the Martin Luther King Jr. National Holiday on November 2, 1983. Coretta Scott King (left), the widow of the assassinated civil rights leader, is in attendance. (Ronald Reagan Library)

and champion of racial justice and equality. Most of the new Republican leaders were from the South and West, many of them former Democratic segregationists who became Republicans in the civil rights era. Although the Reagan and Bush administrations were markedly less supportive of African Americans, race relations became calmer.

A 1990 Gallup poll reported that Americans believed 32 percent of the U.S. population was African American and 21 percent was Latino. The actual statistics were 12 percent African American and 9 percent Latino. Demographers predicted that by 2050 non-Latino white Americans will be a minority. Concern over these real or imagined figures and the new issue called multiculturalism reflected Reagan and Bush policies that widened and reinforced social and economic barriers between American groups. Books, newspapers, magazines, and films explored the continuing debates on bilingual education, Afro-centrism, and affirmative action. Liberals such as Arthur M. Schlesinger Jr., the Kennedy administration historian, denounced this "cult of ethnicity" as separatism, fragmentation, and desegregation weakening society. Conservatives agreed there was a cultural war for the soul of the nation.

Although African Americans only made slow progress in the 1980s, some new leaders stood out. Harold Washington was the first African American to be

African American Conservatives

Conservatism in the African American community in the 1980s was not a new phenomenon. In the early 20th century, Booker T. Washington and Marcus Garvey advocated self-help, entrepreneurship, and conservative policies as prominent African American leaders. Although most African American voters switched to the Democratic Party in the 1932 election as loyal supporters of President Franklin D. Roosevelt's New Deal, they were not a monolithic voting bloc. Some African Americans remained faithful to the Republican Party of Abraham Lincoln because they respected capitalism, free enterprise, and the Protestant work ethic.

The first African American elected by popular vote to the U.S. Senate was the moderate Republican Edward W. Brooke (1967–1979) from Massachusetts. In the 1980s, President Reagan and President Bush encouraged efforts to recruit African American voters to the Republican Party, but with limited success. Reagan appointed an African American Wall Street lawyer, Samuel R. Pierce Jr., as secretary of Housing and Urban Development (1981–1989), and Bush appointed Condoleezza Rice to the National Security Council and Gen. Colin Powell as Chairman of the Joint Chiefs of Staff in 1989. As the African American middle class grew larger and moved to the suburbs, Congress included 40 African American members by 1985. Twelve African American Republicans were nominated for the House of Representatives by 1989, but Gary Franks of Connecticut in 1991 was the first African American Republican elected to Congress since 1978. The rise of neoconservatism in the Republican Party in the 1980s, however, did attract more conservative African American voters, but in 1988 only 6 percent of Republicans were African American.

Clarence Thomas, an African American conservative, was chairman of the Equal Employment Opportunity Commission (1982–1990) where he restricted federal affirmative action policies. In 1991, he succeeded Supreme Court Justice Thurgood Marshall after sensational Senate hearings that attracted a national television audience. Despite accusations that he had sexually harassed a colleague, Anita Hill, while he was EEOC chair, the Senate confirmed him in a close vote (Foskett 2004). Thomas joined Ward Connerly, Glen Loury, Colin Powell, Condoleezza Rice, Thomas Sowell, Shelby Steele, and Walter Williams as leading conservative spokespersons for African Americans in the 1980s.

elected mayor of Chicago (1983), and David Dinkins became the first African American mayor of New York City (1989). The first African American man elected governor was Douglas Wilder of Virginia in 1989. African Americans and Latinos in professional and executive positions were more common than ever before.

Television reflected the changing image of African Americans in the 1970s with several sitcoms, but none survived in the 1980s. One high point for African American viewers was the Emmy-winning *Cosby Show* on NBC (1984–1992), a popular sitcom starring Bill Cosby as a New York City physician married to an attorney. Jimmy Smits created one of the few positive role models for Latinos as a leading character in the hit NBC drama *L. A. Law* (1986–1994). Mexican Americans took pride in the election of Henry Cisneros as the first Latino mayor of a major U.S. city, San Antonio, in 1981. President Bush proudly noted his own Hispanic grandchildren. Despite progress in sports and the racial and multi-ethnic changes that were a constant feature of America society in the 1980s, this was seldom demonstrated on television.

Even northeastern cities as distant from the Mexican border as Boston were changing in ethnic composition. Boston was 68 percent white in 1980, but 59 percent in 1990. Its Latino population increased from 6 percent in 1980 to 14 percent in 2000, due to the arrival of immigrants from Mexico, Central America, South America, and the Caribbean. The city's Asian population also grew from 3 percent in 1980 to 8 percent in 2000. The influx of immigrants made this and many other U.S. cities more diverse, vibrant, and interesting with a tapestry of newcomers who were an economic boon and countered the out-migration to the suburbs or Sun Belt states. The 28.4 million immigrants in the United States arriving from 1980 to 2000, about 10 percent of the population, was the highest percentage in 70 years, and they were the engine driving growth in small businesses and international commerce in every city and state.

Malaise Revisited

The national slump that President Carter identified in 1980 as a malaise, a chronic condition of stagflation with simultaneous price inflation and stagnant economic growth, was a cause for Americans' discontent. In 1989, it returned to haunt President Bush. Mobilized by the Union of Concerned Scientists organized at MIT in 1969, prominent members of the scientific community, including many Nobel Prize winners, had warned since the 1970s against excessive military spending, the dangers of nuclear bombs, and reliance on fossil fuels and nuclear energy. The high cost and the enduring damage to the environment, as well as the social costs of underfunding social welfare and education programs, became evident in the Bush era. His critics demanded fair trading and an increase in minimum wages, and they opposed deals that exported American jobs, but the messianic vision of the New Right and the neoconservatives dominated government policies.

By June 1991, unemployment rose to 7 percent and Alan Greenspan warned a downturn in the economy was inevitable. Eight years of Reaganomics, defense spending, and tax cuts continued under Bush, which had benefited the rich not the middle or lower class. The frozen minimum wage and decreased consumer spending contributed to the declining economy, but President Bush vetoed a bill to extend unemployment benefits. Nevertheless, Bush was popular;

English as the Official U.S. Language

Congress had never considered declaring English as the nation's official language until Republican senator Samuel I. Hayakawa of California introduced a constitutional amendment in 1981. Language diversity has always been common in the United States, and before World War I, bilingual education was popular in many communities, although some states passed laws to encourage English proficiency. The 1980s saw a 40 percent increase in the foreign-born population, but the 1990 census found that 94.2 percent of minority language speakers were bilingual and only 1.8 million Americans, less than one percent of the population, spoke no English at all. However, in some Sunbelt communities, Spanish was so widely spoken that some whites felt alienated. The Latinization of the country was a remarkable demographic shift with 30 million Hispanics in the United States by 1995.

Senator Hayakawa's proposal made no progress in Congress, but since 1981, 22 states adopted some form of official English legislation. A similar effort by Congress to make English the official language of the federal government by statute also failed in 1991. The proponents were most often found in Sunbelt states with large Hispanic populations. The four most populous states—California, Florida, New York, and Texas—had over 40 percent of the nation's Latinos. Arguments for an official-language law included savings in bilingual school budgets, less racial or ethnic conflict, streamlining government operations, promoting citizenship, and unifying Americans. Critics claimed the proposal was simply xenophobic, discriminatory, and unnecessary, but polls showed a majority opposed liberal immigration policies.

a year after Desert Storm his approval rating was over 70 percent. Despite his 1988 campaign promise—"no new taxes"—by June 1990, Bush agreed with bipartisan leaders of Congress to raise taxes to reduce the federal deficit. Conservatives, never satisfied with Bush as an heir of Reagan, were outraged, and in the 1990 midterm elections many Republicans stayed home. The Republicans lost one seat in the Senate and eight in the House. When Bush signed the Democrats' Civil Rights Act of 1991, conservatives saw this as a further betrayal.

Immigrants in the Media

Distorted and inaccurate coverage by the U.S. media contributed to racist stereotypes of Arabs and Muslims as backward and violent. By 1982, the coverage of Israel's invasion of Lebanon and occupation of West Beirut demonstrated greater balance in the media's reporting on Middle East issues. However, some critics attributed this new balance to anti-Israel bias. By 1989, Muslims outnumbered Episcopalians in the United States, but polls showed little public sympathy for

Anti-Muslim Discrimination

Only 12 percent of the world's 1.2 billion Muslims were Arabs, but most Americans confused the two groups. In 1980, the National Association of Arab-Americans reported that its study of U.S. high school textbooks revealed much inaccurate or out-of-date information, negative stereotypes, and omissions about the history of the Middle East. Inaccurate stereotypical images of Arab and Muslim villains were common in U.S. movies and television long before Muslim terrorists attacked Americans in the 1980s. Polls by Louis Harris showed most Americans shared negative opinions (called Islamophobia or Arabophobia) about the Middle East, and this increased after the OPEC embargo led to a world oil crisis in 1973. Although the U.S. Muslim population grew rapidly in the 1980s, the American media continued to portray Arabs and Muslims in an unfavorable light. A survey by Robert Wuthnow in *America and the Challenges of Religious Diversity* (2005) found negative perceptions were most often directed by American Christians toward Muslims, who were described as "fanatical," "violent," "backward," and "close-minded."

This hostility and demonization increased when Iranian revolutionaries (dubbed Islamicists by the media) kidnapped 52 Americans at the U.S. embassy in Tehran in 1974; Libyan diplomats were expelled from Washington as spies in 1981; and 17 Americans died in the 1983 bombing of the U.S. embassy in Beirut. The bias against Islam, expressed in a 1984 *Wall Street Journal* article that warned of an "Islamic war waged against the West, Christianity, modern capitalism, Zionism and communism," led to widespread discrimination and scapegoating. The deaths of 241 U.S. Marines and soldiers in another Beirut bombing in 1983 increased prejudice against all Muslims. Terrorist hijackings of an American TWA airliner and the *Achille Lauro* Italian cruise ship in 1985 and terrorist kidnapping American clergy and journalists in Lebanon added to the outrage.

President Reagan linked the Libyan leader Muammar Qaddafi with terrorism and a worldwide fundamentalist movement. In America's monolithic, anti-Islamic view of the Muslim world, this justified the U.S. bombing of Libya in 1986. By 1985, American-Arab Anti-Discrimination Committee offices and mosques in U.S. cities had been bombed or burned. With little success, South Dakota senator James Abouresk and other prominent Arab Americans condemned this prejudice and violence. However, Christian Right leaders Jerry Falwell and Pat Robertson also expressed anti-Muslim views and conspiracism in apocalyptic language.

Popular movies like *Rollover* (1981), *Hanna K.* (1983), *The Little Drummer Girl* (1984), *Back to the Future* (1985), *Iron Cage* (1986), *The Delta Force* (1986), and *Baby Boom* (1987) saw Hollywood routinely reduce, disparage, and demean the Middle East and its people in a variety of ways. Much of this was based on ignorance; Tim Jon Semmerling explains in *"Evil" Arabs in American Popular Film* (2006) that the stereotypical evil Arab in movies and television was an illusion that reveals more about Americans than Arabs. It also was due to a generally pro-Israel attitude in America. Israel was a democratic nation and our ally, surrounded by hostile Muslim nations and supported by U.S. conservative Christians.

Anti-Muslim sentiment only increased after a terrorist bomb exploded on Pan Am Flight 103 over Scotland, killing 259 passengers in 1988, and after the Persian Gulf War in 1991. Jesse Jackson was one of the few American leaders who attempted personal diplomacy in the Middle East.

the world's fastest growing religion or the Middle East. With the end of the Cold War, the fall of the Berlin Wall, and the dismantling of the Soviet Union, voters turned from traditional Republican issues (defense and national security) to traditional Democratic issues (the domestic economy and pocketbook issues) in the 1990 midterm elections. Small but dedicated human rights organizations like Amnesty International and Human Rights Watch remained critical of the U.S. role in Latin America, Africa, and the Middle East.

The media also reported inaccurately that immigrants refused to assimilate, clung to their own language and culture, and were swelling the ranks of the poor and welfare recipients. Enormous insecurity developed among Americans of European descent as the size of the immigrant population skyrocketed. Conservatives demanded restrictive legislation, violence and hate crimes increased, and even politically moderate citizens were disturbed by these demographic changes. By 1990, over 32 million Americans spoke English as a second language, a one-third increase since 1980, and Spanish was the primary language for half of those 32 million. Schools, banks, advertising, and television revealed the growth of Spanish in the nation. The backlash against increased immigration was reflected in proposals to auction visas, to limit them to people with specific skills, or to require national identity cards.

BIOGRAPHIES

David Ross Brower, 1912–2000

Environmentalist

Born in Berkeley, California, David Brower studied at the University of California in Berkeley and worked at Yosemite National Park in the 1930s where he became a skillful mountain climber. After serving in the Army's 10th Mountain Division in Italy in World War II, Brower was an editor for the University of California Press and for the Sierra Club magazine. Brower served as executive director of the Sierra Club (1952–1969), where he increased membership to 77,000 and exposed environmental exploitation of the land and animals. He is credited with preventing construction of dams on the Grand Canyon and Colorado River. In 1969 he founded and led (1969–1984) the Friends of the Earth, and founded the Earth Island Institute in San Francisco (1982) to promote environmental conservation worldwide. His use of strikingly beautiful landscape photographs in Sierra Club posters and coffee table books created a religion of wilderness. This reoriented Americans' sense of the environment and ecology.

In his long career as an activist, Brower wrote or edited 50 books, including his autobiography *For Earth's Sake* (1990), and was nominated twice for the Nobel Peace Prize. He battled the government and corporations to protect forests, rivers, mountains, and porpoises, and lobbied against nuclear power and pesticides. John McPhee, who wrote *Encounters with the Archdruid* (1971) about Brower, dubbed him the Sierra Club's "preeminent fang" and America's "archdruid." Brower's words chiseled in stone at the National Aquarium in Washington, D.C., read, "We do not inherit the Earth from our fathers, we are borrowing it from our children."

Anne M. Gorsuch Burford, 1942–2004

Public Official

Born in Wyoming, Burford graduated from the University of Colorado at Boulder and earned her law degree there. She was an assistant district attorney in Denver and a lawyer for the Mountain Bell Company. She was a Colorado legislator (1976–1980) when Ronald Reagan appointed her head of the Environmental Protection Agency (1981–1983), the first woman to hold that position. She quickly imposed drastic staff and budget cuts on her own department. Embroiled in controversies with environmentalists, she refused to provide Superfund documents to Congress. She and many of her staff resigned when her Superfund director, Rita M. Lavelle, was indicted and later imprisoned. Burford wrote her autobiography in 1986 and married Robert Burford, the equally controversial director of the Bureau of Land Management. Like James Watt, she expressed the Reagan administration's antipathy to big government and what they considered overregulation of the environment and natural resources to the detriment of economic expansion. Burford died on July 18, 2004.

Lynne Cheney, 1941–

Public Official

Lynne Cheney personified the rising influence of women in the New Right socially conservative agenda in the 1980s. Born in Casper, Wyoming, she married Richard B. Cheney in 1964. After graduating from Colorado College, she earned a Ph.D. in literature at the University of Wisconsin in Madison. As chair of the National Endowment for the Humanities (1986–1983), Lynne Cheney reversed the NEH's liberal tradition in federal grants

Anne Gorsuch Burford, the controversial EPA director under Ronald Reagan, resigned in 1983. (U.S. Environmental Protection Agency)

and authorized more traditional standards for teaching history, but the published guidelines were so liberal that most history professors condemned them and the U.S. Senate unanimously rejected them. Later she worked with the American Enterprise Institute, *Reader's Digest,* and other conservative organizations and was a prominent voice for tradition in the culture wars. As the wife of Secretary of Defense Richard B. Cheney (1989–1993), she was a vocal supporter of Republican Party politics and an outspoken critic of education, post-modernism, multiculturalism, rap music, and video games. When Richard Cheney became vice president of the United States (1988–2006), she continued her advocacy of the conservative social agenda. Lynne Cheney is the author of nine books, including *Kings of the Hill* (1986), *American Freedom* (1987), and *Academic Freedom* (1992).

Barry Commoner, 1917–

Scientist

Born in Brooklyn, New York, Barry Commoner graduated from Columbia University in 1937 and earned a doctorate at Harvard University in 1941. After serving in the Navy during World War II, Commoner became a professor of biology at Washington University for 34 years. By the 1950s, he was a leading critic of nuclear testing and received the International Humanist Award from the International Humanist and Ethical Union in 1970. Commoner founded the Citizens Party when he ran for president in 1980. He is best known for *The Poverty of Power: Energy and the Economic Crisis* (1976) and *Making Peace with the Planet* (1990). Since 1981 he has worked on ecological issues at the Center for the Biology of Natural Systems at Queens College in New York.

Oliver "Ollie" North, 1943–

Public Official

Born in San Antonio, Texas, and raised a Catholic in upstate New York, Oliver North graduated from the U.S. Naval Academy in 1968 and served in the U.S. Marine Corps from 1968 to 1990. On the National Security Council (1981–1986), Lt. Col. "Ollie" North became a favorite of President Reagan who assigned him to help coordinate the invasion of Grenada (1983) and to plan the bombing of Libya (1986). North became famous for his role in the Iran-Contra scandal, a secret and illegal plan to sell U.S. weapons through an intermediary to Iran and to use the profit covertly to aid the Contras in Nicaragua (1985–1986). When this became public in 1986, Reagan fired him, and North testified to Congress in televised hearings (1987). He admitted he had lied to Congress, but his conviction in a federal court was overturned on appeal (1990). North ran for the

U.S. Senate in Virginia (1994) and became a born-again Christian. He is a conservative talk radio host and television commentator (Church 1987).

T. Boone Pickens Jr., 1928–

Businessman

Born in Oklahoma, Thomas Boone Pickens Jr. was the son of a Texas oil man. He graduated from Oklahoma State University in 1951 and worked as a geologist for Phillips Petroleum. By 1956, Pickens founded Mesa Petroleum in Texas but soon moved from oil exploration to the acquisition of large profitable oil companies. By 1981, his firm was the largest independent oil and natural gas company in the world, and he continued with mergers and acquisitions of undervalued or inefficient oil and gas firms. Little known outside of Texas, he appeared on the cover of *Time* magazine on March 4, 1985, in a story about the new trend for hostile takeovers by corporate raiders and greenmailers (Greenwald 1985). Even when these attempted takeover schemes failed, Pickens and his shareholders usually earned substantial profits. His fame as an "entrepreneurial populist" who criticized large inefficient oil corporations spread so quickly that he considered running for president as a Republican in 1988.

An unlikely convert to environmentalism, Pickens became a spokesman for alternative energy, water conservation, and the substitution of natural gas for petroleum. Pickens wrote his best-selling autobiography, *Boone*, in 1987 and donated millions to Texas universities. He also contributed more than $290 million to his alma mater, Oklahoma State University in Stillwater, largely for new athletic facilities and geology programs. One of the most controversial American businessmen in the 1980s, when T. Boone Pickens retired, *Forbes* magazine placed him among the 100 richest men in the nation.

David Stockman, 1946–

Public Official

Born in Texas and raised on a Michigan family farm, David Stockman graduated from Michigan State University in 1968 and studied at Harvard University (1968–1970, 1974). He was elected as a Michigan Republican to the House of Representatives (1977–1981) but resigned to become director of the Office of Management and Budget for President Reagan (1981–1985). Stockman was committed to reducing government spending, overregulation, and waste, but he was widely criticized for saving money by classifying ketchup as a vegetable in school lunch programs. Due to conflicts with Reagan cabinet members, he left the OMB and wrote a book criticizing the Reagan administration, *The Triumph of Politics* (1986). Stockman, criticized by some Republicans as disloyal to Reagan and for advocating the unrealistic 1981 budget cuts for social programs that Democrats exploited, left politics to become a Wall Street investment banker.

James G. Watt, 1938–

Public Official

Born in Wyoming, James Watt graduated from the University of Wyoming in 1960 and earned his law degree there in 1962. He was on the staff of Wyoming senator Milward Simpson and worked for the U.S. Chamber of Commerce and the Department of the Interior and Federal Power Commission before he founded the Mountain States Legal Foundation in 1976. When Ronald Reagan appointed him as the secretary of the Interior (1981–1983), Watt had long been a lawyer, lobbyist, and spokesman for the western coal, oil, gas, and lumber industries. His term in the cabinet was marked by controversy due to his open hostility to environmentalism and his support for the Sagebrush Revolution's agenda of economic development of federal forest and grazing lands. He called environmentalists a left-wing cult and promised we will mine more, drill more, cut more timber. Watt tried to implement the deregulation of environmental laws that Reagan believed were hindering economic growth. In 1983, he banned the Beach Boys from performing at the Fourth of July concert on the National Mall because rock music attracted "an undesirable element." Nancy Reagan, who liked the Beach Boys, suggested to her husband that it was time for Watt to leave. He resigned amid the public controversy with environmental organizations, and in 1996 he pled guilty to withholding documents from a federal grand jury. The environmental movement he castigated had become too deeply embedded in the public mind to be dismissed (Tygiel 2006).

George F. Will, 1941–

Journalist

Born in Champaign, Illinois, George Will graduated from Trinity College in Hartford, Connecticut, earned an M.A. at Oxford University, and a Ph.D. in political science at Princeton University in 1968. After teaching at Michigan State University, the University of Toronto, and Harvard University, he served on the staff of Colorado Republican Senator Gordon Allcott (1970–1972). Will was the Washington editor for the conservative magazine *National Review* (1973–1976) and was a *Washington Post* syndicated columnist since 1974 and for *Newsweek* since 1976. Will won a Pulitzer Prize in 1977 for his erudite commentary. His columns were conservative and factual with frequent references to political philosophy and baseball. In the 1980s, he became a news analyst for ABC news programs.

Will became one of the most widely-read and influential political commentators in the United States. However, his critics pointed out that Will violated the journalist's neutrality by helping Ronald Reagan prepare for his 1980 debate with President Carter. Will has received numerous awards for journalism and is the author of many books, including *The Pursuit of Virtue and Other Tory Notions* (1982), *Statecraft as Soulcraft: What Government Does* (1983), *The Morning After: American Successes and Excesses, 1981–1986* (1986), and *The New Season: A Spectator's Guide to the 1988 Election* (1987).

REFERENCES AND FURTHER READINGS

Barkan, Elliott Robert. 1996. *And Still They Come: Immigrants and American Society 1920 to the 1990s*. Wheeling, Ill.: Harlan Davidson.

Bayor, Ronald H. 1996. *Race and the Shaping of Twentieth-Century Atlanta*. Chapel Hill: University of North Carolina Press.

Bell, Daniel. 1999. *The Coming of Post-Industrial Society: A Venture in Social Forecasting*. New York: Basic Books.

Bernard, Richard M., and Bradley R. Rice, eds. 1983. *Sunbelt Cities: Politics and Growth Since World War II*. Austin: University of Texas Press.

Boston Globe. 2006. "Exxon is asked to pay $92m more for spill," June 2, A2.

Boyer, Paul, ed. 1990. *Reagan as President: Contemporary Views of the Man, His Politics, and His Policies*. Chicago: Ivan R. Dee.

Brands, H. W. 2001. *The Strange Death of American Liberalism*. New Haven, Conn.: Yale University Press.

Broder, David S., and Bob Woodward. 1992. *The Man Who Would Be President: Dan Quayle*. New York: Simon & Schuster.

Brower, David R. 1990. *For Earth's Sake: The Life and Times of David Brower*. Salt Lake City: Peregrine Smith Books.

Brownstein, Ronald, and Nina Easton. 1983. *Reagan's Ruling Class: Portraits of the President's Top One Hundred Officials*. New York: Pantheon Books.

Buchanan, Patrick J. 1988. *Right from the Beginning*. Boston: Little, Brown.

Buchanan, Patrick J. 2004. *Where the Right Went Wrong: How Neoconservatives Subverted the Reagan Revolution and Hijacked the Bush Presidency*. New York: St. Martin's Press.

Burford, Anne M. 1986. *Are You Tough Enough: An Insider's View of Washington Power Politics*. New York: McGraw-Hill.

Cannon, Lou. 1991. *President Reagan: The Role of a Lifetime*. New York: Simon and Schuster.

Carney, Jay. 1986. "Sunbelt Import," *Time,* August 18, 21.

Cawley, R. McGreggor. 1993. *Federal Land, Western Anger: The Sagebrush Rebellion and Environmental Politics*. Lawrence: University Press of Kansas.

Church, George J. 1987. "Ollie's Turn," *Time,* July 13, 22.

Costa, Dora L. 1998. *The Evolution of Retirement: An American Economic History, 1880–1990*. Chicago: University of Chicago Press.

Cumbler, John T. 1989. *A Social History of Economic Decline: Business, Politics and Work in Trenton*. New Brunswick, N.J.: Rutgers University Press.

Daniel, Pete. 2005. *Toxic Drift: Pesticides and Health in the Post–World War II South*. Baton Rouge: Louisiana State University Press.

Daniel, Roger. 1991. *Coming to America: A History of Immigration and Ethnicity in American Life*. New York: HaperCollins.

Davis, Patti. 1992. *The Way I See It: An Autobiography*. New York: Jove Books.

Diggins, John Patrick. 2007. *Ronald Reagan: Fate, Freedom, and the Making of History*. New York: W. W. Norton.

Duffy, Michael, and Dan Goodgame. 1992. *Marching in Place: The Status Quo Presidency of George Bush*. New York: Simon & Schuster.

Easton, Nina J. 2000. *Gang of Five: Leaders at the Center of the Conservative Crusade*. New York: Simon & Schuster.

Ehrenreich, Barbara. 1990. *The Worst Years of Our Lives: Irreverent Notes from a Decade of Greed*. New York: Pantheon Books.

Ehrman, John. 1995. *The Rise of Neo-conservatism: Intellectuals and Foreign Affairs, 1945–1994*. New Haven, Conn.: Yale University Press.

Ellwood, David T. 1988. *Poor Support: Poverty in the American Family*. New York: Basic Books.

Evans, Thomas W. 2006. *The Education of Ronald Reagan: The General Electric Years and the Untold Story of His Conversion to Conservatism*. New York: Columbia University Press.

Farrell, John A. 2001. *Tip O'Neill and the Democratic Century*. Boston: Little, Brown.

Feinstein, Stephen. 2006. *The 1980s from Ronald Reagan to MTV*. Berkeley Heights, N.J.: Enslow.

Fisher, David E. 1990. *Fire and Ice: The Greenhouse Effect, Ozone Depletion, and Nuclear War*. New York: Harper and Row.

Fitzgerald, Frances. 2000. *Way Out There in the Blue: Reagan, Star Wars, and the End of the Cold War*. New York: Simon & Schuster.

Foskett, Ken, 2004. *Judging Thomas: The Life and Times of Clarence Thomas*. New York: HarperCollins.

Friedrich, Otto. 1985. "The Changing Face of America," *Time,* July 8, 22.

Gonzalez, Juan. 2000. *Harvest of Empire: A History of Latinos in America.* New York: Penguin Books.

Goodgame, Dan. 1989. "Calling for an Overhaul," *Time,* October 9, 18–19.

Greenwald, John. 1985. "High Times for T. Boone Pickens," *Time,* March 4, 27.

Greenya, John, and Anne Urban. 1986. *The Real David Stockman: The True Story of America's Most Controversial Power Broker.* New York: St. Martin's Press.

Gregory, James N. 2005. *The Southern Diaspora: How the Great Migrations of Black and White Southerners Transformed America.* Chapel Hill: University of North Carolina Press.

High, Steven. 2003. *Industrial Sunset: The Making of North America's Rust Belt, 1969–1984.* Toronto: University of Toronto Press.

Hill, Dilys M., and Phil Williams, eds. 1994. *The Bush Presidency: Triumphs and Adversities.* New York: St. Martin's Press.

Jenkins, Philip. 2006. *Decade of Nightmares: The End of the Sixties and the Making of Eighties America.* New York: Oxford University Press.

Kelley, Robin D. G. 1994. *Race Rebels: Culture, Politics, and the Black Working Class.* New York: The Free Press.

Kelley, Robin D. G. 1997. *Yo' Mama's DisFunktional: Fighting the Culture Wars in Urban America.* Boston: Beacon Press.

Kingsland, Sharon E. 2005. *The Evolution of American Ecology, 1890–2000.* Baltimore: Johns Hopkins University Press.

Krauthammer, Charles. 2004. "He Could See for Miles," *Time,* June 14, 9–11.

Kruse, Kevin M. 2005. *White Flight: Atlanta and the Making of Modern Conservatism.* Princeton: Princeton University Press.

Kuttner, Robert. 2006. "Here's a Job Americans Would Do," *Boston Globe,* May 27, A15.

Lacayo, Richard. 1986. "Rattling the Gilded Cage," *Time,* August 11, 31.

La Chapelle, Peter. 2007. *Proud to Be an Okie: Cultural Politics, Country Music, and Migration to Southern California.* Berkeley: University of California Press.

Lamm, Richard, and Gary Imhoff. 1985. *The Immigration Time Bomb: The Fragmenting of America.* New York: Truman Talley Books.

Leo, John. 1986. "Sex and Schools," *Time,* November 24, 15–16.

Levy, Peter B. 1996. *Encyclopedia of the Reagan-Bush Years.* Westport, Conn.: Greenwood Press.

Magnuson, Ed. 1985. "Shake-Up at the White House," *Time,* January 21, 12–14.

Magnuson, Ed. 1989. "A 14-State Barrage of Twisters," *Time,* November 27, 17.

Martin, William. 1996. *With God on Our Side: The Rise of the Religious Right in America.* New York: Broadway Books.

McCormick, John. 1989. *Reclaiming Paradise: The Global Environmental Movement.* Bloomington: Indiana University Press.

McPhee, John. 1971. *Encounters with the Archdruid.* New York: Farrar, Straus and Giroux.

Mills, Nicolaus, ed., 1994. *Arguing Immigration: The Debate Over the Changing Face of America.* New York: Simon & Schuster.

Mooney, Chris. 2005. *The Republican War on Science.* New York: Basic Books.

National Coalition for the Homeless, Who is Homeless? http://www.national homeless.org.

Obendorfer, Don. 1991. *The Turn from the Cold War to a New Era, the United Sates and the Soviet Union, 1983–1991.* Baltimore: Johns Hopkins University Press.

Olson, Karen. 2005. *Wives of Steel: Voices of Women from the Sparrows Point Steelmaking Communities.* University Park: Penn State University Press.

Phillips, Kevin. 1969. *The Emerging Republican Majority.* New Rochelle, N.Y.: Arlington House.

Phillips, Kevin. 1993. *Boiling Point: Democrats, Republicans, and the Decline of Middle-Class Prosperity.* New York: Random House.

Pickens, T. Boone, Jr. 1987. *Boone.* Boston: Houghton Mifflin.

Powell, Colin L., and Joseph E. Persico. 1995. *My American Journey.* New York: Random House.

Reagan, Michael. 1988. *On the Outside Looking In.* New York: Zebra Books.

Reagan, Nancy. 1989. *My Turn: The Memoirs of Nancy Reagan.* New York: Random House.

Reeves, Richard. 2005. *President Reagan: The Triumph of Imagination.* New York: Simon and Schuster.

Regan, Donald T. 1988. *For the Record: From Wall Street to Washington.* San Diego: Harcourt Brace Jovanovich.

Rudolph, Barbara. 1989. "No Joyride in 1989," *Time,* January 9, 34.

Sale, Kirkpatrick. 1975. *Power Shift: The Rise of the Southern Rim and Its Challenge to the Eastern Establishment.* New York: Random House.

Sale, Kirkpatrick. 1993. *The Green Revolution: The American Environmental Movement, 1962–1992.* New York: Hill and Wang.

Schaller, Michael. 1992. *Reckoning with Reagan: America and Its President in the 1980s*. New York: Oxford University Press.

Schulman, Bruce J. 1994. *From Cotton Belt to Sunbelt: Federal Policy, Economic Development, and the Transformation of the South, 1938–1980*. Durham, N.C.: Duke University Press.

Semmerling, Tim Jon. 2006. *"Evil" Arabs in American Popular Film: Orientalist Fear*. Austin: University of Texas Press.

Slansky, Paul. 1989. *The Clothes Have No Emperor: A Chronicle of the American 80s*. New York: Simon & Schuster.

Smolowe, Jill. 1989. "El Salvador, The Battle for San Salvador," *Time,* November 27, 18.

Stockman, David A. 1986. *The Triumph of Politics: How the Reagan Revolution Failed*. New York: Harper and Row.

Thompson, Heather Ann. 2001. *Whose Detroit?: Politics, Labor, and Race in a Modern American City*. Ithaca, N.Y.: Cornell University Press.

Thompson, Lawrence L. *A History of HUD,* http://www.hud.gov/library/book shelf12/hudhistory.cfm.

Troy, Gil. 2005. *Morning in America: How Ronald Reagan Invented the 1980s*. Princeton: Princeton University Press.

Tygiel, Jules. 2006. *Ronald Reagan and the Triumph of American Conservatism*. New York: Longman.

Ullmann, Owen. 1986. *Stockman: The Man, the Myth, The Future*. New York: Donald I. Fine.

Vetter, Herbert, ed. 1982. *Speak Out Against the New Right*. Boston: Beacon Press.

Wallis, Claudia. 1989. "Onward, Women!" *Time,* December 4, 17–19.

Wicker, Tom. 2004. *George Herbert Walker Bush*. New York: Viking.

Wilentz, Amy. 1985. "I Will Veto Again and Again," *Time,* March 18, 31.

Wilentz, Sean. 2008. *The Age of Reagan: America from Watergate to the War on Terror*. New York: Harper.

Wilson, William Julius. 1987. *The Truly Disadvantaged: The Inner City, the Underclass, and Public Policy*. Chicago: University of Chicago Press.

Wuthnow, Robert. 2005. *America and the Challenges of Religious Diversity*. Princeton: Princeton University Press.

A Nation of Nations: Families and Diversity in America

OVERVIEW

In a decade sometimes called the age of diversity, the two great pillars of economic security—the family and the workplace—guaranteed much less stability. Public and private benefits, the safety net that protected Americans in economic trouble, eroded in the 1980s as the government and corporate employers reduced income security, retirement pensions, and health care. Free market ideology stressed personal responsibility with Americans free to choose. This had great impact on children and families at a time when the more diverse American family underwent profound changes. One influential conservative critic of liberal trends in the American family was the psychologist James Dobson, who founded the Family Research Council in 1981. He advocated spanking children and opposed multiculturalism, gay rights, and feminism. Other researchers pondered the fate of the family in books such as *What's Happening to the American Family?* (Levitan, Belous, and Grillo 1988).

In the 1980s, the trend was that marriage was no longer the main institution organizing American lives. Greater independence and more flexibility became common as women became less dependent on men. Although most people did marry, separation and divorce rather than death ended most marriages. Americans lived longer and married later, fertility rates fell, single mothers were more common, and more than 60 percent of mothers with children worked outside the home. The American family, especially the 11 percent of families headed by women, seemed to be under siege. For example, the U.S. census showed that

35 percent of women lived without a spouse in 1950, but this increased to almost 50 percent by 1990. This was because women married at a later age, lived with a partner without marrying, lived longer as widows or were divorced and delayed or never remarried, or remained single according to the *New York Times* on January 16, 2006. African American women were more likely to live without a spouse than Hispanic, Asian, or non-Hispanic white women.

The rising consumption of goods and services prompted many mothers to enter the work force. Inflation and slow growth or decline in family earnings also made a woman's income necessary to maintain a middle-class standard of living. Family planning meant more mothers could work and have a career. Some researchers connected working women with historically high divorce rates while others questioned the impact of working mothers on children. Divorce became a pop culture theme in books, movies, and music. Adoption also became more common and more humane, although teenage mothers tended to keep their babies. The new cooperative adoptions led to 60,000 pregnant women selecting the adoptive parents for their children in 1986 (Gibbs, *Time* 1989).

Marriage also may have lost its significance as a rite of passage, but Hollywood viewed the sanctity of the American family as most important in the age of family values. The hit movie *The Big Chill* (1983) struck a chord for many women by portraying a 1960s campus radical who became an unmarried yuppie lawyer yearning to have a baby even without a husband. In *Ordinary People* (1980) Robert Redford provided a cautionary tale about the fragility of an affluent family and the need for communication. *Fatal Attraction* (1987) vilified a desperate career woman but forgave a reckless husband.

Since the failure of Reaganomics, many economists advocated an approach that would lead to greater economic security for families. But macroeconomic growth did not make families in the United States more secure, and median wages stagnated in the 1980s (Orszag 2006). Average family income steadily dropped by half for many, from 7 percent of families in 1970 to 17 percent in 2000. This prevented economic growth and made government intervention into the free market more tempting. The goals of job security and higher living standards for more families required a progressive tax system, better education, more savings, and asset accumulation to create a family nest egg to use in hard times. Those who opposed higher minimum wages, for example, like those opposed to labor unions and government regulation of business and environment, argued this would put the United States at a competitive disadvantage in the global economy. But liberals argued that this view underestimated the power and prosperity of the U.S. economy and the importance of stable families.

The conjugal nuclear family celebrated by the popular culture, with a loving married couple, a strong male breadwinner, and their happy children, the *Ozzie and Harriet* or *Father's Knows Best* families on television in the 1960s, began disappearing in the 1980s. Americans delayed marriage, premarital sex became the norm, and divorce rates increased to 50 percent. Gay parents were also more common in the 1980s. The U.S. census reported that by 2000 about 34 percent of lesbian couples and 22 percent of gay male couples raised at least one child under age 18 in their home. As the *New York Times Magazine* noted on November 19, 2006, since 1980 Americans "are in many cases redesigning 'family.'" Some critics claimed that these changes began earlier, and some argued the ideal never existed for most American families. The changes were attributed to many causes—the civil rights movement, Hugh Hefner's *Playboy* philosophy, no-fault divorce laws, working mothers, modern contraception, the declining birthrate, Helen Gurley Brown's *Cosmopolitan* magazine, the anti–Vietnam War protests, women's liberation, or gay rights campaigns. *Time* magazine noted in its September 10, 1984, cover story, "Making Babies, The New Science of Conception," that in vitro fertilization and new medical procedures made pregnancy a matter of personal choice and timing. Whatever the cause, families and children were different in the 1980s. Even Anita Bryant, the former Miss America who led an antigay rights campaign in Florida, was divorced; she told the *Ladies' Home Journal* in 1980 that she could better understand the frustrations of feminist and gay protestors (Wallis 1984).

Aspirations for self-expression, sexual satisfaction, and personal happiness took hold in the 1980s in ways that had not been possible or were simply deferred in previous decades. Attitudes and behavior had changed and conformity was no longer necessary or in fashion. Demographers predicted that 7 out of 10 Americans would marry eventually, but at a later age. It was clear that the traditional institution of marriage lost its unique social status by the end of the decade. The trend of a declining birthrate, increasing illegitimate births, incidence of female-headed households, delayed marriage, and higher ratio of adults living alone, once considered the hallmarks of socially deviant minority communities, became common in the white majority. Statistics reveal that the birth rate fell from 18.4 per thousand in 1970 to 16.6 in 1990. The divorce rate was 3.5 in 1970, 5.2 in 1980, and 4.7 in 1990. In 1971–1980 about 4,493,300 immigrants entered the United States, and in 1981–1990 the number of immigrants increased to 7,338,000. The percent of unemployed workers rose from 4.9 in 1970 to 7.1 in 1980, and fell to 5.6 in 1990.

Because 6 out of 10 U.S. women were working mothers by 1982, fewer men were the sole breadwinner, and more women had a job providing a source of income, economic power, and self-esteem. Marriage became more egalitarian and companionable than the traditional male-dominant marriage. As Kathleen Gerson noted in *No Man's Land* (1993), the male primary breadwinner was no longer the dominant cultural group, declining to about 14 percent of American families by 1990. This meant men's lives changed in many ways; for example, more men were cooking at home—about 30 percent did so (*Time*, June 2, 1986).

General Mills recognized this change in family life by revising Betty Crocker, its symbol since 1936. In 1982, the *Betty Crocker Working Woman's Cookbook* had responded to the changing role of wives and mothers. Throughout the 1980s,

Betty Crocker had five face-lifts as she grew younger and more modern, and, dressed in a business suit, she appeared to be at home in the office or the kitchen. The sixth edition of the classic *Betty Crocker Cookbook,* published in 1986, presented a new Betty with a distinctly young urban professional appearance, a new version of a familiar symbol who men could trust. Technology also influenced family meals; the microwave oven meant that by 1987, 8 out of 10 U.S. households regularly purchased take-out food to be consumed at home (*Time,* June 2, 1986).

TIMELINE

1980   The U.S. divorce rate reaches 50 percent.

April, the Mariel boatlift brings 125,000 Cuban refugees to Florida.

Asian-Americans are 1.6 percent of U.S. population, or 3.5 million people.

1981   December 28, the first test tube baby is born in the United States.

The Islamic Society of America is founded.

Twenty-one percent of the U.S. foreign-born population are illegal aliens.

President Reagan appoints Sandra Day O'Connor as the first woman on the Supreme Court.

James Dobson founds the Family Research Council.

1982   President Reagan announces the War on Drugs.

The number of unemployed Americans reaches nine million.

Second Wave feminism focuses on the family.

The nuclear freeze movement assembles 700,000 people in New York City's Central Park to protest nuclear weapons.

Chicana feminists organize a national association.

1983   *The Big Chill* movie celebrates the rise of the yuppies.

President Reagan tells an audience of evangelical Christians the Soviet Union is an evil empire.

The Supreme Court overturns an Ohio law requiring a twenty-four-hour waiting period for an abortion.

The number of unemployed Americans reaches 11 million.

The American Islamic College is founded in Chicago.

A Nation at Risk report evaluates poor school performance.

1984   Only 55.7 percent of Americans vote.

Mothers Against Drunk Driving is founded.

The Democrats nominate Geraldine Ferraro, the first female vice presidential candidate.

Newsweek calls 1984 the Year of the Yuppie.

All states permit no-fault divorce.

1985   President Reagan, age seventy-three, is inaugurated as the oldest U.S. president in history.

Antonin Scalia is the first Italian-American to serve on the Supreme Court.

Congress passes an amnesty bill for illegal immigrants.

1986   President Reagan urges more focus on family values in his state of the union address.

The Vatican opposes in vitro fertilization.

September 14, Nancy Reagan leads a national crusade against drugs.

December 19, Howard Beach riot takes place in New York City.

1987   Congress passes the Anti-Drug Abuse Act.

February 4, environmentalists declare a victory when Congress overrides Reagan's veto of the Water Quality Control Act.

March 25, Supreme Court upholds affirmative action.

Miami has the second largest Cuban population in the world.

1988   George H. W. Bush gives a speech at the Republican National Convention in New Orleans calling for a kinder and gentler nation.

Over Reagan's objection Congress passes the plant closing bill to require advance notice of layoffs.

Only 77.7 percent of men are in the labor force.

Congress passes the Civil Liberties Act for Japanese-American internee reparations.

1989   The first conference of Central and North American migration
                  experts is held in Guatemala.

                  President Bush orders the invasion of Panama in the
                  continuing War on Drugs.

                  November 7, Douglas Wilder becomes the first black governor
                  in U.S. history and David Dinkins becomes New York City's
                  first black mayor.

                  The Central Park jogger rape case is heard.

THE AMERICAN FAMILY

Changes

By the late 1980s, average real wages for most American workers declined, especially for the lowest 20 percent of the population. The median income of families headed by men under age 30 declined by 27 percent, approximately the same percentage as per capita income declined in the Great Depression of the 1930s. Men working in manufacturing industries suffered most in the economic turbulence of the 1980s, so their wives entered the work force, especially in nonunion service-sector jobs, to increase family income. Housing costs rose too, by 294 percent for new houses in the 15 years prior to 1987, which increased the need for working wives and mothers. Economic insecurity became the defining feature of the U.S. economy in this decade with structural unemployment and eroding health care and retirement programs. As poverty increased in the 1980s, the working class sometimes turned to crime and drug abuse. In *The New American Poverty,* Michael Harrington contrasted his former New York City neighborhood near Union Square in 1949 with the area in 1984, now full of African American and Puerto Rican criminals and drug dealers. He attributed this change to family disintegration.

Milton Friedman, the most influential economist of the 1980s, advised President Reagan that government spending and taxes could not reduce inflation and restore economic stability, but few accepted Friedman's monetary policies (Diggins 2007). For example, although medical care had improved and expanded to more Americans, rising health costs concerned many families, as *Time* magazine reported in a December 10, 1984, cover story on "Medical Miracles, But How to Pay the Bill?" (Friedrich 1984). Health care was more effective and more available but also more expensive for American families who had depended on their employers for health insurance.

Throughout the 1980s, women of all economic levels, the poor, the middle class, and the rich, steadily gained ground on their male counterparts in the work force. The gap in pay changed very little from the 1950s to the 1970s, but in the

1980s, American women enjoyed a period of sharp increases in pay. It became possible to imagine that women with similar qualifications would make identical salaries as men did. In 1980, women earned about 82 percent as much per hour as men with similar education and experience. By 1990, this rose to 91 percent due to government efforts to reduce sex discrimination. The effect of laws like Title VII and Title IX, which prohibited discrimination in school and at work, became apparent in the 1980s, and this narrowed the pay gap (Leonhardt 2006). However, the glass ceiling, a term coined in 1984, prevented some women from earning the higher salaries men received. The glass ceiling was the informal but widespread and transparent limit by employers on a woman's advance in salary and promotion. It remained in place but had a few cracks by 1990; such limits have also been applied to racial and ethnic minorities.

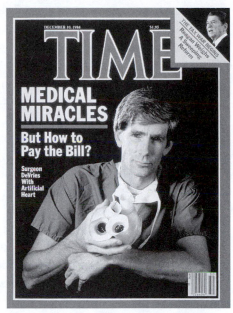

Surgeon William DeVries on the cover of Time *magazine, "Medical Miracles: But How to Pay the Bill?" December 10, 1984. (William Strode/Time Magazine/ Time & Life Pictures/Getty Images)*

The American family also changed as the divorce rate rose to 50 percent in 1980 and then slowly declined. By 1985, every state passed no-fault divorce laws, which made it easier to terminate a marriage, but fewer divorced people remarried than in the recent past. Many women no longer took their husbands' surnames, and lawyers wrote prenuptial contracts for many couples. The age at first marriage also rose for women from 20 in 1960 to 25 in 1980, with men two or three years older. The number of interracial marriages rose from 310,000 in 1970 to 1.3 million in 1990. Couples cohabiting, or living together without marriage, at all ages increased, as did the number of children born out of wedlock, about one in three by 1990. This was more common for college-educated working women than ever before. However, the Centers for Disease Control and Prevention reported that teenage pregnancy and abortion rates increased rapidly in the 1980s. The pregnancy rate for girls ages 15 to 19 rose from 88.8 per thousand in 1980 to 95.9 per thousand in 1990 (Coontz 2005).

Once stigmatized as bastards, children of unmarried mothers were more common and more accepted in the 1980s. State and federal courts gave them more legal protection and the right to support and inheritance from their parents. The differences between "legitimate" and "illegitimate" children diminished and states seldom removed children from unmarried mothers without sufficient cause after the U.S. Supreme Court ruled in *Levy v. Louisiana* (1968) that the 14th Amendment protected the offspring of unwed parents. Although the state had a valid interest in protecting married families, the Court declared that children born out of wedlock had legal claims on their father's estate. Celebrities who had children outside of marriage without shame or stigma became more common in the 1980s, which glamorized this issue to a certain extent.

Globalization also had an impact on the American family in the 1980s. Traditional jobs and industries disappeared, but new opportunities in new technologies that emerged in the shifting economy forced American workers into new or unconventional (often temporary, contract, or short-term) employment in new places. Stephanie Coontz, a historian of marriage and families, noted that the number of children raised by unmarried parents rose in the 1980s, as did the number of families with both parents working. More educated mothers were more likely to be employed, and one child in three was born to an unmarried mother. New in vitro fertilization techniques and the opening of sperm banks to single women in 1980 made delayed pregnancy more possible. More than half of the women in the United States used contraception in 1982, and the average age of mothers having their first baby rose 2.7 years from 1960 to 1992. All of this meant that unconventional families were more common and more acceptable. By 1980, the divorce rate had doubled and changes in legal, medical, economic, educational, and social conditions made American marriage and the family more flexible and diverse than ever before (Coontz 2005).

Family Economics

The decline of the middle class in America in the 1980s became a serious problem. The rising cost of housing, health care, and higher education were not issues that government addressed. Unable to muster congressional support for repealing the most popular New Deal and Great Society federal programs, the Reagan and Bush conservatives opposed unions and federal regulation, cut taxes, and blocked new government programs at the expense of higher federal deficits. This undermined gains to which the poor and the middle class had become accustomed. Liberals insisted tax cuts for the lower- and middle-class workers would permit them to raise their children, pay for college, and care for their elderly parents with less dependence on the government. If the wealthy and the corporations paid their fair share in taxes, the American family would be more secure. But few Americans responded to this liberal message in the conservative 1980s. They expected capital investment, concentrated wealth, tax cuts, and increased personal savings would create prosperity that trickled down to ordinary American consumers. President Bush, who promised a kinder and gentler nation in his 1988 campaign, continued Reagan's supply-side approach through deficit reduction, shrinking government by deregulation, and privatiz-

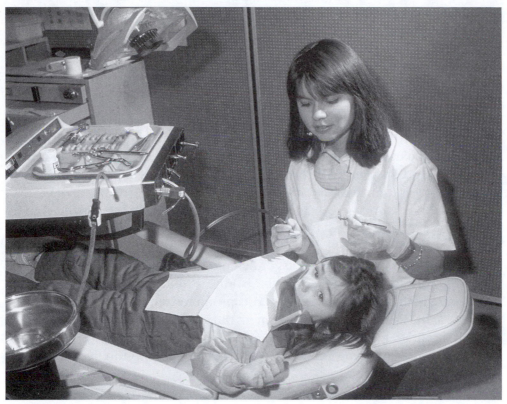

A woman dentist examines a child's teeth in 1985, a new trend as more women entered the medical professions. (Corel)

ing public services, such as reduced federal subsidies for Amtrak trains. He promised not to raise taxes during his campaign and called for local voluntary charity, a thousand points of light, to form a nation of communities helping families in need (Carlisle and Golson 2008).

The 10 largest cities housed one-third of the African American population by 1989, along with most of the other nonwhite populations. Many white middle-class Americans retreated to the suburbs or the Sunbelt. Nonetheless, the 1980s were an unlikely time for conflict because economic and social changes were blurring class, race, religion, and gender lines. Mass education was producing an educated people freer of prejudice than ever before. The mass media and expanding international markets had integrated the United States into an economic community of consumers committed to growth.

In her 1983 book, *Outrageous Acts and Everyday Rebellions,* the feminist leader Gloria Steinem commented on a *Wall Street Journal* series on the advent of the "working woman," which many considered the greatest change in American life since the Industrial Revolution. Ms. Steinem noted that women have always worked. The change was that so many women in the 1980s worked outside the home—an unprecedented 41 percent. Almost 64 percent of working women were single, divorced, separated, or widows working to support themselves and their children, or worked because their husbands earned too little to support the family. Many also worked for personal satisfaction. But increasingly, women worked to avoid falling out of the middle class. Many women suffered a 30 percent decrease in income after divorce or separation.

Other changes in the 1980s that influenced the American family were suburbanization and geographical mobility, especially in the Sunbelt states, which diminished the traditions of ethnic and racial conflict in the older urban centers of the East and Midwest. Also women entered health, retail, and service jobs while factory and manual labor jobs disappeared, leaving working-class men with few options. The percentage of men in the work force across the country declined to 77.7 percent by 1989. Those without high school or college diplomas found few entry-level jobs, so men dropped out of the work force to rely on welfare and disability payments, or fell into drug abuse and crime. This was especially true in urban centers in the Northeast and Midwest for low-skilled men where high housing and energy costs prompted a demographic shift to the Sunbelt. At the same time, the Department of Housing and Urban Development housing program budget declined from $55.7 billion in 1980 to $15.2 billion in 1987. Consequently, rising expectations and declining opportunities created tensions in American families.

Blended Families

Divorce was so common in the 1980s that an estimated half of first marriages ended in divorce after an average of 11 years. Divorce was expensive, costing approximately $10,000, and took one year to complete. About three out of four adults under age 45 remarried within four years, especially those with children. The term "blended family" was coined to describe the new families that were created when divorced parents remarried. About 500,000 adults became new stepparents each year, representing over six million children or 10 percent of all children in the United States. More than half of all children born since 1970 lived in an extended blended family.

The word stepparent was often considered negative, and both adults and children often had problems adjusting to their new family roles. Children sometimes felt the stepparent was an intruder and preferred their biological parents. The adults also faced psychological and economic challenges. Ronald and Nancy Reagan may be a good example of the blended family formed when a divorced man remarried and had difficulties with the children. Celebrating holidays and school graduations or weddings often produced complicated arrangements or conflict for blended family members. Consequently, about 60 percent of second marriages ended in divorce. Third marriages added to the confusion, and lawyers specialized in complicated estate, trust, and inheritance planning for blended families.

Growing Up in the 1980s

Changes in the American family combined with economic turbulence meant that children growing up in the 1980s faced problems and stresses never seen before. For example, increased immigration created a large second-generation population of children and teens, about one in five Americans by 1990, whose assimilation will determine future prosperity and stability in the United States. One social problem that reflected these difficulties was the incidence of high school dropouts. Some states reported one in four teenagers did not graduate from high school. Test scores and the increase in remedial courses on college campuses indicated that many more high school graduates were academically deficient. This was attributed to overcrowded schools, the shortage of qualified teachers, obsolete curricula, and limited access to alternative education programs. *Time* magazine reported that 13 percent of Americans tested by the Census Bureau failed a basic literacy test, and the Department of Education estimated that 17 million illiterates lived in the United States, including high school drop-outs, immigrants, and some high school graduates (Lacayo, *Time,* 1986).

Educators proposed building new schools with modern equipment, new courses, career counseling, flexible classroom hours, expanded kindergartens and preschools, and more study options to include vocational training and work experiences. Higher standards and higher pay for teachers was also a frequent recommendation. But conservative critics opposed teachers' unions and raising local or states taxes to pay for higher school budgets without educational reform. They demanded a longer school day and school year, and they wanted to retrain teachers with a more traditional and rigorous curriculum and more outcome testing, called assessment. In response, federal spending had increased from 8 percent in 1960 to 16 percent in 1985 for public schools while local spending decreased from 51 to 31 percent. This meant greater federal control of local schools in the 1980s, when state educational bureaucracies were "colonized" by Washington (McGuinn 2006).

Reagan had promised to eliminate the Department of Education, decrease the federal role in education, offer tuition tax credits for private schools, create school vouchers, and expand school choice. He accomplished none of these goals in part because the Department of Education published its report *A Nation at Risk* (1983) which concluded that poor public schools put the United States at a military and economic disadvantage. This report confirmed that about 13 percent of all 17-year-olds were functionally illiterate, and this rate was as high as 40 percent among minority teenagers. The College Board's Scholastic Aptitude Tests (SAT) showed a steady decline in scores from 1963 to 1980, and the number and

George H. W. Bush, who promised to be the education president, attends the second working session of the Education Summit in Charlottesville, Virginia, on September 28, 1989. (George Bush Library)

proportion of high scores also dramatically declined. Military and business leaders complained that they spent millions of dollars on remedial education and training in basic skills (reading, writing, spelling, and computation). The problem was serious, but conservatives opposed a larger federal government role in education, teachers unions, and spending hikes. Liberals adopted the opposite positions and opposed school choice and accountability measures. As a result, the Reagan administration accomplished little in public education, and federal and state spending on education increased in 1960–1985 while local spending decreased. President Bush continued Reagan's policies on education and school vouchers, but he claimed to be the "education president" and made school standards and accountability more prominent public issues despite the conservatives' opposition to any federal role in education, to more funding, and even to the Department of Education. Consequently, public school students in the 1980s grew up on a battleground between liberals (and teachers' unions) and conservatives.

Economists noted that adults without a high school diploma were more often unemployed and earned 30 percent less than high school graduates over a lifetime of work. Dropouts also contributed to the rising crime, drug abuse, teenage pregnancy, and public welfare costs. The transformation of U.S. industry in the 1980s meant that few high school dropouts, or even many high school graduates, could achieve middle-class status without postgraduate education or training.

High Education Costs

Access to a middle class lifestyle in the 1980s was heavily predicated on earning a college degree. In 1989, President Bush claimed he would be the "education president" to make American students first in the world in mathematics and science. Yet his 1990 budget sharply reduced student loan funding. Strapped by the rising cost of college, middle-class students and their families found state and federal financial assistance shrinking. Grants, scholarships, and loans were available to the poorest families, but the middle-class student was often ineligible even though college tuition, fees, and living costs increased sharply. Public programs that had served both lower-income and middle-class students shifted their more limited funds to the poorest college students. Legislators found that complaints about inadequate financial aid for families with children in college were more common in the 1980s. The debt burden students had upon graduation from college was heavier each year, and educators noted this influenced their choice of a career. The price tag for a college diploma persuaded many graduates to seek jobs in business rather than in lower-paid teaching or social-service careers. Still the advantages of higher education had increasing appeal, and the number of African American teenagers attending college rose from 16 percent in 1970 to 24 percent in 1988.

Recognizing that the Third Industrial Revolution was based on an explosion of knowledge, some states proposed tax credits or low-interest student loans for middle-class families with children in college and offered more merit-based aid programs. Still many high school students who were not economically disadvantaged found fewer resources available for their college expenses. In 1986, *Time* magazine reported an imaginative program in which dozens of Boston companies raised $5,000,000 to cover tuition costs for public school graduates admitted to college, and then offered the students jobs after graduation. Chicago, Dallas, and Oakland announced similar programs (Lacayo, *Time,* 1986). This was one response to sharp reductions in federal and state student aid, and one effect was to reduce Boston's unemployment rate for adolescents to 4.5 percent, well below the national average for teens of 17 percent.

Despite the rising cost of higher education, the number of college students increased. Although earning a college degree was a demanding, time-consuming, and expensive investment, the benefits were tangible. In 1980, college graduates earned 25.7 percent more in annual income than high school graduates, and this disparity increased to 55.5 percent by 1989, according to the U.S. Census Bureau. This advantage was sustained over a lifetime, especially for those in medicine, law, business, engineering, and computer science. About one-third of college graduates went on to earn an advanced degree in this decade, and the rate of labor force participation rose with the more years of education. The economics of educational and career choices in the United States were more apparent than ever before (Fogg, Harrington, and Harrington 1999).

The Impact of the Cost of College

Good jobs that were once open to smart, ambitious U.S. high school graduates required a bachelor's degree by the end of the 1980s. But as many as one in four high school graduates were academically and economically unprepared for college. Conservative critics like Allan Bloom (*The Closing of the American Mind,* 1987) and E. D. Hirsch (*Cultural Literacy: What Every American Needs to Know,* 1987) aroused a national debate about the inadequate preparation of college students. Making these young people college ready and closing the education gap for poor and minority adolescents was difficult as long as tax-poor cities were dependent on local property taxes to finance public schools. Some states became convinced that investment in early childhood education resulted in savings on future social welfare and criminal justice costs. Enrichment and after-school programs impressed upon students and parents the value of the college degree in the modern U.S. job market. One solution was to direct financial aid to those in need rather than to base assistance on merit.

However, the trend was to shift federal and state funds for American college student aid from grants to loans or tax breaks, and to base financial assistance on merit, not need. This chiefly benefited those who would attend college anyway. It ignored students who needed funds to enroll in college, resulting in an increase of middle-class students in college and a decline in lower-class students. Consequently, there was a shortage of nurses and teachers, for example, in the six New England states, which had 43 community colleges and over 200 public and private colleges in the 1980s. Despite this, the region had lower numbers of high school students who went to college; in Connecticut only 38 percent did so; in Maine, 49 percent; in Massachusetts, 35 percent; in New Hampshire, 44 percent; in Rhode Island, 47 percent; and in Vermont, only 55 percent (Dobelle 2006). This was in contrast to 2005 when more than 68 percent of U.S. high school graduates that year enrolled in a college or university.

THE NEW IMMIGRANTS

Latin American Influx

Jesse Jackson's Rainbow Coalition began as an alliance of African American and white voters, but America in the 1980s was a multicultural, multiethnic polyglot speaking nation. Television acknowledged the mini United Nations character of Brooklyn in Bill Cosby's sitcom *The Cosby Show.* As Gil Troy observed in *Morning in America* (2005), even the Reagan administration accepted the new multicultural United States in pragmatic deals with many racial and ethnic groups. By 1980, more than 11 million immigrants had entered the United States legally since the end of World War II. Americans felt more generous toward new immigrants. Congress liberalized the immigration laws 12 times from 1945 to 1980. The percent of the foreign born in the United States in 1980 reflected the changing nature of immigration. The once dominant Europeans accounted for only 39 percent, but Latin Americans were 33.1 percent and Asians 19.3 percent. By the end of the decade Europeans were only 22.9 percent, Latin Americans were 44.3 percent, and Asians were 26.3 percent of legal immigrants. The 7.3 million immigrants who entered the United States in the 1980s changed the nation as they always had but in new ways that many Americans found disturbing. Most Hispanic Americans were from Mexico, owing to the border's proximity, the tradition of migration north, persistent economic problems in Mexico, and the steady demand for cheap labor in jobs Euro-Americans found undesirable (in farming, industries, restaurants, landscaping, and domestic service). Smaller but growing numbers were from Central and South America, the Caribbean, or Cuba. Most Asians were from the Philippines or China, with smaller numbers from Korea, Vietnam, or India.

Some critics wondered why we admitted immigrants when many American citizens were unemployed. Some suggested that the United States should only admit immigrants with special skills, talents, or wealth. That migration was a global phenomenon involving 175 million people did not appease most Americans. Granting amnesty in 1986 to three million illegal aliens, of whom about 80 percent came from Mexico, remained very controversial. The 1986 amnesty law sanctioned employers for the first time for hiring undocumented workers, and it tightened controls on the Mexican border. Economists argued that immigrants filled service and agricultural jobs that Americans ignored, and they contributed more to the U.S. economy in taxes and spending than they received in welfare payments. Still critics noted that immigrants dominated big-city jobs as janitors and hotel workers, displacing African American workers. Illegal immigration increased by half a million people per year after Congress passed the 1986 amnesty law. But as Nicolaus Mills observed in *Arguing Immigration* (1994), the toy and garment industries in Los Angeles founded in the 1980s by immigrants provided thousands of new jobs.

Political activists in the 1960s and 1970s had conquered de jure discrimination; the problem in the 1980s was de facto institutional discrimination that permeated U.S. society. La Hermandad Mexicana (the Mexican Brotherhood) in Los Angeles and similar community-based organizations challenged the INS for unconstitutional "voluntary" deportation of Mexicans who were denied legal rights. But it was easier to change the law than to change society and the economy. Conservatives in the 1980s, joined by many other American nativists, focused on the more than 20 million illegal or undocumented immigrants who entered the United States between 1945 and 1980. Illegal or undocumented aliens were 21 percent of the foreign-born in the United States. Fears of unemployment, job competition, and declining wages reemerged, and resentment against all immigrants became more common. White Americans felt threatened by religious, racial, and ethnic minorities who sought equality in a pluralistic society. Riddled with misgivings, Americans wondered why these new immigrants were welcomed if they filled our jails and welfare rolls.

In 1980, Miami had the largest percentage of immigrants of any city in the world, and many Florida communities spent millions each year on illegal immigrants in schools and hospitals (Waters and Ueda 2007). However, the shortage of labor in Florida and many other states was relieved by immigrants. Throughout the 1980s growth of the U.S. labor force was largely due to immigrants; for example, the Bureau of Labor Statistics reported 1 in every 17 workers was foreign-born in 1960, but this increased to 1 in 8 by 2000. Foreign-born workers were disproportionately represented in occupations and industries with lower wages and higher risks of injury or death. The Bureau of Labor Statistics also found in 1985 that the foreign born were not more likely to receive government benefits such as state unemployment compensation, food stamps, and pubic assistance. But few critics of the new immigration were persuaded.

The 1980s Melting Pot

Immigration created a society more multicultural than ever before. There were more foreign-born people in the United States: 9.6 million in 1970, but 19.8 million in 1990. In the 1980s, it seemed everyone knew a neighbor, coworker, or classmate who was a Hindu, Sikh, Buddhist, or Muslim. Charlotte, North Carolina, had a new Hindu temple in 1981, and Atlanta built its first one in 1987. Houston had 30 Buddhist temples in the 1980s. About two-thirds of the 3,000 Muslim centers in the United States were built after 1980. America's religious character was changing at the very time the Religious Right championed conservative Christian family values. Although 86 percent of Americans identified themselves as Christians, the United States included 5 million Muslims, 2.5 million Buddhists, 1.3 million Hindus, and millions of Jews, Unitarians, and nonbelievers in 1989.

International adoption increased in the 1980s; about 9,000 U.S. couples or single parents adopted a child from overseas in 1986, often from China, Korea, or Latin America (Nelan 1989). Another remarkable change in the ethnic mosaic was the increased number of Latinos in the United States, growing from 9 million residents in 1970 to 14.6 million in 1980. The 2,000 mile U.S.-Mexico border is unique; no other First World country has a land border with a Third World country. Border crossings accounted for the large number of immigrants from Mexico, as well as those from Central America and South America who entered from Mexico. Although critics of immigration saw Latinos as one group, they were extremely diverse and differed in origins and destinations; most Puerto Ricans settled in the Northeast, Cubans in Florida, Chicanos in California, and Tejanos in Texas. New immigrants from Central America and the Caribbean joined these

Jade Buddha Temple in Houston, 1989. Immigration during the 1980s meant the growth of religions like Buddhism. (Albert Cheng)

groups in the 1980s, but they also were generally poor, with median Hispanic household incomes less than 75 percent of that of Anglos. Lack of education, political weakness, and social and cultural separation were common problems for most Latinos, but by 1980 they mobilized their communities and asserted their rights. Public opinion in 1983 favored sanctions on employers of undocumented immigrants who were believed to cause unemployment, but many businesses depended on or preferred immigrant workers. With a low unemployment rate of about 5 percent, there were few American citizens willing to accept the low wages and difficult conditions in many jobs that illegal immigrants performed.

Prompted by large corporations in 1983, the Reagan administration proposed a temporary guest worker program, but this lacked support in Congress. Latino groups demanded amnesty for undocumented workers, no sanctions on employers, and strict enforcement of labor laws. The 1986 Immigration Reform and Control Act was passed as a compromise, and by 1988, 1.3 million persons had claimed amnesty, most from Mexico. The INS claimed much fraud occurred. In 1988, Wendy's Restaurants in Maryland was the first employer fined for violation of this law. Illegal or undocumented immigrants increased in the 1980s, not only from Mexico but also from Asia, Central America, and the Caribbean. One indication of the growing significance of Hispanic Americans was the first Miss Latino U.S. beauty pageant in 1983, which selected a contestant for the Miss Latin American pageant held in Miami.

By the end of this decade more than 213,000 Jamaicans came to the United States, about 9 percent of that island's population. This forged a West Indian identity, especially in "Caribbeanized" New York City, with a noticeable impact on food, language, religion, and music (Rubin and Melnick 2007). Despite some friction with African Americans, who often resented West Indians' success as entrepreneurs, Jamaicans escaped their country's economic turmoil—largely sweatshop labor and tourism—for U.S. cities. The foreign-born black population of the U.S. grew more than two and a half times by 1980. Although Jamaican immigrants contributed much to the U.S. communities where they settled, in the 1980s they also controlled 40 percent of the drug trade in the United States, according to the Drug Enforcement Agency. Cocaine smuggled from Columbia passed through Jamaica to Europe and America. The *New York Post* blamed the city's crack addiction problem on violent Jamaican drug gangs, which spread to West Virginia by 1988. Rubin and Melnick also reported that Jamaica sent $2 billion worth of marijuana to the United States by the end of the decade, as many reggae songs suggested.

Dominicans first arrived in New York City's Washington Heights section in 1965, but waves of immigrants in the 1980s from the Dominican Republic, an impoverished Caribbean nation of 7.5 million, transformed this working-class neighborhood in north Manhattan. They displaced the Irish and Jewish residents and created a new Hispanic community, the most densely populated neighborhood in the city. About one in three Dominicans was an illegal immigrant who took a dangerous trip in a small boat to Puerto Rico and then posed as a Puerto Rican to come to New York by plane. They joined many Catholic churches and founded small Pentecostal congregations, and they opened grocery and beauty shops or restaurants and travel agencies and worked as street vendors. Many found work in Latin-run garment factories and chains like McDonalds in the Washington Heights Little Dominican Republic ethnic community by word of mouth from friends and relatives (Talwar 2002). About 70 percent of Dominicans were of mixed Hispanic and black ancestry, and they often encountered racial prejudice and had trouble learning English. In 1990, only 39 percent of the Dominicans in New York had a high school diploma, and 6 percent had a college degree. In addition, an estimated 400,000 Haitians lived in the U.S. by 1986, and 70,000 of these in New York City. Drugs, crime, poverty, and overcrowding in the inner city neighborhoods were common problems, as was some conflict with the more established Puerto Ricans in the United States (*Time,* February 17, 1986).

More Diversity

The new phenomenon known as multiculturalism in the 1980s prompted many Americans toward greater acceptance of diverse cultural and social differences. One reflection of this diversity was the requirement in many U.S. colleges that

Illegal Immigration and Jobs

Population growth around the world in the 1980s resulted in increasing immigration to the United States, a problem *Time* magazine reported in its August 6, 1984, cover story, "Mexico City, the Population Curse." The millions of new immigrants who arrived legally in the United States in the 1980s from Mexico, Latin America, Asia, and Africa accounted for the total gain in employment the nation experienced. But illegal immigration had more negative consequences. Illegal immigrants numbered as many as two out of three of those entering the country, estimated to be 3.5 million in 1980 and 5 million in 1987 (Russell 1984). They did take jobs from American workers, although they also filled unwanted jobs and created new jobs. Those most affected by illegal immigration were American workers under age 25, especially the young, native-born men and women without a college degree who were displaced by immigrants entering the labor force at the lowest levels of pay and skills. The *Boston Globe* reported on October 21, 2006, that a study by the Center for Labor Market Studies at Northeastern University found, contrary to some estimates, there was no shortage of unskilled, low-educated workers in the national and state labor markets. The lifetime earning of adults who are not high school graduates declined drastically after 1980, which imposed greater burdens on the taxpayers (Sum and Harrington 2006).

However, the critics of strict enforcement of immigration policies claimed that legal and illegal immigrants usually took jobs that Americans did not want. Studies showed that undocumented immigrants competed most often with low-skilled, low-educated American workers in off-the-books work in agriculture, landscaping, housecleaning, child care, home remodeling, construction, and manufacturing. Often this was in violation of safety, health, wage, and immigration laws. Other critics of strict enforcement of immigration laws included American business leaders who argued that the role of illegal immigrants was a "special and important part of our economic growth" and removing them from the U.S. economy "would be devastating and counterproductive." Thoughtful critics of immigration restriction knew that demonizing illegal immigrants from Mexico, for example, and controlling borders more strictly would increase the cost of everything from landscaping to restaurant meals. The higher costs, if American workers replaced immigrants, would reduce profits, disposable income, investment, and economic growth (Orszag 2006, p. A13).

Despite this debate, most studies of legal and illegal immigration found the newcomers had a positive impact on the U.S. economy. In addition to their energy, creativity, and desire to succeed, immigrants created revenue by spending on housing, education, and consumer goods as well as filling available jobs and paying taxes. Perceptions of immigrants as lazy or taking jobs away from U.S. citizens were old stereotypes. In Texas and California, for example, immigrants had a high level of poverty, about 25 percent in 1989, but a lower level of unemployment than natives. Each year the United States created 300,000 new low-skill jobs that attracted immigrants but authorized only 5,000 visas annually, so the result was increased illegal immigration.

Big Box Discount Stores

In the 1980s the new big box discount stores such as Wal-Mart, Office Depot, Staples, and Home Depot became popular in the United States. Sam Walton, whose 3,500 Wal-Mart discount stores popularized this form of discount merchandising, urged his customers to buy U.S. products in an American store. Later, he was nonplussed when the media exposed an embarrassing secret: Wal-Mart hired illegal immigrants as part-time workers at substandard wages to stock the shelves with low-priced items imported from Third World countries. Critics complained these goods were manufactured for Wal-Mart in brutal working conditions.

Nevertheless, these big box stores reflected America's rampant consumerism. Consumers wielded unusual power in the 1980s; in 1985, they revolted against Coca-Cola's "New Coke." The media covered this minor story as a grassroots revolt by nostalgic consumers who were defending an American symbol and institution. In mammoth shopping malls sprouted across suburbia, customers searched for sales of trendy clothing, faster computers, and new electronic gadgets in one franchise chain store or another. The big box discount store in a suburban or rural mall, with large, free-standing, rectangular single-floor stores surrounded by parking lots, killed off the local Main Street vendors who made the mythical small town a decent place to live, work, and raise children.

Locally owned stores and their employees anchored town and city centers, created new jobs, and generated greater benefits for the local economy than national chains through higher wages for employees, local and state taxes, and purchases from local businesses rather than out-of-state providers. But in the 1980s, many state and local governments wooed the big box retailers with subsidies and tax abatements. Wal-Mart was criticized for permitting senior citizens to park their RVs in the store parking lot overnight because the tourists were loyal customers, despite the lost revenue to local campgrounds. Critics such as the National Trust for Historic Preservation compared Wal-Mart stores to the CVS and Rite Aid pharmacy chains and fast food restaurant chains such as Burger King or McDonalds for their devastating impact on older downtown business district drugstores, cafes, and diners (Mitchell 2006). By 1989, some towns and states, realizing the economic costs in additional police, fire, sewer, water, and highway services, blocked plans for new big box stores. The low-wage, nonunion workers also created new costs in food stamps, welfare, and Medicaid benefits. Others argued against the big box to preserve the rural landscape and to protect the environment and local businesses. Still, consumers seeking bargains at any price found the Big Box stores irresistible.

all students take at least one course about a non-Western culture or an American minority group. These curriculum changes frequently aroused heated debates on campus about the need for diversity, part of what was known as the culture wars. In 1988, critics such as Secretary of Education William J. Bennett charged that the curriculum changes were mere tokenism due to liberal white guilt and were an example of the futility of political correctness. Others claimed the changes were unnecessary because of the increasing numbers of international and non-white students in U.S. colleges and universities. In response, many colleges replaced the History of Western Civilization courses added at the time of World War I with new World Civilization survey courses. Other colleges introduced new ethnic studies and comparative religion courses to meet the demands and to broaden their students' intellectual experiences.

After 1965, federal law gave immigration preference to the relatives of U.S. residents. This meant more chain migration because one legal immigrant could bring his spouse, children, parents, and siblings to America. One immigrant was reported to have brought 83 relatives to the United States (Edwards 2006). By 1989, when migration experts from Central and North America met for a conference in Guatemala City, the refugees were recognized as an international issue more important than illegal immigration.

Latin Americans

The Hispanic American (or Latino) community in the U.S. grew from 78,000 people in 1850 to 18 million by 1980. The number of Mexican immigrants in the United States tripled between 1970 and 1980 and doubled again by 1990. In addition to 15 million people from Mexico, Latinos included 3 million people from the Commonwealth of Puerto Rico, who were exempt from immigration laws. Inexpensive plane fares from San Juan to New York City made the migration process easier. All these Latin Americans shared a language and Roman Catholic heritage but were different from Irish, German, or French-Canadian Catholics in the United States. More like Italian-Americans, they had personal relationships with the Virgin Mary and the saints and less organizational loyalty to their Church. Latinos were a diverse population, not a unified ethnic group.

The largest subgroup of Latinos were 17 million Mexicans, most in Arizona, California, Colorado, New Mexico, and Texas but also found in smaller numbers in many states. Present in the United States before there was a United States, most contemporary Mexican Americans were descendants of the *campesinos* (farmers) who migrated north in the 20th century to find jobs when the economy or politics in Mexico proved too unstable. Their remittances sent back to relatives in Mexico were an important asset in the economy of Mexico. By 1980, Mexican-Americans were the largest foreign-language group in the United States. Many arrived as migrant farm workers in the Southwest. Although Congress

Immigrant farm workers harvest peppers in Gilroy, California. Immigrants were a common and essential agribusiness labor force in the 1980s. (Nancy Nehring)

ended the *brachero* (guest worker) program in 1965, many Mexicans still came illegally as seasonal farm workers. The *mojados* (undocumented aliens) often were exploited by employers because they feared *la migra* (U.S. Immigration and Naturalization Service) and could not complain about job conditions, wages, or housing. The impact of the 1986 mass amnesty law actually increased the number of illegal immigrants in the 1980s, and the INS reported 75 percent of the 3 million people legalized were Mexican. Then they could bring family members by the chain migration process into the United States. This created a long wait for visas, increased INS budgets, more border control problems, and high costs for local and state governments where the immigrants settled. Population growth and economic problems in Mexico probably caused more illegal migration north where millions of acres of new land were irrigated for commercial agriculture.

Most Americans of Mexican origin lived in Texas and California urban centers, or in rural areas of Colorado and New Mexico. For historical reasons, they were suspicious of the Catholic Church but piously devoted to patron saints and the Virgin. Their families were close and extended, bound by culture and language. Gathered in urban barrios, they suffered discrimination and poverty, which strained family relationships. By 1980, *Chicanismo,* a pride in being Mexican-American, stimulated the community as did Chicano activists, writers, singers, and actors. Their major leader was Cesar Chavez who promoted nonviolent economic action. His United Farm Workers organization based in Delano, California, was more a moral crusade than a labor union. Chavez appealed to the conscience of America in a successful five-year national consumer boycott of California grapes. On the other hand, President Reagan recognized the political clout of Mexican-Americans, who took pride in his appointment of Lauro Cavazos, former president of Texas Tech University, as Secretary of Education. He was the first Hispanic to have a cabinet position (1988–1990).

The influence of Mexicans on the United States is most clearly seen in the popularity of Mexican food and restaurants, exceeded only by Italian and Chinese restaurants, since 1980. Californians and Texans were the first Americans to enjoy Mexican food, and the first English-language Mexican cookbook dates to 1914. Taco stands were common in the West and Southwest by 1930, but this new cuisine became a national trend when the Taco Bell chain opened in California in 1954. It became the leading Mexican fast food restaurant business by 1980 with 1,333 stores in 45 states. As a result, the words taco, salsa, nacho, and burrito entered the American language in the 1980s and changed the national diet. Julia Child, the popular French chef on PBS, supported the trend toward ethnic and regional foods, and President Reagan invited Paul Prudhomme, another PBS television chef, to cook his New Orleans Creole cuisine for the Group of Seven heads of state at the economic summit in Virginia in 1983.

Puerto Ricans were the second largest subgroup of Latinos, numbering about 3 million people, primarily in New Jersey and New York. Coming from the Commonwealth of Puerto Rico, they were not immigrants but U.S. citizens and descendants of the rural poor who moved to the mainland since 1900. Although the 4 million people in Puerto Rico supported independence movement at times, most were satisfied to be citizens of the United States. Inexpensive plane fares from San Juan to New York or Boston made their migration easier, but lacking education and skills and speaking only Spanish, many Puerto Ricans in the 1960s were trapped in urban poverty in the United States when they arrived as economic refugees. They lacked a firm ethnic identity, and the debate over statehood or independence for Puerto Rico retarded nationalism, as did the social disruption of relocating from rural agrarian society to urban industrial life. The racial differences that were not an issue at home divided Puerto Ricans by color on the mainland. In the 1980s, many white Puerto Ricans were unsympathetic to demands by black Puerto Ricans for integration. Nearly half of the Puerto Ricans on the mainland lived in poverty, did not speak English, and found the American emphasis on education, competition, and individual achievement alien to their culture. They preferred to speak Spanish and to shop in a neighborhood *bodega* (grocery) or *botanica* (herb and medicine store) rather than in supermarkets. By 1980, many were still poor, and only 1 in 10 Puerto Ricans in the mainland United States was employed in a professional, technical, or management job.

Cubans were the third largest Latino group in the United States, numbering over one million people who left Cuba when Fidel Castro's communist government came to power in 1959. Concentrated in Florida, these political refugees were usually welcomed by the U.S. government and quickly gained legal status. At first they were the well-educated professionals from the middle and upper classes of Cuba, but by 1980, many poor rural Cubans arrived as "boat people." Still devoted to the fate of Cuba and politically conservative, the Cuban-Americans generally made very successful adjustments to life in the United States. As Cuba's population grew from 8.4 million in 1970 to 10.6 million in 1990, the Castro government allowed some dissidents to leave Cuba. In 1983, more than 125,000 Mariel Boatlift people arrived in Florida, including physically and mentally disabled people that Cuba wanted to expel and some criminals. The American media exaggerated the number of criminals among these refugees, but fewer than 350 later committed serious crimes in the United States.

The Cubans transformed Florida and dominated Miami with *panaderias* (bakeries), *famacias* (pharmacies), *mueblerias* (furniture stores), and *bodegas* (groceries). Since 1960, these émigrés were mostly middle class with a strong entrepreneurial tradition reflected by 20,000 independent businessmen in the Latin Chamber of Commerce, Rotary Club, Lions Club, and Kiwanis Club organizations throughout Florida. They dominated the state's construction, service, hotel, tourist, and garment industries as well as Cuban restaurants, bars, radio stations, and newspapers. Fiercely anti-Communist, most Cuban-Americans became patriotic citizens and conservative Republicans. Miami had the second largest number of Cubans of any city in the world by 1987.

American industry leaders who had much influence in Washington in the 1980s insisted that they needed workers, and immigrants knew that wages in California, for example, were four times higher than at home in Mexico. However, as U.S. inflation and unemployment rates increased in the 1980s, illegal immigration became a national issue. The Mexican government generally ignored this problem because migration prevented lower-class turmoil and created a cash flow in the form of remittances sent home, which offset Mexico's trade deficit with the United States.

Immigrants from Asia

About 7.2 million Asian Americans lived in the United States by 1990, or 2.9 percent of the population, which was an increase of 107.8 percent from 1980 census figures of only 1.5 percent. Hawaii, California, and New York had the largest Asian populations, but Asians were also residents in many other states, especially Florida, Illinois, Massachusetts, New Jersey, Texas, Washington, and Virginia.

Since the 1840s, some Chinese lived in the United States but entered mainstream society less than any other ethnic group. In reaction to racial prejudice, they lived in segregated urban neighborhoods, which they self-governed with their own social and welfare societies. They worked hard, saved money, avoided publicity, and remained apart from white America. When Congress eliminated immigration quotas, the Chinese-American population increased to more than 700,000 by 1980. New immigrants and native-born Chinese-Americans seized opportunities in the United States, with 25 percent in college or professional jobs by 1980. Regarded as a model minority, the Chinese valued academic success but some colleges imposed hidden quotas on Asian applicants to maintain diversity and to benefit white students.

Despite some cultural friction between the older Chinese and the new immigrants, the country's Chinatowns in big cities could not house all the newcomers, including ethnic Chinese refugees from Vietnam. Their assimilated children confronted discrimination and were politically active and moved into middle-class suburban communities. Most Chinese-Americans retained the community's ties and spoke Cantonese, Mandarin, or a regional dialect, and many were Buddhists, Confucians, or Taoists. They no longer looked for an eventual return to China and instead became patriotic Americans, but they tended to marry within their own group and retained a separate identity. Since the 1930s, Cantonese cuisine was very popular in the United States, but by the 1980s, Joyce Chen (1917–1994), an immigrant to Massachusetts from Beijing, popularized new Hunan and Szechuan style Chinese food, partly as a result of her popular PBS television program *Joyce Chen Cooks*.

Another spectacular Chinese immigrant success story was An Wang (1920–1990), who came from Shanghai to Boston in 1945. He earned a Ph.D. in physics at Harvard University and founded Wang Laboratories in Boston in 1951. His contributions to computer technology made electronic calculators and desktop minicomputers practical. Dr. Wang employed 30,000 workers in 1985 until IBM's revolutionary PC dominated the industry. In 1983 Wang founded the Wang Center for Performing Arts in Boston and was a leader in many philanthropies (Kenney 1992).

Like the Chinese, the Japanese population in the United States was small and separate until immigration laws changed in 1965. About 320,000 people of Japanese origin lived in the United States in 1941, most in Hawaii. About 110,000 Japanese Americans on the mainland were interned in federal camps during World War II because they were suspected of not being loyal to America. The Supreme Court upheld this action in a 1944 decision, and those interned lost $400 million of their property.

In 1952, Congress ended the ban on immigration and citizenship for Japanese and other Asians, and by 1980, approximately 150,000 Japanese entered the United States. As the Japanese-American community grew to 750,000, most had remarkable academic and economic success. Unlike the Chinese, Japanese immigrants after 1945 were absorbed into American society with little cultural conflict and their children smoothly entered mainstream society. Japanese-Americans in the 1980s were sensitive to discrimination and stereotyping and quick to protest any bias. They rejected the older generation's isolation and

President Reagan signs the Reparations Bill, also known as the Civil Liberties Act, before a group of Japanese-Americans on August 10, 1988. The Act granted $20,000 in compensation to each surviving World War II internee. (Ronald Reagan Library)

submission as they enjoyed middle-class prosperity. Many Japanese-Americans took satisfaction in the Civil Liberties Act of 1988, which granted $20,000 in compensation to each surviving World War II internee.

Another Asian group, the Filipinos, arrived in America by 1900 to find work in service and agricultural industries, but numbered only 175,000 by 1960. After 340,000 arrived in the 1970s, their numbers grew to 600,000 by the 1980s. Several West Coast cities had large Filipino communities, but compared to the Chinese and Japanese, they suffered much poverty and discrimination. They were divided internally by language; some spoke Visayan, others Tagalog or Ilocan. When Cesar Chavez founded his own union for Mexican-Americans, the immigrants from the Philippines merged the AFL-CIO Agricultural Workers Organizing Committee with Chavez's union to form the United Farm Workers in California and elected a Filipino American leader, Philip Verna Cruz, as vice-chairman. Like the Chinese and Japanese, the Filipinos respected the patriarchal family with an authoritarian father and obedient, ambitious, and successful children. Discrimination in American society was a problem, as was the American emphasis on equality, freedom of expression, and individualism, which was at odds with Filipino culture. But these strains on Asian-American families and communities were less significant than the arrival of so many new Asian immigrant in the 1980s.

After the Vietnam War (1964–1975), an estimated 132,000 refugees fled from Vietnam. Over 125,000 Vietnamese were airlifted by the U.S. military to government bases in Guam, Thailand, Wake Island, Hawaii, and the Philippines. Many entered the United States with special INS status and were settled in Arkansas, California, Florida, and Pennsylvania refugee centers, but many Vietnamese relocated in California and Texas. Polls showed only one in three Americans welcomed them. In the 1980s, a second wave of refugees fled Communist control of Vietnam, often escaping in small boats. These "boat people" were sheltered in asylum camps in Thailand, Singapore, Hong Kong, or the Philippines. When Congress passed the Refugee Act of 1980, the Vietnamese government and the United Nations established an orderly departure program that allowed legal emigration for humanitarian reasons or to reunite families. After 1981, about 500,000 Vietnamese came to the United States, and their children adapted more quickly to American society than many Asian immigrants. The immigrants from Vietnam who were ethnic Chinese (called the overseas Chinese) reinvigorated Chinatowns, but Little Saigon areas also developed in San Jose, Houston, Washington, D.C., and in California with small businesses, restaurants, cafes, and beauty shops. Some Chinese Americans complained about Vietnamese youth gang crime in their Chinatown business districts. Laos and Cambodia also contributed immigrants to the United States at the same time the Vietnamese arrived.

Vietnamese-Americans varied widely in education, occupation, and income levels; some engaged in fish and shrimp industries in Texas, Louisiana, Alabama, and Mississippi, others worked in California's Silicon Valley computer industry, or in the professions and small businesses. Despite friction with other Asian-Americans and with racist whites, they became the fifth largest Asian immigrant group in the United States, after the Chinese, Filipino, Asian Indian, and Korean, numbering 1.2 million in the 2000 census. Reflecting these changes in society, Asian-American women, who had placed greater emphasis on racism than sexism, began to support the feminist movement in the 1980s, marching for the ERA and participating in 1984 and 1988 voter registration drives.

Another legacy of the Vietnam War were immigrants from Thailand who numbered only 44,000 in 1980. More than 64,000 Thais arrived by 1990, and more than 66 percent of them lived in Los Angeles. Other Thai-American communities were established in Houston and Philadelphia, which often included people from Laos. The Buddhist temple served as the community center for Thai-Americans by offering Thai language, music, and culture classes for the children of immigrants. The Thai New Year water festival attracted some Americans, and the popularity of Thai restaurants with American yuppies was one of the most striking features of 1980s cuisine.

Asian influences on American culture include the ubiquitous Chinese restaurant, but in the 1980s, Japanese sushi, Indian curry, and Vietnamese pho noodles became fad foods. Martial arts and kung fu had long been popular, and

Boat People

In his acceptance speech at the Republican national convention on July 16, 1980, Ronald Reagan invoked "the boat people of Southeast Asia, of Cuba and Haiti" coming to "this island of freedom, here as a refuge for all those people in the world who yearn to breathe freely." In 1983, the Cuban government responded by allowing religious and political dissidents, the mentally and physically disabled, and some criminals to leave Cuba on the Mariel boatlift. In six months about 125,000 Cubans left the port of Mariel, about 20 miles from Havana, on 500 boats of various sizes in April and May. The U.S. Coast Guard initially prevented them from landing in Florida but had to rescue many of the refugees at sea and settle them in federal government camps created for this emergency. Most of these boat people became productive American citizens (Waters and Ueda 2007).

The term "boat people" also includes Haitian and Dominican refugees from the island of Hispaniola. The bottom dropped out of the Dominican economy in 1982, and the United States reduced sugar quotas by 70 percent from 1981 and 1987, which contributed to the economic distress. Corruption, poverty, inflation, strikes, riots, and political unrest were chronic problems although tourism grew in the late 1980s. Illegal immigration to the United States dramatically increased, and many Haitians crossed the Mona Channel to Puerto Rico in small boats, and then came to the U.S. mainland. The Reagan administration refused to admit Haitian refugees in 1982, and Associate Attorney General Rudolph Giuliani argued they were economic migrants not political refugees. They were returned to Haiti or detained in refugee camps despite widespread criticism. The 1986 overthrow of Haitian dictator Jean-Claude "Baby Doc" Duvalier led to more illegal immigration. In 1990, President Bush ordered thousands of refugees detained at Guantanamo, Cuba, or returned to Haiti. Unlike Cubans, who were seen as political refugees from communism, the Haitians and Dominicans were treated by the United States as economic refugees to be returned or incarcerated. Nonetheless, New York had 1 million Dominicans and Haitians by 1989.

Other boat people were refugees from Vietnam, Laos, and Cambodia who escaped their communist government in boats of all types. Thousands landed in Hong Kong, the Philippines, or other Southeast Asia ports after harrowing voyages and pirate attacks. After long periods in United Nations relocation camps, many entered the United States legally, some to join the 134,000 refugees from Vietnam admitted to the United States by the Ford administration in 1975.

Hollywood exploited this in action movies such as *Shaolin Temple* (1982) with Jet Li, *Heart of Dragon* (1985) and *Police Story* (1986) with Jackie Chan, and *Kung Fu: The Movie* (1986) with David Carradine. Amy Tan's novel *The Joy Luck Club* (1989) and Maxine Hong Kingston's novels *China Men* (1980) and *The Woman Warrior* (1989) were very influential. In sports, tennis champion Michael Chang, figure skater Kristi Yamaguchi, and gymnast Amy Chow were sources of pride for many Americans. I. M. Pei designed the Pyramids of the Louvre in Paris (1989) and Maya Ying Lin designed the Vietnam Veterans Memorial (1982) in Washington, D.C.

Other New Hispanic Immigrants

An exodus of Central Americans continued through the 1980s; many were applicants for political asylum who only needed to make a claim that they faced a "well-founded fear of persecution" at home to obtain INS asylum status. Fleeing through Mexico to the U.S. border, most arrived in Texas or California. In 1988, one INS office in Texas received 1,700 asylum applications a week. By 1989, over 100,000 Nicaraguans lived in the Miami area, and few were willing to return home because of political persecution and civil war between the socialist Sandinistas and the right-wing Contras. Most immigrants spent their savings to travel north and supported relatives in Nicaragua with money earned in the United States. They usually applied for political asylum when the Immigration and Naturalization Service classified them as "out of status aliens" who "entered without inspection," so they were not illegal immigrants but had an ambiguous status. They first arrived in Miami in 1981 as Contras supported by the CIA until Congress prohibited this aid. Some Contra exiles in Florida were wealthy conservatives who anticipated the defeat of the Sandinista government, but most were poor and uneducated refugees.

Guatemala, Central America's largest nation with 10 million people, suffered a violent history under the brutal Gen. Efrain Rios Montt and Gen. Romeo Lucas in 1980–1987. Between 1978 and 1985, 500 university students and professors were killed by the army or government death squads, 100,000 children orphaned, and 38,000 people disappeared. From 1960 to 1996 as many as 250,000 Guatemalans died in more than 600 massacres and murders by the police and soldiers or from torture and political assassinations. The police and army also controlled the drug trade, transferring cocaine from Colombia to the United States. This distraught nation had little access to health care and education, the highest rate

Table 6.1. Selected Immigrants to the United States, 1986 and 1989 (percentage of total)

Country	1986 %	1989 %
Cambodia	2.20	0.60
China	4.20	3.00
Columbia	1.90	1.40
Cuba	5.50	0.90
Dominica	4.40	2.40
El Salvador	1.80	5.30
Guatemala	0.90	1.70
Haiti	2.10	1.30
India	4.40	2.90
Iran	2.70	1.90
Jamaica	3.30	2.20
Korea	5.90	3.10
Laos	1.30	1.10
Mexico	11.10	37.10
Philippines	8.70	5.20
Vietnam	5.00	3.50

Source: Migration Information Source, http://migrationinformation.org/Global Data/countrydata/data.cfm.

of juvenile malnutrition, and the worst human rights record in the Western Hemisphere in 1988. As a result, about one million Guatemalans fled to the United States, most settling in New York, Chicago, Los Angeles, and San Francisco. Because the Reagan administration considered their country's repressive government to be pro-American, the INS rejected 9 out of 10 applications for political asylum and declared them economic, not political, refugees. Consequently, more than 40 percent of the undocumented Central Americans in the United States were Guatemalans (Garcia 2006). Some arrived with a tourist or student visa and simply remained, but most came illegally via Mexico seeking a safe haven. They sent home $700 million a year to family and friends, remittances that amounted to about 15 percent of that country's gross national product. About half of these immigrants lived in California, where some of the teenagers became involved in violent gangs and drug dealing in Los Angeles.

Immigrants from El Salvador were another large group from Central America who arrived in the 1980s when civil war disrupted their homeland. From 30,000 immigrants in 1970, they grew to 100,000 in 1980, and about 560,000 Salvadorans lived in the United States by 1989, or one-sixth of the citizens of El Salvador. They were the fourth largest Latino group in the nation. Many worked hard to send money home, approximately $790 million in annual remittances by Western Union or other means by 1990. Most were poor young people (ages 20 to 49) who settled into Hispanic communities in New York, California, Texas, or Washington, D.C., and fewer than 5 percent ever returned home. In the United States, many of these new Hispanic immigrants pretended to be Mexican to avoid deportation to their war-torn homeland.

Arriving in the United States, Cubans, Mexicans, Guatemalans, and other immigrant groups from Latin America were surprised to find that they were considered Hispanic or Latino by the government. Most Americans did not understand that Hispanic or Latino ethnic groups were as different from each other as Europeans were. They shared language and religion, for the most part, but little else. Each group had their unique dialect, accent, history, culture, cuisine, dress, and traditions. Often they brought to the United States rivalries and suspicions that prevented cooperation with one another as a Latin-American community. By 1990, for example, Latinos amounted to 13 percent of the voters in California but they elected very few public officials. Cubans, on the other hand, were more active in Florida politics, especially on conservative issues.

An estimated 10 million illegal immigrants arrived in the 1980s, many as refugees from South or Central America, as depicted in the film *El Norte* (1983). As a result, the U.S. Hispanic population increased by 53 percent in the 1980s to become the nation's largest ethnic group (22 million) by 1990. Business lobbyists advocated for lax enforcement of immigration laws because they wanted low-wage workers. Conservatives objected to illegal entry by so many poor Latinos and refugees from repressive governments in the Dominican Republic and Haiti, or Central America. In 1986, Congress passed a law offering amnesty

Coyotes y La Migra

More than 4.4 million immigrants entered the United States legally in the 1970s, and this trend increased to 7.3 million in the 1980s. An uncounted number of immigrants entered illegally, most crossing the long Mexico-U.S. border from Latin America or Asia. In comparison, an estimated 300,000 people entered the U.S. illegally from Canada. Professional guides, or *coyotes,* charged immigrants a hefty fee to cross the 2,000-mile (3,200-km) border from Mexico into the United States. Despite intensified efforts to control this problem, the Immigration and Natural-ization Service (*la Migra*) and U.S. Border patrol estimated that *coyotes* brought more than a million illegal immigrants each year into California, Arizona, and Texas. Many of these immigrants were victims of crimes en route (rape, robbery, and murder) or were abandoned in the desert by the *coyotes.* In July 1980, the *New York Times* reported the case of 13 immigrants from El Salvador who died cross-ing the border into Arizona. They had each paid $2,500 to a *coyote* to guide them from Mexico into the United States, but when things went wrong, they were aban-doned to die of dehydration and heat exhaustion where they were hiking just 50 miles west of Phoenix. Such tragedies became common in the 1980s. Most *coy-otes,* whether American or Mexican citizens, were not prosecuted because local courts were swamped with criminal cases. They were caught and released or re-turned to Mexico, except when major crimes were involved. Conservatives, es-pecially in the Southwest, demanded more intensive border patrols and proposed constructing a fence to deal with this problem.

to illegal immigrants who had resided in the United States since 1982. The law also penalized employers of undocumented aliens. In many states, the impact of millions of poor, uneducated illegal immigrants and their children was eco-nomically burdensome because the states were compelled to provide bilingual education, police, and health services to these groups. When Congress passed the Immigration Reform and Control Act (1986), which offered undocumented aliens the right to become resident aliens, 1.4 million people complied by the 1988 deadline. Of these, 71 percent were from Mexico, but the *coyotes* contin-ued their grim trade.

Some Supreme Court decisions had the additional effect of encouraging em-ployers to hire the 8 million illegal immigrants in the United States because the law denied them National Labor Relations Board protection from low pay, un-safe conditions, or the right to union membership. By 2000, 28.4 million immi-grants lived in the United States, a 43 percent increase since 1990. This was more than 10 percent of the total population, the highest percentage in 70 years. As the white population aged, the immigrants provided a young, vibrant workforce and an economic boon to the economy as they started small businesses, rehabilitated housing, and stimulated international commerce. The economist Robert J. Samuelson warned in a *Newsweek* article that poor illegal uneducated immigrants had profited employers but became a burden for local and state government and increased competition for low-wage American workers (Samuelson 2006).

The New Nativism

One result of the white ethnic revival of the 1970s was the creation in the 1980s of a new national myth based not on the Pilgrims landing at Plymouth Rock in 1620 but on millions of European immigrants landing at Ellis Island. In this view, America was a nation of humble but heroic immigrants who struggled to build a modern society. White ethnics claimed a history of toil and trouble and rejected any responsibility for injustices suffered by racial minorities. American culture reflected this new nativism in widespread attitudes of ethnocentrism and xenophobia underlying the triumph of the Christian Coalition and the New Right in the 1980s. For example, Arabs were depicted as evil people in films and television programs. Ethnic stereotypes also dehumanized Africans, Asians, and Latinos. Conservative Protestants were most likely to criticize religious pluralism and to believe in religious exclusivity. Calls for English as the official language and tighter border controls were specific examples of this New Nativism. Although illegal or undocumented immigration statistics were largely a product of the INS bureaucratic process, nativist and many conservative Americans focused on the slightest change in these numbers to decry it as a threat to the nation. They saw immigration, especially from Mexico, as the biggest threat to U.S. culture, security, and sovereignty.

Although Hispanic-Americans encountered considerable prejudice, much of this anti-immigrant backlash was directed at immigrants from Asia. Many nativists saw Asians, who were only about 4 percent of the U.S. population, as non-Christians who were inassimilable and unwilling to adjust to U.S. society. The largest groups among the 10 million Americans from Asia were the Chinese (23 percent), followed by Filipinos (18 percent), Indians (16 percent), Vietnamese (11 percent), Koreans (10 percent), and Japanese (8 percent).

Immigration's Impact on Marriage and Media

In this new multicultural America of the 1980s, marriage became more exogamous than ever before. Increasingly, white Americans married outside their race, religion, and class. In the post-Vatican II Catholic Church, American Catholics were more likely to live within mixed marriages than Protestants. The sociologist Andrew Greeley noted in *Religious Change in America* that 20 percent of Catholics but only 10 percent of Protestants were in mixed marriages by 1985. Americans questioned all forms of authority, including religion, and discarded

During the 1980s Americans increasingly married outside their race, religion, and class. (North Georgia Media)

long-term taboos and traditions. Changing marriage patterns reflected this more diverse and ecumenical society but also contributed to the rising divorce rate. Couples of the same background were less likely to divorce than those in exogamous or interchurch and interethnic marriages, although the *Journal of Marriage and Family* reported that men and women rarely mentioned religious differences as a cause of divorce (Cleek and Pearson 1985). This meant that marriage in the United States in the 1980s became a largely secular institution over which religious institutions had less control. Interreligious and interracial marriage became more frequent and socially acceptable as influences for endogamy declined. Increased immigration meant a wider diversity in marriage partners for more Americans. More than 2 percent of marriages in 1990 were interracial, and ethnic diversity among spouses was much higher.

Another indication of the growing diversity of the U.S. population was the number of foreign-language media in America. The University of Massachusetts in Boston, for example, counted 73 ethnic media outlets in New England, including television programs, radio, cable TV, newspapers, newsletters, magazines, and online web pages. The ethnic media reached about 51 million adults through more than 700 sources across the country and assisted immigrants in becoming acculturated to America. Ethnic media did not compete with mainstream media; on the contrary, it filled a role by covering news that English-language media overlooked (Kilburn 2006).

Religious Pluralism and Immigration

Religious pluralism in the United States increased in the 1980s due to immigration and the secular nature of modern life. The Christian Coalition and New Right found this distressing. Pat Robertson bemoaned the fact that the U.S. was importing Hinduism, and Randall Terry claimed only a wave of intolerance for non-Christian faiths would save the nation. Exclusivists, those who regard their own faith as the only true faith, were a minority, estimated at 20 percent of Americans. There were incidents of vandalism and violence against Hindu, Sikh, and Islamic places of worship, but many cities had examples of ecumenical and interfaith cooperation, and by 1989 about one-quarter of Americans were non-Christians. Those claiming to be Christians peaked at 86 percent in 1989 and began to decline. Religious pluralists, those who accepted all organized faiths as legitimate (if not true), represented a majority of Americans. Clearly the United States was the most religiously diverse nation by the end of the decade.

Hispanic and West Indian immigrants in the 1980s introduced Santeria, a faith most Americans found strange and even primitive. Immigrants from Asia and the Middle East were usually Buddhists, Muslims, Sikhs or Hindus. A surprising number of American Jews and Christians found Buddhism, Hinduism, or Islam so attractive that they became converts. The estimates of the number of Anglo Muslims in the United States range from 20,000 to 50,000 (Smith 1999).

On the other hand, separation of church and state was widely accepted and secularization was a pervasive concept by the 1980s. Many Christians, Jews, Muslims and others struggled to adhere to their faith and the expectations of secular society. The issue of prayer in public schools was hotly debated, although the courts ruled it was unconstitutional and a growing number of Americans favored some type of school prayer. Freedom of religion for prison inmates was a related issue, and in the 1980s many correctional systems accommodated new demands for religious practices.

Events

One positive feature of immigration to the United States in the 1980s was known as the brain drain (Bowen 1986). A British government study revealed that universities in the United Kingdom lost 1,404 faculty and staff members to American universities or industries in 1985. The overproduction of American Ph.D.s in the 1975–1985 period had ended, and the imminent retirement of many senior

Racial Violence in the 1980s

In 1982, white teens killed Willie Turks, an African American transit worker in the Gravesend section of Brooklyn, as he was driving home from work. In 1984, Bernard Goetz, the "subway vigilante," became a symbol of public frustration over urban crime after he shot four African American teens who tried to rob him on a Bronx subway. Many saw Goetz as a hero because they believed the police were ineffective in protecting the public from crime. In 1989, when a 28-year-old New York City investment banker was beaten and raped while she was jogging in Central Park, the media touted this tragedy as an example of rampant African American crime. It was attributed to a gang of African American teens practicing a gang ritual they called "wilding." After a court convicted them, a serial rapist confessed and other evidence cleared the teens of this crime, but the public fear of racial crime in the city had increased.

Despite progress in racial equality in sports, for example, these incidents demonstrate the racial violence and fear so common in the 1980s. Gang violence in Los Angeles, Washington, D.C., and New York evoked "fear laced with guilt, anger tinged with racism" (Lamar 1986). Many of these violent ghetto youths fathered children out of wedlock and committed crimes as rites of passage, a new lost generation "hanging out on street corners, talking tough, listening to music boxes, dealing drugs, slipping into lives of crime." This was explained in part by economics and education. The poverty rate for African Americans was 31 percent, compared to 11 percent for whites, and as many as half the young African American males in major cities were undereducated (18 percent dropped out of high school) and unemployed (40 percent of African American teens). Although African American men were only 6 percent of the U.S. population, they composed half the male prison population.

Another controversial racial incident occurred at Howard Beach in the Queens section of New York City on December 19, 1986. Teenagers in this predominantly Italian American community attacked three African American men who were believed to be stealing a car. One African American man was killed by a passing motorist's car while fleeing his pursuers, another man was hospitalized after being beaten with baseball bats, and a third man escaped. When this case attracted national media attention, Gov. Mario Cuomo appointed a special prosecutor to ease local tensions amid claims of a racial riot. Twelve white youths were indicted on charges ranging from second-degree murder to assault and inciting a riot. The Ku Klux Klan advertised in Howard Beach but was unsuccessful in organizing whites in this community, while the court cases lasted four years. Howard Beach remained in the minds of many Americans a sinister example of racial prejudice or racial crime (Hynes and Drury 1990).

African American conservatives such as Glenn Loury adopted a "blame the victim" attitude, noting the African American teen gang members' "attitudes, history, criminal-arrest records and other qualities" made them difficult to employ.

Continued on next page

Racial Violence in the 1980s, Continued

Others blamed the social pathology caused by public welfare and moral decline, or the migration of middle-class African Americans to the suburbs, which deprived urban teens of positive role models. Michael Harrington offered an explanation in *The New American Poverty* that the "huge migration from the rural south . . . was much too great for a society that was switching from smokestacks to services" (Harrington 1984). Drug dealing provided high wages and self-esteem for poor young African American, Latino, and white men outside the mainstream, but this fueled crime and violence in cities. This contributed to the breakdown of families, teenage pregnancy, and a cycle of poverty. Liberals and conservatives debated the solution to racial violence in the 1980s, but experts on both sides agreed that joblessness and poverty were the main causes of crime.

The incidence of crime and the effects of the crackdown on crime were reflected in the U.S. Department of Justice reports on violent crime rates. They were very high in the 1980s, more than twice as high as in 2005. New high-security "super-max" prisons, like those in Marion, Illinois, and Pelican Bay, California, opened by 1989 to incarcerate high-risk inmates. A disproportionate number of inmates were African American or Hispanic, and the number of women sent to prison rapidly increased in the 1980s. Criminologists speculated that females were committing the same crimes as men did because of new ideas about equality for women. In their zeal to win the War on Drugs, some officials exceeded their authority in a sexist and racist prenatal health program in 1989. The Charleston, South Carolina, police and prosecutors cooperated with the Medical University of South Carolina to eliminate drug abuse by pregnant women. This included nonconsensual drug testing of pregnant patients, which led to the arrests of about 60 women, one of whom went into childbirth handcuffed to the hospital bed. The women investigated were poor and African American while white women using drugs during pregnancy were overlooked.

The victims of crime were most often unmarried African American and Hispanic men and least often married whites. Most prison inmates had abused drugs or alcohol, and 8 out of 10 drug users were white, but most of those arrested for drug offenses were nonwhite. Since the Supreme Court restored the death penalty in 1976, more than half those under sentence of death were nonwhite men. Arrests, crimes reported to the police, court trials, firearm-related offenses, drug offenses, and prison sentences all increased sharply in federal and state courts in the 1980s (U.S. Department of Justice).

American professors made these young and well-educated immigrants very welcome. The National Science Foundation counted 1,001 scientists and engineers who came from Britain in 1986, lured by higher salaries, superior research facilities, and more professional opportunities. The INS also reported increasing numbers of educated people from Ireland and Israel who overstayed their visas to work as professionals in America. As the number of international students attending graduate schools in the United States increased, many of these young scholars saw no need to return home and preferred to remain after earning their degrees.

Some immigration experts even proposed luring immigrants with specialized skills and training to the United States by facilitating their visa, green card, and citizenship status as Canada and other countries had done. About one-quarter of the immigrants who arrived in the 1980s had college degrees, a human capital migration of highly educated professionals and technical workers. The brain drain from China, Cuba, Korea, India, the Philippines, and the Soviet Union included scientists, engineers, physicians, and other skilled workers for U.S. university, health care, electronics, and management jobs. Many immigrants from Asia were often better educated than the U.S. population; by the 2000 census, 44 percent had a college degree compared to 24 percent of all Americans. One estimate found more than 6,000 immigrant Muslim physicians living in the United States in 1980. By 1989, about one in three engineers and scientists working in California's Silicon Valley had been born abroad, including immigrants from Britain, China, India, Israel, Lebanon, Peru, Poland, and Vietnam (Iyer 1985).

American popular culture also reflected the new international, interracial society in the 1980s as Sushi bars and new Cuban, Vietnamese, Indian, Korean, and Thai restaurants opened in major cities. Cable television companies offered Spanish-language channels, and most cities had foreign-language radio programs. Banks, hospitals, public transportation systems, and government agencies offered information in foreign languages. The term mixed marriage no longer only referred to a Catholic who married a Protestant or Jew, but more likely to interracial or international couples.

Native Americans

Sociologists have long claimed that overt racism is more common where the majority feels threatened by a sizable minority. This may explain the racial discrimination Native Americans encountered in the Sunbelt states in the 1980s. Native Americans constituted the most numerous minority in most western states, especially in areas bordering Canada, where few Latinos, African Americans, or Asian-Americans lived. Casual use of racial epithets for Native Americans, and the misunderstanding by whites that reservation land, fishing or hunting rights, and exemption from some taxes were a form of welfare and reverse discrimination only added to the problems. Long after African Americans in the South won civil rights and acceptance by whites, Native Americans in Montana and other western states routinely encountered racial prejudice and official acts of discrimination in registering to vote. In 1986, a federal court ordered a new system of elections in Montana to protect the constitutional rights of Crow and Cheyenne voters whom Congress had enfranchised in 1924.

However, by 1980, the decline of racism and revival of ethnic pride led to claims by many individuals and groups that they were Native Americans. The Bureau of Indian Affairs (BIA) developed a process for these claims for tribal membership and recognition. This trend was also inspired by the interest in public benefits for members of tribes in the 1980s, especially casino gambling and land claims. Native American descendant recognition recruitment organizations stimulated petitions for tribal recognition by people with dubious claims to Indian heritage. The Maryland Commission on Indian Affairs, responding to claims in 1987 by Piscataway people for tribal recognition, proposed a state law regulating the process. The debate continued throughout the 1980s as the *Baltimore Sun* reported on September 30, 1993. New Jersey, Connecticut, New York, Massachusetts, and Rhode Island encountered similar efforts as Native American minorities asserted their rights in the 1980s. It had become popular and profitable to be a minority.

Native Americans in the Southeast had long been neglected, but North Carolina had the largest Native American population in the South, and one of the largest in the United States by 1980. Although the BIA only recognized one tribe in North Carolina, the state recognized seven other communities as tribal entities. The eastern band of Cherokees lived in the Great Smoky Mountains, but most other Native Americans lived in Piedmont near the Virginia border and on the coastal plain near South Carolina. Since 1960, all North Carolina Native Americans had pressed for democratic rights as they entered industrial jobs and were energized by the civil rights and Red Power movements and pan-tribal or kin networks. When North Carolina established a state Commission of Indian Affairs in 1977, the way was clear for state funds to support Native American cultural activities in arts, crafts, historical preservation, and pow-wows. By 1980, about 15,000 North Carolina Native Americans were urban residents and enjoyed more economic prosperity, but all Native American communities continued to struggle with poverty, prejudice, and social problems in this decade. However, Native Americans' pride in their culture assumed many forms in the 1980s. In some states, courts and corrections officials accepted demands by Native American inmates for recognition of their religions.

Gambling and Native Americans

After the Cabazon Indians began offering high-stakes bingo on their reservation in 1983, local and California state officials repeatedly went to court to stop this illegal gambling. Arthur James Welmas, chairman of the small Cabazon Band of Mission Indians, won a 1987 decision by the U.S. Supreme Court that laid the foundation for the Native American gaming industry. The ruling that states could not regulate gambling on reservations led to prosperity and political power for hundreds of tribes. By 1980, other Native American people opened tax-free cigarette and liquor stores on reservation land until the Supreme Court ruled that states could collect taxes on tobacco products sold to non–Native Americans on the reservations. In response to controversies in many states, Congress passed the Indian Gaming Regulatory Act in 1988, which opened the way for Indian gambling casinos across the United States. This brought new jobs and recognition to Native Americans (Lane 1995).

Just as concerns about the impact of immigration led Congress to pass the Immigration Reform and Control Act in 1986, the expanding drug epidemic led to the Anti-Drug Abuse Act in 1988. This law created the White House Office of National Drug Control Policy. William J. Bennett was appointed by President Bush as the director, known as the drug czar. Bennett's goal was to eradicate illicit drug use, trafficking, manufacturing, and drug-related violence, crime, and health problems. Smuggling drugs into the United States had become an international issue. By 1990, the United States had the largest prison population in the world.

RELIGIONS IN AMERICA

Acknowledging Diversity

Americans in the 1980s continued to regard the United States as a Christian nation despite the significant presence of Muslims, Buddhists, Hindus, Jews, Mormons, and other non-Western or non-Christian religions. Although Americans claimed to respect the religious faiths of non-Christians, most people had little understanding of these faiths. Many Americans accepted cultural pluralism without making an effort to appreciate the new religious and cultural diversity in this country. Few bothered to learn much about these minority religions or to engage in constructive dialogue with them, although the right of diverse groups to worship freely was generally accepted. The impact of immigration aroused considerable discussion in the 1980s but more in terms of racial and ethnic differences than in terms of religious differences. Because American culture is a product of a distinctive Christian (largely Protestant) tradition, this heritage created many tensions about religious diversity. By 1990, the United States had new populations of 527,000 Muslims, 401,000 Buddhists, 227,000 Hindus, 23,000 Taoists, and 13,000 Sikhs.

One controversy in religion occurred in 1989 when the National Endowment for the Arts (NEA) granted $15,000 to Latino artist Andres Serrano for his photograph *Piss Christ,* an image of a crucifix submerged in urine. The artist insisted this was a criticism of religion degraded by kitsch, but members of Congress and the Religious Right were outraged that a federal agency funded this "sacrilege." Senators Jesse Helms and Alfonse D'Amato denounced the image as blasphemy, but when liberals defended it as artistic freedom and freedom of speech, another culture wars battle resulted. Although some clergy defended Serrano, conservatives also criticized his *Madonna and Child II* (1989) image.

The changing role of women in American society had an influence on religion by the end of this decade. There was an increasingly prominent representation of females as a sacred symbol in most religions. In Judaism, the Conservative and Reform theologians revised prayer books to emphasize the female in sacred matters, the role of matriarchs, and the feminine attributes of God—compassion, forgiveness, understanding, and love. The first female rabbis appeared in 1974. Roman Catholics saw major trends in the worship of the Virgin Mary as the mother of Jesus. Women served as lectors and on parish councils, and the altar girl was more common. Catholics heard more demands for the ordination of women. Most Protestant churches accepted women as ministers, and in general, women assumed more visible roles in most parishes and churches in the 1980s (Allitt 2004).

Religious Pluralism and Diversity: Religious Conflict and Ethnocentrism

Approximately three out of four American adults self-identified as religious in polls but did not necessarily belong to or attend a place of worship. About 8 out of 10 Americans identified as a Christian, but the presence of millions of non-Christians made obsolete the deeply-rooted idea that the United States was or should be a Christian country. How Americans adapted to this new reality became a key issue in the 1980s. Many claimed to respect the faiths of others, but few Americans understood very much about those religions. Diversity was assumed to be good, a positive feature of the multicultural society, and even one that strengthened U.S. society. But many questioned how well Americans were moving beyond tolerance, respect, and civil liberties to acceptance of other religions and cultures.

Immigration increased dramatically in this decade; in sheer numbers it grew from 4.4 million people between 1971 and 1980 to 7.3 million people between 1981 and 1990. The origins of these immigrants also changed from Europe to Latin America and Asia. Partly as a result of immigration, the U.S. population increased from 203.3 million people to 248.6 million people in 1990. Imports exceeded exports during this period. For many Americans these changes, attributed to the new global economy, seemed strange and even troubling. Increasing ethnocentrism, xenophobia, and nativism led to racial or religious conflict and more so-called hate crimes.

Christianity

American Protestants in the 1980s often referred to themselves as Christians, especially those in conservative, evangelical, and fundamentalist churches. This reflected the born-again Christian movement (about 7 percent of all adults) and the policies of the New Right and organizations such as the Christian Coalition. The mostly all-white traditionalist Southern Baptists became the largest Protestant church in the 1980s. Mainstream or liberal Protestants used the term Christian less often and emphasized their denominational affiliation, for example, Episcopal, Unitarian, or Presbyterian. Christians in the United States, the Roman Catholics and Protestants, amounted to about 76 percent of all Americans by 1989. Although most Americans did not attend religious services regularly, many held a traditional belief that the United States was a Christian nation.

The chaplains who opened state legislature and congressional sessions were Protestant ministers and Catholic priests, or occasionally rabbis. Hotel rooms provided Bibles. The issue of prayer in public schools remained a controversial and perennial topic in politics. Since 1957, the U.S. currency has borne the words "In God We Trust." The news media routinely reported on church events and remained deferential to church leaders. Clearly, religion, usually Christian religion, was a well established feature of U.S. society during the 1980s.

Roman Catholics

Anti-Catholicism was so deeply rooted in American history that few Americans realized that Roman Catholics predated Protestants in North America by more than a century. They numbered only 40,000 in 1790 but became the largest religious denomination in the United States by 1860. After the election of John F. Kennedy as president in 1960, American Catholics had entered mainstream U.S. society and no longer felt themselves to be a minority or an immigrant church. By 1989, Catholics numbered about one-fourth of the population and grew rapidly as Hispanic immigrants, about 57 percent Catholic, arrived. The films of Catholic directors like Robert Altman, Francis Ford Coppola, Martin Scorsese, and John Huston used the rituals of Catholicism to argue that this distinctive spiritual outlook coexists with American visions and values. Hollywood made these movies—like *The Verdict* (1982), *Agnes of God* (1985), *Prizzi's Honor* (1985), and *Mass Appeal* (1986)—because American audiences were still curious about the arcane rituals of the Roman Catholic Church.

Since the Second Vatican Council in 1965, the Catholic hierarchy had encouraged ecumenicalism and outreach to other religions. The popular, conservative, anticommunist Pope John Paul II (1978–2005) visited the United States in 1979 and 1987, which did much to diminish anti-Catholicism and to promote his faith. Americans of all faiths grieved when the Pope was shot in Rome in 1981

Pope John Paul II talks with President Ronald Reagan and his wife Nancy at the Vizcaya museum in Miami, Florida, on September 10, 1987. (Ronald Reagan Library)

by a Turkish radical. But U.S. Catholics, like Protestants, had liberal–conservative conflicts; traditionalists preferred the Mass in Latin and not eating meat on Friday, and Gallup polls indicated that three-quarters of American Catholics followed their own conscience rather than the moral teachings of their Church on social issues such as divorce, abortion, contraception, homosexuality, and other sexual or family issues. Attendance at parochial schools, Mass, and confession declined, but Pope John Paul II confirmed traditional church doctrines. Conversely, conservative Catholics found they had much in common with the Christian Coalition and the New Right, who welcomed their cooperation (O'Toole 2008).

Judaism

Jews were the main challenge to the American idea that this was a Christian society. Because of the important role American Jews had in educational, economic, and cultural achievements, they occupied a central place despite pervasive anti-Semitism. Even the Holocaust, depicted in the Oscar-winning film *Sophie's Choice* (1982), was not an important issue to most Americans. In the 1960s, most American Protestants and Catholics had avoided social interaction with Jews while conceding to them a third option as a major religion. The term Judeo-Christian was used to convey the belief that all three faiths had much in common. In public discourse, Americans routinely spoke of churches and synagogues by the 1980s. Approximately 5 million Jews lived in the United States in the 1980s, but this was a declining population due to a lower birth rate, high intermarriage rate (40 to 50 percent) with non-Jews, and the fact that only one in three families raised their children as Jews. For many American Jews, their ethnicity was Jewish, but fewer than half belonged to a synagogue and one-quarter joined another religion. On the whole, they tended to support liberal causes and social reform, although some prominent Jews took conservative positions. Anti-Semitism had declined since 1960, and was unacceptable in most social circles in the 1980s, but anti-Semitic crimes remained a regular feature in newspaper and television reports every year.

When the Soviet Union allowed Jews to emigrate in 1988, about 19,000 Russian and Ukrainian Jews came to the United States (Nelan 1989). This increased to 80,000 the next year, which expanded the American Jewish population, especially in New York City, Boston, Chicago, Los Angeles, and San Francisco. Pressured by Israel, in 1989 the United States imposed a limit of 50,000 Soviet Jews per year in an effort to encourage migration to Israel. Many of these political refugees were part of the intellectual brain drain benefiting the United States, but some brought the Russian Red Mafia criminal organization to New York. Unlike most American Jews, who were liberals, the Soviet Jews arriving in the 1980s tended to be more conservative. American Jews were also surprised by the support Pat Robertson, Jerry Falwell, and the New Right expressed for Israel. The result was that the United States had the largest Jewish population in the world but one that was more secular and more diverse (Bowen 1989).

The Church of Jesus Christ of Latter-day Saints

The Mormon Church, officially known as the Church of Jesus Christ of Latter-day Saints, expanded rapidly in the 1980s due to a high birth rate and extensive proselytism. Founded by Joseph Smith in New York in 1830, the Mormons established their main colony in Salt Lake City, Utah, by 1847 under the leadership of Brigham Young. Although Mormons follow many of the tenets of Christianity, they are not a Protestant denomination and remain outside the mainstream Judeo-Christian organizations of U.S. Protestant, Catholic, and Jewish faiths. By the 1980s, they numbered about 12 million members in the world and became the fourth largest religious body in the United States with 4 million members. Most of the Church's income is from collections (called fast offerings), annual tithes (or 10 percent of a member's income), and income from investments and real estate. By 1990, this was estimated at $30 billion, including land, an insurance company, a large radio chain, and a daily newspaper in Utah.

Since 1978, African Americans have been accepted as full members of the church, which stimulated Mormon missionary efforts under the leadership of the church president Spencer W. Kimball (1973–1985) and his successor Ezra Taft Benson (1985–1994). The Mormon lifestyle is rigorous, with no alcohol, tobacco, caffeine, or gambling; limits on homosexuality; and formal clothing required at weekly worship. Public welfare is discouraged, but church social welfare programs are extensive.

The practice of polygamy, which the church condemned in 1890, remained the most well-known and controversial aspect of this church and led to much skepticism about Mormonism by many Americans. Although most Mormons were patriotic conservative Republicans, many Catholics and Protestants, especially conservative evangelicals in the New Right, considered them to be a cult because they follow nonbiblical scripture and accept direct revelation. The LDS church also had a more flexible policy on abortion, which they discouraged but did not ban. Because of their own history as a persecuted minority, the Mormons defended freedom of expression for all minority groups and favored teaching evolution and the separation of church and state more than evangelical leaders like Pat Robertson. Euthanasia and school prayer were other issues on which Mormons were divided. The most well-known Mormons in the 1980s represented the diversity of this faith—Republican senator Orrin Hatch (1977–), Democratic senator Harry Reid (1985–) and Democratic representative Morris Udall (1961–1991). Mormons lived in every region but were most numerous in the Western states (Millet 2007).

American Muslims

It is unclear how many Muslims lived in the United States in the 1980s because no statistically valid survey was taken; estimates range from 500,000 to 3 million. Two out of three Muslims were immigrants to the United States or were the children of immigrants. Conversion, chiefly by African Americans and American women who married Muslims, meant that by the end of this decade four out of five American Muslims were born in this country. Arabs from Syria or Lebanon had been in the United States since 1875 but in very small numbers. But the first Muslims in the United States were an unknown number of Islamic Africans, perhaps as high as 20 percent, brought from West Africa as slaves by 1800 (Smith 1999).

The slaves were compelled to become Christians, but in the 1980s, thousands of African American Christians joined Elijah Muhammad's Nation of Islam that Louis Farrakhan revived. In addition, at this time Arabs who were Muslims (or Islamic) began to arrive in growing numbers from the Middle East, North Africa, East Europe, Asia, and the Caribbean. Most settled in New York, New Jersey, Illinois, and California. A high birth rate and the increasing number of international students from Asia and the Middle East attending U.S. colleges and universities added to these Islamic communities.

U.S. foreign policy in the Middle East had a profound impact on the prejudice faced by the Muslims from 60 nations living in the United States. American movies in the 1980s portrayed Muslims in a comical or disparaging manner, as in *Cheech and Chong's Next Movie* (1980) and *Wrong Is Right* (1982), or as terrorists in *Wanted Dead or Alive* (1987). Bias in the media and in U.S. school textbooks added to the anti-Muslim prejudice, and many Americans erroneously believed that all Muslims were Arabs and all Arabs were Muslims. Practicing their faith in the secular United States was often a problem.

There are almost one billion Muslims in the world, about 20 percent of the world population, and most are not Arabs. By 1980, about 1.5 percent of the U.S. population was Islamic, estimated at 3.3 million people, who worshipped in 600

The controversial Nation of Islam leader Louis Farrakhan speaks at a rally at Madison Square Garden in October 1985. (Stephen Ferry/Liaison/Getty Images)

mosques or Islamic centers (Haddad 1991). Many arrived in the 1960s from Palestine, Egypt, Syria, Lebanon, Iraq, Malaysia, Albania, Yugoslavia, or the Soviet Union. By 1987, U.S. colleges and universities admitted over 150,000 Muslim students, and as many as 75,000 American women married Muslims and converted to Islam. Thousands of African Americans in the Nation of Islam added to the number of Muslims in America. By the end of the decade, Muslim populations were established in New York, New Jersey, Pennsylvania, Michigan, Texas, California, and New Mexico. American support for Israel and foreign relations in the Middle East frequently provoked anti-Muslim attitudes and occasional violence and crime against Muslims in the United States.

RAINBOW NATION: MULTICULTURALISM, RACE RELATIONS, AND CRIME

Threats on the Homefront

By 1988, many Americans felt they were inundated by crime as the media focused a spotlight on violent criminals, a disproportionate number of them African

American or Hispanic. The War on Drugs meant that 6 out of 10 prison inmates in 1989 were convicted of drug offenses, often nonviolent and minor. The dominant political issues of the past had disappeared from view as the Soviet Union dissolved and communism collapsed. Lee Atwater, George Bush's campaign manager in 1988, created a television spot linking Massachusetts governor Michael Dukakis, the Democratic presidential nominee, with Willie Horton, an African American man in a Massachusetts prison for the rape and assault of a Maryland woman while out on a prison furlough. This TV ad made Willie Horton a household name, and the presidential campaign became a referendum on law and order. Experts claimed Bush won 54 percent of the vote because of this issue.

Responding to the public outcry for a crackdown on crime, many states revised laws on capital punishment after the Supreme Court ruled in the *Furman v. Georgia* case (1972) that a jury-imposed death sentence was racially biased. The death sentence was constitutional, and 40 of the 50 states imposed death sentences. With the Court's approval, hundreds of convicts were executed, a majority of them poor African American or Hispanic men. By 1984, 12 states had cracked down on crime; New York mandated long sentences for drug offenses and California limited parole and imposed mandatory sentences. Consequently, the U.S. prison population increased from 10,000 in 1970 to 503,000 in 1985 and 750,000 in 1990, largely composed of young African American and Hispanic male drug offenders. Many prisons were filled beyond capacity, forcing corrections officials in 19 states to grant 18,617 prisoners early release in 1985 (*Time,* June 6, 1986).

The international drug smuggling business, much of it from Colombia to the United States, expanded rapidly in the 1980s, and urban youth gangs sold these drugs on the streets. By 1989, Los Angeles had 150,000 teenagers in more than 900 gangs, whose income was mostly from dealing drugs. Their automatic weapons made drive-by shootings a regular feature in newspapers and television news broadcasts in New York, Washington, D.C., Los Angeles, and moved to Atlanta and other Sunbelt cities. William Bennett, the new drug czar appointed by President Bush, had a $2.5 billion budget to control the drug epidemic, but the Bush administration opposed gun control legislation to placate conservative supporters. Violence between African American, Hispanic, and Asian gangs in schools and on the streets became a major problem for the police (Carney, *Time,* 1986).

Crime

The war against drugs had few victories in the 1980s. Hollywood glamorized drug use in films like *Less than Zero* (1987), *Bright Lights, Big City* (1988), and *Slaves of New York* (1989), and cocaine or crack reached epidemic proportions in poor African American and Hispanic urban neighborhoods. Much crime, especially robbery, burglary, auto theft, shop lifting, purse snatching, and mugging, was by drug addicts. Ghetto and barrio youths out of school and unemployed found drug dealing and drug use attractive. By 1990, government on all levels spent $15 billion a year in the war against drugs, about 75 percent of this for police, courts, and prisons. The crackdown on illegal immigration was in part a crack-down on drug smuggling. But many experts agreed most crime was due to poverty, unemployment, and lack of education. They said stable families, good schools, and good jobs—not prisons—were the solutions to prevent crime and violence.

According to the U.S. Department of Justice, African Americans were more likely to be murdered than whites, and most African American murder victims were killed by African Americans. The residents of poor urban neighborhoods, most of whom were law-abiding, were the victims of most crime in the 1980s. The destabilizing effect this violence had on communities caused people to flee to the suburbs, businesses to close, and neighborhoods to deteriorate in a de-structive cycle. American society produced goods but not good jobs with good wages. The gap between society's haves and the have-nots widened. Critics like Clarence Thomas complained that adolescent parents became grandparents before age 40, high school dropouts turned to drugs and crime, and rap music glamorized violence. African American communities were under siege, but most white communities were immune and indifferent (Foskett 2004).

Events

The $16 million Reagan inaugural was "the costliest in the country's history," with the rich and powerful from American business arriving by so many pri-vate jets that Washington National Airport could not accommodate them all (Abrams 2006). In the middle of an economy with double-digit unemployment and double-digit inflation, American conservatives and corporate elites celebrated the Reagan Revolution in 1981. The new mood was consumption and materi-alism. Skeptical of government planning, the triumphant neoconservatives be-lieved poverty would be overcome only by sustained economic growth free of federal and state restrictions on business. But Reagan, rooted in the New Right, was successful because he won over the center as an amiable, pragmatic, and accommodating leader. Democrats underestimated him as an aging movie star, but his model was Franklin Delano Roosevelt more than Calvin Coolidge.

The most striking feature of the 1980s economy may have been bipolarization, with more high income jobs and more low income jobs, as middle income jobs decreased dramatically. This was seen in the employment decline in heavy manufacturing industries, blue-collar occupations, and the employment in-crease in high technology manufacturing and service-producing industries, the white-collar occupations. In 1973, for example, 43 percent of U.S. full-time wage workers were employed in blue-collar occupations, compared with only 35 percent in 1982. The economy was dynamic but seemed to create the wrong types of jobs. Readjusting to the new global economy was painful for many American families.

Conservatives and Multiculturalism

Irving Kristol, Gertrude Himmelfarb, Norman Podhoretz, and like-minded liberals became disillusioned by 1980 with social changes in the nation. Michael Harrington coined the term neoconservatives to describe these leaders of the rightward drift of his fellow intellectuals. But this group also included people like the movie star Charlton Heston, who had expressed reservations about the liberal agenda since President Johnson's Great Society and the War on Poverty in the 1960s. Multiculturalism was one issue they abhorred because it increased tensions between racial, ethnic, and social classes. Neoconservatives charged that promoting separatism and special privileges for the poor, immigrants, and minorities violated the principles of equal opportunity. Heston vigorously objected to the National Endowment for the Humanities celebration of many cultures. He criticized the assumption of the superiority of certain groups, rejecting the dominant culture and assimilation "to the point where the ethical foundations of Western Civilization are now in question" (Raymond 2006).

Neoconservatives blamed academics and the media for imposing multiculturalism on society as politically correct. They urged Americans to return to traditional Anglo-American family values and to retain unchanging political ideals in the volatile post–Cold War era that ushered in the conservative resurgence and the Reagan Revolution in the 1980s. Celebrating individuality, they saw multiculturalism promoting division and hate, not tolerance and approval. As always, America attracted young ambitious immigrants, but in the 1950s 53 percent of immigrants were from Europe, and in the 1980s only 11 percent were Europeans while the large numbers came from Asia or Latin America. Most Americans took a conservative position on this, and most polls showed a majority favored limits on immigration for a variety of reasons. Blaming immigrants for economic problems was a conservative habit; President Hoover had blamed Mexicans for California's high unemployment in 1930.

Although liberals emphasized the economic issues, the conservative opposition to immigration concentrated on deeper cultural issues. Some pointed out that immigration was successful in the past because the nativist backlash limited immigration levels and gave preference to more assimilable groups from European countries. President Reagan's adviser Patrick Buchanan saw the United States as a Christian Anglo-American nation with core values threatened by the new immigrants. He considered the Third World to be a vast global underclass filled with the social pathologies seen in U.S. ghetto communities rather than a

Green Card Marriage Fraud

In 1986, Congress passed the Immigration and Marriage Fraud Amendment Act to prevent fake marriage schemes. Each year about 160,000 immigrants married U.S. citizens, which qualified them for a visa, an INS green card, and citizenship. In some cases the immigrant paid an American (sometimes as much as $25,000) to enter into the false marriage, and they divorced after receiving the important green card. One survey by the Immigration and Naturalization Service (INS) estimated 30 percent of the marriages they investigated in the 1980s were sham marriages, but later studies reported only 8 percent were fraudulent.

When the INS suspected fraud, investigators separately interviewed both parties, who were expected to answer as many as 200 questions providing explicit, intimate details about their relationship to prove the marriage was legitimate. A two-year testing period or conditional residency was imposed sometimes to verify that the couple intended to live in a real marital relationship and to prove this intention by their actions. An alien found guilty of a fraudulent marriage was deported, and the U.S. citizen or permanent resident who conspired with an alien to evade immigration laws by means of a fraudulent marriage was charged with a federal crime. Those found guilty of this felony were liable to five years imprisonment and/or a $250,000 fine. Some Americans operated a commercial enterprise, marrying and divorcing one immigrant after another for hefty fees. In other cases, Americans took a vacation to a foreign country, during which they were paid to marry an alien. Hollywood depicted this scheme in the romantic comedy *Green Card* (1990).

problem of advanced industrial nations (Diggins 2007). Much of the conservative criticism focused on Latinos more than Asians, whom many saw as model minorities with strong family values (Abrams 2006).

The American Immigration Control Foundation was founded in Virginia in 1983 by conservatives devoted to reducing uncontrolled immigration. Among the books they published was Lawrence Auster's *The Path to National Suicide* (1990), which argued that multiculturalism was not merely an effort to be more inclusive of U.S. historic minorities but rather a misguided attempt to overcome the educational deficiencies of African Americans and other minorities. Auster claimed it was a radical ideology to systematically dismantle America's national identity.

African Americans and Multiculturalism

The civil rights movement diminished in the 1980s, but Jesse Jackson was a presidential candidate, Colin Powell was chairman of the Joint Chiefs of Staff,

African American Conservatives

Only 14 percent of African American voters supported Reagan in the 1980 election, but the conservative atmosphere influenced many African Americans. One indication of the conservative influence was the establishment of 400 private Christian schools for African American children from Atlanta to Los Angeles. African American churches and organizations started these small Christian academies as a growing number of African American parents shunned public schools. African American enrollment in traditional private schools and independent secular schools also increased in the 1980s, according to the *Christian Science Monitor* (Spaid 1996). Most students came from middle-class families who valued a Christian environment and learning about African American history.

Popular culture revealed the influence of African American conservatives in the popular TV sitcom, *The Cosby Show,* which reflected the Reagan-era emphasis on traditional family values. With a stable, middle-class black family headed by a physician father and a lawyer mother, this 1980s top-rated show appealed to every demographic group and challenged African American stereotypes. Dr. Cliff Huxtable, like President Reagan, was a charming and nostalgic man who listened to his smart wife, and everyone lived in a prosperous nation that had moved beyond the civil rights era. *The Jeffersons* was a similar TV program that featured a successful middle-class African American businessman and his smart wife.

A new vanguard of conservative dissident African American leaders emerged in the 1980s, especially Clarence Thomas, Walter Williams, Thomas Sowell, Shelby Steele, Robert Woodson, and Glenn Loury. They argued that racism alone did not create poverty and social problems, and that the older civil rights era leaders were wrong to focus on racial grievances and white guilt to win political rights and power. Dysfunctional behavior by African Americans perpetuated poverty and dependency, but self-criticism, African American dignity, and self-reliance could end the ghetto-specific culture of poverty. Just as Ronald Reagan said government was the problem, they claimed African Americans were the victims of liberal state intervention. Clarence Thomas, the head of the Equal Employment Opportunity Commission, opposed affirmative action programs and condemned the African American addiction to the narcotic of dependency (Foskett 2004).

Michael Jackson became a superstar, and Bill Cosby had the most popular television sitcom. African Americans joined the middle class in unprecedented numbers. Racism still blocked talented African Americans from many opportunities but less often than ever before and overt racial bias became politically incorrect or socially unacceptable. The celebration of multiculturalism, or cultural pluralism as it was sometimes called, recognized the contributions of African Americans to American society and gave status to all African Americans. Diversity entered mainstream thinking in the 1980s but not always in predictable ways.

For example, Hollywood depicted the troubled romance between an African American man in Mississippi and an Asian Indian woman from Uganda in the 1980s in *Mississippi Masala* (1992).

However, some African Americans objected to the inclusion of new immigrants into multicultural programs in schools, correctly seeing that as immigrants assimilated into U.S. society, they displaced African Americans who arrived in America in 1617. Affirmative action, which overwhelmingly benefited white women, now also embraced Asian and Hispanic minorities to the detriment of African Americans. Some African Americans resented the new immigrants' success and targeted Korean shops in urban riots, as seen in Spike Lee's movie *Do the Right Thing* (1989). Unionized African American hotel workers and office janitors often were replaced by non-union Hispanic workers in many cities, further exacerbating tensions. By 1982, the closing of large industrial manufacturing firms (including Chrysler, Ford, General Motors, Goodrich, Uniroyal, U.S. Steel, Goodyear, and Firestone) in metropolitan Los Angeles eliminated 70,000 blue-collar jobs, many held by African Americans living in the middle-class city of Compton. As unemployment increased, poverty, crime, gang violence, and drug dealing made Compton a slum where African Americans competed with Asians and Latinos for the dwindling number of jobs. For many African Americans these new immigrants were only a problem and competitors for jobs (Waters and Ueda 2007).

Multiculturalism in Southern California

The United States admitted 8.6 million immigrants in the 1980s, more than any decade since 1900–1910. About 11 percent of them, or 750,000, indicated their destination was California. For example, the principal destination of six of the eight largest immigrants groups in 1987—Chinese, Filipinos, Indians, Koreans, Vietnamese, and Mexicans—was California, and only Cubans and Dominicans settled primarily in other states. Migration from across the nation and the world has shaped this state more than most. More than half of the Golden State residents were not California natives, and approximately 22 percent of the state's population was foreign born, of whom one-quarter were Latino. The celebration of the Los Angeles bicentennial in 1981 made clear the history of the city and the state began when pioneers from Mexico settled in this area in 1781. Modern immigrants from Mexico in 1900–1930 made East Los Angeles the largest barrio in the United States, with 100,000 people by 1940. In the 1980s the agricultural fields of the Imperial Valley and the San Joaquin Valley and the industries of Los Angles continued to attract Mexican immigrants (Romo 1983).

By 1989, about 40 percent of Los Angeles's 9 million people were foreign-born, half did not speak English at home, and one-quarter spoke Spanish. The Korean population in Los Angeles County was 150,000, but the Latino population

A group of Chinese men socialize in the Chinatown section of Los Angeles, ca. 1980. (Joseph Sohm/Visions of America/Corbis)

was 3 million, and African Americans outnumbered whites. This metropolitan area had 2.8 million foreign-born residents by 1990, compared to 575,000 in Orange County, 360,000 in San Bernardino, 428,000 in San Diego, 337,000 in Oakland, 347,000 in San Jose, and 441,000 in San Francisco. These major metropolitan areas were crossroads for many networks of peoples and cultures, which created an expansive urban object mocked as "sixty suburbs in search of a city" (Waters and Ueda 2007).

Only 7 percent of Latinos in Los Angeles had a college degree compared to 27 percent of the whites, and 61 percent of the Latinos lacked a high school diploma. Lower education levels invariably meant lower income, and 750,000 Latinos under age 18 lived in poverty in 1989. Reductions in social services and welfare benefits in the 1980s had the heaviest impact on these poor and uneducated Latino families. These Latinos had minimum wage jobs (about 24 percent) and lived in less stable communities with lower levels of grassroots political activity. Adjusting to life in California took time, but one striking change was that, by 1980, over 40 percent of Latino marriages were exogamous. This was evidence that the multicultural society was becoming more socially acceptable.

In the 1980s, Watts and Compton, the best-known African American neighborhoods in Los Angeles, became media shorthand for racial problems in the wake of economic restructuring, labor market disintegration, and gang violence.

One study by the Department of Housing and Urban Development in 1982 listed the previously middle-class suburban city of Compton as a "disaster area" (Sides 2005). Southern and East Coast African Americans who had migrated there in hope of home ownership and economic stability were often disappointed by the decline of these relatively small communities within a larger multiethnic population. Music, dance, and art were areas in which cultural crossover between African American, Latino, and Asian people was most evident, but ethnic rivalry and competition for jobs became an overwhelming issue (Hull 1987).

Much about California multiculturalism was misunderstood because social science studies of migration were biased by nationalism and saw immigration and assimilation into mainstream U.S. society only as a social problem. The racial traditions of the South and the North helped to amalgamate European immigrants into white supremacy. But a long history of anti-Mexican and anti-Asian politics achieved a similar result in California. Laws created categories of "illegal" immigrants, and California's African Americans lived with this legacy of misapprehending migration from Latin America, Asia, and Southern or Eastern Europe. Even the notorious "black" city of Compton was 42 percent Latino by 1989.

The Watershed Decade

The 1980s was a watershed decade in which the nation's attitude changed from idealism and worry to optimism and materialism. Ronald Reagan's sunny vision may have been the greatest influence for this change, but he was less a revolutionary than a conciliator, to the relief of his critics and to the dismay of his most conservative supporters. As Lizabeth Cohen noted in A Consumer's Republic, inequality of income grew enormously in the 1980s, much of it traceable to Reagan's new economic policies. One example was the huge corporate debt resulting from the entrepreneurs' merger movement in the 1980s. But Americans responded to and remembered his optimistic message not his economics (Cohen 2003). However, spending on public welfare declined in 1981 but increased after 1984.

The number of federal employees increased more rapidly in the 1980s than in the 1970s. Federal spending as a percentage of the gross domestic product rose in the 1980s. This indicates that the Reagan administration had only a mixed record without the major social impact it promised and claimed. Triumphantly reelected in 1984, Reagan championed some emotional issues, especially school prayer and abortion, with support from conservatives and fundamentalist religious organizations but without support from a majority of Americans. Reagan used his power to reduce taxes and government regulation even when that did little to restore the economy. Military forces were increased to impose U.S. policy on the world even when that had seldom proved effective.

One reason the conservative renaissance failed to accomplish more in the 1980s was the rise of neoconservatism. Irving Kristol, editor of *Public Interest* and a leading spokesman for the neoconservatives, wrote *Reflections of a Neo-conservative: Looking Back, Looking Ahead* in 1983 which pointed out the reasons why neoconservatives did not always support the Reagan or the New Right agenda. Kristol was detached from middle-class society and accepted liberal-democratic capitalism only as a pragmatic step. He favored public welfare and economic growth to obtain political and social stability, not for the production of material goods. He did not think the United States could or should impose democratic government on other nations by military force. As unsentimental critics of liberals and conservatives, the neoconservatives demanded a rational republican virtue that the Reagan Revolution lacked, and they often appeared to focus only on the decline of the United States. At the same time, many critics predicted that Japan was destined to overtake the United States as the world's foremost economic power, especially because it seemed to be free of the social and ethnic problems that plagued America. The Japanese visited the United States in increasing numbers as tourists and to invest in U.S. corporations and land, aided by an ever-strengthening yen. The yuppie gourmet boom made sushi popular with Americans for the first time, and Japanese cars outsold Detroit's automobiles. The purchase of Rockefeller Center and Columbia Pictures by Tokyo corporations was an unsettling reminder of the decline of U.S. financial hegemony and Japan's simultaneous rise, fueled largely by Japan's $52 billion trade surplus with the United States. Japan was a conspicuous star in the 1980s while the United States was bogged down in political and business scandals (Buckley 1992).

In 1987, British historian Paul Kennedy wrote a bestselling book *The Rise and Fall of the Great Powers* that suggested the U.S. was following the examples of Rome, Spain, France, and Britain into imperial decline. After World War II, a new term—the American century—was used to describe the U.S. superpower status, but Kennedy argued the United States had lost its military and economic superiority and was not prepared for the new era of globalization and power sharing. Although the Cold War ended in 1991, the increasing U.S. budget deficit, the growing gap between the rich and the poor, divisive culture wars, business competition from other nations, and massive legal and illegal immigration into the United States amounted to a fatal crisis. In the 1980s, America had slipped from being the largest creditor nation to being the world's largest debtor. In contrast to previous generations, American children could no longer expect to earn more than their parents had. All of this troubled soul-searching Americans at the very time Ronald Reagan was trying to restore the nation's image and confidence.

The media widely discussed Kennedy's book, usually disagreeing with his pessimism. In 1990, Joseph Nye wrote a thoughtful book rebutting Kennedy.

Bound to Lead: The Changing Nature of American Power dismissed the rivalry of Japan and the European Union and predicted the United States would not decline but would continue as the world's only superpower while overcoming its problems. Nye pointed out that immigration reflected the international appeal of American culture, especially popular culture's penetration into other countries in the 1980s. This, more than military power, made the United States very influential.

This controversy and concern brought the debate back to children and families. Both Kennedy and Nye agreed that innovation, flexibility, and adaptation were essential to America's strength, and this depended on educating our children for the Third Industrial Revolution, or what some called postindustrial society. Although most pundits agreed that education was important, the 1980s economic and family disorders meant that one-quarter of U.S. students did not graduate from high school. Standardized test scores indicated another quarter were academically deficient. Remedies proposed included school reform and a longer school day or year. But the United States also compensated for this deficiency by importing talent by the brain drain; nearly one-fifth of the engineers in the United States in the 1980s were immigrants. The debate over the decline of the United States continued as Kennedy claimed the United States would decline but slowly, and Nye predicted decline was unlikely.

Despite the doomsayers and liberal criticism of the Reagan era, the nation made much progress in the 1980s. The 270 million people in America had a genius for invention, and innovation improved communications drastically as personal computers, fax machines, and cell phones became ubiquitous. Transportation networks were completed, including the last section of the interstate highway system linking New Hampshire and Vermont in 1982, and were constantly improved. Daily life in the United States amazed the world as more than adequate food, water, clothing, housing, education, medical care, and entertainment became a matter of course for most Americans. Women, gays, lesbians and racial, religious, and ethnic minorities enjoyed more tolerance and equality than ever before. Social Security and Medicare helped keep poverty among the elderly relatively low. The characteristic American optimism that Ronald Reagan personified was restored, along with idealism and faith in our stable democratic government on all levels.

Coming into power in 1980, the conservatives quickly learned that compromise was the essence of politics, and public opinion moderated many of the most extreme plans of the Reagan revolution. The moderate Midwestern conservatives represented by President Gerald Ford (1974–1977) had been overshadowed in the 1980s by the neoconservatives and the New Right, but they remained the core of the Republican Party. The liberalism of the New Deal may have ended, but its legacy was too deeply rooted to disappear. This was evident in Speaker of the House Tip O'Neill's adroit restraint of the conservative agenda in Congress. This proved that the issue of fairness still resonated in the minds of the majority of Americans, and government was still the institution we often castigated but relied upon.

Reaganomics, the popular name for President Reagan's philosophy of supply-side economics, which combined tax cuts, less government spending, and a balanced budget with an unregulated marketplace, ushered in some stability and prosperity but was no panacea. Some 216 million Americans, about 8 out of 10, lived in comfortable suburbs or sprawling communities outside a city. Certainly problems remained in 1989; among them, poverty, crime, drug abuse, racism, environmental degradation, failing schools, family instability, uncontrolled immigration, corporate greed, corruption and waste in government, and the modern curse of ennui or alienation from one's own community. These issues predated Reagan and Bush, who seemed to encourage "hard-heartedness, self-absorption, materialism, and a peculiar kind of self-righteous decadence" (Troy 2005). Reagan did replace the malaise and stagflation of the 1970s with an adaptive economy generating millions of new jobs and restoring America's image as a superpower, despite the persistence of many social problems (Longley 2007). But these problems also outlasted the Reagan and Bush eras.

BIOGRAPHIES

William J. Bennett, 1943–

Public Official

Born in Brooklyn, New York, William Bennett attended high school in Washington, D.C., and graduated from Williams College in 1965. He earned a Ph.D. in philosophy at the University of Texas in Austin in 1970 and graduated from Harvard Law School in 1971. After serving as director of the National Humanities Center in North Carolina (1976–1981), President Reagan appointed Bennett as chairman of the National Endowment for the Humanities (1981–1985) and later as Secretary of Education (1985–1988). President Bush appointed him as the first director of the Office of National Drug Control Policy, or drug czar (1988–1991).

As secretary of education, the blunt-spoken and conservative Bennett was critical of Stanford University for caving in to radical students who demanded curriculum reform in 1988. This was one memorable incident in the culture wars that ensnared Americans in the 1980s, when conservatives resisted the inclusion of non-Western multicultural topics in the academic curricula. Jesse Jackson supported the Stanford students and faculty, but Bennett, the moralist of the Reagan administration, championed the traditional curriculum, proclaiming in the *National Review* that "the West is the culture in which we live." Denouncing professors as tenured radicals, his conservative allies defended the traditional education that their critics derided as "not so great books" by racist, sexist, imperialist dead white males. He gained much attention for his claims that the nation was in a cultural decline. The multiculturalists won this campus civil war but at the cost of imposing a new politically correct atmosphere (Levy 1996, 35).

Moving to the newly created position of drug czar in 1988, Bennett had little more success. Reagan was critical of permissiveness and the climate of lawlessness he attributed to the pervasive drug culture, but he preferred to use surrogates—his wife or Bill Bennett—in his War on Drugs. By 1980, only 35 percent of high school seniors surveyed considered marijuana harmful, and movies like *Cheech & Chong's Nice Dreams* (1981) made pot seem cool. Reagan expanded the budget for curtailing drug smuggling from $853 million in 1982 to $1.5 billion in 1986 but cut the funds for drug treatment by $74 million. In 1983, crack cocaine imported from the Bahamas quickly became popular with 5 million American users. Although Bennett boasted that daily pot smoking among high school seniors dropped from 1 in 9 in 1979 to 1 in 30 in 1987, the United States consumed 60 percent of the world's illegal drug supply in 1989 (Troy 2005). Bennett politicized morality as if it was a conservative possession, and President Bush continued this emphasis on ethics and family values, although moderate and liberal Americans dismissed this message as more rhetoric.

William Bennett is a frequent television commentator and a prolific author. Among his most influential books are *To Reclaim a Legacy: A Report on the Humanities in Higher Education* (1984), *What Works, Schools Without Drugs* (1986), *Our Children and Our Country: Improving America's Schools and Affirming the Common Culture* (1988), *The Book of Virtues* (1993), and *The Devaluing of America: The Fight for Our Culture and Our Children* (1994). He was considered a likely candidate for president in 1996 but later was a syndicated radio talk show host. He became again controversial when the media revealed that he had lost millions gambling in Las Vegas.

Ivan Boesky, 1937–

Financier

Ivan Boesky was a Wall Street investment manager accused of serious crimes in 1986. Born in Detroit, he graduated from Michigan State University and Detroit School of Law, and by 1986 was a leading arbitrageur who made a plea bargain with the Securities and Exchange Commission and Rudolph Giuliani, the U.S. Attorney in New York, to repay $100 million for insider trading on Wall Street; he also served two years in prison. The *Time* magazine cover story on December 1, 1986, "Wall St. Scam—Making Millions with Your Money—Investor "Ivan the Terrible" Boesky," outlined his crimes. This enormous scandal shocked the U.S. investment community and involved some of the biggest investment firms on Wall Street. It involved takeover battles between the Gillette Company and Revlon Inc., and the T. Boone Pickens' merger with the Unocal oil company in

1985. Most of the major Wall Street brokerage firms had been used by Boesky in his various frauds.

Arbitrage meant secretly buying stock in a company that was threatened by a takeover before the stock price rose and then reselling the stock at an inflated price as a result of their purchases with funds from junk bonds and an investment banker. Arbitrageurs usually bought stock illegally after hours or when normal trading was suspended under exchange rules and SEC regulations. Whether the takeover succeeded or not, arbitrageurs or corporate raiders like Boesky reaped large profits.

Although Deputy Secretary of the Treasury Richard Darman and other key members of the Reagan administration believed corporate executives should be subjected to the discipline of the marketplace, the result was to drive companies into debt or to move overseas, and U.S. jobs were lost as a few rich criminals increased their personal fortunes. Boesky testified against Michael Milken and other white-collar criminals. The Boesky scandal shook public confidence in Wall Street, but his message that "greed is healthy" suited the self-indulgent era Tom Wolfe parodied in his novel *Bonfire of the Vanities* (1987).

Joyce Chen, 1917–1994

Chef and Restaurateur

Born in Beijing, China, as Liao-Jia-ai, she immigrated to Massachusetts in 1949 with her husband, where she was known as Joyce Chen. While her husband studied at Harvard, Chen raised her family in Cambridge and introduced friends to southwestern China's regional cuisine, which was different from the more popular Cantonese food. By 1958, she opened her first restaurant in Cambridge and attracted the interest of the PBS TV chef Julia Child. She published the *Joyce Chen Cookbook* in 1962 and began a popular WGBH television program, *Joyce Chen Cooks,* in 1966. To introduce high quality Hunan and Szechuan style foods, she assisted many Chinese chefs in immigrating to the United States, and she founded Joyce Chen Products in 1971, the leading source of Asian cookery equipment and food products in the nation. By the 1980s, Joyce Chen was a successful business leader and cultural liaison for the United States and China. When she retired in 1986, she had introduced a variety of Chinese cuisine with chili peppers, shallots, garlic, ginger, and peppercorns previously unknown in the United States.

Henry G. Cisneros, 1947–

Public Official

Born in San Antonio, Texas, Henry Cisneros was one of five children of a middle-class Hispanic family whose roots were in the American Southwest for 300 years, but his maternal grandfather had emigrated from Mexico during the revolution in 1900. After graduating from Texas A&M University in 1968, he married his high school girlfriend, Mary Alice Perez, earned a master's degree in urban planning at Texas A&M, and became the youngest person ever appointed a White House fellow. He earned a master's degree in public administration at Harvard University and a doctoral degree from George Washington University (1975). Cisneros was the youngest person elected to the San Antonio city council in 1975–1981, and as mayor in 1981–1989, he was the first Mexican-American to head a major U.S. city. He was praised for attracting high-tech companies to the city to provide more jobs and improve the economy. In 1982 he was selected as one of the "Ten Outstanding Young Men of America," and he was seriously considered for the 1984 Democratic vice presidential nomination. He later served as Secretary of Housing and Urban Development (1993–1997). During the 1980s, HUD had been seriously mismanaged, and racial tensions, homelessness, and deteriorating housing projects had been neglected. Cisneros won accolades from housing experts across the nation for transforming this scandal-ridden agency into one that worked to eliminate racial segregation and poverty in inner cities. Hispanics took great pride in his achievements, despite his resignation from HUD over extramarital and financial affairs. Cisneros also headed a Spanish-language television network.

Milton Friedman, 1912–2006

Economist

Milton Friedman was the most influential economist in the United States in the 1980s. Born in New York City to a working-class Jewish family who emigrated from Ukraine, he graduated from Rutgers University in 1932 and the University of Chicago in 1933 before earning a Ph.D. at Columbia University in 1946. Teaching economics at the University of Chicago (1946–1976), Friedman developed the Chicago School of Economics and won the Nobel Prize in economics (1976). By 1977, he worked at the Hoover Institution at Stanford University until he died in San Francisco in 2006.

He was best known for *A Monetary History of the United States* (1963), in which he argued the importance of the money supply over government fiscal policy by taxes and spending or investments in determining consumption and output. Unlike most economists since the New Deal, the conservative Friedman favored supply-side policies and limited government management of the economy. He said the Depression of the 1930s was not a failure of the free enterprise system but a failure of government. As a libertarian, he advocated the volunteer army, ending the draft in 1973, a negative income tax to replace public welfare, privatizing Social Security, school vouchers, and the decriminalization of drugs and prostitution. As a member of President Reagan's Economic

Economist Milton Friedman, a champion of the free market economy, has had a profound impact on 20th-century economic thought through his many books and years of teaching. He was awarded the Nobel Prize in Economics in 1976 for his contribution to understanding monetary policy. (University of Chicago News Office)

Policy Advisory Board in 1981, he convinced Reagan to allow the brutal 1981–1982 recession to end double-digit inflation and to rely on monetary policy, not Keynesian policies, to create economic stabilization. Friedman shaped the views of American conservatives in the 1980s by emphasizing the power of the marketplace and the inability of the government to improve the economy. He received the Presidential Medal of Freedom and National Medal of Science (1988). Most Americans knew Friedman's ideas about free markets and personal liberty from his columns in *Newsweek* magazine (1966–1984) and his PBS television series *Free to Choose* (1980).

Michael Milken, 1946–

Financier

Michael Milken was the senior executive vice president of New York City's Drexel Burnham Lambert investment firm and was the guru of the junk bond at his Beverly Hills office. Born in Encino, California, he was educated at the University of California, Berkeley, and the University of Pennsylvania. His firm was Wall Street's most profitable investment house in 1983–1985, and Milken earned over $50 million a year by issuing junk bonds. In 1986, the Securities and Exchange Commission began a broad investigation of insider trading, financial manipulation, and fraud. This resulted in the fourth largest drop in the Dow Jones index on record. Junk bonds were high-interest risky investments that provided much of the funds for the Wall Street boom in the mid-1980s. Investment managers like Milken provided funds for takeover bids by corporate raiders and insider trading. Milken's innovative financing promoted pioneers in the cable television, cellular phone, entertainment, and hotel industries. However, when Ivan Boesky testified against him, Milken pled guilty to five SEC charges in 1990, paid a $200 million fine, and served 22 months in prison. Milken later continued his long career in philanthropy.

Mitch Snyder, 1946–1990

Lobbyist

Mitch Snyder was an advocate for the homeless in the United States after a career in advertising on Madison Avenue in New York City and a federal prison sentence for auto theft. Influenced by two Catholic priests he met in prison, fathers Philip and Daniel Berrigan, Snyder joined the Community for Creative Non-Violence (CCNV) in 1973 in Washington, D.C. He operated a soup kitchen, thrift store, medical clinic, and halfway houses for the homeless, many of whom were deinstitutionalized mental patients and Vietnam War veterans. Snyder was arrested many times for anti–Vietnam War protests and demonstrations at the White House to obtain federal funds for the poor. He wrote *Homelessness in America: A Forced March to Nowhere* (1982), which made homelessness a national public issue. His passionate advocacy for homeless people who froze to death on city streets in the 1980s led Snyder and CCNV members to occupy abandoned federal buildings in Washington, D.C., to shelter hundreds of people overnight. He also made public fasts to force the Reagan administration to renovate a building as a shelter. On the eve of his reelection in 1983, President Reagan promised funds to renovate the building. But the problem of homelessness was spreading; riots erupted in New York City's Thompkins Square in 1988 when police cleared the park of homeless people. Mitch Snyder's colorful and effective career was depicted in a TV movie, *Samaritan: The Mitch Snyder Story* (1986), which was nominated for an Academy Award. However, after suffering personal and professional problems, Snyder committed suicide in 1990. Victoria Rader reviewed his career and legacy in *Signal Through the Flames: Mitch Snyder and America's Homeless* (1986).

Sam Walton, 1918–1992

Businessman

Born on an Oklahoma farm and raised in Missouri, after graduating from the University of Missouri in 1940, Sam Walton served in the U.S. Army and in 1945 operated a Ben Franklin variety store in Arkansas. There he pioneered his discount merchandizing practices, buying wholesale goods from the lowest-priced supplier for high-volume retail sales. Other innovations were profit sharing for employees, check-out counters at the front of the clean, well-lit store, and building larger stores in key locations. Walton opened the first Wal-Mart store in Rogers, Arkansas, in 1962 and expanded the chain of big box discount stores—some, by 1987, as large as 70,000 to 200,000 square feet when most department stores were about 40,000 square feet. Wal-Mart was soon the world's largest retailer in the United States and operated in Canada, Britain, Germany, Mexico, Brazil, Argentina, China, and South Korea.

In 1985, Walton opposed communism in Central America by offering college scholarships to Central Americans attending Christian colleges in the United States in the hope that exposure to American capitalist and Protestant Christian values would prevent the spread of communism. *Forbes* magazine ranked Walton as the richest man in the United States in 1985, a genius who recognized and catered to the rampant American consumerism. He transformed the retail business as the largest private employer in the United States. In 1992, President George H. W. Bush awarded Sam Walton the Presidential Medal of Freedom as one of the most influential Americans in the 20th century. Walton wrote his autobiography, *Sam Walton, Made in America* (1992), and he and his family were active philanthropists, especially for Presbyterian churches, charter schools, and neoconservative causes.

However, the big box discount stores that Sam Walton built were criticized for their deleterious impact on the environment and business districts in local communities. Some critics questioned Wal-Mart practices of demanding state and local government subsidies and tax abatements before opening a new store and hiring 1.2 million nonunion undocumented workers at low wages. The company imported goods produced in sweatshop Third World conditions, had vigorous antiunion policies, used racial and gender discrimination in promoting employees, and relied on low-wage part-time workers who qualified for Medicaid and food stamps because Wal-Mart offered no affordable benefits.

An Wang, 1920–1990

Physicist and Entrepreneur

An Wang was born in Shanghai and earned a Ph.D. in physics at Harvard University in 1948. Dr. Wang worked with Howard Aiken, who founded the world's first computer science program at Harvard, and they launched the computer industry in New England. In 1951, Wang Laboratories in Boston and Lowell made magnetic core memory practical and later produced the electronic calculator and a popular desktop computer by 1965. Wang had 30,000 employees by 1986 manufacturing a series of workstations for schools and laboratories. Competition from the giant IBM severely impacted Wang's company in 1989. However, he remained a prime example of how the Asian brain drain benefited the U.S. economy in the 1980s. Dr. Wang and his family were prominent philanthropists and founders of the Wang Performance Center in Boston.

Ellen Willis, 1941–2006

Writer and Journalist

Born in New York City, Ellen Willis graduated from Barnard College and the University of California, Berkeley. By 1970, she was the first pop music critic for the

New Yorker and in the 1980s wrote for *The Village Voice, The Nation,* and *Rolling Stone*. Willis was best known as a feminist critic of antipornography feminism, calling it sexual puritanism, moral authoritarianism, and a threat to free speech. In 1981, she coined the term pro-sex feminism and founded the pro-choice street theater group No More Nice Girls. Among her books is *Beginning to See the Light* (1981), but Willis may have been most remembered for her essay, "Hell No I Won't Go: End the War on Drugs" in *The Village Voice* on September 19, 1989. She argued that the Reagan and Bush War on Drugs was unconstitutional and that drugs should be decriminalized because they were a social or medical problem but not a legal one. The antidrug crusade led to gang violence in African American and Latino neighborhoods, and funding police, courts, and jails instead of social welfare programs failed to eliminate the causes of drug abuse. Willis, a professor of journalism at NYU, analyzed religion, sex, film, pop music, and religion in her long career.

REFERENCES AND FURTHER READINGS

Abrams, Richard M. 2006. *America Transformed: Sixty Years of Revolutionary Change, 1941–2001*. New York: Cambridge University Press.

Allitt, Patrick. 2004. *Religion in America since 1945: A History*. New York: Columbia University Press.

Almirol, Edwin B. 1985. *Ethnic Identity and Social Negotiation: A Study of a Filipino Community in California*. New York: AMS Press.

American Experience, *Test Tube Babies,* http://www.pbs.org/wgbh/amex/babies/.

Auster, Lawrence. 1990. *The Path to National Suicide: An Essay on Immigration and Multiculturalism*. Monterey, Va.: American Immigration Control Foundation.

Baltimore Sun. 1993. "Casino plan encounters skepticism," September 30, 6.

Bloom, Allan. 1987. *The Closing of the American Mind: How Higher Education Has Failed Democracy and Impoverished the Souls of Today's Students*. New York: Simon and Schuster.

Bowe, John. 2006. "Gay Donor or Gay Dad?" *New York Times Magazine,* November 19, 67–73.

Bowen, Ezra. 1986. "Defecting to the West," *Time,* June 30, 12–14.

Buckley, Roger. 1992. *U.S.-Japan Alliance Diplomacy, 1945–1990*. New York: Cambridge University Press.

Carlisle, Rodney P., and J. Geoffrey Golson, eds. 2008. *The Reagan Era: From the Iran Crisis to Kosovo*. Santa Barbara, Calif.: ABC-CLIO.

Carney, Jay. 1986. "Sunbelt Import," *Time,* August 18, 28.

Cleek, Margaret Guminski, and T. Allan Pearson. 1985. "Perceived Causes of Divorce: An Analysis of Interrelationships," *Journal of Marriage and Family* 47:179–193.

Cohen, Lizabeth. 2003. *A Consumer's Republic: The Politics of Mass Consumption in Postwar America.* New York: Knopf.

Conti, Joseph G., and Brad Stetson. 1993. *Challenging the Civil Rights Establishment: Profiles of a New Black Vanguard.* Westport, Conn.: Praeger.

Coontz, Stephanie. 2005. *Marriage, A History: How Love Conquered Marriage.* New York: Penguin Books.

Dallek, Robert. 1984. *Ronald Reagan: The Politics of Symbolism.* Cambridge, Mass.: Harvard University Press.

Diehl, Kemper, and Jan Jarboe. 1985. *Cisneros: Portrait of a New American.* San Antonio: Corona.

Diggins, John Patrick. 2007. *Ronald Reagan: Fate, Freedom, and the Making of History.* New York: W. W. Norton.

Dinnerstein, Leonard, Roger L. Nichols, and David M. Reimers. 2003. *Natives and Strangers: A Multicultural History of Americans.* New York: Oxford University Press.

Dobelle, Evan. 2006. "Reforming Education across New England," *Boston Globe,* December 1, A19.

Duffy, Michael, and Dan Goodgame. 1992. *The Status Quo Presidency of George Bush.* New York: Simon and Schuster.

Edwards, James R. 2006. *Two Sides of the Same Coin: The Connection Between Legal and Illegal Immigration.* New York: Center for Immigration Studies. Available at http://www.cis.org/articles/2006/back106.html.

Finger, John R. 1991. *Cherokee Americans: The Eastern Band of Cherokees in the Twentieth Century.* Lincoln: University of Nebraska Press.

Fogg, Neeta P., Paul E. Harrington, and Thomas F. Harrington. 1999. *The College Majors Handbook.* Indianapolis: JIST Works.

Foskett, Ken. 2004. *Judging Thomas: The Life and Times of Clarence Thomas.* New York: Morrow.

Friedman, Milton. 1987. *The Essence of Friedman.* Stanford, Calif.: Hoover Institution Press.

Friedman, Murray. 2005. *The Neoconservative Revolution: Jewish Intellectuals and the Shaping of Public Policy.* New York: Cambridge University Press.

Friedrich, Otto. 1984. "One Miracle, Many Doubts," *Time,* December 10, 23–24.

Garcia, Marina Cristina. 2006. *Seeking Refuge: Central American Migration to Mexico, the United States, and Canada*. Berkeley: University of California Press.

Gerson, Kathleen. 1993. *No Man's Land: Men's Changing Commitments to Family and Work*. New York: Basic Books.

Gibbs, Nancy. 1989. "The Baby Chase," *Time*, October 9, 15–18.

Gilgoff, Dan. 2007. *The Jesus Machine: How James Dobson, Focus on the Family, and Evangelical America Are Winning the Culture War*. New York: St. Martin's Press.

Goodgame, Dan. 1985. "In West Hollywood: Exotic Mix," *Time*, December 16, 12.

Greeley, Andrew. 1989. *Religious Change in America*. Cambridge: Harvard University Press.

Haddad, Yvonne Y., ed. 1991. *The Muslims of America*. New York: Oxford University Press.

Harrington, Michael. 1984. *The New American Poverty*. New York: Holt, Rinehart and Winston.

Hirsch, E. D. 1987. *Cultural Literacy: What Every American Needs to Know*. Boston: Houghton Mifflin.

Hoff, Joan. 1991. *Law, Gender and Injustice: A Legal History of U.S. Women*. New York: New York University Press.

Hull, Jon D. 1987. "Life and Death with the Gangs," *Time*, August 24, 42.

Hynes, Charles J., and Bob Drury. 1990. *Incident at Howard Beach: The Case for Murder*. New York: Putnam.

Iyer, Pico. 1985. "Impact Abroad," *Time*, July 8, 12.

Jacobs, Meg. 2005. *Pocketbook Politics: Economic Citizenship in Twentieth-Century America*. Princeton: Princeton University Press.

Kennedy, Paul M. 1987. *The Rise and Fall of the Great Powers: Economic Change and Military Conflict from 1500 to 2000*. New York: Random House.

Kenney, Charles C. 1992. *Riding the Runaway Horse: The Rise and Decline of Wang Laboratories*. Boston: Little, Brown.

Kilburn, Will. 2006. "Same ol' Melting Pot, New Recipe," *Boston Globe*, December 31, 3.

Klein, Herbert S. 2004. *A Population History of the United States*. New York: Cambridge University Press.

Kristol, Irving. 1983. *Reflections of a Neoconservative: Locking Back, Looking Ahead*. New York: Basic Books.

Lacayo, Richard. 1986. "Spreading the Wings of an Idea," *Time,* September 22, 11–12.

Lamar, Jacob V. 1986. "Today's Native Son," *Time,* December 1, 31–33.

Lane, Ambrose. 1995. *Return of the Buffalo: The Story Behind America's Indian Gaming Explosion.* Westport, Conn.: Bergin & Garvey.

Leonhardt, David. 2006. "Scant Progress on Closing Gap in Women's Pay," *New York Times,* December 24, 1, 18.

Levenstein, Harvey. 1993. *Paradox of Plenty: A Social History of Eating in Modern America.* New York: Oxford University Press.

Levitan, Sar A., Richard S. Belous, and Frank Grillo. 1988. *What's Happening to the American Family?: Tensions, Hopes, Realities.* Baltimore: Johns Hopkins University Press.

Levy, Peter B. 1996. *Encyclopedia of the Reagan-Bush Years.* Westport, Conn.: Greenwood Press.

Longley, Kyle, Jeremy D. Mayer, Michael Schaller, and John W. Sloan. 2007. *Deconstructing Reagan: Conservative Mythology and America's Fortieth President.* Armonk, N.Y.: M. E. Sharpe.

Mahler, Sarah. 1998. "Lives at Crossroads: Salvadorans in the U.S." *Hemisphere.* September 22. Available at http://www.accessmylibrary.com/comsite5/bin/pdinventory.pl.

Mangum, Garth L., Stephen L. Mangum, and Andrew M. Sum. 2003. *The Persistence of Poverty in the United States.* Baltimore: Johns Hopkins University Press.

McGuinn, Patrick J. 2006. *No Child Left Behind and the Transformation of Federal Education Policy, 1965–2005.* Lawrence: University Press of Kansas.

McLaughlin, Steven. 1988. *The Changing Lives of American Women.* Chapel Hill: University of North Carolina Press.

Migration Information Source, *Global Data Center,* http://migrationinformation.org/GlobalData/countrydata/data.cfm.

Migration Policy Institute, *Migration and Development in El Salvador,* http://migrationinformation.org/.

Millet, Robert L. 2007. *The Vision of Mormonism.* St. Paul, Minn.: Paragon House.

Mills, Nicolaus, ed. 1994. *Arguing Immigration.* New York: Simon and Schuster.

Mitchell, Stacy. 2006. *Big-Box Swindle: The True Cost of Mega-Retailers and the Fight for America's Independent Businesses.* Boston: Beacon Press.

Nelan, Bruce W. 1989. "Soviet Union," *Time,* October 9, 24–25.

Nye, Joseph S. 1990. *Bound to Lead: The Changing Nature of American Power.* New York: Basic Books.

Oakley, Christopher Arris. 2005. *Keeping the Circle: American Indian Identity in Eastern North Carolina, 1885–2004.* Lincoln: University of Nebraska Press.

Olson, James Stuart. 1979. *The Ethnic Dimension in American History.* New York: St. Martin's Press.

Orszag, Peter. 2006. "Cool-headed, Warm-hearted Economics," *Boston Globe,* December 3, E9.

O'Toole, James M. 2008. *The Faithful: A History of Catholics in America.* Cambridge: Harvard University Press.

Portes, Alejandro, and Ruben G. Rumbaut. 1990. *Immigrant America: A Portrait.* Berkeley: University of California Press.

Portes, Alejandro, and Ruben G. Rumbaut. 2001. *Legacies: The Story of the Immigrant Second Generation.* Berkeley: University of California Press.

Rader, Victoria. 1986. *Signal through the Flames: Mitch Snyder and America's Homeless.* Kansas City, Mo.: Sheed & Ward.

Raymond, Emilie. 2006. *From My Cold, Dead Hands: Charlton Heston and American Politics.* Lexington: University Press of Kentucky.

Reeves, Terrance J., and Claudette E. Bennett. 2004. *We the People: Asians in the United States, Census 2000,* Special Reports, December. U.S. Department of Commerce. Available at http://www.census.gov/prod/2004pubs/censr-17.pdf.

Reimers, David M. 1985. *Still the Golden Door: The Third World Comes to America.* New York: Columbia University Press.

Rogozinski, Jan. 1999. *A Brief History of the Caribbean: From the Arawak and Carib to the Present.* New York: Penguin.

Romo, Ricardo. 1983. *East Los Angeles: History of a Barrio.* Austin: University of Texas Press.

Rubin, Rachel, and Jeffrey Melnick. 2007. *Immigration and American Popular Culture.* New York: New York University Press.

Russell, George. 1984. "People, People, People," *Time,* August 6, 16–17.

Samuelson, Robert. 2006. "Dodging Immigrations Truths," *Newsweek,* May 17, 11–12.

Sehgal, Ellen. 1985. "Foreign Born in the U.S. Labor Market: The Results of a Special Survey," Bureau of Labor Statistics, *Monthly Labor Review* 108 (7): 18–24. Available at http://www.bls.gov/opub/mlr/1985/07//art3abs.htm.

Sides, Josh. 2005. "Straight into Compton: American Dreams, Urban Nightmares, and the Metamorphosis of a Black Suburb," *American Quarterly* (Winter): 85–105.

Smith, Jane I. 1999. *Islam in America.* New York: Columbia University Press.

Spaid, Elizabeth Levitan. 1996. "Blacks Eschew Public Schools for Classrooms with Scripture," *Christian Science Monitor,* August 21, 9.

Steinem, Gloria. 1983. *Outrageous Acts and Everyday Rebellions.* New York: Holt, Rinehart and Winston.

Sum, Andrew M., and Paul E. Harrington. 2006. "Two Kinds of Immigration," *Boston Globe,* October 16, A9.

Takaki, Ronald. 1993. *A Different Mirror: A History of Multicultural History.* New York: Little, Brown.

Takaki, Ronald, ed. 1994. *From Different Shores: Perspectives on Race and Ethnicity in America.* New York: Oxford University Press.

Talwar, Jennifer Parker. 2002. *Fast Food, Fast Track: Immigrants, Big Business, and the American Dream.* Boulder, Colo.: Westview Press.

Time, "Making Babies, The New Science of Conception," September 10, 1984, 7–9.

Time, "Elusive Dreams in Exile," February 17, 1986, 29.

Time, "Business Notes Images," June 2, 1986, 19.

Time, "American Notes Prisons: Running Out of Room," June 6, 1986, 33.

Trimble, Vance H. 1990. *Sam Walton: The Inside Story of America's Richest Man.* New York: Dutton.

Troy, Gil. 2005. *Morning in America: How Ronald Reagan Invented the 1980s.* Princeton: Princeton University Press.

U.S. Department of Justice, Bureau of Justice Statistics, *Key Crime & Justice Facts at a Glance,* http://www.ojp.usdoj.gov/bjs/glance.htm.

The Village Voice, 50th Anniversary Special, http://www.villagevoice.com/specials.

Wallis, Claudia. 1984. "The New Origins of Life," *Time,* September 10, 6–9.

Waters, Mary C., and Reed Ueda, eds. 2007. *The New Americans: A Guide to Immigration Since 1965.* Cambridge: Harvard University Press.

Willis, Ellen. 1992. *No More Nice Girls: Countercultural Essays.* Hanover, N.H.: University Press of New England.

Wills, Garry. 1987. *Reagan's America: Innocents at Home.* Garden City, N.Y.: Doubleday.

Wuthnow, Robert. 2005. *America and the Challenges of Religious Diversity.* Princeton: Princeton University Press.

People and Events in the 20th Century

THE 1900s

THE 1910s

THE 1920s

THE 1930s

THE 1940s

THE 1950s

THE 1960s

THE 1970s

THE 1980s

THE 1990s

1980s Index

About the Authors

Peter C. Holloran, PhD is an associate professor of history at Worcester State College in Worcester, Massachusetts. Born in Boston and a Cambridge resident, his published works include *Boston's Wayward Children: Social Service for Homeless Children, 1930–1930* (Northeastern University Press, 1994) and the *Historical Dictionary of New England* (Scarecrow Press, 2003) and the *Historical Dictionary of the Progressive Era* (Scarecrow Press, 2008). He is also an editor of the *Journal of Popular Culture* and Secretary of the New England Historical Association.

Andrew E. Hunt is an associate professor in the Department of History at the University of Waterloo in Waterloo, Ontario. Born in Canada, raised in the United States, and living once again in Canada, Hunt focuses on post–World War II U.S. history, teaching courses on the civil rights movement, the Vietnam War, and rock 'n' roll. He is currently researching and writing two books, one on Sen. George McGovern, the other on President Ronald Reagan. He is the author of two previous books, *The Turning: A History of Vietnam Veterans against the War* (New York: New York University Press, 1999) and *David Dellinger: The Life and Times of a Nonviolent Revolutionary* (New York: New York University Press, 2006).